OIL F

M000306891

Oil for Food

*The Global Food Crisis and
the Middle East*

ECKART WOERTZ

OXFORD
UNIVERSITY PRESS

OXFORD
UNIVERSITY PRESS

Great Clarendon Street, Oxford, OX2 6DP,
United Kingdom

Oxford University Press is a department of the University of Oxford.
It furthers the University's objective of excellence in research, scholarship,
and education by publishing worldwide. Oxford is a registered trade mark of
Oxford University Press in the UK and in certain other countries

© Eckart Woertz 2013

The moral rights of the author have been asserted

First published 2013
First published in paperback 2015

Published in the United States of America by Oxford University Press
198 Madison Avenue, New York, NY 10016, United States of America

British Library Cataloguing in Publication Data
Data available

Library of Congress Cataloging in Publication Data
Data available

ISBN 978–0–19–965948–7 (Hbk.)
ISBN 978–0–19–872939–6 (Pbk.)

In memory of Ulrich Wörtz

Preface for Paperback edition

Writing about a contemporary event like the global food crisis of 2008 and the Gulf countries' reaction to it is necessarily a moving target. Two years after *Oil for Food* was written, there have been further developments, so the publication of the paperback provides an opportunity to revisit some of the book's arguments.

The title *Oil for Food* tried to encapsulate three major dimensions of food security in the Middle East and in the Gulf region in particular: First it describes the very essence of food security in a region that is the largest food net-importer of the world and relies on direct and indirect oil revenues to pay for such imports. Second, it illustrates the strategic nature of food, its importance for national interests, and the unrealistic self-sufficiency aspirations that have guided national policies as a result. Third, it points to the heavy reliance of modern food systems on hydrocarbon inputs like fuels and fertilizers. These factors have played a major role in the history of modernization of agriculture in the Gulf region as well, and have resulted in unsustainable levels of water consumption.

The strategic dimension of food in the Middle East has been further demonstrated by events in Syria and Iran. As the Syrian uprising morphed into outright civil war the Assad regime used food as a weapon in an attempt to starve rebel-held areas into submission.[1] Syria has also been vulnerable to food trade disruptions. Food has been excluded from sanction regimes, but financial transactions have not. This compromised the ability of the Assad regime to find takers for its wheat tenders. Traders were wary about its ability to pay its bills from frozen accounts. Rebel groups also used taxation of the food trade as a source of income.

The travails of the Syrian regime are echoed by the challenges of Iran when it was shut out of the international banking system. To circumvent sanctions it took payments for oil and gas exports in non-convertible Indian Rupees and via gold imports from Turkey. At one point it even negotiated oil-for-food barter deals with Pakistan.[2] Other regimes in the region undoubtedly took notice of these incidents. They pointed to their own vulnerabilities, which are described in chapter 4 of this book, like the United States' withdrawal of P.L 480 food aid to rein in Nasser in the 1960s, its contemplated food embargo in retaliation to the Arab oil boycott in the 1970s, or the multilateral UN embargo against Iraq from 1990 until 2003 and the related Oil-for-Food Program.

---

[1] *Foreign Policy*, 17 April 2014.
[2] *Reuters*, 28 June and 9 August 2012; 15 February, 21 February, and 12 April 2013.

Against this historical backdrop aspirations of self-sufficiency in the region are understandable, but unrealistic. Even tiny and wealthy Qatar has downsized its ambitious plan for futuristic self-sufficiency with "iPad farms" that use solar based desalination, hydroponics, and vertical farming. Instead of planting 70 percent of its food by 2023, its revised food security Master Plan now only speaks of 40–60 percent and a vague medium term time horizon. Even that might be too optimistic. Growing this amount of food in the desert does not make economic and ecologic sense. International consultancy companies make a killing by planning the next white elephant and playing to the Gulf's inclination to look for technical fixes, but when all is said and done there is no alternative for MENA countries to embrace the reality of food import dependence.

Egypt's plan for wheat self-sufficiency has not fared better. Wheat production has hardly increased since 2011/12. Domestic political turmoil might not have helped, but there are also resource constraints to increase production. There is an argument to be made for using scarce water resources for more valuable economic pursuits and foster the kind of inclusive economic diversification that can pay for future food imports while providing sufficient food accessibility for the poor. The scenario in Egypt is different. The country depends on a financial lifeline from Gulf countries to pay its bills. Such help is given for political reasons as Saudi Arabia and Iran are locked in a rival bid for regional hegemony, which has increasingly sectarian undertones.

The fact that the IMF, *The Economist*, and the World Economic Forum have concurred with critics from the left in identifying social inequality as an issue of major global concern is not without irony. It points to a deep-seated crisis of capitalism. Inequalities in Egypt and other parts of the MENA have increased as well. Economic liberalization since the Mubarak era primarily benefited a small group of regime clients. Food security in the MENA is not so much an issue of strategic vulnerability or agriculture, but of inclusive economic development and food accessibility. Qatar might have the highest per capita income of the world; the Nepalese construction workers that had to take refuge in their country's embassy after not being paid for months were food insecure.

As it did during the Cold War, Egypt uses its strategic position and a certain nuisance value in the acquisition of external rents. Otherwise its income from tourism has declined and its slim manufacturing base struggles to compete with Asia in mass markets like textiles and southern European countries that have gained competitiveness after bringing down production costs. Egypt has hoped to develop its natural gas reserves to make up for the shortfall in oil revenues after it became an oil net-importer at the end of the 2000s. However, instead of growing, its natural gas production has declined while domestic consumption continued to rise. Egypt will become a gas net-importer soon. It is plagued by power shortages and already had to resort to emergency deliveries of LNG from Qatar. Similarly, Syria's oil production has plummeted since 2012. Its erstwhile plans to develop into a gas-trading hub now appear a flight of fancy given the security situation. Yemen's oil and gas sector has also been affected by the country's internal turmoil.

Dependence on direct and indirect hydrocarbon revenues in the MENA thus goes far beyond the Gulf countries, while the old ways of throwing oil money at economic problems is unsustainable. This raises questions about the future affordability of food imports. The unconventional oil revolution in the US has been portrayed as a major threat to the economic and strategic position of the MENA over the last two years. This is exaggerated. Even in the hypothetical event of complete US oil self-sufficiency, the MENA would still be crucial to quench Asia's energy thirst. The US would maintain an indirect dependence on MENA oil because of the latter's role in price discovery of a fungible commodity that is traded in a unified, global market.

There is also a considerable convergence of interests: Producers of unconventional oil in the US need high prices to cover their costs and stay in business; MENA countries need them to maintain domestic spending. In the advent of a sudden price decline the US might rather cooperate with OPEC than seeking to prevent the latter's efforts at price stabilization. By far the gravest threat to oil revenues in the MENA is growing domestic consumption that compromises export capacities. Another threat would be a resurgence of Iraqi oil production if that happened along the optimistic lines that the Iraqi government envisages. This would constitute a much larger supply addition than those of US tight oil from shale formations and would cause downward pressures on prices. However, it is an unlikely scenario given the current security situation. There has been a resurgence of US refining and petrochemical production, which is of particular concern for Europe's competitive position, but so far growth rates of petrochemical production in the Gulf and Asia continue to be higher than in the US. When they will level out it remains to be seen how the competitive landscape of an increasingly globalized industry will develop.

While the vulnerability of other MENA countries to food price shocks is obvious, the position of Gulf countries is more comfortable given their reserves of oil and foreign exchange. Predictions about their imminent demise seem exaggerated as no strong reform coalition is in sight. The domestic bourgeoisie is coopted and apolitical, the working class foreign, policed, and docile, the military weak and coup-proofed, and the national citizenry still sufficiently sedated by the rent fed nanny state. It is also held together by sectarian fear mongering and is given limited avenues of participation via wasta networks and petitioning in majlis gatherings. With countries like Syria and Libya in free fall the allure of the Arab Spring has faded, but regimes in the Gulf are clearly concerned about spill over effects, as their authoritarian repression of dissent has shown. Twitterati and poets have been jailed. In this situation food prices are regarded as crucial for domestic stability. The reflex after the global food crisis of 2008 to increase public spending remains intact. Cutting of food subsidies is not very likely. They are smaller in absolute terms than those for fuel and electricity and their value for legitimacy is considerable. In contrast to energy subsidies that mostly benefit middle and upper classes with a high ownership ratio of cars and appliances, subsidies on staple foods are self-targeting as poor people spend a higher share of their incomes on these items. The strategic subsidies to Egypt show that Gulf countries are also willing—to a degree—to help cash strapped allies to maintain such spending.

As its reliance on world markets grow, the MENA faces increasing competition for food imports from China. China increased its imports of animal feedstock like soybeans over the last decade and eased its traditional stance of self-sufficiency for grains for human consumption in 2014 by allowing a modest reliance on imports. Contrary to conventional wisdom it has not invested much in actual farmland. Its focus is more on food trading and processing to ensure food safety standards and to cater to the increasingly varied diets of its population. Among such recent investments have been Tnuva, the Israeli cheese and consumer foods supplier, US pork producer Smithfield Foods, the UK breakfast brand Weetabix, and Australian wine-maker Hollick. Chinese grain trader COFCO has spent $1.5 billion on a stake in a sugar, soybean, and wheat joint venture with Hong Kong based Noble Group. China prepares to compete with the Cargills and Nestlés of this world rather than gobbling up farmland in the upstream sector.

There are some large food processing companies in the Gulf that operate internationally like Kuwait based Americana. Gulf countries have also shown a similar, if more subdued interest in trading companies as I describe in the book, but compared with China they have arguably less capacity to put such strategies to work.

MENA countries and China have dramatically increased their share in global food imports. According to the Production, Supply and Distribution (PSD) database of the United States Department of Agriculture the MENA accounts for almost a third of globally traded cereals; this dominance is even stronger when only net-imports are considered. Here the MENA's share stands at 44 percent. Net-imports of cereals have increased from 58 million tons in 2006/07 to 92 million tons in 2013/14. It is followed by East Asia, whose net-imports increased from 38 million tons to 66 million tons. A concomitant rise of net-exports in the former Soviet Union states, Australia/Oceania, South America, South Asia, and Europe and a continuously large share of North America have met this demand growth. Supplies from Sub-

Saharan Africa have had no role in this trade; it is also a large and growing net-importer with 29 million tons. Seven years after the global food crisis the media image of large-scale land investments in Africa by Gulf Arabs and the Chinese fails to show up in the trade statistics.

Oil for Food has argued that there is a disconnect between media reports about land grabs and actual implementation on the ground. It has been criticized for it, predictably, largely by reiterating the conventional wisdom. Yet, if at all, the implementation gap has grown. When Gulf countries have really put money on the table it has been in developed agricultural markets like Australia or Argentina, rather than in challenging investment environments in Africa. Companies that have actually started projects there face considerable problems along the lines described in chapter 8 of this book. In Ethiopia, Emami Biotech has failed; the Indian investor Karuturi, which has developed into a poster child land-grabber in the media, faces serious economic difficulties. Even the Saudi Star project of well-connected billionaire Al-Amoudi is in trouble as he has admitted to the media.[3] Saudi Arabia's crack down on illegal migrant workers in 2013 with the expulsion of over 100,000 Ethiopians has not bought it goodwill in the country and relations between the two countries are more subdued than they were two years ago.

The skepticism about the reliability of media reports is now more widely shared. The flagship publication of the International Land Coalition, the Land Matrix has substantially revised its overall estimate of land investments; it got rid of some paper projects and now allows for differentiation according to implementation status. This shows that many signed projects have in fact not started. There have also been revisions to the upside, the Gulf projects in north Sudan that have seen some degree of realization were not part of the database as *Oil for Food* has pointed out and they are now included.

The *Journal of Peasant Studies* dedicated a special issue to methodologies of land grab research in 2013. Caution against quantitative fixations was widespread amidst calls for more qualitative studies that take into account peculiarities of target and investor countries and differentiate between various types of land, tenure, and farming systems. This was also one of the conclusions in the edited volume *The Global Land Grab: Beyond the Hype* by Mayke Kaag and Annelies Zoomers (Zed Books 2014). As vast parts of the social sciences march to a naïve quantitative drumbeat there is a certain urge to put a number on everything and run a regression analysis. Yet, hopefully, more qualitative studies will shed light on the diverse realities of commercial pressures on land, whether by foreign or domestic investors.

Skepticism about quantitative exaggerations aside, I hope it is clear that I do not doubt the potential threats posed by large-scale agro-investments, like

---

[3] *Bloomberg*, 3 December 2013; see also *Al Monitor*, 9 December 2013; *The Reporter*, 23 November 2013.

displacements of smallholders and pastoralists. Land grabs do happen, just not on the scale as is often assumed. As far as they have happened in the case of the Gulf countries, I have pointed them out in this book and mentioned when preemptive displacements have been used to clear land for investors as happened in Ethiopia.

Having said that, I believe there should be room for more middle ground in a fervent debate that sometimes oscillates uncritically between romantic views of subsistence farming and slick project designs that are coated in hyperbolic language and unrealistic profit expectation of 30 percent and more. Africa is the only continent that has yet to witness a demographic transition. Its food production per capita declined between 1980 and 2000 and has hardly moved upwards since. Many of its farmers are food insecure and unable to feed its growing urban population. There is need for agricultural investments and Gulf countries might be able to play a positive role if they moved away from their real estate centered mentality. Formal land ownership is not key for a successful farming project; bringing on board local populations and smallholders is. Project designs with joint equity or contract farming are more likely to do that trick than fully owned plantations.

While future food security in the MENA will increasingly rely on food imports, domestic agriculture remains important. With blue water resources already (over) allocated, greater attention will need to be paid to rainfed farming and improved management of green water resources. It is worth recollecting some of the lessons of Australian dryland farming and its application to the MENA that Lynne and Brian Chatterton outlined in their reference work *Sustainable Dryland Farming* (Cambridge University Press 1996).

Hence, I would like to end on a positive note. Considerable potential exists to make MENA societies more equitable and food secure while managing their resources more sustainably. Neo-Malthusian tales that try to explain social conflict in the MENA (e.g. Syria and Darfur) as a result of drought and ecological limitations are misplaced and woefully neglect socio-political origins of such conflicts. Humans have choices and are capable of adaptation. The environment is not an external variable that would transform itself mechanically into socio-political outcomes.

There have been a few publications since *Oil for Food* was published that contain further valuable information about related topics, among them are *The Gulf Monarchies and Climate Change* by Mari Luomi (Hurst 2012), *The GCC Economies* edited by Mohamed A. Ramady (Springer 2012), *Environmental Politics* in Egypt by Jeannie Sowers (Routledge 2013), *The Political Economy of Arab Food Sovereignty* by Jane Harrigan (Palgrave Macmillan 2014), two summary reports about GCC land investments in Cambodia and Ethiopia by Ben Shepherd for the Center for International and Regional Studies at the Georgetown University School of Foreign Service in Qatar (2012 and 2013), "The Role of Drought and Climate Change in the Syrian

Uprising" by Francesca de Chatel (*Middle Eastern Studies*, Vol. 50/4, 2014), and a number of working papers by Jim Krane about domestic energy consumption in the GCC. Finally, *Middle East Food Security*, which was edited by Zahra Babar and Suzi Mirgani (Hurst, Oxford University Press 2014) deals with food security in the wider Middle East including countries like Egypt, Iran, Jordan, Lebanon, and Yemen.

The text of the book has remained largely unchanged, there have only been some minor revisions to address ambiguities and increase readability in light of current events. For future developments and debates you can consult the website www.oilforfood.info.

Barcelona, July 2014

Preface

My grandmother loved her grandchildren dearly, but when it came to food security, there were qualifications. She was ready to chase us on the fragile outer branches of the apple trees on her ancestral land to make sure that all fruits were harvested in fall. Then she conserved them and put them with the other jars in the cellar where they would collect dust. She belonged to a generation that had lived through World War I as children and through World War II as adults; she better wanted to be prepared.

As a spoiled brat of *Wirtschaftswunder* prosperity, my enthusiasm to work the land usually faded after a couple of hours. Yet when I suggested to her that the menial labor of her offspring was a misallocation of resources, that the war was over, and that there were supermarkets now, she would smile knowingly and steadfastly refuse to take chances.

Of course she knew that there were supermarkets now. She went to one every day. She didn't get her bread from the land. My grand-uncle had given up farming; other relatives only practiced it part time and had moved on to work in the factory or open a restaurant.

When I lived in Dubai during the better part of the 2000s there were supermarkets too. Loads of them. Yet when the global food crisis struck in 2008, I would encounter similar memories and concerns. Gulf politicians had grandmothers, too. The global food crisis was not just about trade statistics, inequalities, and environmental sustainability. It was also about the collective memories that inform decision-makers.

That's why this book deals with issues that seem to be far removed from the global food crisis like the fragile supply situation during World War II, the failed attempt to develop Sudan as an Arab bread-basket in the 1970s, or wheat farming in the desert and the emergence of a Saudi agro-lobby. The book only ends where my research started: an explanation of Gulf agro-investment, why so few projects have been implemented, and why there is such a disconnect with the media hype around land grabs. Everything before is an exploration of those collective memories. I gradually worked myself back in time, grinding through archives and leading interviews. The work was tremendously rewarding and I hope I can share some of the curiosity that I have gathered in the process.

This book wants to fill some blanks in the increasingly rich literature about the political economy of the Arabian Peninsula and its history. But I hope that it is written in a sufficiently accessible style to be of interest for journalists and practitioners, too, who deal with the issue of food security in governments,

NGOs, and international organizations. It is important to cast a wide net; the questions that the global food crisis has raised did not come on us suddenly in 2008. They start earlier. *Oil for Food* is not only the story of Gulf agriculture and food security, it is also the story of a global food system that is highly dependent on hydrocarbon inputs and unsustainable in its current form.

This book would not have been possible without my fellowship at Princeton University. I am grateful to Bernard Haykel of the Near Eastern Studies Department for inviting me to the Oil, Energy and the Middle East Program, and to Robert Socolow and the Princeton Environmental Institute for co-hosting me during my time at Princeton. Thanks also to my colleagues who made my stay there such a pleasant one, to the Transregional Institute for an extraordinary lecture series, and to the unsung heroes of Firestone Library, who either have every book on the planet or get it for you from somewhere.

Other institutions were tremendously helpful, too. The Gulf Research Center and its chairman Abdulaziz Sager supported the early stages of this research. Conferences at the Center for International and Regional Studies at the Georgetown University School of Foreign Service in Qatar, at Sultan Qaboos University in Muscat, at Gezira University in Sudan, and at the Emirates Center for Strategic Studies and Research in Abu Dhabi provided helpful insights. I want to thank them exemplarily in lieu of the various conferences and institutions where I have been allowed to discuss the issue of food security and shape my research agenda. I am also greatly indebted to all the people at NGOs, farming operations, companies, ministries, and sovereign wealth funds who patiently listened to my nagging questions and shared their views and insights with me. Most of them have been rendered anonymous; exemplarily I want to thank Turki Faisal al-Rasheed for our inspiring and at times controversial discussions on Saudi agriculture. A big thank you to the staff at the various archives, Presidential Libraries, and paper collections who helped me during my research. The discussions with my colleagues at the Barcelona Centre for International Affairs (CIDOB) were always stimulating when finishing the final manuscript. Also thanks to Johann Sebastian Bach and his Goldberg Variations, I did not know that one can listen to the same music so often.

Nate Hodson and Ben Shepherd read Part I and Part II of the manuscript in full and provided helpful critique. Tsering Wangyal Shawa designed the maps and brought my slightly chaotic suggestions patiently on board. John Fanning helped with the website for this book (www.oilforfood.info). Harry Verhoeven and Martin Keulertz provided invaluable guidance on Sudan and water issues respectively. Steffen Hertog shared his legendary newspaper archive with me and commented on parts of the draft, so did Robert Springborg, Guido Steinberg, Clemens Breisinger, Robert Vitalis, Giacomo Luciani, Wolf Lorleberg, Toby Jones, Matias Margulis, Cyrus Schayegh, Francis Ghilès,

Alden Young, Shoibal Chakravarty, and three anonymous reviewers for Oxford University Press. This book would not be the same without their invaluable comments. Any mistakes are mine of course.

My editor Adam Swallow was supportive of the project all along and helped me to firm up the draft. Aimee Wright, Jo North, and the copy editing team at Oxford University Press gave the book its current form. The oil-for-food story is diverse with sometimes surprising twists and angles. If chapters are read separately it is suggested to read the conclusions of the preceding chapters as an introduction to the following ones.

Finally, a big hug to my wife Chantal, for her love and patience when I had my head in the clouds writing this book. Also thanks to my parents who years ago supported my choice of Middle Eastern studies, which doesn't pay as good as banking but is so much more fun. I want to dedicate this book to the memory of my father, Ulrich Wörtz; I wished he had been around a little while longer.

Barcelona, July 2012

Acknowledgements

I acknowledge copyright for the following articles, parts of which have been used for the book: "Arab Food, Water, and the Big Landgrab that Wasn't," *The Brown Journal of World Affairs*, Vol. 18, Issue 1, Fall/Winter 2011, 119–132; "The Governance of Gulf Agro-Investments," *Globalizations*, Vol. 10, Issue 1, 2013; "The Global Food Crisis and the Gulf's Quest for Africa's Agricultural Potential," in Tony Allan, Martin Keulertz, Suvi Sojamo, and Jeroen Warner (eds.), *Handbook of Land and Water Grabs in Africa: Foreign Direct Investments and Food and Water Security* (London and New York: Routledge 2012), 102–117; "The Gulf, the Maghreb and Sub-Saharan Africa: Cooperation for Food Security?" in Francesc Badia i Dalmases (ed.), *Transitions in North Africa in Times of Scarcity: Finance, Employment, Energy & Food. The Mediterranean in a Multipolar World up to 2030*. Barcelona Centre for International Affairs (CIDOB) in cooperation with OCP Foundation, Barcelona, March 2012, 17–24. The copyright for the maps of Sudan and the Middle East belongs to Tsering Wangyal Shawa.

Contents

Figures and Maps   xxiii
Tables   xxv
Acronyms and Abbreviations   xxvii
Note on Transliteration   xxxi

Introduction   1

1. The Gulf Food Security Predicament   9
   1.1 The Middle East and the Global Food Crisis of 2008   9
   1.2 Social Contract, Subsidies, and Price Controls   12
   1.3 Malthus not ante portas: Domestic Agriculture and the
       Lack of Water   16
   1.4 Global Food Prices: Paradigm Shift or Not?   19
   1.5 Consumption Patterns and Self-Sufficiency Ratios   26
   1.6 Structure of Food Imports: Product Groups and
       Countries of Origin   28
   1.7 Conclusion   32

Part I. Gulf Food Security: History, Political Economy, and Geopolitics

2. Ethiopian Wheat and American Tires: Gulf Food Security
   and World War II   35
   2.1 On the Margins: Gulf Agriculture before World War II   36
   2.2 The Allied Middle East Supply Center (MESC)   43
   2.3 Food, Legitimacy, and Strategy in the Gulf   47
   2.4 Inflation, Transport, and Food Security   54
   2.5 Beyond the War: Water, Sedentarization, and Power   57
   2.6 Conclusion   61

3. Rise and Fall of the Blooming Desert: The Self-Sufficiency Illusion   63
   3.1 White Elephants and Horses: The Al-Kharj Farm   63
   3.2 Opposition and Ecology   67
   3.3 Create Two, Three, Many Al-Kharjs   69
   3.4 Self-sufficiency and the Saudi Wheat Bonanza 1970s–1990s   75
   3.5 Wheat or Water   83
   3.6 Agricultural Development in the Smaller Gulf States   88
   3.7 Cereal Programs Elsewhere: Egypt, Iran, Syria, and Sudan   97
   3.8 Conclusion   104

4. The Food Weapon: Geopolitics in the Middle East   107

4.1 Food for Peace and Gangsterism by Cowboys: Saudi Arabia
vs. Nasser's Egypt   109
4.2 We Freeze, They Starve: Counter Threats to the Oil Embargo   114
4.3 US Current Account, Inflation, and Food Politics   120
4.4 The Grain OPEC   126
4.5 The Reagan Doctrine of Agricultural Trade   130
4.6 No Oil, No Food: Iraq in the 1990s   134
4.7 Conclusion   138

Part II. Gulf Food Security and International Agro-Investments

5. The Global Land Grab Phenomenon   143
5.1 Patterns of Agricultural Expansion   146
5.2 Asians, Arabs, and Asset Managers: The Different
Investor Types   150
5.3 Land Grabs and Social Conflict   154
5.4 Conclusion   160

6. The Sudan Bread-Basket Dream   161
6.1 Surplus, Statehood, and Development   161
6.2 The Gulf and the Sudan Bread-Basket Vision   171
6.3 Gulf Capital Buying In   174
6.4 The Basket Case   179
6.5 The Aftermath of a Failure: 1980s and 1990s   187
6.6 The Bread-Basket Reloaded: A Dam Program and an
"Agricultural Revival" in the 2000s   189
6.7 Conclusion   193

7. Return to the Future: Current Gulf Agro-investments   195
7.1 Targeted Countries and Crops   197
7.2 The State as Facilitator: Differences between GCC Countries   207
7.3 The Investors: Sovereign Wealth Funds, State-owned
Companies, and the Private Sector   217
7.4 Conclusion   225

8. Explaining the Implementation Gap: Money, Water, and Politics   227
8.1 A Land Grab that Wasn't   227
8.2 The Global Financial Crisis and the SWF Meltdown   231
8.3 Framework Conditions, Water Stress, and Climate Change   233
8.4 Resource Nationalism, NGOs, and Hydropolitics   244
8.5 Conclusion   253

9. Oil-for-Food Policies?   255
9.1 Domestic Policies: Oil, Diversification, Water   255

9.2 Multilateral Regimes: WTO, G20, International Storage,
     and Climate Change   258
9.3 Bilateral Relations   264

References   269
Index   303

Figures and Maps

Fig. 1.1. Top five food exporters to the GCC countries by traded item (2008)   30

Fig. 3.1. Harvested crops in Saudi Arabia (2006)   79

Fig. 7.1. Number of announced Gulf agro-projects and MoUs (2008–11)   197

Fig. 7.2. Gulf development funds: total cumulative financial assistance
(end 2007)   220

Map 2.1. The Middle East   37

Map 6.1. Sudan and South Sudan   163

Tables

Table 1.1. Oil and gas dependence of GCC economies in 2010   10

Table 1.2. Population growth and fertility rates in the Middle East, 2010–50   12

Table 1.3. Vulnerability to food price shocks in the GCC countries, 2007   15

Table 1.4. Food security levels and mineral wealth: Arab League states, Turkey, and Iran   18

Table 1.5. Consumption patterns, share in total dietary energy consumption, 2005–07   27

Table 1.6. Self-sufficiency ratios of Gulf countries and Sudan in 2008   28

Table 2.1. Pre-war diets in international comparison   46

Table 3.1. Timeline of agricultural subsidy regimes in Saudi Arabia   74

Table 3.2. Urbanization rate of Saudi Arabia   81

Table 3.3. Cultivated area in the Gulf   89

Table 6.1. Net disbursement of economic aid to Sudan from major donors, 1972–79   177

Table 8.1. Governance rankings of selected target countries   235

Table 8.2. Water resources, virtual water trade, and net food trade in selected target countries   239

Acronyms and Abbreviations

AAAID	Arab Authority for Agricultural Investment and Development
ADFD	Abu Dhabi Fund for Development
ADIA	Abu Dhabi Investment Authority
AFESD	Arab Fund for Economic and Social Development
AMF	Arab Monetary Fund
AOAD	Arab Organization for Agricultural Development
ARAMCO	Arabian American Oil Company
ARP	Agricultural Revival Programme (Sudan)
BADEA	Arab Bank for Economic Development in Africa
CASOC	California Arabian Standard Oil Company
CGIAR	Consultative Group on International Agricultural Research
CPI	Corruption Perception Index or Consumer Price Index
EDBI	Ease of Doing Business Index
FAO	Food and Agricultural Organization of the United Nations
Feddan	4,200 m^2 or 1.038 acres or 0.42 hectares
FSI	Failed States Index
GCC	Gulf Cooperation Council (Saudi Arabia, UAE, Kuwait, Bahrain, Qatar, Oman)
GCR	Global Competitiveness Report
GDLA	Global Dry Land Alliance
GMO	Genetically Modified Organisms
GSFMO	Grain Silos and Flour Mills Organisation
HA	Hectare
HDI	Human Development Index
ICARDA	International Center for Agricultural Research in the Dry Areas
IFAD	International Fund for Agricultural Development
IFDC	International Fertilizer Development Center
IFPRI	International Food Policy Research Institute
IIASA	International Institute for Applied Systems Analysis
IIED	International Institute for Environment and Development
IRRI	International Rice Research Institute
IsDB	Islamic Development Bank
ISI	Import-substituting industrialization

IMF	International Monetary Fund
KAISAIA	King Abdullah Initiative for Saudi Agricultural Investment Abroad
KFAED	Kuwait Fund for Arab Economic Development
KIA	Kuwait Investment Authority
LDC	Least Developed Countries
MBPD	Million Barrels per Day
MENA	Middle East and North Africa
MESC	Middle East Supply Center
MoA	Ministry of Agriculture
MoAW	Ministry of Agriculture and Water
MoIWR	Ministry of Irrigation and Water Resources
MoW	Ministry of Water
MoWE	Ministry of Water and Electricity
MoU	Memorandum of Understanding
NFU	National Farmers Union
NIF	National Islamic Front (Sudan)
OAU	Organization of African Unity
OIC	Organization of the Islamic Conference
OFID	OPEC Fund for International Development
PIF	Public Investment Fund
PPP	Purchasing Power Parity
QIA	Qatar Investment Authority
QNFSP	Qatar National Food Security Programme
RAI	Responsible Agricultural Investments
SAAB	Saudi Arabian Agricultural Bank
SAGIA	Saudi Arabian Government Investment Authority
SAMA	Saudi Arabian Monetary Agency
SAR	Saudi Arabian Riyal
SCAIAP	Saudi Company for Agricultural Investment and Animal Production
SFD	Saudi Fund for Development
SME	Small and Medium-sized Enterprises
SOCAL	Standard Oil of California
SWF	Sovereign Wealth Fund
SYP	Six Year Plan (Sudan)
TNC	Transnational Company
UKCC	United Kingdom Commercial Corporation
UNDP	United Nations Development Programme

UNCTAD	United Nations Conference on Trade and Development
USGS	US Geological Service
WEF	World Economic Forum
WTO	World Trade Organization

Note on Transliteration

For Arabic transliterations, the style of the *International Journal of Middle East Studies* (IJMES) is used with the following exceptions: names and locations with well-known English spellings (e.g. Nasser, Riyadh), spellings that are used by living persons and companies to write their name in English, and spellings of names from archival sources. The article Al- is capitalized when it stands at the beginning of a name.

Introduction

When Talib Kanʿan polled the audience of his talk show on the Arabic satellite channel *Al Arabiya* about priorities of Arab food security, diversifying foreign supplies was one of the proposed solutions. In February 2010, right after the global food crisis, this was not unreasonable, given the high food import dependence of the Middle East, but it achieved only modest approval ratings. Taking steps to address desertification and the lack of water did not fare any better; only 11 percent of the audience saw them as a threat to food security in the Arab world. Poverty and lacking access to available food was not even offered as an issue. Instead, visions of autarky loomed large. Increased domestic food production, Arab economic integration, and regional cross-border investments achieved stellar acclaim.

The deeply ingrained sensitivity about food self-sufficiency in the Arab world is reminiscent of the discourse about energy independence in the West. Historic precedence informs the threat perception. Dependence on food imports during World War II was fragile. An embargo-happy US politicized food trade in the 1970s. Domestic agro-lobbies in the Middle East also like to sing the praises of self-reliance in order to defend subsidies and access to scarce resources like water.

During the global food crisis of 2008, food prices skyrocketed and food exporters announced export restrictions. As a result, agricultural investments have moved to center stage of strategic considerations in the Middle East. Privileged access to food production is seen as a cornerstone of food security, if not at home for reasons of limited water resources and arable land, then at least in countries that are geographically close and beckon with established political and cultural ties like Sudan and Pakistan. If "drill baby drill" is regarded as a panacea for the energy challenge by some in the US, "plant baby plant" is the rallying cry of an equally convinced crowd in the Middle East.

Such slogans fly in the face of limited factor endowments. Enhanced oil recovery, hydraulic fracturing, and new drilling on the one hand and improved farming technologies on the other might be able to improve self-sufficiency, but will never be able to attain it. Calls for energy independence from the Middle

East have been a fixture in US campaign politics since the Nixon administration. Yet they overlook the obvious energy interdependence between the largest oil consumer and the largest oil exporter of the world.[1] Similarly, the food import dependence of Middle Eastern countries will not disappear. Ironically, the US constitutes a large part of this dependence, alongside other grain exporters like Canada, Russia, and Australia. Oil and wheat are strategic commodities that have occupied the minds of governments on both sides.

Water scarcity has rendered self-sufficiency but a dream. Since the 1970s, the Middle East as a whole cannot grow its required food supplies from renewable water resources anymore. Extremely water-scarce parts of it like Israel, Palestine, and desert Libya lost this ability in the 1950s already. So did the Gulf countries.[2] Their recourse to mining of fossil water aquifers is unsustainable and the day of reckoning is drawing closer. Saudi Arabia has decided to phase out its subsidized wheat production by 2016. Groundwater depletion is an even more pressing issue in the Middle East than contentious cross-border sharing of surface water along the Nile, Euphrates, Tigris, and Jordan.[3] As agriculture consumes around 80 percent of water, the easiest way to save it is to reduce agricultural production and direct scarce water resources to more urgent or more valuable uses in the residential, industrial, and service sectors.

Rather than leading to Malthusian Armageddon, the lack of local water has been compensated by "virtual water" that is embedded in imports of cereals and other foodstuff. The virtual water trade has added the equivalent of a second river Nile to the region's water balance. It is a necessary precondition for food security in the Middle East and will increase in importance in coming years. Population growth will only level out after 2050 and domestic agriculture will stay flat at best. As long as other countries produce enough exportable surplus and the Middle East has the money to pay for it, there should be no problem—provided food accessibility of poor people is guaranteed by sufficient entitlements like income, access to resources, and government transfers if need be.

In its standard definition of food security the FAO not only stresses the physical, social, and economic access of "all people, at all times" to sufficient food; the food has to be safe and nutritious as well to enable a healthy and active life.[4] Most Middle Eastern countries have sufficient export earnings and migrant remittances to cover food imports. Their problem is not so much a lack of calories, but of micronutrients like iron and vitamins (Table 1.4). The food security situation is only alarming or extremely alarming in a few Arab League countries like Yemen, Sudan, Somalia, and Mauritania. In fact, the

---

[1] Al-Faisal 2009.   [2] Allan 2001: 5f.
[3] Alterman and Dziuban 2010.   [4] FAO 2010b: 8.

most water-scarce countries in the Gulf are the best off.[5] If anything, they have a problem with too many calories—their per capita ratios of diabetes and obesity are among the highest in the world.

Still, the perception of Gulf countries is one of threatened food security. With oil prices above $100 per barrel, rising food prices in the wake of the global food crisis were easy for them to stomach. They did not face the same challenges like their poor cousins in the rest of the Arab world. Their balances of payments were not stretched and they had the means to intervene in local food markets to stabilize prices. However, the export restrictions imposed by food exporters like Argentina, Russia, India, and Vietnam had an immense psychological impact. Gulf countries now face the specter that some day they might not be able to secure enough food imports at *any* price, even if their pockets are lined with petrodollars. This has reinforced the impression that food security is too important to be left to markets. Meanwhile, the political realities of the Arab food security debate have prompted approaches that are unsustainable and expensive.

The oil-for-food trade-off will be a determining factor for Middle East food security over the coming decades. Oil and gas revenues supply the bulk of the foreign currency that finances the growing food imports of the region, not only in the Gulf countries, but also in other exporter nations like Algeria, Libya, Iraq, Iran, the two Sudans, and Yemen. Furthermore, oil revenues reach the poorer neighbors of the Gulf countries indirectly in the form of aid, investments, and remittances by expatriate workers. They affect balance of payments and import options.

Oil and gas are also indispensable input factors of modern, globalized agriculture, which has grown dramatically since World War II and the Green Revolution in the 1960s. Mechanization, irrigation, and distribution networks need fuel. Nitrogen fertilizer from natural gas is crucial to feed seven billion people. Other links between oil and food include the economics of biofuels and the impact of pollution and climate change on agricultural production capacity. The Middle East does not only play a prominent role in global oil markets as producer but also in global food markets as consumer. It imports almost a third of globally traded cereals.[6]

International farmland investments are at the heart of the global food security challenge and put the Middle East in the spotlight of overlapping global crises in food, finance, and energy. Foreign agro-investments in poor countries that are food net importers like Sudan, Ethiopia, Pakistan, or the Philippines are controversial. They might compromise these countries' domestic food security and infringe upon customary land rights of smallholders

---

[5] Breisinger et al. 2012.
[6] Average 2008/9–2011/12 for all Arab League countries plus Turkey, Israel, and Iran. Data from USDA 2012b.

and pastoralists. There is an urgent need to structure investments with consideration of such stakeholders. Given the amount of publicity that Gulf land investments have attracted, two things are striking: (1) five years after their announcement few projects have been implemented; and (2) very little is known about the Middle East investors themselves. An increasing number of academic studies focus on the target countries. Less work has been done on the sources of investment. As far as they figure, accounts are based on secondary sources in English-speaking media that often take inflated numbers about land investments at face value. Why have Gulf countries started to undertake such investments? What role does their political economy of food play and what capacity constraints do they face? Why do they mistrust international markets? What geopolitical implications are behind the current investment drive? And why has there been such a gap between announcements and actual realization of projects?

This book sets out to provide answers to these questions. It analyzes how the history of food security in the Middle East informs decision-makers today. It examines how food import vulnerability has developed in the countries of the Gulf Cooperation Council (GCC), how it is perceived, and how it is managed. It pays particular attention to Saudi Arabia, the world's biggest oil exporter and the largest GCC country with the most extensive agricultural sector. The Gulf countries are in focus as they share similar factor endowments and have been the most prominent international agro-investors in Sudan and elsewhere. Dealing extensively with other important countries in the Middle East like Egypt or Iran would require separate books, yet the story of Gulf food security here is told in a wider regional context. Comparisons are made and other countries are included in the discussion. Food security can be analyzed from different angles, globally, regionally, nationally, or on a household level. The focus of this book is regional and national. Nevertheless, it tries to identify vulnerable segments of the population and links Gulf food security with the global picture by illustrating how international actors have played a role in regional developments.

Chapter 1 maps out the Gulf food security predicament and situates it in the context of the global food crisis of 2008. It discusses whether there has been a paradigm shift to structurally higher food prices and outlines the international playing field that the GCC countries are facing as they increasingly need to satisfy their food needs from abroad. The importance of food accessibility for political legitimacy of the region's rentier states is discussed, beside the crisis of domestic agriculture, the water situation, and the structure of local diets. Finally, import dependence is analyzed in detail by food items and countries of origin.

The three chapters that follow in Part I outline the history of Gulf food security. Chapter 2 shows how regional food trade was important for Gulf food security before World War II, even though the region was on the fringes of agricultural development in the wider Middle East. This was also apparent during the war when famines were only averted by supplies from the Allied Middle East Supply Center in Cairo. The experience of import disruptions and insufficient infrastructure for food distribution is imprinted on the memories of decision-makers. It has informed their self-sufficiency aspirations and international agro-investments in the 1970s as well as today. World War II and its aftermath also laid the foundation for the modernization of agriculture and established a legacy of state-led development.

Chapter 3 traces the steady rise in irrigation and mechanization of agriculture in the decades after World War II, particularly in Saudi Arabia. Sedentarization, land distribution, and control of water were important tools of political power and nation building. While there was an interest in using agriculture for economic development and increased self-sufficiency, many projects were in fact subsidized white elephants that served to distribute oil rents to clients. This chapter analyzes the establishment of pilot farms in Al-Kharj and the gradual development of agricultural institutions in the overall Saudi development process. Particular attention is given to the Saudi program of wheat self-sufficiency that was launched in the 1970s and took off in earnest in the 1980s. While agricultural developments in the small Gulf states were more subdued because of limited land and water resources, aspirations were substantial, especially in the UAE under Sheikh Zayed. The desire for self-sufficiency is also illustrated by means of comparison with cereal programs in other Middle Eastern countries such as Egypt, Iran, Syria, and Sudan.

Chapter 4 turns to the international stage. Food trade has been used as a political weapon in the Middle East several times. In the 1960s, the US withdrew subsidized food aid under the Food-for-Peace program (P.L. 480) to influence Egyptian foreign policy. In the 1970s, it threatened food embargoes in retaliation against the Arab oil boycott. Saudi Arabia reacted with a barter proposal to Australia that aimed at obtaining privileged bilateral access to food in exchange for oil. The US also contemplated a "Grain OPEC" to extract political favors from oil exporters and to improve its balance of payments. There has been a depoliticization of the food trade out of commercial considerations since the 1980s, yet the UN embargo against Iraq in the 1990s showed the Arab world the disastrous effects of a multilateral cut-off of food supplies. The chapter analyzes these episodes from the perspective of Gulf policy-makers and shows how they motivated a desire for self-sufficiency. It also illustrates why embargoes mostly failed to achieve their policy goals and only led to trade diversion.

The four chapters of Part II analyze Gulf food security in its global dimension. The historical aspects that have been developed in Part I are used as a backdrop for current Gulf agro-investments, which are put into the context of the global food crisis and earlier investment attempts in the 1970s.

Chapter 5 introduces the phenomenon of global farmland investments that have made headlines since 2008. Declining growth rates of agricultural productivity, inequalities, meatification of diets, the use of biofuels, population growth, climate change, and ecological degradation all threaten food security on a global level. The motivation and capacities of Gulf investors are compared with other international investors like China and Western financial institutions. Basic problems of such land investments are discussed and potential conflicts with local stakeholders are outlined.

Chapter 6 analyzes the failed attempt to develop Sudan as Arab bread-basket in the 1970s. Gulf governments hoped that Sudan with its huge land mass and considerable water resources could alleviate the vulnerability of imports and the threat of the food weapon. These plans failed at the time, but many have resurfaced with the global food crisis of 2008. This chapter takes a detailed look at the institutions involved in the 1970s. Sudan's agricultural sector, forms of land tenure, and the reasons for the failure of the bread-basket dream are analyzed. Yet a reloaded version of it appeared on the stage when the Sudanese government launched a massive dam program and announced plans for an "agricultural revival" (*al-nahda al-zira'iyya*) in the 2000s.

After the global food crisis, international agro-investments by Gulf countries have been placed back on the agenda. This time, investors have looked beyond Sudan. Chapter 7 gives an overview of announced projects, targeted countries, and institutions involved. It analyzes local conditions and political backlash in countries like Sudan, Ethiopia, Pakistan, and the Philippines. The role of sovereign wealth funds (SWFs) and the interplay of state and private sector are crucial in the political economy of such investments. Different GCC approaches are highlighted, most notably in Saudi Arabia and Qatar, which have the highest degree of institutionalization for international agro-investments.

Dispelling some of the widespread media hype around international land deals, chapter 8 analyzes why there has been such a gap between announced Gulf agro-investments and their actual implementation. Gulf investors have identified challenging business environments, political instability, and infrastructure shortcomings as impediments. Some target countries face similar climatic constraints as the Gulf countries. Water stress compromises their development capabilities and climate change will likely exacerbate existing problems. On a political plane, established agro-exporters have been anxious to keep agricultural resources national while smallholders and grassroots movements in poorer developing countries have resisted agro-investments. Gulf countries could also become parties in delicate hydropolitics along the Nile, Euphrates, and Indus should they actually implement projects on a large scale.

Chapter 9 concludes and offers a speculative outlook. Food security in Gulf countries is about managing import dependence. Self-sufficiency is no longer an option because of water scarcity. Foreign agro-investments in developing countries can be one piece of the puzzle, but they may end up stillborn like previous attempts in Sudan in the 1970s. Win-win situations will only prove possible if the interests of stakeholders in targeted countries are safeguarded. Apart from this, Gulf countries will need to look at other areas to guarantee food security. They can improve cooperation with institutions like the WTO. They can work on international storage solutions in order to prevent a renewed occurrence of export restrictions. They can improve water security with domestic policies. They can reduce unhealthy diets and overconsumption of calories. They can also ensure revenue streams by stretching the lifetime of their oil reserves and preserving the value of their overseas assets. Ultimately, the future of food security will hinge upon food imports and the ability to pay for them. Hence, broad-based participation in economic diversification, not domestic agriculture, is at the heart of the Gulf food security challenge.

1

The Gulf Food Security Predicament

1.1 THE MIDDLE EAST AND THE GLOBAL FOOD CRISIS OF 2008

The year 2008 was inauspicious for food security in the Middle East. Saudi Arabia started to phase out subsidized wheat production for lack of water. Iran temporarily rivaled Egypt as the largest wheat importer of the world after a drought reduced its harvest. Rising food prices diminished the purchasing power of urban classes and led to protests in several cities of the region. The countries of the Nile Basin Initiative were unable to reach an agreement about water security and the allotment of Nile waters. Egypt and Sudan were pitted against sub-Saharan riparians.[1] In Syria, several hundred thousand people left the land in the Eastern provinces after a drought wreaked havoc and 70 percent of livestock herds perished. Iraq's agriculture continued to be devastated after decades of neglect, sanctions, and war.

Just as the limits of domestic agriculture became apparent, the reliability of global food markets began to falter. Food exporters announced export restrictions after a commodities boom affected their own food security. International cooperation for market stabilization was lacking. Old fears resurfaced about geopolitical disruptions of food supplies. The export restrictions proved to be temporary, but the psychological damage was done. For at least a short time, even oil exporters with massive petrodollar reserves were unable to buy food as they pleased on the open market.

Gulf countries reacted with four different responses to the food crisis: (1) to buffer the impact of food inflation, they increased subsidies and public sector wages, implemented price controls, and handed out direct payments to the national population; (2) they increased strategic storage of basic food items; (3) they introduced water saving technologies in domestic agriculture and phased out water intensive crops; and (4) they announced a flurry of international agro-investments that aimed at securing privileged access to food production via bilateral arrangements.

---

[1] Mekonnen 2010: 428.

Oil and Diversification

All of these measures require money that still comes directly or indirectly from oil, with additions from natural gas. In the Gulf countries, hydrocarbon revenues in 2010 constituted on average 46 percent of GDP and around three-quarters of government revenues and total exports (see Table 1.1). The hydrocarbon share of the UAE is relatively low, partly because of more economic diversification, partly because of a high share of re-exports in total trade. Bahrain's hydrocarbon share of GDP is low because production peaked in 1977 and because the country achieved some success with diversification in sectors like finance and tourism. The shares of Kuwait and Saudi Arabia are higher. In comparison to the 1970s, there has been diversification and oil dependence has declined, but it has inched up again in the 2000s because of rising oil prices.[2]

Pure quantitative measures have their shortcomings. They do not differentiate between non-oil activities that are mere derivatives of rent distribution like government jobs or real estate, and true diversification sectors like logistics, renewable energies, or heavy industries. When oil prices are decreasing, quantitative measures signal diversification. When they are increasing, a proof of statistical diversification becomes all but impossible, even if there are successful examples of new economic activity beyond the oil upstream sector. Qualitative aspects of diversification can only be judged on a disaggregated level.[3] Gulf countries have managed to create new industries and have put the infrastructure in place to expand these sectors, yet for the foreseeable future the importance of oil income will remain paramount.

As oil production matures, economic diversification will become more important to facilitate food imports. This is already apparent in Oman and Bahrain where oil production has peaked. In less well-endowed countries with

Table 1.1. Oil and gas dependence of GCC economies in 2010 (estimates, shares in %)

	Saudi Arabia	UAE	Kuwait	Qatar	Bahrain	Oman
Hydrocarbons/GDP	52	34	52	57	25	54
Hydrocarbons/Gov. revenues	90	76	81	55[b]	85[c]	85
Hydrocarbons/Exports	86[a]	35[a]	95	90	75[c]	66

Source: IMF 2012, 2011a–f. GDP figures from IMF 2011f.
(a) Includes refined products
(b) Investment income of state-owned hydrocarbon companies is subsumed under non-hydrocarbon revenues and the investment income of state-owned companies in total. The latter's share in government revenue was 25 percent in 2010
(c) Actual shares, not estimates

[2] Beutel 2012; Malaeb 2006.   [3] Luciani 2012b.

larger populations like Yemen, Egypt, or Syria, the role of hydrocarbons is still substantial. Egypt has turned into a net oil importer at the end of the 2000s. Before production plummeted because of civil war, Syria remained a small net exporter of crude oil, but its overall petroleum balance in value terms has been negative since 2008, as it needs to import refined products. Yemen's exports will also soon be a thing of the past as production declines and consumption rises. All three countries have hoped to increase natural gas exports to make up for part of the oil revenue loss.[4] There is also an indirect dependence on oil revenues in the form of migrant remittances, transfer payments, and investments from rich Gulf countries. A substantial part of Egypt's Suez Canal fees also comes from passing oil tankers. When oil income, other exports, and remittances are not enough to purchase food imports, hardship and reliance on food aid can ensue. In this sense the term "oil for food" describes a reality that goes beyond the temporary Iraqi sanction regime of the 1990s and its Oil-for-Food program in whose context it was first used. Economic diversification is crucial for the sustainability of food imports in the long run. Uneven distribution of income, logistic shortcomings, regional conflicts, and refugees can all exacerbate the situation. The UN's World Food Program (WFP) is currently active in Yemen, Iraq, Iran, Syria, Egypt, Algeria, Sudan, Somalia, and the occupied Palestinian territories.[5]

Population Growth

Food imports will grow to feed more people and accommodate diets that are more varied. The Middle East still has one of the highest population growth rates in the world (see Table 1.2). In West Asia, which comprises the Arabian Peninsula, the Mashreq, Iran, and Turkey, the average of 1.88 percent is considerably higher than for the world (1.1 percent) or even the less developed countries excluding China (1.52 percent). Yet this average consists of very heterogeneous population growth profiles. Many countries are in the middle of a demographic transition. In Iran, the fertility rate has plummeted from 5.6 children per woman in 1985–90 to currently 1.59. Turkey, Algeria, Tunisia, Morocco, Lebanon, and the smaller Gulf states also have fertility rates at or below the replacement level of 2.1. Population growth will continue, as it takes time until youth cohorts pass through a population pyramid. But eventually growth will slow down. In some countries like Lebanon, Iran, and Oman it will turn negative by 2045–50 according to the projections of the UN Population Division.

---

[4] See the respective country analysis briefs of the US Energy Information Administration (EIA) at <http://www.eia.gov>, accessed 8 July 2012.
[5] See the WFP website <http://www.wfp.org/countries>, accessed 5 April 2012.

Table 1.2. Population growth and fertility rates in the Middle East, 2010–50 (estimates)

	Population (million)			Total Fertility Rate			Population Growth (%)		
	2010	2030	2050	2010–15	2025–30	2045–50	2010–15	2025–30	2045–50
West Asia	232	320.4	395.4	2.85	2.49	2.22	1.88	1.36	0.87
Saudi Arabia	27.5	38.5	44.9	2.64	2.01	1.67	2.13	1.21	0.56
UAE	7.5	10.5	12.2	1.71	1.49	1.59	2.17	1.22	0.43
Oman	2.8	3.6	3.7	2.15	1.57	1.49	1.89	0.75	-0.13
Egypt	81.1	106.5	123.5	2.64	2.2	1.88	1.67	1.08	0.53
Turkey	72.8	86.7	91.6	2.02	1.76	1.69	1.14	0.63	0.08
Lebanon	4.2	4.7	4.7	1.76	1.59	1.64	0.73	0.33	-0.21
Algeria	35.5	43.5	46.5	2.14	1.72	1.66	1.36	0.67	0.16
Iran	74	84.4	85.3	1.59	1.34	1.61	1.04	0.31	-0.15
Yemen	24.1	41.3	61.6	4.94	3.63	2.75	3.03	2.38	1.75
Iraq	31.7	55.3	83.4	4.53	3.71	2.96	3.1	2.45	1.82
Sudan and South Sudan	43.6	66.9	91	4.22	3.29	2.54	2.39	1.9	1.34

Source: United Nations 2010.

Population growth in the UAE is fueled by predominantly male migration and is expected to be relatively high despite a birth rate below replacement level. Egypt, the most populous country, and Saudi Arabia occupy a middle rank. Their fertility rates will fall to and below replacement level in 2025–30. Population growth in Saudi Arabia is expected to peak in 2065. Birth rates are still high in Yemen, Iraq, Sudan, and the occupied Palestinian territories. Their population growth will remain robust beyond 2050. To accommodate more people with food imports and some domestic production will be a challenge. Food availability and accessibility are crucial for maintaining legitimacy. Even if food inflation has not led to outright hunger, it has reduced people's purchasing power. It played an important role in the Arab Spring and governments in the region are concerned about its impact on political stability.

1.2 SOCIAL CONTRACT, SUBSIDIES, AND PRICE CONTROLS

In the US, 45 million people receive food stamps, one out of seven Americans.[6] Affordable food is an important part of the social contract in any country. The Middle East is no exception. If anything, welfare provision there is even more important for legitimacy. The unwritten ruling bargain of Gulf rentier states is

[6] *The Economist*, 14 July 2011.

no taxation and no representation. The state enjoys relative autonomy as a result of oil rents. It does not require tax income and does not grant participation in return. Yet there is a sense of mutual obligation. The state buys political acquiescence by redistributing oil rent. Citizens are rewarded in the form of public sector jobs, government contracts, and transfer payments. This social contract came under pressure in the 1980s and 1990s due to high population growth and low oil prices. Since the public sector could not guarantee the necessary job creation for a burgeoning youth population, developing the private sector became official government policy. Still, the basic premise of the deal remains in place. During the Arab Spring, welfare payments were used to pre-empt public discontent and calls for more participation.[7]

Food inflation hits lower income groups particularly hard because they have to spend a higher share of their disposable income on food. There were food-related riots in 48 countries during the 2007/2008 spike in food prices.[8] Riots of this sort have not been reported in the Gulf, but there has been criticism. In a rare sign of political opposition, a number of high-ranking Saudi clerics warned that inflation could "have a negative impact on all levels, causing theft, cheating, armed robbery and resentment between rich and poor."[9]

Gulf countries are autocracies and have suppressed dissent in the wake of the Arab Spring. Yet the prevalent pattern is still one of inducement and soft coercion. Debates in majlis gatherings, the social media, and even in some newspapers can be lively and there are limited avenues for informal participation. Regimes need to heed some sort of public opinion and food plays no minor role in it as the following episode from Saudi Arabia illustrates. Mohammad al-Qunaybit, a member of the consultative body Majlis al-Shura and newspaper columnist, became a vocal public critic of food price inflation. Stopping short of criticizing the king himself, he argued that "the king's advisers are creating a cloud of confusion around him." In the ensuing public debate the Minister of Commerce and Industry Hashim Yamani made the mistake of acting too nonchalantly by replying that there were nineteen types of rice and "it [was] not compulsory for people to eat the most expensive." King Abdullah's reaction was to fire Yamani, install a rice subsidy, and increase government salaries. At the same time, Qunaybit was informed that he should change his tone.[10]

Subsidy Programs and Price Controls

Fuel, electricity, and water subsidies constitute the bulk of subsidy payments in the Gulf, but food subsidies are not far behind. Saudi Arabia has substantial

---

[7] Breisinger, Ecker, and Al-Riffai 2011.　　[8] Brinkman and Hendrix 2010.
[9] *Gulf News*, 17 December 2007.　　[10] Lacey 2009: 305.

food support schemes in place, comparable to Egypt and Iran. In addition to food for human consumption, the government subsidizes imports of barley and other livestock fodder. These subsidies have been handled flexibly. The government raised and reduced them drastically depending on the development of world market prices. The rice subsidy that King Abdullah put in place in 2007 was later eliminated in order to stop profiteering by traders.[11] In 2011, rising world market prices rendered a price ceiling for barley fodder all but meaningless. A black market developed and sent livestock prices soaring ahead of the inflation prone Ramadan season. After public pressure, the government raised the barley subsidy in order to bring subsidized import prices in line with the set price ceiling.[12]

Other Gulf countries also intervene, but in a less systematic fashion. Qatar was reluctant to introduce food subsidies in 2008; instead, it implemented food price controls in 2011 alongside pay hikes for government employees.[13] As part of a general subsidy package in the same year, the Kuwaiti ruler announced 14 months of free staple foods for nationals, who already enjoy subsidies on such items. Whereas the Saudi subsidies affected the general price level, this ad hoc measure did not benefit the expatriate population of the emirate. The same is true for the public sector pay hikes that various Gulf countries have enacted since 2008. Expatriates are primarily employed in the private sector. The various subsidy regimes did not insulate Gulf countries from the pass through of global food price rises. In the UAE it was particularly high and above the global average.[14] With the exception of the UAE and Yemen, food prices in the MENA countries are also downward-sticky and tend to remain on elevated levels after global price corrections. The UAE does not have a system of consumption subsidies like Saudi Arabia, but it has tried to rein in food inflation through price controls for staple foods. This led to complaints by retailers about ensuing losses and the need for cross-subsidies. Without global food prices falling or the government making up for losses via subsidies, the price controls were criticized. Some retailers stopped offering certain goods, as their prescript sales prices did not cover their costs.[15] In fact, the Abu Dhabi government later granted selected subsidies to state-owned food processor Agthia to make up for grain price inflation.[16]

---

[11] Mousa 2009, 2010.
[12] *Saudi Gazette*, 17 July 2011; *Arab News*, 21 July 2011.
[13] WikiLeaks cable 08DOHA422, US Embassy in Doha, 4 June 2008; *Gulf News*, 7 September 2011.
[14] Ianchovichina, Loening, and Wood 2012: 18.
[15] *The National*, 5 and 27 July 2011.
[16] *The National*, 27 July 2012.

Migrant Workers and Vulnerability to Food Price Shocks

Statistics in the GCC often lack detail and reliability. This is particularly true for the UAE. The IMF, banks, and international think tanks have questioned inflation statistics in the past.[17] The share of food in the general Consumer Price Index (CPI) is 26 percent in Saudi Arabia, 14.3 percent in the UAE, and 18 percent in Qatar and Kuwait.[18] This is comparable to OECD countries and below the developing world where people often spend more than 40 percent of their income on food. Yet the devil is in the detail that official statistics lack. There are segments of the population that are more exposed to food price inflation. A survey by Bayt and YouGov, a recruitment firm and a polling company, found that most people in the GCC spend between 10 and 20 percent of their income on food, but there were also cohorts of about 10 percent of the samples that spent 30 to 50 percent and more on food (see Table 1.3).

In reality, this share might be higher due to sample bias. The survey was conducted online and poorer blue-collar workers often do not have internet access or are illiterate. People with a monthly income of less than $1001 represented 26 percent of the samples and Asians 31 percent. There are no official population breakdowns according to ethnicity in the GCC and the figure is highly political, but in all likelihood, the share of both groups in the actual population is higher. Asians often work as blue-collar workers and domestic servants in the GCC. In the UAE, Qatar, and Kuwait they are the majority.[19] They have suffered most from high inflation rates. Delays in wage

Table 1.3. Vulnerability to food price shocks in the GCC countries, 2007 (share of income spent on food, % of total sample)

	Saudi Arabia	UAE	Kuwait	Qatar	Bahrain	Oman
Sample size	2081	3129	903	422	151	135
Less than 11%	22	24	14	24	23	13
11–20%	38	44	46	43	39	40
21–30%	15	12	18	11	14	13
30–50%	10	7	9	7	6	19
More than 50%	1	1	2	0	3	3
Don't know/Can't say/N/A	13	13	11	15	16	10

Source: Bayt.Com and YouGov Siraj 2007: 34.

[17] *Arabian Business Magazine*, 26 March 2009; Bertelsmann Transformation Index 2010; IMF 2007.

[18] Sfakianakis 2008: 4; *KUNA*, 7 April 2012.

[19] According to estimates, expatriates constitute 37 percent of the GCC population on average. Their share ranges between 20 percent in Oman, 27 percent in Saudi Arabia, 64 percent in Kuwait, and up to 81 percent in the UAE. Kapiszewski 2006: 4. Asians constitute the largest

payments and difficult working conditions have repeatedly led to wildcat strikes, mostly in the UAE but also in other Gulf countries. Migrant workers lack formal channels to make their voice heard and officials have identified them as a security threat on numerous occasions. The GCC General Secretary did so publicly in 2005 and in 2008, the Bahraini Minister of Labor chose to describe Asian labor migration as "a danger worse than the atomic bomb or an Israeli attack."[20] Still, authorities are inclined to address their grievances to safeguard stability. During the food crisis of 2008 officials were particularly concerned about the price of rice, their main staple food.[21] Amartya Sen's research about historical famines in India and Ethiopia has contributed to viewing food insecurity as a political and social construct, whereas earlier it was mainly regarded as a technical issue of agricultural productivity and food distribution.[22] Lack of entitlements and food accessibility on a micro-level, amid food availability on a macro-level can be an issue in the Gulf region as well, even though its shining metropolises appear remote from disaster stricken famine areas.

1.3 MALTHUS NOT ANTE PORTAS: DOMESTIC AGRICULTURE AND THE LACK OF WATER

Gulf countries are food secure—mostly. Their per capita incomes are comparable to developed countries. Qatar has the highest in the world, ahead of Luxemburg, Singapore, and Norway. Export earnings cover food imports many times over. The infrastructure to distribute food is available and meets international standards. Income distribution is unequal and there are vulnerable segments of the population, but no one goes hungry as long as wages are paid and markets are supplied.[23] Food accessibility is often ensured by subsidies. If anything, there is a problem with an excessive intake of calories, unhealthy dietary patterns, and a lack of physical exercise. The Gulf has one of the highest per capita rates of obesity and diabetes in the world. Obesity

share of expatriates, followed by non-local Arabs and Westerners. An article in *Al-Bayan* on 29 October 2008 claimed to be based on government sources and put the share of Indians, Pakistanis, and Bangladeshis in the UAE population at 59 percent alone.

[20] Janardhan 2011: 102.

[21] Interviews, Dubai, May 2008.

[22] Sen 1981. For a similar argument about famines in the late nineteenth century see Davis 2001: 5–63.

[23] In the wider Middle East income inequality is comparable to Asia and lower than in Latin America and Africa; Noland and Pack 2007: 67. There is no Gini coefficient data for the Gulf countries, but anecdotal evidence suggests that inequalities are high. This applies not only to migrant labor but also to poor nationals, particularly in Saudi Arabia.

rates have trebled since 1980.[24] The dietary change towards greater shares of meat and dairy products, processed foods, and sugar that is currently observable in emerging markets like China and India began in the region in the 1970s already.

On the Global Hunger Index (GHI) 2011 of IFPRI et al. the MENA countries do not score badly and show a low risk of hunger with values at or below 5, with the exception of Sudan (21.5), Yemen (24), and Mauritania (12.7), which have values that signal serious or alarming risk.[25] Yet the three equally weighted categories of the GHI, percentage of the undernourished among the general population and prevalence of underweight and mortality among children younger than five, indicate calorie shortages. They do not capture lack of micronutrients like iron or vitamins as good as the prevalence of stunting (height for age), which also indicates other important aspects like clean drinking water and access to health care. The IFPRI report *Beyond the Arab Awakening* of 2012 uses stunting as an indicator for food security on the micro-level and here the situation is less sanguine (Table 1.4).

Between 15 and 25 percent of Arab children under five are too short for their age, but only 5 to 15 percent are underweight.[26] Even in Gulf countries like Saudi Arabia, Oman, and Bahrain stunting is a serious issue with prevalence rates close to 10 percent. As there is a concomitant obesity epidemic this comes as a surprise. It is further complicated by the fact that stunting and obesity not only happen on opposite sides of the social spectrum, the rich and the poor, but also in poor households as a result of calorie rich but micronutrient poor diets. The same person can even experience both conditions over her lifetime. If a mother experiences serious malnutrition in the womb or until the age of two, her metabolism will change permanently and will be geared towards storing spare calories as fat for a rainy day. If her diet improves due to economic growth or government subsidies for calorie rich food like bread and sugar, she will become obese, while her children will be stunted. The co-occurrence of obesity, micronutritional deficiencies, and stunting is a worldwide phenomenon, but nowhere as common as in the Arab world. In Egypt, the share of obese people in the general population is 30 percent—all in a country that faces a serious food security challenge. The lack of micronutrients, not lack of calories or self-sufficiency, is the main food security issue in most Middle Eastern countries and the Gulf region.

For the oil rich Gulf countries, low food production per capita does not matter if world markets stay open. Yet their production is not so low after all.

---

[24] Alpen Capital 2011: 22. The obesity rate in Saudi Arabia stays at 36 percent, in the UAE at 34 percent, and in Kuwait and Bahrain slightly lower at 29 percent. Globally, Saudi Arabia and the UAE are among the top five countries with diabetes prevalence with a share of roughly 13 percent.

[25] IFPRI, Concern Worldwide, and Welthungerhilfe 2011: 49f.

[26] For the following see *The Economist*, 3 March 2012; Ghattas 2012; Ruel 2012.

The Gulf Food Security Predicament

Table 1.4. Food security levels and mineral wealth: Arab League states, Turkey, and Iran

	Macro food security: Food imports in % of total exports + net remittances[a]	Micro food security (% of stunted children[a])	Overall food security (average of macro and micro food security)[a]	Food security risk[a]	Food production per capita (2000, international $)[b]	GDP per capita (PPP, US$, 2011e, rounded)[c]
Oil exporters						
Saudi Arabia	4.0	9.1*	6.5	Low	104	24,000
Kuwait	2.4	3.8[4]	3.1	Low	55	40,700
UAE	3.4	–	–	Low	114	48,600
Qatar	2.0	4.0*	3.0	Low	n/a	102,900
Oman	6.2	9.6*	7.9	Low	n/a	26,300
Bahrain	2.9	9.0*	5.9	Low	n/a	27,400
Iraq	–	27.5[3]	–	Serious	n/a	3,900
Iran	2.4	16.6*	9.5	Moderate	246	12,300
Algeria	7.3	15.6*	11.4	Serious	111	7,200
Libya	3.4	21.0[5]	12.2	Moderate	133	13,900 (2010)
Sudan	8.4	37.9[3]	23.2	Alarming	148	3,000
Yemen	15.4	59.6[3]	37.5	Ex. Alarming	44	2,500
Oil importers						
Egypt	8.7	30.7[6]	19.7	Serious	199	6,500
Syria	9.7	28.6[3]	19.2	Serious	237	5,100
Jordan	13.9	8.3[4]	11.1	Serious	120	5,900
Lebanon	16.5	15.0*	15.7	Serious	258	15,600
Morocco	8.2	21.6*	14.9	Serious	163	5,100
Tunisia	6.5	9.0[3]	7.7	Moderate	220	9,600
West Bank & Gaza	31.9	11.8[5]	21.9	Serious	135	2,900 (2008)[d]
Somalia	–	42.1[3]	–	Alarming	–	600 (2010)[d]
Mauritania	20.6	24.2[6]	22.4	Alarming	–	2,200
Djibouti	42.3	32.6	37.4	Ex. Alarming	–	2,700
Comoros	49.2	47.0	48.1	Ex. Alarming	–	1,200
Turkey	2.0	13.9*	8.0	Moderate	–	14,600

Source: (a) Breisinger et al. 2012; (b) Breisinger et al. 2010; (c) IMF 2011g; (d) CIA Factbook
PPP = Purchasing Power Parity
*estimates for 2008; [1] = 2003; [2] = 2005; [3] = 2006; [4] = 2009; [5] = 2007; [6] = 2008

Perceived vulnerability of food imports has motivated the desire for self-sufficiency. Saudi Arabia embarked on a costly program of subsidized wheat production in the 1970s that made it the world's sixth largest wheat *exporter* by the beginning of the 1990s.[27] Its livestock sector consumes about 40 percent of globally traded barley today. The smaller UAE also developed visions of self-reliance under its late ruler Sheikh Zayed, against the odds of even more limited water resources. Subsidized agriculture has been a means to foster alliances. Alongside import licenses, sponsorship schemes, government contracts, and land grants, it has been used to reward clients and buy political acquiescence.[28]

Subsidized agriculture in Saudi Arabia was able to keep pace with population growth in the 1980s and 1990s. The food gap between domestic consumption and production that rose dramatically in the 1970s did not significantly widen. However, renewable water reserves were not enough to sustain this momentum. Vast production gains were achieved by mining fossil water aquifers. These are now running dry, and Gulf agriculture is becoming unsustainable. In light of this, Qatar has reformulated the self-sufficiency vision and aims at domestic production with futuristic means such as hydroponics and greenhouses that are run with solar-based desalination. Thus, Qatar hopes to produce up to 70 percent of its food by 2023.[29] For a small, very wealthy city-state, this might be possible at a high price, but for larger countries like Saudi Arabia, this is not an option. Desalinated water is too expensive for agriculture. It supplies 85–99 percent of drinking water in Kuwait, Qatar, UAE, and Bahrain. In Oman and Saudi Arabia this share was still below 50 percent by the mid-2000s but has inched up to 70 percent in the latter case.[30]

All GCC countries now recognize that water scarcity is a problem. However, discussions often revolve around technical fixes since water subsidies are regarded as an entitlement that is too sensitive to be touched. Nonetheless, some decisions against vested interests have been taken. In 2007 Saudi Arabia announced the phasing out of wheat production by 2016. The subsidized agricultural schemes in the country are economically unfeasible and ecologically unsustainable. In contrast to the 1970s the development of domestic agriculture has ceased to be an option in the quest for food security. Dependence on food imports will rise in an increasingly volatile global market environment.

1.4 GLOBAL FOOD PRICES: PARADIGM SHIFT OR NOT?

The global food crisis that began in 2008 is reminiscent of the food price spikes at the beginning of the 1970s that led to the World Food Conference in 1974.

[27] Richards and Waterbury 2008: 163.   [28] Luciani 2005.
[29] *Gulf Times*, 20 February 2011.
[30] Dawoud 2007: 31, 39ff; *Saudi Gazette* 1 September 2012.

Now, as then, Malthusian fears as exemplified in the Club of Rome reports are widespread.[31] Now, as then, there is a wave of international initiatives to spur agricultural growth. Now, as then, Gulf countries face a rising food gap and consider developing Sudan as an Arab bread-basket.

The food crisis of the early 1970s and accompanying Malthusian fears subsided and gave way to low commodity prices in the 1980s and 1990s. Agricultural development disappeared from the radar screens of policy-makers. Cheap food was taken for granted again. By 2005, most developing countries were investing only about 5 percent of public revenues in farming. The share of Western aid related to agriculture declined by three-quarters between 1980 and 2006.[32]

Is the food crisis of 2008 different? Are high food prices here to stay? The rising global interest in farmland investments and a flurry of political initiatives would indicate yes. The OECD and FAO estimate that global food production will need to increase 40 percent by 2030 and 70 percent by 2050 to meet anticipated demand. During the coming decade, food prices are expected to remain considerably above their former long-term averages.[33]

The argument for a structural shift in food prices is often repeated. Population growth, biofuel demand in developed countries, and dietary changes in emerging markets like China impact the demand side. On the supply side, waste along the logistic chain remains high, the productivity gains of the Green Revolution have petered out, and erosion, water stress, and climate change affect production. The available bank of uncultivated land is limited and input factors like oil and fertilizers have become more expensive.[34] City dwellers now outnumber the world's rural population and the cost of food distribution is set to rise.

Apart from fundamental supply and demand factors, there is evidence that the steep rise in trading of financial derivatives caused increased food price volatility. If financial investors were only active on the long end of the market, like pension funds usually are, they also contributed to higher prices as they constituted additional demand.[35] The deregulation of agriculture since the 1970s has been another factor in increased food price volatility, whatever the inefficiencies of the old system were. The storage of staple crops for price stabilization has diminished with the breakdown of international commodity agreements in the 1970s, the inclusion of agriculture in the Uruguay round of the GATT in 1986, and the decoupling of farm subsidies from price support schemes. The latter happened in the US in

---

[31] Meadows and Club of Rome 1972; Meadows, Randers, and Meadows 2004.

[32] *The Economist*, 19 November 2009.

[33] OECD-FAO 2009: 62, 2010: 32.

[34] Brown 2009: Chapters 1–3.

[35] Hernandez and Torero 2010; Schutter 2010a.

1996 and in the EU in 2003 in the wake of the reform of the Common Agricultural Policy (CAP).[36]

The Stuttering Agricultural Treadmill

A sustained upward trend in food prices would be a fundamental paradigm shift. Temporary price spikes notwithstanding, food prices have been falling in real terms since the 1860s.[37] Only since the late 1980s has this trend leveled out somewhat.[38] Production growth was fueled by land expansion until the early twentieth century and by a productivity explosion after World War II. Mechanized agriculture, intensive livestock production, and mineral fertilizer application have proven Malthus wrong. World population did grow dramatically, but food production grew even more. The long-term trend of falling prices in real terms has forced producers to increase productivity via capital investments to stay competitive. This kept farm prices on their downward trend as supplies continued to outpace demand. The latter was also hampered because of persistent poverty levels, especially in the developing world. The "agricultural treadmill" (Cochrane) has made mechanized farming a victim of its own success: Productivity gains transformed into lower prices, necessitating a constant need to scale up production in order to avoid revenue loss.[39]

The large majority of small-scale farmers were bystanders or losers in this process. Either they were confined to subsistence farming and low productivity, or they entered the agricultural treadmill and were spat out if they failed to scale up their operations. In the US, about a quarter of the population lived on a farm in 1930. Nowadays the number of full-time farmers is about half that of the prison population. Those still farming have been spectacularly productive. Mechanized operations in the US and elsewhere have produced structural grain surpluses since World War II. They have fed growing cities, not only in their own countries but also in the Middle East and other parts of the developing world. Small-scale farmers in the Third World did not figure as producers in this trade. If their traditional production systems failed or they were not able to compete with heavily subsidized and mechanized farming operations in the developed world, their food security was compromised. Either they received food aid or they migrated to the cities and generated other income. Otherwise, the purchase of "cheap" food from the mechanized sector would have been out of their reach.[40]

---

[36] Winders 2011.   [37] Johnson 1999.
[38] Piesse and Thirtle 2009.
[39] Cochrane 1958.
[40] Weis 2007: 25ff, 82; Friedmann and McMichael 1989.

The agricultural treadmill is stuttering in quantitative output terms, even though its pace might continue for those who are in it because of rising input costs. Wheat and rice yield growth has roughly halved since the 1990s. This is serious as it accounted for 80 percent of production increases in these items between the 1960s and 1980s.[41] Increased yields contributed 70 percent of global agricultural production growth between 1961 and 2005, the expansion of cultivated land only 23 percent, and the intensification of cropping patterns 8 percent.[42] Productivity growth by traditional means like fertilizer, irrigation, and improved seed variants is still happening, but has declined in developed agricultural regions. The same is true for developing countries that have applied Green Revolution technologies since the 1960s, including India, China, and Mexico. Apart from decreasing marginal returns, the Green Revolution is threatened by ecological backlash that is partly of its own making. Only sub-Saharan Africa and some countries in Latin America might be able to achieve larger productivity gains by a more widespread application of such technologies.[43] An article in *Foreign Affairs* in 2010 argued that Africa was "agriculture's final frontier" and that a belated Green Revolution there would be essential for global food security.[44]

Cornucopians vs. Malthusians and the Agricultural Question

Economists are usually Cornucopian optimists. The idea of absolute resource constraints is alien to them. Increased scarcity leads to higher prices, which cut demand, spur innovation, and make new production facilities economically viable. Once the supply side reaction sets in, prices revert to mean. Instead of a paradigm shift, the normal inner workings of markets would govern. Proponents of resource pessimism have been ridiculed when their dire predictions have failed to materialize, whether it was peak coal fears in nineteenth-century Britain or peak oil projections today.[45] An article in 1974 detected six waves of food supply pessimism since Malthus' *Essay on Population* in 1789, the last one triggered by the food crisis of the early 1970s.[46] From this perspective, the global food crisis of 2008 would be just the seventh wave of such pessimism. It

---

[41] Bruinsma and FAO 2003: 46; OECD-FAO 2010: 102, 110.

[42] Deininger et al. 2011: 10.

[43] World Bank 2007: 51ff.

[44] Thurow 2010. See also Paarlberg 2008.

[45] For fears about "peak coal" in the nineteenth century see Radetzki 2010; Smil 2006. For past predictions about imminent peak oil that have passed without signs of precipitous production declines see Maugeri 2006: 206; Adelman 2004.

[46] "The Sixth Wave: The World Food Question and American Agriculture," *Foreign Agriculture*, 28 October 1974.

paints Malthusianism as an apocalyptic cult that proves nothing except that millennialism is somehow wired into the human DNA.

An established discourse argues that further agricultural productivity gains would be possible if a "gene revolution" were allowed to run its course.[47] Paul Collier believes that policy-makers could sustain agricultural production growth "indefinitely" by encouraging technological innovation.[48] Seeds of Genetically Modified Organisms (GMO) have predominantly been used in the US and a small group of other countries. Genetic modification has focused on a few crops (mainly corn, soybeans, and cotton) and traits (mainly insect resistance and herbicide tolerance).[49] There is no evidence so far that GMO would be able to achieve comparable productivity gains like the Green Revolution did in the past.[50] The field of GMO research has been left to private corporations whose technology is tailored to large-scale commercial farms, not to small-scale farmers in the developing world. This affects what is researched and for which beneficiaries.[51] The World Bank and IFPRI see GMO as context and technology specific. For a beneficial impact, orphan crops like cassava, millet, or sorghum and other traits like drought resistance would need to be addressed and proprietary technologies would need to be made accessible through more public sector research and inclusive growth policies.[52] Inequality of land ownership is one of the reasons why the Green Revolution in Latin America has produced less tangible benefits, but more environmental damage than in Asia, as Robert Paarlberg, a proponent of GMO, points out.[53] Any application of a new agricultural technology like GMO would not happen in a social void either. Meanwhile, an influential report by the International Assessment of Agricultural Knowledge, Science and Technology for Development (IAASTD) under the auspices of the United Nations and the World Bank emphasized the social and economic roots of poverty and hunger. It downplayed widespread discussions about GMO and other technological fixes and concluded that small-scale farming adapted to agro-ecological niches is more suitable for Third World countries than industrial agricultural models.[54]

Hence, a purely technical analysis of production figures and food availability is insufficient. Food insecurity is above all a socio-political problem of

---

[47] Glover 2010; Paarlberg 2008; Richards et al. 2010.

[48] Collier 2008.

[49] World Bank 2007: 177. About half of the GMO acreage is planted in the US, followed by Brazil and Argentina. The EU opposes GMO and so do many African governments, possibly out of fear for EU export markets.

[50] Brown 2009: 8.

[51] Runge and Runge 2010; Paarlberg 2010: 172f.

[52] World Bank 2007: 177ff.; IFPRI 2006; Nelson et al. 2009.

[53] Paarlberg 2010: 59–62.

[54] IAASTD 2009: 17, 67. For a critique of the report see Paarlberg 2010: 66.

distribution and equity in the production process. The world food system theoretically produces 1.5 times enough food for all people, but is organized around the poles of obesity and hunger.[55] Globalization, increased food miles, and waste along the logistic chain are part of a system that is highly dependent on hydrocarbon inputs. Transnational corporations (TNCs) like Monsanto, Cargill, or Nestlé have increasingly dominated the value chains of this global food system. They control the supply of input factors like seeds and fertilizers, dominate trade of bulk commodities, and then process them into packaged foods. The share of profits in the food system that farmers earn has been constantly decreasing since World War II. An increasing number of people in the developed world and in emerging markets thrive on unhealthy diets with large shares of meat, sugar, and processed foods, while those in the developing world who lack incomes and entitlements are exposed to price spikes in staple foods, which form a large part of their budgetary spending.

Even if one were ready to discard the concerns of advocacy groups about the impact of large-scale farming and GMO on biodiversity and the food sovereignty of farmers, the assumptions of Cornucopian optimists would seem to be overblown. It is unlikely that GMO could help the agricultural treadmill return to its old pace of output growth. Productivity gains not only face decreasing marginal growth, they are also threatened by ecological degradation that is partly of modern agriculture's own making. The food for 400 million people is grown by overpumping of aquifers and rivers, most notably in the south west US, India, East Asia, and south east Australia.[56] Intensive cultivation, tillage, and lack of drainage have led to erosion, salination, and soil exhaustion. Excessive use of fertilizer and run-off into rivers and the sea severely affects marine life and water quality.

Climate Change, Meatification, and Biofuels

Agriculture is not only affected by climate change, it is also causing it through emissions of methane from livestock and of nitrous oxide from fertilizer and manure. After the energy sector, agriculture is the single most important source of greenhouse gas emissions, contributing 15 percent of the total. If the impact of deforestation were added, which is often a result of agricultural expansion, this share grows to 26 percent.[57] Impact estimates of climate change on agricultural production are fraught with uncertainty. Much will depend on to what extent a carbon fertilization effect will materialize.[58] Yet,

---

[55] Weis 2007: 13, 169.   [56] Brown 2009: 14.

[57] World Bank 2007: 17.

[58] Müller et al. 2009. Carbon fertilization is the increase in yields as a result of increased concentration of carbon dioxide in the atmosphere.

reasonable consensus exists that the impact will be substantial, that the worst effects will set in after 2050, and that losses in output capacity will be particularly high in the Middle East and developing countries in the tropical belts of Africa, Latin America, and South Asia.[59]

Relief from the demand side of food markets could come from an accelerated demographic transition, less meat consumption, waste reduction, and changes in biofuel production. Reining in financial speculation could also take heat out of food markets. After the global financial crisis, financial markets are going through a process of re-regulation that might reverse the liberalization of commodity trading that occurred in the 2000s. Meat production needs over 10 times more land, 11 times more fossil fuels, and 100 times more water than a comparable production of plant-based calories.[60] About two-thirds of the world's arable land is dedicated to livestock production, either in the form of pasture or farmland to grow fodder.[61] A more plant-based diet and a switch to animal proteins with higher feedstock conversion efficiency like poultry or fresh water aquaculture could reduce this impact.

High oil prices and government policies have promoted biofuels as an alternative to petroleum. This has led to significant shifts in acreage towards crops for biofuel use.[62] Biofuels are expected to contribute an additional 30 percent to grain price increases by 2020 if governments achieve announced targets.[63] Thereafter there could be a reduction of their impact on price depending on the speed with which second generation biofuels are introduced. These do not rely on food crops, can be planted on poorer soils, and have considerable drought resistance (e.g. Jatropha). Third generation biofuels in the form of algae would not compete with food production at all since they can be planted in saltwater.[64] Apart from biofuels there is also increasing demand for biological raw materials that can be processed into bio-plastics, bio-lubricants, and pharmaceuticals. The impact of biofuels on food prices could be lower than expected if growing resistance against their use prompts governments to withdraw support. However, if oil prices remain high enough, biofuels will crowd out food production even in the absence of subsidies. This is particularly true for the more competitive ethanol production from sugar in Brazil.

University of Manitoba professor Vaclav Smil regards the Haber-Bosch process of nitrogen fixation, which was invented in 1909, as the single most important invention of our time, far more important than the car, the

[59] Cline 2007; Fischer et al. 2005; IPCC 2007; Knox et al. 2011; Müller et al. 2009, 2011; Nelson et al. 2009; World Bank 2010b.
[60] Pimentel and Pimentel 2003; Robbins 2001: 294.
[61] Weis 2007: 40–4; Rifkin 1992.
[62] World Bank 2008.
[63] Fischer et al. 2009: 151.
[64] Sheehan et al. 1998.

telephone, or the computer. Nitrogen fixation has allowed for the production of mineral fertilizers and the agricultural productivity revolution of the twentieth century. In 2001, Smil estimated that even the most efficient organic farming could only sustain 60 percent of the world population.[65] Solutions to the global food crisis will require modern agricultural techniques, but they will need to be more sustainable than the current ones. Fertilizers, pesticides, and water can be used more effectively with the help of precision farming.[66] Technological change has to be adapted to ecological constraints and the aspirations of small-scale farmers who are orphans of agricultural development policies. There is room for more shades of gray in a heated debate between agro-ecological purists and advocates of a brave new world of agricultural engineering.

How agricultural change will play out is impossible to predict, but there is convincing evidence of a paradigm shift towards structurally higher food prices. The old order of the agricultural treadmill and declining food prices in real terms has become shaky. Structural grain surpluses in the North at subsidized rates are not as readily available anymore for the importing countries of the Middle East. OECD countries have dealt with their dependence on energy imports by monitoring market developments and transport security. Diversity of supply has been of particular importance in managing exposure. Gulf countries must also manage supply of their food imports. What is needed? From where will they get it? How will it reach them? These are essential questions for them.

1.5 CONSUMPTION PATTERNS AND SELF-SUFFICIENCY RATIOS

Food balance sheets as used by the FAO and the Arab Organization for Agricultural Development (AOAD) measure production, change in stocks, and net trade and put the results in relation to population numbers. They do not indicate wastage and often do not capture subsistence production and micronutrient deficiencies accurately. Actual dietary intake by household and gender might differ considerably and can be better identified by surveys. Still, food balance sheets are the closest method one has to get a picture of the food provision of a country on a macro-level.

Wheat and rice constitute around 40 percent of caloric consumption in the largest GCC countries (see Table 1.5). This is considerably higher than in the

[65] Smil 2001: 204.
[66] Paarlberg 2010: 115ff.; Conway 1998; Conway and Barbier 2009; Conway and Pretty 2009.

Table 1.5. Consumption patterns, share in total dietary energy consumption, 2005–07 (%)

Food items	Saudi Arabia	UAE	Kuwait	USA	India	China	Sudan
Wheat	27	29	23	16	22	20	15
Rice (milled equivalent)	11	13	17	2	31	27	1
Sugar (raw equivalent)	10	11	10	9 + 8[c]	8	2	10
Oils[a]	11	5	10	15	7	4	3
Corn	6	–	1	3	2	2	1
Sorghum, millet, and other cereals	5	–	–	–	5	4	33
Vegetables[b]	3	9	9	4	6	11	6
Dates	5	2	1	–	–	–	1
Poultry meat	4	6	7	5	–	2	–
Mutton and goat meat	1	2	4	–	–	–	2
Meat other	1	1	–	6	–	11	2
Milk (whole and skimmed)	5	5	3	6	4	2	15
Butter, ghee	1	2	2	1	3	–	–
Eggs	–	1	2	1	–	2	–
Cheese	–	1	1	4	–	–	1
Fruits, other[d]	–	1	–	1	1	–	–
Total	90	88	90	81	89	87	90
Misc.	10	12	10	19	11	13	10

Source: FAO 2011c.
(a) Oils from corn, palm, sunflower, soybean, or groundnut
(b) Includes pulses, potatoes, tomatoes, and others
(c) 8 percent stands for other sweeteners
(d) Oranges and mandarins in the US, bananas in India

US, but lower than in developing nations like China or India. Sorghum consumption, which dominates in Sudan, plays only a minor role in Saudi Arabia, where wheat is of particular importance, accounting for 27 percent of dietary intake. Despite such high consumption, the kingdom was still close to self-sufficiency in wheat in 2008 (see Table 1.6). Since then it has started to import growing amounts as it phases out domestic production. In other GCC countries, cereal cultivation is largely non-existent and import dependence is close to total, especially in the case of rice. This is also true for oils, whose relative consumption is high in the Gulf. Import dependence for other food items such as poultry, fruits, and vegetables is also substantial, although self-sufficiency ratios can be as high as two-thirds or more. The numbers for fruits and vegetables need to be treated with caution though, given the very cosmopolitan display of such items in supermarkets in the Gulf. They probably constitute relative rather than absolute truths. Self-sufficiency ratios in fruits and vegetables are likely to remain relatively high, as domestic agriculture is reoriented to these more value added crops with the help of water saving technologies like greenhouses and drip irrigation.

Table 1.6. Self-sufficiency ratios of Gulf countries and Sudan in 2008 (%, rounded)

	Saudi Arabia	UAE	Kuwait	Qatar	Bahrain	Oman	Sudan
Cereals (total)	20	1	2	1	0	6	75
Wheat and flour	96	0	1	0	0	1	27
Corn	8	0	10	7	0	0	95
Rice	0	0	0	0	0	0	54
Barley	0	0	1	2	0	54	0
Potatoes	98	10	32	0	0	30	99
Pulses	0	10	0	0	0	0	85
Vegetables	88	38	66	20	30	46	100
Fruits	67	66	27	23	22	82	98
Sugar (refined)	0	0	0	0	0	0	86
Fats and oils	1	0	0	0	0	0	102
Meat (total)	55	21	38	23	43	22	100
Red meat	41	12	71	28	72	19	100
Poultry meat	58	23	25	19	21	23	100
Fish	50	72	36	67	154	162	95
Eggs	117	51	63	37	58	54	98
Milk and dairy products	31	17	10	7	7	163	97

Source: Arab Organization for Agricultural Development (AOAD) 2009.

Investment banks expect a continuous shift towards protein rich diets and more fruit consumption in the Gulf. Dairy demand in particular is expected to increase.[67] Food imports will continue to rise over the coming decade. The US Department of Agriculture (USDA) projects that in 2021 Saudi Arabia will be one of the largest rice importers worldwide alongside the Philippines, Indonesia, Iran, the EU, Bangladesh, and Iraq. It will continue to be the world's largest barley importer, followed by other Middle Eastern countries like Iran, whose imports will grow even faster. The Middle East and developing countries in Africa will account for about half of the total increase in global wheat trade and will absorb half of globally traded poultry, with Saudi Arabia one of the largest importers.[68]

1.6 STRUCTURE OF FOOD IMPORTS: PRODUCT GROUPS AND COUNTRIES OF ORIGIN

If there is political turmoil in an oil-producing country, consumer nations take notice. Experts in think tanks and talking heads on television ponder the risk

[67] Alpen Capital 2011; NCB Capital 2010.
[68] USDA 2012a.

of supply disruptions and possible alternatives. For Gulf countries, the origin of their food imports is of similar importance. Figure 1.1 illustrates their food import dependence at the height of the global food crisis in 2008.[69] Wheat and rice are the most important dietary contributors, followed by sugar and oils. Barley and corn are crucial as fodder for the substantial livestock industry in GCC countries. The same is true for alfalfa, which figures as part of the statistics for oilseeds. Poultry is the most important animal protein source in Gulf diets followed by live animals. Fruits, vegetables, and dairy products also play a prominent role in the diversification of diets.

Import profiles of GCC countries differ considerably from internationally dominant export countries. Gulf countries get more than half of their rice from India and about a quarter from Pakistan. The US and the largest exporters worldwide, Thailand and Vietnam, are underrepresented, because they do not produce the basmati rice variety that is preferred in the Gulf. Basmati is mainly grown in the northern Punjab region. About three-quarters of the Indian basmati rice harvest goes to the Gulf.[70] As India and Pakistan have their own domestic food security issues this is a concern. India is still a food net exporter in value terms, but in the 1990s, productivity gains of the Green Revolution leveled out and lagged behind population growth for the first time since the 1960s. Pakistan is already a net food importer in both value and calorie terms. Like south and central India, it faces a physical water shortage. As its staple food is wheat, not rice, it restricted exports of this item in 2008, not of rice like India. India tried to accommodate Gulf countries by imposing export restrictions only on South Indian coarse rice varieties. Basmati rice was exempted, but additional export duties were put on it. Saudi importers threatened to sue Indian exporters for a breach of commitments and started negotiating for alternative supplies from Pakistan and Thailand.[71] In terms of value, rice constitutes the largest food import item in the GCC, followed by poultry, barley, and dairy products.

GCC wheat imports come from a wider variety of countries and there has been greater variation of suppliers over the years. In contrast to rice, wheat is a truly global commodity. It encompasses only a few varieties that are traded in large volumes on futures exchanges. A substantial percentage of global production (18 percent) is traded across borders. Rice on the other hand is not as uniform with more than 800 different varieties. Rice futures traded in Bangkok are no comparison to wheat futures traded in Chicago in terms of traded volume or market impact. Less than 6 percent of global rice production is

---

[69] Trade and food related statistics are not as up to date as GDP and other statistics. As of June 2012, the latest available Trade Map data breakdown by partner country was 2008 on an aggregated GCC level using mirror data.

[70] Sfakianakis 2008: 17.

[71] Riyadh Chamber of Commerce and Industry 2009.

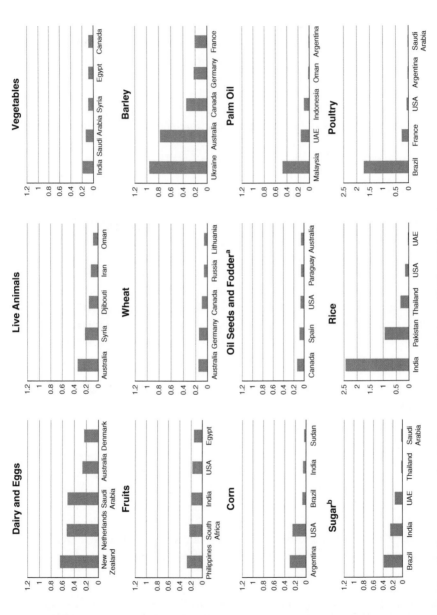

Fig. 1.1. Top five food exporters to the GCC countries by traded item (2008, US$ billion)

Source: International Trade Center 2012.

(a) Includes oleagic fruits, seeds, alfalfa (lucerne), hay, clover, and other fodder

(b) Includes sugar confectionary

traded across borders. Rice markets are more volatile because of this lack of liquidity. A harvest failure in one country is much more difficult to balance through trade. India and China alone account for over half of global rice production and Asia for three-quarters. Most of it is consumed domestically. The importance of rice for Asia's food security is paramount.[72] This showed during the global food crisis, when exporters like Thailand and Vietnam enacted export restrictions that led to panic buying by importers such as the Philippines or Indonesia.

In value terms, Gulf wheat imports trail behind other food items because wheat's unit price is relatively low and Saudi Arabia has only started to import growing quantities since 2008. India used to be the most important supplier with 40 percent shares but its wheat exports to the Gulf have plummeted since 2005.[73] Important suppliers are Australia, Germany, and Canada. Russia's role declined after its export embargo in 2010 and because of quality issues like lower protein content. The US managed to become Saudi Arabia's number three supplier by 2011.[74]

Brazil produces about 20 percent of the world's sugar and is responsible for more than a third of global exports. It is also the Gulf's most important supplier. The country has an extensive biofuel program and half of its sugar production is converted to ethanol. Thus, there is a direct substitution link between oil and sugar prices. The UAE does not produce any sugar, rice, or palm oil, but appears in the data as a supplier because it is a re-export hub for the Gulf region. Apart from re-exports, Saudi Arabia's modest contribution to sugar imports might come from the export of date confectionary, as confectionary is itemized together with sugar.

Brazil also exports close to $2 billion of poultry meat per year to the Gulf and dwarfs all other suppliers. The market for live animals is of particular importance during 'Aid al-Adha, when sheep and goats are slaughtered all over the Muslim world to celebrate the end of the annual pilgrimage season. The trade in live animals is largely regional with the exception of Australia. Syria, Iran, and countries on the Horn of Africa dominate supplies to the Gulf. Palm oil is by far the most important edible oil in the Gulf and is mainly imported from Malaysia and Indonesia beside UAE re-exports. The most important fruit suppliers are the Philippines, South Africa, India, the US, and Egypt with approximately similar shares.

The Gulf region is a large importer of fodder for its livestock industry. Saudi Arabia constitutes an astounding 40 percent of worldwide barley imports.[75] In

---

[72] For an historical overview see Bray 1994.

[73] Woertz 2010.

[74] ESCWA and IFPRI mimeo 2012; *Saudi Gazette*, 8 June 2012.

[75] Saudi Arabia's share has ranged mostly between 30 and 45 percent since the mid-1980s. In the 2000s, the share has been mostly at and above 40 percent. USDA 2012b.

terms of other food items, the Gulf's global share is modest, but its barley demand can move markets. The Ukraine, Australia, Canada, and the EU have been major suppliers. Argentina and the US have been the most important suppliers of corn, Spain and the US for green fodder, and Paraguay for soybeans. As Gulf countries are forced to phase out water intensive alfalfa production, green fodders will need to be increasingly imported and rank high in their foreign agro-investment strategies.

In sum, there is a striking disconnect between major food suppliers and preferred agro-investment destinations of Gulf countries. Among the most prominent target countries, only Pakistan is a major supplier with its rice exports. The Philippines and Egypt have exported fruits to the Gulf, but this is not as strategic as rice or wheat. Sudan has exported some livestock and corn, but the amounts were hardly crucial. Ethiopia and other sub-Saharan countries have only provided limited amounts of tropical fruits, tea, and coffee to the Gulf. They are food net importers like most target countries. As will be seen, major food exporters have either figured less prominently in Gulf agro-investments (e.g. Australia, Ukraine, Brazil, and Kazakhstan) or not at all (e.g. Canada, Western Europe, and the US).

1.7 CONCLUSION

Gulf countries are heavily dependent on food imports, but because of their substantial oil revenues they are food secure. The widespread equation of food security with food self-sufficiency in the region is misleading as long as Middle East countries can afford to pay for food imports and markets stay open. The main food security issues relate to micronutritional deficiencies, obesity, and unhealthy diets. There is a strong likelihood that food prices will remain at elevated levels. This is due to a paradigm shift fueled by factors like population growth, changing diets, financialization of food markets, and increased biofuel production. At the same time, modern agriculture is negatively affected by environmental degradation and climate change, to which it contributes to no small extent. Gulf countries face increased reliance on world markets at a time when their reliability has diminished. This has prompted them to seek agro-investments in countries that do not contribute meaningful quantities to their food requirements and are in fact food net importers themselves. Such investments are controversial and not without precedent. They were tried in Sudan during the food crisis of the 1970s and failed. To understand the motivation for such international agro-investments, one must examine the history of Gulf agriculture and the geopolitics of food trade in the Middle East as it has developed since World War II.

Part I

Gulf Food Security: History, Political Economy, and Geopolitics

2

Ethiopian Wheat and American Tires: Gulf Food Security and World War II

Vulnerability to food import disruptions has been part of the collective consciousness in the Gulf throughout the twentieth century. In the case of the aging Saudi rulers, it is actually part of their individual memory. World War II offers an interesting case study for how such memories have shaped policies in subsequent decades. It constituted the apogee of a regional food trade that had developed since the nineteenth century and gave way to an international system of food surplus disposal by developed countries after the war. The war period also established a legacy of state intervention and state-led development models. The Gulf saw its first projects of mechanized agriculture and the importance of food policies for political legitimacy became apparent.

The Arabian Peninsula had always imported cereals from Middle Eastern producers and India, but a sheikh at the beginning of the nineteenth century would not have been concerned with the grain harvest in Australia. This started to change by the end of the century. With the repeal of the protectionist British Corn Laws in 1846 and the dramatic decline in transport costs after 1870, long-distance trade of cereals expanded. A true global wheat market developed that went far beyond earlier exchanges during the Roman Empire or the early modern era.[1] Beside coal, the industrial revolution was fueled by imported grains that fed Britain's workers. Main suppliers were Russia, the US, India, and Australia. By 1880, the UK imported a majority of its grain supplies.[2]

The Suez Canal was completed in 1869. The introduction of railways, steamships, and the telegraph reduced transport costs and enhanced market access in the Middle East. Trade in colonial export crops like cotton, wine, silk,

---

[1] Wheat supplies from Egypt and Sicily were important for the provision of Rome and its armies, but such trade was only a niche and self-sufficiency the norm. Erdkamp 2005. Until railway lines opened up interiors in the nineteenth century, long-distance trade in cereals was confined to the sea. Even in the Mediterranean with its long coastlines it accounted for only 8 percent of overall grain consumption in the sixteenth century. Braudel 2000: Vol. 2, 62.

[2] Morgan 1979: 3, 36; Friedmann and McMichael 1989.

and opium expanded, as did the regional trade in cereals.[3] Extensively planted cereals constituted about 80 percent of crops. Half of them was for subsistence while the other half was sold on local and regional markets. Livestock production was also extensive; apart from Egypt, fodder cultivation was not common. The Gulf was part of this emerging regional system. By the turn of the century, its populace relied to a considerable extent on imported foodstuff and needed money to pay for it. Rudimentary polities were emerging that perceived import dependence as a strategic liability. Food provisions to clients and people became an important tool for aspiring rulers to enhance legitimacy.[4] By World War II, the strategic liability of food import dependence became clear. The Middle East was exposed to import disruptions, financial shortages, and weak transportation infrastructure that hampered food distribution.

The precarious supply situation during World War II was a defining moment that shapes Gulf countries' quest for food security today.[5] Like the politicized food trade of the 1970s and the export restrictions of 2008, it continues to inform policy-making. The events of the period also shaped the development of modern agriculture in the Gulf countries that went on to an unsustainable strategy of self-sufficiency in Saudi Arabia in the 1980s and 1990s.

2.1 ON THE MARGINS: GULF AGRICULTURE BEFORE WORLD WAR II

Agriculture in the Gulf countries first developed on the fringes of the wider Middle East. Its agro-sociological make-up was different from its neighbors in the north and east of the region. Nomadism and tribal structures were more prevalent, irrigation agriculture was confined to a few oases, and rain-fed agriculture was absent, apart from mountainous regions in the Asir, Yemen, Oman, and the northern part of today's UAE (see Map 2.1). The Gulf was not involved in a quasi-colonial export trade. It did not witness the implementation of large-scale private landownership and the rise of absentee landlords as

---

[3] Issawi 1982, 1995; Owen 1993. Egypt, Turkey, and Iran were centers of cotton cultivation in the nineteenth century. Sudan followed in 1925, when Great Britain introduced the Gezira irrigation scheme in the south of Khartoum in 1925. Wine was produced in the Levant, tobacco in Turkey and Syria, silk in Mount Lebanon and Iran. The latter was also a major producer of opium, as was Turkey. Export crops yielded on average three times higher profit margins than wheat. For the development of the Red Sea grain market see Serels 2012.

[4] For the role of urban food provisioning in state building of Morocco in the late nineteenth and early twentieth centuries see Holden 2009.

[5] Remarks of QNFSP Chairman Fahad al-Attiya at the Middle East Institute, Washington, DC, 25 January 2010.

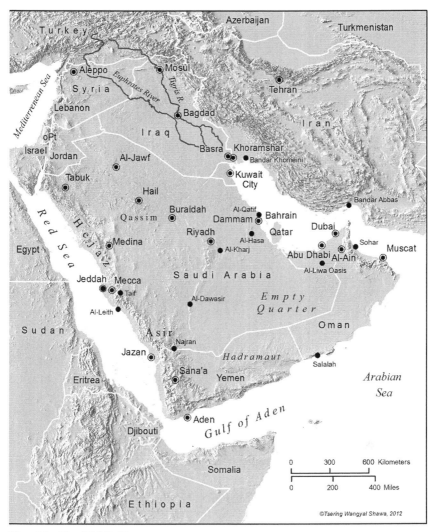

Map 2.1. The Middle East

oPt = occupied Palestinian territories

in Egypt or Iraq. Its few urban agglomerations like Jeddah or Mecca were small. Industrialization attempts as in Egypt in the 1920s would have been unthinkable.[6] Still, in addition to trading food with its neighbors, the Gulf had also experienced some technological changes by the twentieth century.

Before the advent of oil, basic standards of living in the Gulf were vastly different. Population and economic growth have been tremendous. The first

---

[6] Davis 1983.

overland roads in Saudi Arabia were only constructed in the 1950s, and the UAE—today a major air hub—had only an unpaved landing strip until the 1960s. Population numbers were small. In 1950, Qatar had 25,000 inhabitants, Bahrain 116,000, Kuwait 152,000, the area that later became the UAE 70,000, Oman 456,000, Yemen 4.3 million, and Saudi Arabia 3.1 million.[7] What are now major metropolitan centers were little more than large villages.[8] As late as World War I, commerce and sedentary lifestyles were still challenged by tribes and raiding parties that pillaged caravans. Piracy ravaged the Gulf coast, challenging British and Ottoman authority. The weak Ottoman government only asserted itself in occasional expeditions to raise taxes and conscripts.

The Gulf's natural endowment has been particularly challenging for agriculture. Before the advent of the oil-driven motor pump, the severe lack of rainfall and absence of rivers confined farming to a few oases and privileged spots.[9] Water for agriculture was only available in monsoon affected regions (Asir, southern Hejaz, Salalah), areas close to wadis (Wadi Fatima, Sirhan, Najran) or in the vicinity of artesian wells (Al-Hasa, Al-Qatif, Khaibar, Al-Ain). If scarcity of water hampered agriculture, its occasional abundance was a problem as well. Flash floods in the wake of rare but intense winter rainfalls could wash away entire farms that were built close to wadis or in sinks to reach underground water.[10]

To make matters worse, winter rains were often followed by locust swarms, which bred in the swamplands of East Africa, parts of the Arabian Peninsula, the Rajputana Desert in India, and along the coasts of the Gulf. Combating them only became viable with the development of modern communication lines and political coordination. Addressing this challenge was a focal point of the Middle East Supply Center (MESC) and British development agencies in the years 1942–7.[11]

Against these natural odds people eked out a living on the Arabian Peninsula. In Asir and Yemen farmers made use of terraces to take maximum advantage of run-off water from the eastern slopes of the Red Sea mountain ridge, which are less steep than the slopes in the west. The US agricultural mission that visited Saudi Arabia in 1942 found terraces in excellent condition and concluded, "The Western world, especially the United States of America,

---

[7] United Nations 2010. Lloyd gives a considerably lower number for the population of Oman during the war years with only 80,000 inhabitants. Lloyd 1956: 66.

[8] Jeddah had 30,000 inhabitants after World War II, Riyadh 60,000, Mecca 80,000 and San'a 25,000. Lloyd 1956: 355. Abu Dhabi was indeed a village with only a few thousand inhabitants. For a contemporary account of life in Abu Dhabi in the post-war period see Al-Fahim 1998.

[9] Philipp 1984: chapter 2.

[10] Steinberg 2004.

[11] Wilmington 1971: 123–6; British Information Services 1951: 17f.

can learn much about soil and moisture conservation from the mountain farmers of Saudi Arabia."[12]

Farming in the orchards of the mud-walled oases was intensive and the shadows of irrigated date palms were used to plant fruits (e.g. peaches, melons, figs), vegetables (e.g. pumpkins, eggplant), and lucerne as fodder for camels and horses.[13] Cereals like wheat, sorghum, barley, and some millet were grown as well, particularly in the terraced fields of the Asir, but these had to be supplemented by imports. British India was the main supplier of rice, wheat, and cotton goods. Basra and Egypt delivered rice and barley. The latter struggled to compete with the seaborne grain trade from India and Iraq but was the dominant supplier of sugar for Jeddah.[14]

On the Gulf coast, fish was the main source of protein. Beside pearls, fishing was a mainstay of the economy and was licensed by the ruler. In the Trucial States (Oman and today's UAE) 60 percent of the fish harvest was exported to the hinterland as dried fish or fertilizer in the 1950s and 1960s.[15] The pearl trade was paramount in generating the income that allowed for the import of rice, sugar, and other consumer goods like tea, coffee, textiles, and wood.[16] Hunting game added to caloric intake until the advent of automatic weapons and four-wheel drive vehicles decimated wild animals. In 1952, the former Dutch representative in Jeddah, Daniel van der Meulen, deplored the "motorized slaughter" of the Oryx gazelle. Overhunted beyond human needs it did not stand the chance it had had when hunting was still carried out on horseback.[17] Ostriches were already extinct. Only occasional eggshells in the desert bore testimony to their former presence.[18]

In good years, the oases of Al-Hasa and Al-Qatif were able to produce a surplus, which was exported to Najd in the interior.[19] Dates had long served as the main staple for populations in central Arabia, but by the beginning of the twentieth century, they were replaced by rice, at least for the upper echelons of

---

[12] Fakry and Twitchell 1943: 140.

[13] Steinberg 2004: 81–5.

[14] Ochsenwald 1982: 67ff.; Lloyd 1956: 66; Serels 2012:79f. Sudan still played a role as a grain supplier to Jeddah at the beginning of the nineteenth century before it was crowded out. Statistics before World War II are guestimates. After World War I new suppliers appeared. In the 1930s, France supplied most of the flour to Jeddah and the Red Sea coast. India, Iraq, Australia, and Transjordan followed with small quantities. Rice mainly came from Rangoon and some of it from Calcutta. Sugar was imported from Europe, Java, and Egypt and coffee from East Africa and Yemen. Ryan to Eden, 29 February 1936, "Annual report 1935," in Tuson and Burdett 1992: Vol. 6, 41.

[15] Heard-Bey 1982: 173.

[16] Abdullah 1978: 103; Al-Naqeeb 1990: 55ff.

[17] Meulen 1957: 210.

[18] Heard-Bey 1982: 172.

[19] Philby 1928: 217. Najd describes the central lands of Saudi Arabia ranging from the borders of the Empty Quarter to the northern frontiers without the western mountains and eastern coastlands. Riyadh is its center.

urban society. On the Red Sea coast, wheat and millet also played an important role.[20] In contrast to the large oases in Al-Hasa and Al-Qatif, the Trucial coast was not self-sufficient in dates, especially after more and more people took up pearl fishing and neglected farming. Around the turn of the century, additional dates were imported from Ottoman Iraq and from Persian ports across the Gulf.[21]

The oases in the Trucial States used sophisticated irrigation systems involving *falaj* (pl. *aflaj*), subsurface canals that date back to pre-Islamic times. The advent of the motor pump and more rewarding opportunities in the wake of the oil boom damaged the communal water management of the *falaj* culture. Some *aflaj* had already fallen out of use by the 1950s and 1960s.[22] A similar fate was in store for the terraced fields of Yemen and the Asir.[23]

In the mid-1920s, central Arabian agriculture slowly modernized through the drilling of wells and the import of motor pumps. The Saudi king abolished import duties on agricultural machinery in 1928 and established a system of installment payments for their purchase in 1930. Yet the impact of this technology remained marginal. The pumps were used for greening the gardens of royals and notables rather than for farming.[24] Only later did their use become widespread.

Regional Food Trade

In the nineteenth century, the British established political and economic hegemony in the Gulf region and superseded indigenous forms of commercial exchange in the Indian Ocean. Steamships began to serve the region's ports in the 1840s and connections became more regular than with sailing boats that relied on seasonal monsoon winds.[25] The Arabian Peninsula was along the trade route to India and was integrated on the fringes of a British dominated world economy with trade of luxury goods like frankincense and coffee along the Red Sea coast and the pearl trade on the Gulf coast.

Regional food trade increased. By 1935, wheat production in the Middle East had recovered from World War I and the Great Depression. About 4 percent of the harvest was traded across borders and the region regained its position as a wheat net exporter, which it had before the war. Anatolia, Iraq, Transjordan, and Egypt were major producers.[26] In the Arabian Peninsula, town dwellers and Bedouins lived in symbiosis through the trading of

---

[20] Steinberg 2004: 82; Ochsenwald 1982: 67f.; Lloyd 1956: 66. For austere, date-based diets of Bedouins in the post-war period see Thesiger's account of his travels in the Empty Quarter 1945–50. Thesiger 1959.
[21] Heard-Bey 1982: 177.   [22] Heard-Bey 1982: 177ff.
[23] Nugent 2003.   [24] Philipp 1984: 13–17.
[25] Al-Naqeeb 1990: 51ff.   [26] Schatkowski-Schilcher 1989: 247f.

livestock, hides, milk, wool, and butter ghee in exchange for cereals, dates, tea, coffee, weapons, textiles, timber, and luxury goods like spices or watches. The distinction between town dwellers and nomads was not absolute. There were semi-nomadic lifestyles in addition to the various forms of cooperation.[27]

To finance food imports, the Arabian Peninsula entertained a vast regional trade network. In the Hejaz, the annual pilgrimage was its commercial life-blood. The Hajj season offered opportunities to extract various fees from pilgrims and to trade sheep, pearls, salt, slaves, and coffee for consumer goods. Most of the trade consisted of re-exports from Yemen and Africa, with only a fraction originating in the Hejaz itself.[28] The slave trade came under pressure from the English and the Ottomans during the second half of the nineteenth century.[29] Its importance decreased even though slavery remained legal in Saudi Arabia until 1962, in the UAE until 1963, and in Oman until 1970. Camels were exported to Syria, Egypt, and Iraq, horses to India and Iraq. In Najd, seasonal labor migration to the cities on the Gulf coast was a means of acquiring currency for food imports. The pearl fishing business thrived until the 1930s, when the Great Depression and the invention of artificial pearls by the Japanese led to its decline.[30] The horse and camel trade was also badly hit in the 1930s. Najd started to export fewer horses to Iraq than it imported. Camel demand in Egypt was decimated as dietary preferences changed and the motorcar superseded the "ship of the desert" as a means of transport. Alternative camel exports to Italians in Eritrea offered only a short respite.[31] New ways of generating cash were needed. Karl S. Twitchell, the American engineer and intermediary who led the US agricultural mission of 1942 even investigated whether exporting camel wool to the US for carpet making would be viable in order to provide Bedouins with income.[32]

An important part of the region's revenue came from political sources rather than commercial ones. External rents provided cash income for the rulers of the Gulf long before the advent of oil. The arrival of great powers in the region and Britain's policy of indirect rule offered opportunities for the collection of strategic transfer payments. The smaller sheikhdoms along the Gulf coast began receiving British stipends in the nineteenth century. Ibn Saud did so from 1915, albeit on a smaller scale than his rival Hussain, the Sharif of Mecca, whom he would depose in 1925.[33]

The importance of food trade for Gulf rulers was evident during World War I. The Entente forces imposed a maritime blockade on the Ottoman Empire.

---

[27] Steinberg 2004. [28] Ochsenwald 1982; Al-Naqeeb 1990: 54.

[29] Ochsenwald 1980. [30] Steinberg 2004: 83.

[31] Calvert to Eden, 26 June 1936, "Economic Survey of Saudi Arabia," in Tuson and Burdett 1992: Vol. 6, 691.

[32] Twitchell to Colonel Eddy, 28 July 1944, Twitchell Papers, Box 5, Folder 1.

[33] Kostiner 1993: 55–62.

No food reached the ports of the Mediterranean and the Red Sea and the trade routes into Kuwait were controlled. By 1916, there was full-blown starvation in Greater Syria. Half a million people perished by the end of the war.[34] Lebanon was particularly affected because it lacked significant cereal production. Its agriculture was oriented towards mulberry trees and silk exports.

Against this backdrop, Hussain, the Sharif of Mecca, turned to the British. Beside money and weapons, grain exports to the Hejaz were a political priority for him. At the beginning of the war he promised Britain, "We shall not turn against her or aid her enemy" if she would only facilitate the necessary grain imports.[35] With the Ottomans unable to guarantee food security in the Hejaz, the region was left to the mercy of the British, who reopened limited food exports to Jeddah in May 1915. The promise of British food imports in the face of disaster was instrumental in instigating the Arab Revolt a year later. In contrast, tribes in northern Transjordan were reluctant to join the uprising. They were more self-sufficient in food production and the Ottomans were in a more dominant position by controlling the markets that were crucial for their subsistence.[36] The Ottomans also diverted grain deliveries from Syria to the south in order to buy the allegiance of tribes.[37] Transjordan and the Arabian Peninsula were thus in a privileged position in comparison to Greater Syria. Maritime trade routes in the Red Sea and the British-controlled Gulf were open, and the British and the Ottomans vied for Arabian allegiance with grain supplies.

Bargaining for external rents and subsidies was important for Ibn Saud as well. His rudimentary polity was constantly threatened by insolvency.[38] The income from taxation of date farming in the oases of Al-Hasa and Al-Qatif was not sufficient to finance his military forays on the Arabian Peninsula. The archival sources paint a ruler persistently hustling the British for loans and refusing to repay old ones. By 1932, his finances had gone "from bad to worse."[39] The pilgrimage to Mecca was the most important source of revenue after the conquest of the Hejaz in 1925, but the number of pilgrims fell from 130,000 at the end of the 1920s to only 40,000 by 1931. Fewer people were able to afford the expensive journey because of the Great Depression.[40] In debt with local business families and in search for new sources of revenue, the king was happy to sign an oil concession with Standard Oil of California (SOCAL) in 1933. The British Iraq Petroleum Company (IPC) had only shown luke-warm interest. SOCAL went on to found a subsidiary, the California Arabian Standard Oil Company (CASOC), which was renamed the Arabian American

---

[34] Schatkowski-Schilcher 1992.   [35] Teitelbaum 2001: 71f.
[36] Tell 2000: 43f.   [37] Schatkowski-Schilcher 1992: 239.
[38] Vitalis 2007: 4ff; Jones 2010: 28.
[39] Ryan to Simon, 26 February 1933, "Annual Report 1932," in Tuson and Burdett 1992: Vol. 5, 33.
[40] Lacey 1981: 228.

Oil Company (ARAMCO) in 1944. The redistribution of oil rents became essential for maintaining the legitimacy of the Al Saud. Free food distribution was an important part of the ruling bargain. During World War II, about half of all food imports of Saudi Arabia were distributed as charity. Another quarter was used by the palace and as payment for the administration. Only the remaining quarter was sold for money in the marketplace.[41]

2.2 THE ALLIED MIDDLE EAST SUPPLY CENTER (MESC)

During World War II, the Gulf became more integrated into the wider Middle East with the establishment of the Allied Middle East Supply Center (MESC) in Cairo. The MESC was created in April 1941 as a clearing-house to coordinate agencies that dealt with civilian supplies in the Middle East. It played a decisive role in securing food supplies to the Arabian Peninsula, which was included in its operational responsibility in March 1942 alongside Iraq and Iran. Due to the war effort, shipping capacity was limited. Deliveries were threatened by delays, loss, and last-minute diversions. To make matters worse, the Mediterranean was closed for Allied merchant shipping because of Italy's entry into the war, the initial successes of the German U-boat campaign, and the British withdrawal from Greece in April 1941. Supply convoys to the Middle East had to take the long detour around the Cape of Good Hope, which added six to seven weeks to their journey. Once supplies were delivered, overland transport was more complicated because the infrastructure at the south of the Suez Canal was less developed than in Alexandria. The Mediterranean was reopened for Allied commercial shipping only with the end of the North African campaign in June 1943 and the development of effective counter-measures against the U-boats.[42] Scarce shipping capacity was used for military purposes and imports of civilian goods were reduced to a minimum. Supply disruptions had to be managed to avoid economic disintegration, hunger, and political unrest. As J. M. Landis, the senior American representative to the MESC from 1943–5, put it, "A peaceful Islam was essential to the defense of Suez . . . [and] a peaceful Islam could not be assured if it were permitted to starve."[43]

---

[41] Stonehewer-Bird, General Distribution, 5 February 1940; Jeddah to Baxter, FO London, 31 December 1943, in Tuson and Burdett 1992: Vol. 7, 192, 353.

[42] Wilmington 1971: 153; Lloyd 1956: 138.

[43] Landis 1945: 65. During World War I, the Ottoman Sultan had used his nominal title of Caliph to call on a global jihad against the Entente. The fears that Muslim subjects of the Commonwealth might follow this call never materialized. Yet, the idea of a monolithic Islam obviously still loomed large among decision-makers. When pushing for financial support for Ibn Saud, State Department officials and US business interests were inclined to attribute a

The solution was to foster local procurement and regional trade. Local production capacities in industry, raw material provision, and agriculture were raised. The MESC not only managed shipping and trade with the outside world, it also functioned as an economic planning and development agency in the interior. After market-based approaches failed, it applied more interventionist measures like centralized procurement in the countryside and pro-rationing in the cities. Heydemann and Vitals point out that the MESC thus was "the central mechanism behind the diffusion of Keynesian notions of economic planning in the Middle East," whose influence lasted well beyond the end of the war.[44] As in Latin America, the war situation enabled import-substituting industrialization. Imports declined from 5.5 million tons in 1941 to 1.5 million tons in 1944, while intra-regional trade in the Middle East grew from 7 percent of overall trade in 1938 to 33 percent during the war.[45] Beside industrial projects, the MESC improved forestry, agriculture, and animal husbandry. It combated plant pests and converted cotton acreage to cereal production.[46] The increased acreage did not lead to significantly higher output though, since reduced nitrate fertilizer imports from Chile had led to a decline in yields.[47]

The MESC reported directly to the Ministry of War Transport in London. Originally British, it became a joint Anglo-American institution in May 1942, about six months after the US entered the war. Officially, it was only an advisory institution without bureaucratic machinery of enforcement. Its principal channels of influence were recommendations to the Allied governments and local authorities in the Middle East. Although it lacked executive powers, its control over shipping space provided some mechanism of sanctioning. Its head, Robert Jackson, used this with great dexterity to cajole governments into following his suggestions.[48] The MESC took direct control of goods that were deemed strategic, including grain, sugar, fats, oils, meat, canned milk, fish, coal, tires, pharmaceuticals, tea, and coffee. Only the distribution of non-strategic overseas goods was left to commercial channels. Under the guidance of the MESC, the United Kingdom Commercial Corporation (UKCC) acted as the sole importer, storage facilitator, and distributor of strategic goods. The MESC was thus in a unique position to control and direct supplies in these

---

pan-Islamic influence to him, that was outsized in comparison to his limited means of power. Twitchell to Henry Field, Washington, 25 September 1941, Twitchell Papers, Box 4, Folder 1; Miller 1980: 23, 39.

[44] Heydemann and Vitalis 2000: 103, 121.

[45] Wilmington 1952: 147. Part but by no means all of this increase could be attributed to a decrease in total foreign trade.

[46] Wilmington 1971: 119.

[47] Heydemann and Vitalis 2000: 125; Hunter 1953: 182.

[48] Wilmington 1952: 45 and 151. For a detailed outline of the administrative procedures see Hunter 1953: 172–8.

strategic items all along the logistic chain. A centralized system of food storage was essential to react flexibly in cases of emergencies. Imports and stocks were pooled to avoid the decentralized and expensive holding of three-months' reserves in each Middle Eastern country, which would have been necessary otherwise.[49]

The focal remit of the MESC comprised the Fertile Crescent, the Lower Nile Valley including northern Sudan, and the Arabian Peninsula. Cyrenaica and Tripolitania were added to this group after the Allies conquered them. An outer circle consisted of Iran and Cyprus in the north, and Ethiopia, Eritrea, southern Sudan, and the Somalias in the south. It also included Turkey in some instances, before it passed out of MESC jurisdiction after 1942.[50] Through its scope, the MESC helped establish the widespread use of the term "Middle East," which, as E. M. H. Lloyd, economic adviser to the British Minister of State in Cairo in 1943 and 1944, points out, had been used only infrequently and without clear definition before.[51] Once the British set up a military command in Cairo in 1939 and decided to give it the name Middle East it increasingly superseded the term Near East, which had been more common and mostly used to describe Bulgaria, Greece, Turkey, the Levant, Palestine, and Egypt.

Food Trade under the MESC

The Egyptian cereal crisis in the spring of 1942 brought the country perilously close to famine. Social unrest could have thwarted the Allied defense preparations against the German Afrikakorps under Lieutenant-General Erwin Rommel, who was preparing for a new offensive west of Tobruk. German artillery was heard in Alexandria and the MESC was evacuated to Jerusalem. Beside Cairo, there were food riots in Tehran, Damascus, and Beirut, while children in the Gulf sheikhdoms reportedly died for lack of milk.[52] A region-wide crisis was averted at the last minute when 350,000 tons of wheat were shipped in, the harvest came in three weeks earlier, and a new compulsory grain collection scheme in Egypt surpassed expectations. The shock hit close to home, however, and agricultural issues became a priority for the MESC.[53]

---

[49] Wilmington 1971: 90, 118.

[50] Wilmington 1971: xviif. Turkey was not under Allied control, but absorbed grain exports from Syria. After 1942, a separate Allied committee looked after these import requirements. The MESC administered Syria and Lebanon only indirectly via the Spears Mission, which was set up by the British to oversee relationships with the two countries that were formally still governed by French mandatory authorities. Lloyd 1956: 4; Heydemann and Vitalis 2000: 121, 104.

[51] Lloyd 1956: 3. See also Wilmington 1971: 2.

[52] Wilmington 1971: 25.

[53] Lloyd 1956: 129; Wilmington 1971: 115f.

Table 2.1. Pre-war diets in international comparison (approximations)

Item	Middle East	Italy	USA
Kilos per year:			
Grains, as flour	165	177	90
Roots, pulses, and nuts	15–25	59	71
Sugar and syrup	11	7	49
Fats and oils	5	12	22
Meat, eggs, and fish	15	33	85
Fruits and vegetables	100–200	84	184
Milk and cheese	50–100	42	177
Calories per day	2,200	2,689	3,164
Protein (grams per day)			
Total	70	86	90
Animal	10–12	20	52

Source: Lloyd 1956: 15, based on FAO 1949, 1951.

On balance, the Middle East was self-sufficient in staple foods in normal years. Iraq even exported large quantities of barley as feedstock to the UK before the war.[54] While the Middle East was a small net exporter of cereals, it was a net importer of sugar and oil seeds. The region's imports of coffee, tea, and canned food were broadly offset by earnings from exports of citrus fruits from Palestine and dates from Iraq.[55] However, there were regional imbalances and a need for additional imports to offset crop fluctuation, weak local trade links, and insufficient infrastructure. There were also inflexible local dietary habits with regard to certain grain types. Theoretically possible substitution was not easily achieved.

The Arabian Peninsula, Palestine, and to a lesser extent Cyprus were especially dependent on outside deliveries.[56] Regional trade in barley, mainly from Iraq, substituted their pre-war imports of wheat from Canada and Australia.[57] The challenge for the MESC was to convince the countryside, where there was no rationing, to sell its surplus to the towns, where food had to be rationed. Exact pre-war figures about nutrition do not exist. They are completely absent for the Arabian Peninsula. Lloyd relies in his account on FAO "approximations" after the war (see Table 2.1). The diet in the Middle East consisted largely of bread grains, which accounted for around two-thirds of caloric intake. Consumption of sugar and fats in the region was only about a quarter of the US at that time. For meat, fish, and eggs it was only a sixth.

[54] Lloyd 1956: 171. Average annual barley exports to the UK were 200,000 tons between 1934 and 1939.
[55] Lloyd 1956: 7, 14.
[56] Wilmington 1971: 18; Hunter 1953: 180.
[57] Collingham 2011: 129f; Jackson 2006: 166.

Despite limitations in certain food types, dietary intake of the Middle East compared favorably to other developing countries like India. Dairy products, fruits, and vegetables accounted for a relatively large share of the diet.

2.3 FOOD, LEGITIMACY, AND STRATEGY IN THE GULF

The MESC gained great importance for deliveries of foodstuffs and other essential goods to the Gulf from 1942 on, when it assumed responsibility for this part of the Middle East. By 1943, it was practically the sole supplier of essential items.[58] About 70 percent of Saudi Arabia's total imports were staple foods and textiles.[59] The war aggravated the notoriously difficult financial situation of Ibn Saud. Pilgrim numbers were only a third of what they had been at the end of the 1920s and the nascent production of oil and gold was interrupted. SOCAL and its subsidiary CASOC could not bring its oil to market and maintain production because shipping space and scarce input factors like steel were directed towards the war effort. Yet Ibn Saud pressed for a continuance of royalty payments as advances on future oil sales. British stipends were his only other remaining source of income. His revenues were not enough to cover royal lifestyle profligacy and import sufficient food and goods, which were crucial in maintaining tribal loyalties via handouts.[60]

On the one hand, the oilmen at SOCAL were worried about the stability of Saudi Arabia. In the end, their concession was not much more than a personal contract with a desert king and relied on the latter's political standing. On the other hand, their Saudi venture did not generate cash flow as long as oil production was idled. Advances on future oil sales looked like a risky business proposition. They sought to deflect this risk by lobbying for US government support to Ibn Saud.[61]

James A. Moffet, chairman of another SOCAL subsidiary, the Bahrain Petroleum Company, started to lobby the US government in April 1941 on behalf of CASOC for financial aid to the Saudi king. He was a friend and adviser of President Roosevelt for whose election campaign he had raised millions of donations. Moffet told Roosevelt that up to 300,000 people were relying on direct food handouts in Saudi Arabia after a drought in 1940. Without immediate financial assistance, Ibn Saud would be unable to "feed

---

[58] Jordan to Eden, 15 February 1944, "Annual Report 1943," in Tuson and Burdett 1992: Vol. 7, 26.
[59] Mejcher 1989: 112.
[60] Lacey 1981: 264f.; Miller 1980: 35; Vitalis 2007: 64.
[61] Miller 1980: 34–46.

and maintain control of his people." The stability and "independence" of the Saudi kingdom and its "prestige in the Arab world" were at stake.[62]

Roosevelt's initial reaction was positive and the State Department suggested to offer Lend-Lease aid to Saudi Arabia.[63] Yet the Moffet proposal did not go through despite months of deliberations. It got bogged down in technical matters and inter-agency discussions. There were legal impediments for accepting untapped oil as collateral, and the navy declined an alternative proposal to buy petroleum products from Saudi Arabia, because of their low octane and high sulfur content.[64] Roosevelt was also afraid of the political backlash among isolationist circles inside the US if he granted Lend-Lease aid to Saudi Arabia at a time when the US was officially still neutral.[65]

Saudi Arabia did not rank high on the US priority list yet. It was regarded as a British sphere of influence—and obligation. The US was reluctant to "embark on a purely political loan in an area where we are not directly concerned to any great extent."[66] President Roosevelt finally declined the Lend-Lease request and wrote to his Federal Loan Administrator Jesse Jones, "Jess—Will you tell the British I hope they can take care of King of Saudi Arabia. This is a little far afield for us! F.D.R."[67]

The American refusal after months of deliberations personally angered Ibn Saud, because Saudi Arabia was in dire need of tires, trucks, and agricultural machinery.[68] The US diplomats in Cairo and at the State Department looked for ways to placate the king with compensatory measures. The US agricultural mission that was sent to the kingdom in 1942 played a prominent role in these deliberations alongside non-financial aid in the form of material deliveries.[69] The diplomats and the oilmen were wary of giving the impression that Saudi Arabia was an exclusive sphere of British interests, foreshadowing the rivalry between the US and the UK over influence in Saudi Arabia towards the end of the war.[70]

---

[62] Moffet to President Roosevelt, Washington, 16 April 1941, FRUS 1941, Vol. III, 624–7.

[63] Lacey 1981: 261. The Lend-Lease Act was promulgated on 11 March 1941. It allowed for the delivery of war-relevant materials to Allied nations at a time when the US was officially still neutral. Only in December 1941 would the US enter the war.

[64] Murray to State, 10 May 1941; State to Kirk, Cairo, 22 August 1941, FRUS 1941, Vol. III, 633, 646.

[65] Miller 1980: 44.

[66] Memorandum of Conversation by John D. Jernegan, 7 August 1941, FRUS 1941, Vol. III, 644.

[67] Jones to State, 6 August 1941, FRUS 1941, Vol. III, 643. Miller argues that there might have been a gentleman's agreement that the UK provided $10 million funds to Ibn Saud out of its own Lend-Lease loans to circumvent the legal and bureaucratic impediments on the US side. Miller 1980: 45, 234, footnote 55.

[68] Stonehewer-Bird, Jedda to FO, 15 November 1942, FO 371/31462.

[69] Miller 1980: 47, 52.

[70] Miller 1980: 50f.

Thus, Saudi Arabia mainly relied on financial aid from the British and CASOC at the beginning of the war. In 1941 and 1942, the UK paid the Saudi king £3 million annually and CASOC advanced £750,000 each year for post-war oil sales.[71] The British had decided in 1940 to raise their financial assistance in order to ensure Saudi Arabia's "benevolent neutrality."[72] Their motivation was hardly humanitarianism. Food allotments and import controls were used to establish "the minimum level at which the Beduin [*sic*] can exist and yet remain loyal."[73]

Reliance on external rents from Britain and CASOC did not prevent Ibn Saud from playing both sides in the build-up to the war.[74] His son Faisal, who was Minister of Foreign Affairs, visited nearly every large European capital in 1932 in an effort to raise funds. In 1933, the king let the British know of his flirtations with the Soviets, whom he would need to approach should the British not come through with monetary assistance.[75] Later he would seal an arms deal with Mussolini, open diplomatic relations with Germany in January 1939, and sign a treaty of friendship and trade with Japan.[76] In the first two years of the war, the Allies could never be really sure of Saudi Arabia's allegiance. A memorandum remarked, "If [the Saudi king] saw it was to his advantage to play along with the Axis powers he would undoubtedly do so."[77] Flirtations aside, Germany's interest in the oil of the region was limited for strategic reasons. It could not have defended maritime supply lines and had embarked on a synthetic fuel program in the 1930s already.[78] As the war raged on it was also less successful and Saudi Arabia leaned more and more towards the Allied side, but officially, it remained neutral and declared war on the Axis powers only in 1945.

The food situation was of paramount importance to the Saudi government. Food prices spiraled in 1940. The British embassy in Jeddah asked for a release of Indian supplies because there was not enough food in the country.[79] However, there was reluctance to increase deliveries. The British feared that additional supplies might be re-exported to Italian East Africa. They did not trust Saudi assurances to control dhow traffic in the Red Sea and crack down on smuggling. Quotas for food exports from Sudan and Egypt were

---

[71] For estimates based on NARA files see Lacey 1981: 263, 589.

[72] Stonehewer-Bird, Jedda, dispatch, 1 August 1940 and Memorandum of the Foreign Office, "The Neutrality of Saudi Arabia," 8 July 1940, FO 371/24590.

[73] War Cabinet Middle East Supplies Committee, Note by the Joint Secretary, "Middle East Supply Center. Organisation and Present Policy," 28 December 1942, 8f, FO 371/35495.

[74] Lacey 1981: 257f.

[75] Ryan to Simon, 26 February 1933, in Tuson and Burdett 1992: Vol. 5, 23.

[76] Lacey 1981: 257f.

[77] Memorandum of Conversation by Alling, Assistant Chief of the Division of Near Eastern Affairs, Washington, 29 April 1941, FRUS 1941, Vol. III, 629.

[78] Mejcher 1989: 125f.

[79] Jedda to Foreign, New Delhi, 18 February 1940, FO 371/24590.

implemented based on average deliveries over the preceding three years. Quotas for Indian deliveries followed suit. Ibn Saud took this personally and saw it as a sign of British mistrust.[80]

Italy entered the war in June 1940 and its navy disrupted Red Sea traffic from Eritrea. Saudi Arabia's west coast was cut off for six weeks, and communications with Egypt were interrupted for three months.[81] Jeddah merchants were badly hit and the British proposed a convoy system to prevent the continued isolation of the city.[82] Only on 26 March 1941 were the quotas lifted after the military situation allowed for a more complete control of sea-lanes.[83] British troops gained the upper hand against Italy in the East African war theater. The port of Massawa in Eritrea fell and the Italian navy in the Red Sea was destroyed. Haile Selassie was reinstated as emperor in Addis Ababa in May 1941, and by November 1941, the last pockets of Italian resistance in Gondar had been defeated. On 11 April 1941 President Roosevelt declared the Red Sea and the Gulf of Aden a combat-free zone and therefore open to US commercial vessels.[84] Still, imports remained limited, as Egypt and Sudan were unwilling to deplete their stocks of food, petroleum, and lubricants, and released supplies only gradually.[85]

As the refusal of Lend-Lease aid in 1941 had demonstrated, US interest in the Gulf and Saudi Arabia was lukewarm at the beginning of the war. Before 1942, it did not have a physical presence in Jeddah. A non-resident ambassador in Cairo was responsible for the kingdom. US interest began to shift in 1942. With German advances in North Africa and Russia, Saudi Arabia's importance increased because of its strategic position. The Red Sea was a gateway to the Suez Canal and the Gulf a warm-water supply line for Allied deliveries to the Soviet Union. The War Department in Washington also became interested in air routes across the peninsula.[86]

---

[80] Stonehewer-Bird, Jedda to Cairo, 8 September 1940; Lampson, Cairo to Jedda, 12 September 1940; Aden to Cairo, 21 September 1940; Stonehewer-Bird, Jedda, General Afar Distribution, 30 September 1940; Lampson, Cairo, Limited Afar Distribution, 2 October 1940; Secretary of State to Government of India, Commerce Department, 19 November 1940, FO 371/24590; Stonehewer-Bird, Jedda, Distribution B, 5 February 1941, FO 371/27256.

[81] Stonehewer-Bird to Eden, 20 March 1941, in Tuson and Burdett 1992: Vol. 7, 12.

[82] Lampson, Cairo to FO, 10 March 1941, FO 371/27256.

[83] Ministry of Economic Warfare letter, 26 March 1941, FO 371/27256.

[84] Italy had nine destroyers and eight submarines in the Red Sea at the beginning of the war. Churchill 1950: 89. With the surrender of Vichy-controlled Madagascar and French Somaliland (today's Djibouti) in 1942, there was complete Allied control of the East African coastline. Apart from the threat of German forces in the West of Egypt, the Allied position in the Middle East saw a number of other improvements in 1941. Control of Syria was wrested from Vichy France, the pro-Axis Al-Kailani coup in Iraq was foiled, and Iran was occupied after the Shah had shown tacit endorsement of German advances. Jackson 2006: chapter 8, 247, 340ff. See also Kirk 1953: 41–56; Hubbard 2011.

[85] Ministry of Economic Warfare letter, 26 March 1941, FO 371/27256.

[86] Miller 1980: 52.

Most importantly Saudi oil finally appeared on the strategic map of the American government. The US produced a whopping 63 percent of global oil supplies (3.8 mbpd). Energy tsar Harold Ickes was concerned about domestic peak oil and was anxious to find alternative sources of production. Saudi Arabia moved to the center stage of US strategic thinking. It was declared "vital to the defense of the United Sates" when it was finally granted Lend-Lease aid under executive order no. 8926 in February 1943.[87] The US government sent the oilman Everette Lee DeGolyer on a mission to the Persian Gulf to appraise the region's oil reserves. Upon his return in early 1944, a member of his delegation confided to State Department officials that Gulf oil was indeed the "greatest single prize in all history."[88] The US strengthened its diplomatic ties with Saudi Arabia by upgrading the US representative in the legation in Jeddah to the status of Minister in 1943, and in 1944, it opened a consulate in Dahran.[89]

America was no longer willing to leave Saudi Arabia to British interests alone. In April 1944, the US representative in Cairo cabled to the State Department, "The indications are that Saudi Arabia is rapidly becoming an active battle ground in the implementation of two systems of foreign policy— the British . . . and the American." While the former was regarded as colonial, wont to keeping countries in perpetual economic dependence, the American system would aim at self-reliance of "backward countries" and was the only guarantor of "a stable world order."[90] Henceforth British activities in Saudi Arabia were viewed with suspicion, including an anti-locust campaign, training of the Saudi military by Jordanian trainers, and simple roadworks. US diplomats suggested that the US should take over the financing of Saudi Arabia from the UK, instead of sharing the burden of the Saudi subsidy equally, which had been agreed upon in 1944.[91]

The Bengal Famine of 1943 and the Gulf

The Gulf food situation in 1943 was dire because the massive Bengal famine led to the loss of rice imports from India. With the Japanese occupation of Burma in 1942, the British Empire had lost the largest rice exporter at that time. Burma had been crucial for deliveries to India and Ceylon. Now both countries had to draw on supplies from Egypt to substitute that loss at least partly.[92] However, Amartya Sen has pointed out that the Bengal famine cannot be explained by loss of Burmese exports or Indian harvest failures

---

[87] Lacey 1981: 263.   [88] Yergin 1991: 393.   [89] Abdullah 1978: 201.
[90] Kirk to State, Cairo, 25 April 1944, FRUS 1944, Vol. V, 690.
[91] Moose to State, Jidda, 30 April 1944, FRUS 1944, Vol. V, 696.
[92] MESC to Ministry of War Transport, 3 March 1944, MAF 83/1342; Wilmington 1971: 127.

alone. There was enough food in India, but more and more people could not afford it because they lacked funds and entitlements.[93] War-related inflation, bureaucratic neglect, and racial prejudice contributed to the famine. The situation was aggravated because of hoarding and a deliberate policy of limiting storage in Bengal in order to complicate a possible Japanese advance from Burma. Leo Amery, the Secretary of State for India, deplored Churchill's "Hitler-like attitude" towards India, who would reply to an urgent request to release stocks that if food was so scarce "why Ghandi had not died yet."[94] The famine only ended when the government in London finally decided to send one million tons of grain supplies to India in order to bring down prices.[95]

The treatment of India and the incompetence of the colonial and local governments there were in contrast to the situation in the Middle East. The MESC's management of food supplies was more professional and there was an inclination to pre-empt protests by releasing supplies. When the Bengal famine led to the freeze of rice exports to the Gulf in February 1943, the local population protested the resulting changes in diets from rice to grain. Authorities feared that the pearl fishermen who used to sail every May for four to five months might stay at home and create trouble should they not get their usual diet of rice, dates, and fish. The MESC scouted for alternatives and managed to gradually reopen rice supplies via Iraq in March 1944.[96]

The Allies were also quick to airdrop food supplies in the Netherlands in March 1945, when a famine struck those parts of the country which they had hitherto failed to liberate. This led Indian Viceroy Wavell to complain about a racial bias in food distribution. He remarked that food supplies were flowing "when the starvation [was] in Europe."[97] In comparison to India, it seems that the Middle East was not put into the lowest bracket of such hierarchies in food distribution. The region also benefited from the Allied "Germany First" policy. Its strategic importance was higher as it was closer to Europe and a crucial transit region for war supplies. Still, paternalistic attitudes were not absent. When Qatari sheikhs complained about sugar rations and the quality of wheat, barley, and sorghum supplies, the British representative replied brusquely that they "were lucky to get anything to eat" and that an increase in sugar rations was out of the question. He saw markets as well supplied and blamed Qatar for abetting smuggling to

---

[93] Sen 1981. More recent research argues that the harvest of winter rice in 1942 had largely failed and that there was a more serious problem of food availability than Sen has portrayed. Thus, it would not have been only a problem of food accessibility. Whether for reasons of greed or because of real shortages, rice markets dried up. Collingham 2011: 147; Tauger 2003.

[94] Mishra 2007.

[95] James 1997: 581.

[96] Lloyd 1956: 66f. For a discussion of the different attitudes by British representatives in the Middle East and India see Collingham 2011: 152f.

[97] Collingham 2011: 152, 176.

Al-Hasa, Kuwait, and Iran.[98] Contrary to these official records, Qatari octogenarians remember that people died of hunger at that time. Out of destitution, people wrapped goatskins around stones, dried them around a fire, and then ground and ate them.[99]

Food Trade Partners: Ethiopia, East Africa, and the Middle East

The food trade with India is an example how the Middle East was part of a larger inter-regional procurement and allotment scheme. Beside South Asia it included East Africa and Ethiopia. East Africa offered logistic advantages for supplies to the Middle East because the Mediterranean remained closed for commercial shipping until 1943. The responsibility of imports to East Africa was in the hands of the East African Governors' Conference, but its exports played an important role for the MESC. In a position paper of the British War Cabinet that outlined the MESC's strategy by country, it was argued in 1942 that East Africa should "produce to the maximum as markets would be found."[100] Jeddah and Aden flour requirements were partly met by Ethiopian deliveries.[101] The Hadramaut faced starvation after a harvest failure in 1943, which was averted by bringing in special wheat and millet supplies from Ethiopia.[102] In spring 1945 the British ambassador in Washington remarked, "Maximum use will still have to be made of Ethiopian cereals."[103] They were scheduled to supply the Red Sea coast of the Arabian Peninsula, while US shipments would be used to supply the Gulf coast.[104] Yemen in the north of the British Protectorate of Aden remained largely self-sufficient in cereals and other foodstuffs until the end of the war. It did not make any calls on the MESC during that time. It was even able to export some millet to Saudi Arabia.[105] Kenya developed into an important food supplier to Allied troops in the Middle East, particularly of corn.[106] Sudan only made a few calls on the MESC during the war and stabilized its food situation by growing more wheat and exporting less millet. Its exports of cottonseeds actually helped mitigate an acute shortage of oils and fats in Egypt. The shortage arose in 1943–4 as a

---

[98] Report on visit to Qatar by Hickinbotham, 25–27 November 1943, in Tuson 1991: Vol. 6, 594.

[99] Interview with Fahad al-Attiya and Sheikh Hamad bin Ali bin Jassim al-Thani, Chairman and Vice-Chairman of QNFSP, Doha, 15 November 2011.

[100] War Cabinet Middle East Supplies Committee, Note by the Joint Secretary, "Middle East Supply Center. Organisation and Present Policy," 28 December 1942, 10, FO 371/35495.

[101] Ministry of Food to British Food Mission, Ottawa, 3 March 1944, MAF 83/1342.

[102] Lloyd 1956: 65.

[103] British ambassador in Washington, draft letter, undated, FO 371/45524.

[104] Various correspondence, USRSA, Vol. 1, 321ff., 353, 379ff.

[105] FO to Lampson, Cairo, 22 February 1941, FO 371/27256; Lloyd 1956: 63f.

[106] Collingham 2011: 197.

result of the shift of cotton to cereal acreage.[107] Overall, the Middle East was a net importer of wheat, sugar, and oilseeds, while it exported barley and rice to other countries such as India, Ceylon, and the Balkans after the Allies had expelled the Axis powers from there in 1944. The most important surplus countries within the sphere of influence of the MESC were Egypt for rice and Iraq for barley. Syria and Lebanon managed to churn out a modest barley and wheat surplus in some years, but on a much smaller scale.[108]

The MESC expected the food situation in 1944–5 to be worse than in 1943 because of an anticipated 20 percent reduction in the barley harvest in the Middle East. Price controls would need to continue to prevent speculation and hoarding.[109] The MESC refused more barley deliveries to India, arguing that it would need them for the Persian Gulf. The barley was mainly procured from Iraq and to a lesser extent from Egypt and Syria. Main recipients were Palestine, the Gulf coast, and the British army, followed by Malta, Cyprus, and Jeddah.[110]

During the war, there were also overseas supplies of cereals to the Middle East from Australia, the US, and Canada. These were of better quality than the Ethiopian grains about which the Saudis were constantly complaining and half as expensive. But scarce shipping capacity prevented larger inflows.[111] As the shipping crisis eased towards the end of the war, the grain surpluses of these countries would increasingly find their way to the Middle East and US export interests actively lobbied against the import restrictions of the MESC.[112] Still, it was mostly regional trade that prevented famines in the Middle East during the war.

2.4 INFLATION, TRANSPORT, AND FOOD SECURITY

A major challenge of the war economy in the Middle East was inflation. The decline in purchasing power threatened the food security of the poor. Between 1939 and 1945, prices increased up to 600 percent, with great variations from country to country: Sudan had the lowest, Iraq, the Levant, and Iran the highest inflation.[113] A system of rationing and price controls was put in

---

[107] Lloyd 1956: 30.

[108] Lloyd 1956: 358f.

[109] MESC to Ministry of War Transport, 3 March 1944, MAF 83/1342.

[110] MESC to Ministry of War Transport, 24 February 1944, MAF 83/1342.

[111] Ethiopia was an important cereal supplier under wartime conditions, but it was doubted that "economic exportation of staple crops" would be possible because of its underdeveloped transport and communication infrastructure. Keen 1946: 9.

[112] Lloyd 1956: 96.

[113] Compared to a price index of 100 in 1939 the indices in 1945 stood at 293 in Egypt, 254 in Palestine, 620 in the Levant States, 390 in Iraq, 699 in Iran, and 160 in Sudan. Hunter 1953: 187.

place to prevent inflation and speculation, but it did not solve the underlying problem. A constant growth in military expenditure led to an increase in money supply without a concomitant increase in the availability of goods for civilian purchase.

Inflation, and particularly food inflation, was an overarching concern at the second Middle East Financial Conference in 1944 in Cairo. In order to contain it, excess liquidity had to be siphoned off. To this end, taxes were increased. In countries like Egypt that had some semblance of a capital market, government loans were offered to the public, not unlike war bonds in the US or the UK. However, rural populations had no history of saving in paper money and government certificates. Because of the shortage of civilian consumer goods like coffee or watches, they had little incentive to part with a tangible asset like food in exchange for a financial instrument of dubious purchasing power. Many had not forgotten that during World War I, monetary exchange had broken down in Greater Syria, and food could only be purchased with gold.[114]

To procure sufficient amounts of food for Middle Eastern towns, another solution had to be found. Hoarding of precious metals had a tradition in the Middle Eastern countryside, so the Allies embarked on an experiment of gold sales in 1943 and 1944 to mop up excess liquidity. They also hoped that a fall in the price of gold would bring down the general price level and that the gold sales would reduce the amount of necessary paper note issues for military expenditure. Overall, the gold sales policy proved successful and fears that it would undermine foreign exchange controls or the value of local paper currency did not materialize.[115] Like the import-substituting policies of the MESC, the sales demonstrated the influence of Keynes, who had famously brandished gold as a "barbarous relic." They were directed by economist R. F. Kahn who had been a colleague of Keynes at Cambridge University and had reported to him while the latter was a director of the Bank of England.[116]

Saudi Arabia, Ethiopia, and Yemen were in a peculiar situation, since they did not have paper currencies but instead used precious metals. The Saudi representative at the Middle East Financial Conference claimed that his country had not witnessed inflation because its currency was based on the Silver Riyal. However, the value of the Silver Riyal decreased against gold during the war. Its relative supply increased, as several million ounces of silver were minted that Saudi Arabia had received under the Lend-Lease program.[117]

---

[114] Schatkowski-Schilcher 1992: 241.

[115] Lloyd 1956: 208–17.

[116] Heydemann and Vitalis 2000: 129.

[117] Memorandum of Conversation, W. Leonard Parker, Washington, 17 July 1943, FRUS 1943, Vol. IV, 878. The silver deliveries addressed a shortage of coins and were meant as a "shot in the arm" for a modernization drive of Bedouin society until oil revenues would set in. Until

Inflation in staple foods was limited only in gold terms. Supplies were fairly regular and the Arabian Peninsula did not witness the kind of military spending seen farther north in the Middle East. Furthermore, there was some deflationary effect in 1943 when less gold came into the country because of a dull pilgrimage season. Only consumer goods like textiles rose steeply in price due to their limited availability as a result of import controls.[118] Ibn Saud lamented, "Sky rocketing of prices since the war [have prevented] the Bedouin from buying rice and cloth even when it could be imported."[119] In sum, inflation on the Arabian Peninsula was more benign than in other parts of the Middle East, but entitlement shortages and limited purchasing power were serious and affected food security, especially of rural segments of the population.

Food security was also threatened by insufficient infrastructure. The Gulf lacked adequate transport and storage capacities. The Mosul–Aleppo railway line was largely used for westward transportation of grains from the Syrian Gezira. It could not accommodate Iraqi barley exports to the Red Sea coast and other areas to the west. They had to be shipped via the port of Basra.[120] The ports of Kuwait and the Trucial States were not suitable for large ships. The British decided to use Bahrain for deliveries and organize further transport along the Gulf coast with dhows.[121] In Saudi Arabia, the transport facilities of Ras Tanura were insufficient to distribute foodstuffs to the entire country. Additional use of Jeddah on the Red Sea coast was essential.[122]

Shipping of grains from Sudan was hampered by poor infrastructure and climatic conditions. Transportation was restricted to the dry season. Like in Bengal, Sudanese storage facilities had been curtailed at the beginning of the war for "reasons of strategy," presumably to prevent supplies to Italian armies in case of an occupation.[123] Sudan bordered the Italian colonies of Ethiopia, Eritrea, and Libya and was attacked in September 1940. Kassala in the east was occupied and the British had only a thin contingent of the Sudan Defence Force standing between the Italians and Khartoum.[124]

In 1944, several dry seasons decimated the camel stock in Saudi Arabia, and dependence on motor vehicles for the transport of food increased. Ibn Saud

---

well into the 1950s the US tried in vain to recuperate the silver loans as the Saudis argued they thought they were a non-repayable gift. See various correspondences in USRSA Vol. 5, 553–6 and Vol. 6, 157, 630, 669.

[118] Lloyd 1956: 187f.

[119] Memorandum of Statement made by His Majesty Abdul Aziz al Saud at Riyadh, 1 July 1945, USRSA, Vol. 1, 59.

[120] MESC to Ministry of War Transport, 24 February 1944, MAF 83/1342.

[121] MESC to Ministry of War Transport, 15 January 1944, MAF 83/1342.

[122] Stonehewer-Bird, Jedda to Government of India, 11 July 1940, FO 371/24590.

[123] War Cabinet Middle East Supplies Committee, "Middle East Supply Center. Organisation and Present Policy," Note by the Joint Secretary, 28 December 1942, 7, FO 371/35495.

[124] Jackson 2006: 207f.; Kirk 1953: 41.

warned the US that famine in the interior would be imminent if no additional vehicles were delivered.[125] He had been worried as early as 1942 that a lack of transportation impeded food supplies to the remote areas bordering Iraq and Transjordan, reducing his authority there.[126] By 1945, Colonel Eddy, the US ambassador in Jeddah, reported, "Stability and order of Arabia are threatened by the transport crisis." He pressed that cars and spare parts were a "Priority No.1" [*sic*] for the Saudi king.[127] Apart from multi-wheel trucks for hauling food supplies, status-conscious Saudi royals also worried about the lack of appropriate means of personal transport. Passenger cars could not be part of Lend-Lease deliveries and had to be purchased by the notoriously cash-strapped Saudis. In a letter to Colonel Eddy, Ibn Saud complained that he had to cancel his yearly pilgrimage for lack of transport, and when he did decide to travel to the Hejaz in order to welcome the Egyptian King Faruk, he and his entourage were obliged to use supply trucks.[128]

2.5 BEYOND THE WAR: WATER, SEDENTARIZATION, AND POWER

Once the MESC went beyond being a war-related emergency organization and began to fulfill the functions of a development agency, its staff increasingly felt that it should continue to operate as an institution after the end of the war. A number of surveys and conferences helped formulate a vision of a post-war planning stage. Among them was a conference about Middle East Agricultural Development held in Cairo in February 1944.[129] It discussed the introduction of new seeds, irrigation, and tillage practices, argued against "feudal" land tenure, and called for the establishment of a Middle East Council of Agriculture that would coordinate regional efforts at research and development.[130] Officials hoped to build on the nascent regional economic integration, over which the MESC had presided.

Development strategies and import-substituting industrialization (ISI) were at the center of optimistic international debates. The groundwork for institutions like the FAO, the World Bank, and the IMF was already laid by the end of the war. In his State of the Union address in 1941, President Roosevelt

---

[125] Moose to State, Jidda, 29 April 1944, FRUS 1944, Vol. V, 694.

[126] Memorandum of Conversation, Ibn Saud and Minister, Jeddah, 6–10 December 1942, in Preston, Partridge, and Yapp 1997: 387.

[127] Eddy to Cairo, 24 February 1945; Eddy to State, 9 February 1945, USRSA Vol. 1, 15, 11.

[128] Ibn Saud to Eddy, Jeddah, 31 January 1945, USRSA Vol. 1, 12.

[129] Wilmington 1952: 146–9; Philipp 1984: 20; Middle East Supply Center (MESC) 1944.

[130] Keen 1946. The other two strategic surveys that were published after the war were Worthington 1946 and Allen 1946.

spoke of "freedom from want" as one of four essential freedoms. The United Nations Conference on Food and Agriculture in Hot Springs, Virginia in 1943 that led to the foundation of the FAO picked up on this theme. Heydemann and Vitalis argue that the MESC pioneered ideas of Keynesianism and ISI in the Middle East. It introduced policies and institutional approaches that would shape the Middle East in the post-war decades.[131]

Ultimately, the hopes of MESC staff to become part of an unfolding story of international institutions and function as the regional outlet of development efforts did not materialize. Competing American and British interests made cooperation difficult. US export interests perceived the import-substituting tendencies of the war years as burdensome. The UK on the other hand was worried about the competitiveness of its own exports. It was anxious to reduce a Sterling overhang with Middle East creditors that had resulted from war-related deliveries. The nascent wave of decolonization made a paternalistic institutional set-up by Western powers also hard to imagine. The MESC was dissolved on 1 November 1945.[132]

Still, American and British experts continued to assist local governments after the war. In terms of importance, agricultural projects on the Arabian Peninsula were not on the same scale as irrigation projects in Sudan, Egypt, Iraq, or Jordan. They were not even mentioned in project overviews by British government publications.[133] However, American efforts in Saudi Arabia were more extensive, and the impact was substantial, especially in light of developments after the 1970s. At one point, the US also contemplated an "imaginative project" that would have fostered pan-Arab integration of agricultural resources in the style of the MESC by strengthening food exports from the Fertile Crescent to the east of Saudi Arabia.[134] Yet, in the end, national project designs and the integration of the Middle East in the international food regime of Western surplus disposal dominated in the post-war decades.

Abdullah al-Sulaiman, the Saudi Finance Minister between 1929 and 1954 and by far the most important non-royal during that time, initiated the first government-funded large-scale farm in Al-Kharj in 1937–8. Southeast of Riyadh, it was situated at the junction of several wadis with alluvial soils. Saudi Arabia has an extensive system of underground currents that form in the west from rainfall in the Tuwaiq Mountains. They sink down to the

---

[131] Heydemann and Vitalis 2000. For the MESC as pioneer of regional integration see Owen 1999; Wilmington 1971: 158. ISI was the gold standard of development theories at that time. It only fell out of favor in the 1970s and 1980s after increasing balance of payments problems of developing countries. Export orientation superseded it. Arndt 1987: 72ff.; Little 1982: chapter 3.

[132] Wilmington 1971: 165, 1952: 162. For a critique of Wilmington and a more benign view of US–UK competition see Lloyd 1956: 97f.

[133] British Information Services 1951: 7–18.

[134] Notes from the Conference on President's Point IV Proposals for the Near East, confidential, 29 January 1959, Eddy Papers, Box 11, Folder 11 (Near East, 1959).

underlying limestone table and travel eastwards where they feed the artesian wells of the Al-Hasa and Al-Qatif oases. In Al-Kharj several open water pits were formed by the collapse of the surface limestone table.[135] The Al-Kharj farm introduced pumps to enhance exploitation of these water resources. As a model farm, it was meant to encourage the expansion of mechanized agriculture. Apart from providing fresh produce to his palace, Ibn Saud hoped that the project would start a modernization drive and contribute to domestic food supplies by quadrupling his country's farm output.[136] Another rationale for mechanization was the settlement of nomads, which would allow for greater control, leading to the transformation of Saudi Arabia "from a Bedouin to an agricultural economy."[137]

Toby Jones has outlined how the mastery of oil and water resources was crucial in shaping the modern Saudi state. A political bargain was struck to control an assertive clergy, recently conquered tribal areas, and an unruly army. Benefits like water, food, and public services were exchanged for political quiescence. The settlement of nomads was an early policy of Ibn Saud and was important for his military conquest of the Arabian Peninsula: "The Saudis used water, land, and agriculture as incentives to recruit, maintain, and control their armies."[138] A settled army could be called upon and be kept in check more easily than wandering nomads. The distribution of land and water resources was a means to share the spoils of conquest. The settlement policies marked the beginning of Saudi Arabia's transformation from a tribal society to a modern territorial state with a unified national market and distribution system.

Taxing date farmers in the eastern oases of Al-Hasa and Al-Qatif was important in the early stages of the Saudi state, before vast oil revenues had materialized. After the conquest of the Hejaz in 1925, pilgrimage revenues were added as a primary revenue source. This was not enough, however. Successful rent seeking from foreign donors was crucial for the sustenance of basic forms of administration in the pre-war era, as Robert Vitalis has pointed out. It was not efficient tax collection by a developed bureaucracy as Kiren Aziz Chaudhry has argued.[139] British stipends and US advances on oil sales kept a notoriously cash-strapped ruler afloat, as the Saudi king himself

---

[135] Sanger 1947: 186; Crary 1951: 369–79; Twitchell 1944: 380; Fakry and Twitchell 1943: 98–104; Twitchell 1958: 71; Lippman 2004: 180–8; Report on Al-Kharj Agricultural Project, 7 April 1952 and Summary on Al-Kharj by Sam J Logan, February 1986, Mulligan Papers, Box 8, Folder 10.

[136] Sanger 1954: 58.

[137] Memorandum of Conversation, W. Leonard Parker, Washington, 17 July 1943, FRUS 1943, Vol. IV, 878.

[138] Jones 2010: 8.

[139] Vitalis 1999; Chaudhry 1997: Part I.

was ready to admit.[140] Full-fledged state building would only accelerate in the 1950s and 1960s with increasing availability of oil rents.[141]

After Ibn Saud returned from his Kuwaiti exile and reconquered Riyadh from the Rashidis in 1902, he encouraged the settlement of nomads. His goal was to stop raids and establish land rights in order to allow for enhanced political control and commercial expansion. The first Bedouin settlement was founded in 1912. By 1930 some 200 so-called *hijar* (sing. *hijra*) were built. They housed cells of the Ikhwan fighting force, where loyalty amongst group members and towards Ibn Saud was nurtured instead of traditional tribal affiliations. Agricultural development was an important part of this strategy. Ibn Saud sent money, seeds, and other forms of agricultural support to a number of villages to attract wandering Bedouins. In 1929, he cracked down on the Ikhwan after their zealotry endangered his building of alliances in the conquered Hejaz and the safety of his frontiers with Iraq and Jordan. Subsequently a number of the *hijar* were destroyed, but others would continue to receive grants for decades. The basic strategy of sedentarization remained intact.[142]

The abolition of collective tribal control over grazing lands in 1925 centralized power. The confiscation of collective lands did not make the tribes obsolete, but it did give the king authority over tribal leaders as he could control access to grazing grounds and determine migration patterns.[143] This system was formalized in 1952 when the earlier Land Registration Law of the Hejaz was extended to Asir, Najd, and Al-Hasa. Corresponding to the notion of Islamic law that land belongs to God and can only be claimed if and as long as it is cultivated, the law stipulated title documents or proof of continuous land use. As neither could be provided in many cases, large swathes of land fell under the control of the state. Regional emirs often acted as intermediaries until 1960. Afterwards, control was completely centralized. The transformation of land rights gave the state a land bank, which it would use in consecutive waves of land allocation from the 1960s to the 1980s.[144]

Despite the early sedentarization policies, Saudi Arabia remained largely a society of Bedouin pastoralists during World War II, though one with growing centralized control. The FAO estimated in 1953 that 66 percent of the

---

[140] "To establish order and sweep away traitors, as a young man I leaned on the assistance of Britain. Your American oil company has brought new methods and machinery to develop resources under the soil, and your agriculturalists are showing us other hidden resources in water and seed." Memorandum of Statement made by His Majesty Abdul Aziz al Saud at Riyadh, 1 July 1945, USRSA, Vol. 1, 59.

[141] Hertog 2010: 39, 49, 76, 265.

[142] Habib 1978; Safran 1985; Al-Rasheed, Madawi 2010: 56–9; Fabietti 1982; Bronson 2006: 29–32.

[143] Chaudhry 1997: 173.

[144] Chaudhry 1997: 173.

population were nomads, 12 percent farmers, and 22 percent urban dwellers.[145] The State Department endorsed a US agricultural mission in 1941 in order to make up for lost ground in the wake of Roosevelt's denial of Lend-Lease aid to Saudi Arabia earlier that year. In doing so, it hinted at "Ibn Saud's known anxiety to settle his nomads on the land and to discover and develop the water and agricultural resources of Saudi Arabia."[146]

Ibn Saud regarded the work of the agricultural delegation as "vital for [his] country."[147] His Allied counterparts including Karl S. Twitchell were less sanguine about the commercial potential of agriculture in Saudi Arabia. They thought that the "principal purpose of such a mission would be political."[148] Agricultural development aid was perceived as a tool to further strategic aims, similar to the increase of the British subsidy at that time. Meanwhile the Saudi king regarded agriculture and the provision of water as a development priority, necessary for the "happy life" of his country.[149] Yet, land distribution was biased towards larger farms and well-connected royals and businessmen from Najd. Traditional small-scale farmers were pushed aside. Model irrigation projects were used to water countryside retreats, plant fodder for the king's horses, and provide food for his palace. There was an upper-class bias with a leisure component in such development projects. Referring to valuable rugs in the three royal palaces in Al-Kharj, British officials quipped that there was "a larger area under carpets than . . . under cultivation."[150]

2.6 CONCLUSION

The Gulf became increasingly integrated into a system of regional food trade from the late nineteenth century. The provision of food was an important element of fostering legitimacy for the nascent Saudi state. To finance food imports, acquiring external rents from outside powers and good relations with them were crucial. British stipends and royalty advances by the American oil company CASOC/ARAMCO quickly surpassed the pilgrimage as the most important source of government revenue. Sedentarization, agriculture, and water distribution were integral parts of the Saudi state building project and

---

[145] Twitchell 1958: 21.

[146] Alling to Welles, Washington, 27 September 1941, FRUS 1941, Vol. III, 650.

[147] Ibn Saud to Roosevelt, 13 May 1942, FRUS 1942, Vol. IV, 567.

[148] The British Embassy, Washington, Viscount Halifax to FO, 29 May 1941, in Burdett 1998: 703.

[149] Translation of Note from Saudi Arabian Government, 4 July 1945, Riyadh, USRSA, Vol. 1, 57.

[150] Jeddah to Baxter, FO London, 31 December 1943, in Tuson and Burdett 1992: Vol. 7, 353. See also Vitalis 2007: 70f.

transformed the social fabric of the country. The motor pump, introduced in the 1920s, was often used to irrigate leisure gardens, but it also began to affect traditional forms of agriculture and water management. There was a growing rivalry between the US and the UK for influence in Saudi Arabia towards the end of World War II. The MESC was pivotal in ensuring food supplies to the Arabian Peninsula during the war. It also enhanced integration within the Middle East and with East Africa and South Asia. Its legacy would go beyond the war, as it laid the groundwork for many agricultural and economic developments in the post-war years.

Rise and Fall of the Blooming Desert: The Self-Sufficiency Illusion

3.1 WHITE ELEPHANTS AND HORSES: THE AL-KHARJ FARM

The Al-Kharj farm was a pet project of the ruler and Finance Minister Sulaiman was a driving force behind it. It was a signature project for agricultural development in Saudi Arabia and foreshadowed the belief in large-scale farming and technical fixes that would characterize the self-sufficiency drive of the 1980s. Sulaiman first visited Al-Kharj with a team of Western geologists in 1938. An Iraqi scientific mission followed up with a visit to the project site in 1939 and cultivation began.[1] In 1942, the previously mentioned agricultural mission from the US traveled all over Saudi Arabia to explore the potential for increasing food production. Beside mechanization and irrigation, they recommended the free distribution of land and seeds. The three-man delegation was headed by Karl S. Twitchell, a geologist and mining engineer who did extensive surveying work for water, minerals, and oil in Yemen and Saudi Arabia during the 1920s and early 1930s. Originally hired by American businessman Charles R. Crane, Twitchell helped negotiate the first Saudi oil concession for the Standard Oil of California (SOCAL) in 1933, developed the Mahd al-Dhahab gold mine for the newly formed Saudi Arabian Mining Syndicate, and became a close adviser to the Saudi king.

The delegation arrived in Jeddah together with the first resident US representative in Saudi Arabia, James S. Moose Jr., who opened the permanent US legation in Jeddah, marking the growing American interest in the Peninsula. After its visit to Al-Kharj, the agricultural delegation recommended weed and pest control and drainage work in order to leach salts out of the ground. Sites for the water-intensive cultivation of long-staple cotton, barley, and wheat were identified.[2] The delegation also recommended the application of mineral fertilizer. A first batch of 90 tons of ammonium sulphate arrived in the

---

[1] Philipp 1984: 18.   [2] Fakry and Twitchell 1943: 99–103.

kingdom in 1942. It reportedly increased wheat yields in Al-Kharj from 900 to 2,700 pounds per acre.[3]

The last Iraqi left the project in 1942 and Saudi Arabia turned to Egypt for help. However, the Egyptian agricultural experts did not like the climate and living conditions. They left soon after arriving and the farm fell into disrepair. At the request of the king, ARAMCO grudgingly supplied some management services to the project in 1943–4 and installed pumps for a fee. The company was not entirely happy with this arrangement, as agriculture was not its core business. Nor was it pleased to drill for water outside areas with oil exploration prospects. At times, it withheld knowledge about water aquifers in order to avoid such requests.[4] Yet for the king, drilling of water holes was important to build alliances in tribal areas. For ARAMCO it was politically advisable to comply. Later, tribal leaders would appeal directly to ARAMCO's Arabian Affairs Division with requests for water holes, threatening to take the issue to the regional authorities (*amirate*) if ARAMCO refused to comply, which ARAMCO would typically do "if it [could] be done without undue expense."[5]

Robert Vitalis has argued forcefully that ARAMCO was not the benevolent driving force behind the Al-Kharj project as it has often been portrayed. Rather the farm was an initiative by the Saudi elite. US government assistance towards the end of the war was far more important than ARAMCO's role. ARAMCO formally took over the management responsibility of Al-Kharj only in 1950 and then only for a few years.[6] In 1944, a second and larger US agricultural mission visited Saudi Arabia. Under the auspices of the Foreign Economic Administration (FEA), a project team was sent "to contribute to Saudi Arabia's self-sufficiency in food," as Richard H. Sanger, a Saudi specialist in the State Department put it.[7] The Al-Kharj project faced several setbacks, including locusts and the delayed arrival of equipment. The most important impediment was resistance by the local population, which was motivated by religious prejudice, the collision of traditional views with a patronizing attitude of American personnel, and the negative effects of the project on small-scale farmers.

---

[3] Twitchell 1958: 28f.

[4] Philipp 1984: 20; Lippman 2004: 184. ARAMCO's role as a preferred trouble-shooter for the government continues to this day and it is regularly tasked with non-core business activities like building universities or stadiums.

[5] "Rub' Al-Khali Water Wells 1961–1962," James P. Mandeville Jr. to William E. Mulligan, Dahran, 17 March 1962, Mulligan Papers, Box 3 Folder 11; "Bedouin Complaint about Reduction in Flow of Rub' Al-Khali Water Wells," James P. Mandeville Jr. to William E. Mulligan, Dahran, 17 March 1962, Mulligan Papers, Box 3, Folder 12.

[6] For an overview of literature and contemporary company sources with a more benevolent view of ARAMCO's role, including Lippman (2004), see Vitalis 2007: 11–18, 70–4, 283 footnote 27, 295 footnote 16.

[7] Sanger 1954: 60; Sanger 1947.

The local judge, Abdulaziz ibn Baz, angrily opposed the project in 1944. He would go on to become grand mufti of Saudi Arabia in 1993, gaining some fame outside the country for maintaining that the earth is flat.[8] On the agricultural mission, he claimed the king violated his duties as a Muslim ruler by bringing non-believers into the country. The wives of Western experts who had accompanied their husbands working on the project would morally corrupt the local women, he argued. He also complained that the Americans would hire and fire Saudis as they pleased and would use precious water resources extensively.[9] Meanwhile, the rural population was hesitant to adopt new techniques like the introduction of the long hand shovel, wider spacing of trees, and the usage of camel dung as fertilizer. They argued that the old ways had served their forebears well.[10] It is easy to portray this resistance as stubbornness of parochial mindsets, but Lackner points out that the "patronizing attitudes" of the American advisers also caused resistance, as "they failed to recognize any value to traditional agricultural methods, and insisted that the only correct way to do anything was their way."[11]

The conflict between the conservative Ibn Baz and Ibn Saud over the latter's pet project was forcefully decided in favor of the king. Ibn Saud took Ibn Baz by his side and asked an assembly of ʿulamaʾ whether it was his right in accordance with Islam to bring in foreign experts. After he received their approval, he gave Ibn Baz twenty-four hours to reconsider his opinion, otherwise he would be beheaded. Ibn Baz gladly complied and went home to Al-Kharj richly endowed and honored by the king.[12]

Twitchell regarded Al-Kharj and the neighboring Khafs Daghra as relative successes. The introduction of new farming techniques was easier since there had been a traditional farming population already. In other places, an originally nomadic population had difficulties adapting to a farming lifestyle. The US agricultural mission in 1942 noted that Bedouins were less careful with water resources than traditional villagers, did not care sufficiently for date palms after planting them, and planted more than the land could support.[13] Twitchell remarked to the Dutch chargé d'affaires in Jeddah, van der Meulen, that many Bedouins regarded it beneath their dignity to practice farming and become sedentarized. "Some Saudi nationals of a different point of view and

---

[8] Ibn Baz had been blind since the age of eight. After meeting with the first Saudi astronaut, Prince Sultan bin Salman, who told him that he had seen the earth from space and that it was round, he seems to have taken this possibility into consideration, as he stopped making his flat earth assertion, albeit he never officially retracted it. Lacey 2009: 87–90.

[9] Steinberg 2002: 605; Steinberg 2005: 25f.; Lacey 2009: 9f.

[10] Sanger 1954: 67; Philipp 1984: 23.

[11] Lackner 1978: 186.

[12] Steinberg 2002: 604ff.

[13] Fakry and Twitchell 1943: 96, 111, 131.

character will have to [be] imported to such places," he argued.[14] Still, he deemed Ibn Saud's sedentarization policy sufficiently successful and told van der Meulen that he was careful not to be overtly critical of failed Ikhwan settlements. He did not want to mix too much "history" into the report of the mission. Others were less charitable about Ibn Saud's agricultural policies. British officials regarded Al-Kharj as an "expensive white elephant."[15]

By mid-1946, the dissolution of the Foreign Economic Administration led to the withdrawal of the Al-Kharj project team. The US government told Ibn Saud that he would need to finance the project henceforth out of his rising oil revenues, as oil production had resumed with the end of the war.[16] Ibn Saud continued the project with the help of US experts whom he had recruited via ARAMCO. Al-Kharj was expanded to 1,200–1,400 ha and new activities like livestock and poultry production were added. Two-thirds of the production of the project went to Ibn Saud's household and one third to the Crown Prince for distribution to various constituencies.[17]

Al-Kharj was not a priority for the ARAMCO management that formally took over responsibilities in 1950. Only a system of shadow prices allowed the project to show a profit. An audit report in 1954 recommended corrective measures and summed up the situation dryly: "Cost accounting for the Al-Kharj centers of operations...has not been considered necessary by the Aramco-Farms management."[18] There were also technical deficiencies. Excessive irrigation and cramped spacing led to crop loss.[19] After the death of Ibn Saud, the management of Al-Kharj was transferred to the new king, his eldest son Saud. ARAMCO returned to the old arrangement of supplying services for a fee and tried to stay out of the limelight. After coming to power, King Faisal gave the project to the Saudi construction tycoon Muhammad bin Laden, who was equally lackadaisical in taking care of the project. The American project manager Sam Logan, who left Al-Kharj in frustration in 1959, suspected that Bin Laden only took over because he feared he otherwise might lose government contracts elsewhere.[20]

[14] Twitchell to van der Meulen, 14 August 1944, Twitchell Papers, Box 5, Folder 1.

[15] Jordan to Eden, 9 February 1945, in Tuson and Burdett 1992: Vol. 7, 35.

[16] Philipp 1984: 23.

[17] Philipp 1984: 25; Lipsky 1959: 216. Others have also mentioned deliveries to ARAMCO and markets in Riyadh, yet deliveries to the royal family seem to have been dominant. Crary 1951: 377; Lippman 2004: 187; Mildred Montgomery Logan, "The Arabs Call Me Madam Sam," *The Cattleman*, January 1952, 22, 62f.; Mildred Montgomery Logan, "I Like Being the Garden of Eden's First Lady," *The Cattleman*, October 1957, 30, Mulligan Papers, Box 8, Folder 10.

[18] Arabian American Oil Company, Dhahran, KSA, 28 August 1954, "Condensed Executive Audit Report Al-Kharj Farms, 1954," 3, Mulligan Papers, Box 8, Folder 10.

[19] Sanger 1954: 62.

[20] Summary on Al-Kharj by Sam T. Logan, February 1986, Mulligan Papers, Box 8, Folder 10; Lippman 2004: 188.

Al-Kharj demonstrated that it was not easy to transplant farm models of the southwest US into similar climate zones without bringing the local population on board and accommodating their traditional styles of agriculture.[21] Van der Meulen visited Al-Kharj again in 1952. He found it "inexcusable" that Al-Kharj had not been adapted to local traditions and capacities after the improvisational years of the war. Machines were doing most of the work. There were hardly any laborers. Only some guards on horseback were roaming the fields to deter pilferers and prevent Bedouins from feeding their camels off planted greenstuffs.[22] The horses in Al-Kharj were neglected. Interest in them faded with the appearance of flashy motorcars. The traditional small-scale farmers were pushed aside and asked to settle elsewhere as the Al-Kharj project required large open spaces to be plowed by machines. Its farms had become "royal, princely and plutocratic interests."[23]

3.2 OPPOSITION AND ECOLOGY

Not just religious prejudice and narrow-minded traditions motivated opposition against Al-Kharj and other agro-projects, but social grievances also. Abdullah al-Malhuq, the private secretary of a landlord in Dammam, criticized "agricultural feudalism" in an unusually outspoken article in the Hejazi semi-weekly *Al-Bilad al-Sa'udiyya* in 1949.[24] There was increasing land concentration in the 1930s. Royalties and their trusted allies amassed tracts in prime spots that were suitable for irrigation, such as Al-Kharj and the oases of Al-Hasa and Al-Qatif. The king, his brother, and the Minister of Finance Sulaiman owned the bulk of the land in Al-Kharj.[25] The largest farms in Al-Hasa belonged to Sunni absentee landlords from Hofuf and the neighboring Al-Mubarraz in the 1950s, while small farmers and farm laborers were predominantly Shiites. Absentee landlordism in the oasis dated back to Ottoman times and the practice of granting fiefs to Janissary leaders, but a further concentration of landownership had taken place under the Al Saud.[26]

There was little concern for water scarcity and sustainability. Once water was drilled, artesian wells started to flow day and night, turning date groves into swamps, which were ideal breeding grounds for malaria.[27] Twitchell noticed that with the exception of Al-Kharj the drainage work that had been recommended by the US agricultural mission in 1942 had not been undertaken fifteen

---

[21] Philipp 1984: 49.   [22] Meulen 1957: 207f.   [23] Meulen 1957: 213.
[24] Vitalis 2007: 71.   [25] Vitalis 2007: 71.
[26] Jones 2010: 108, 270, footnote 42; Vidal 1954; Anscombe 1997.
[27] Meulen 1957: 216.

years later. Cultivable land was lost to salination.[28] With sinking water tables, drilling of deeper wells and stronger motor pumps were required. This was affordable for the government and its rich benefactors, but not for small-scale farmers. Their fields ran dry and they lost their livelihoods.[29] Thus, modern agro-projects like Al-Kharj contributed to increasing income disparities and polarization in the countryside.[30] When the Hofuf Agricultural Project was set up in 1948 American experts were asked revealing questions by local residents: "Will . . . [the] produce be available for all?" "Can these new methods of farming be used by the poor as well as the rich?"[31]

Water was essential for the regime to ensure control and buy allegiance. When the Tapline to Lebanon was finished in 1948, Bedouins would flock to the "unfailing watering places" at the five water pumping stations of the oil pipeline.[32] While this was not the reason why ARAMCO had built the water stations it did grant the government greater control of the nomads. New modes of consumption proliferated and with them a motivation to acquire money for things such as clothes and food stuff. Similarly, the Ghawar oilfield drew thousands of Bedouins into its orbit in the 1950s because of guaranteed water supplies around the gas–oil separator plants.[33] Others would move to Riyadh because water was provided by drilled wells and the king distributed food. When the city became more and more crowded, poverty stricken, and unhygienic, royals and other privileged people moved to the countryside. The green belt of Riyadh was sacrificed to accommodate the spatial needs of the growing city. Ibn Saud set the trend when he moved out of the town to a palace in Al-Murraba'. In Al-Kharj he built a mud-walled palace as well. Other royals followed and the countryside became gentrified with desert developments. The best known was the garden of Ibn Saud's successor Saud who built "a hundred-acre pleasaunce of lawns and flower-beds," where he took great pride in showing visitors the illuminated fountains in his garden while operating the fountainheads himself.[34]

Water tables sank rapidly, the result of neglect and ignorance on the part of rulers, local populations, and foreign experts. Asked by van der Meulen about the lack of sustainability and the danger of falling water tables, one expert replied, "Thirty wells more and I leave this God-forsaken country for good."[35]

---

[28] Twitchell 1958: 22.

[29] Meulen 1957: 216; Lipsky 1959: 209.

[30] Philipp 1984: 30f. For the water crisis in the Wadi Fatima that was caused by new water projects see Katakura 1977: 32f., 42.

[31] Sanger 1954: 69. See also Meulen 1957: 206ff., 213.

[32] Meulen 1957: 199f.

[33] Jones 2010: 77ff.

[34] Philby 1959: 135; Jidda to State, "Philby Skeptical of Saudi Arabia's Progress under Faisal," 5 November 1950, USRSA, Vol. 5, 549.

[35] Meulen 1957: 217.

Advisers of the king on the other hand were not fazed by the prospect of dwindling groundwater resources, fully trusting technical fixes and Western engineering ingenuity.[36] Unconventional solutions for water supplies were contemplated as early as the 1950s such as piping water from the Tigris, Nile, or the mountains of Turkey. More exotic ideas included cloud seeding, towing of icebergs from the Antarctic, and closing the Straits of Hormuz in order to create a fresh water lake over time.[37] German experts actually put experiments with cloud seeding into practice on a private farm of Sulaiman in the north of Jeddah.[38] These fancy plans never came to fruition, but the technical fixes would come in the form of desalination and drilling deeper into fossil water aquifers. The former provided potable water to the cities, the latter irrigation water for agriculture. By the 2000s, the limits of these technical fixes became increasingly apparent. The energy demand and the costs of desalination are high and aquifers had run dry.

3.3 CREATE TWO, THREE, MANY AL-KHARJS

The idea of Al-Kharj was to transfer desert farming methods as practiced in Arizona, New Mexico, and Southern California to similar climatic conditions in Saudi Arabia.[39] Albert L. Wathen of the first US agricultural mission had spent much of his professional life in this part of America. When the project in Al-Kharj was short of irrigation equipment in 1943, the State Department dispatched him on a special mission to the southwest of the US. He had to identify machinery on Indian reservations that belonged to the US government and could be made available for shipment to Saudi Arabia under the recently approved Lend-Lease aid.[40] King Saud often visited Al-Kharj and compared it to what he had seen during a trip to Arizona in 1947 when he was still Crown Prince. There was a widespread "me too" effect among royal landowners in importing modern farming and irrigation know-how.[41] Four years after the war Twitchell suggested to Muhammad Alireza, a prominent Jeddah merchant, a list of destinations for a three-month convertible trip in the US. The irrigation projects of the west, including the Imperial Valley and

---

[36] Meulen 1957: 218.

[37] Pampanini 2010: 6; Meulen 1957: 218. For an entertaining description of the iceberg initiative in the mid-1970s by a nephew of the Saudi king see Jones 2010: 1f.

[38] Philipp 1984: 36.

[39] Sanger 1947: 180, 190.

[40] State to Kirk, Cairo, Washington, 11 March 1943, FRUS 1943, Vol. IV, 863. Wathen was Chief of the Engineering Branch of the Bureau of Indian Affairs of the Department of the Interior (erroneously termed "Office" in this FRUS source).

[41] Sanger 1954: 66; Meulen 1957: 209.

the Roosevelt Dam, ranked high on the agenda.[42] It is a sad irony that such irrigation projects above the Ogalalla aquifer or along the Colorado River today face problems similar to those in Saudi Arabia. Overexploitation of water resources is not sustainable.[43]

Al-Kharj inspired several other model farms. The Kilo Ten Government Farm was set up in 1948/9 ten kilometers away from Jeddah. It was different from Al-Kharj in that it concentrated on seed and fertilizer testing, greenhouses, and other new technologies. For reasons that are not clear, it did not finish its testing programs as planned. Four other follow-up projects to Al-Kharj were planned in Al-Hasa, Al-Qatif, Taif, and Wadi Fatima in the southern Hejaz at the site of a country getaway of Minister of Finance Sulaiman. After a series of interruptions, only the one in Al-Hasa was institutionalized as Al-Hofuf Agricultural Research Company in 1956. The company later became the Regional Center for Animal Nutrition and Breeding.[44] The lack of implementation prompted British observers to doubt the resolve of the Saudi government. They argued that "The Saudis would . . . like . . . someone to do all the work and finance it for them; [but] when they realize that they are not going to get the irrigation schemes etc., for nothing, they are unlikely to do very much about them."[45] This assessment was incorrect. The Saudi drive to build up agriculture continued. From 1945 to 1953 further research was undertaken on surface and groundwater reserves, irrigation potential, and dam building. The Saudi Arabian Mining Syndicate, ARAMCO, the US Geological Survey, the US Department of Agriculture, the US Technical Cooperation Administration, and the FAO were all involved. The wide representation of American agencies was not accidental. The rivalry between the UK and the US for influence in Saudi Arabia at the end of the war had been clearly decided. Still reeling from the war, the UK was in no position to compete in terms of funding. By 1947, the Saudi king told the Americans that he wished to deal with them and with them only when it came to financial and technical assistance. When the US wanted to refer Saudi Arabia to the World Bank for long-term financing of projects, a Saudi delegation to Washington replied that Ibn Saud did not want his country to become "internationalized" and that "he did not wish to be indebted to countries other than the United States."[46]

[42] Twitchell to Muhammad and Ahmad Alireza, Connecticut, 16 July 1949, Twitchell Papers, Box 1, Folder 1. Other destinations included sightseeing locations like Yellowstone Park, mine sites, and industrial plants. For the Alireza family see Field 1985: chapter 1. Muhammad Alireza was founder of the Jeddah Chamber of Commerce and would later become Minister of Commerce.

[43] Reisner 1993.

[44] Philipp 1984: 26; Crary 1951: 382.

[45] British Embassy Jeddah No. 1163/16/50, confidential dispatch, 23 October 1950, FO 957/97.

[46] Memorandum of Conversation, Henderson, Washington, 17 January 1947, FRUS 1947, Vol. V, 1329ff.

Oil revenues grew from $10.4 million after World War II to $56.7 million in 1950. In the same year, Saudi Arabia was able to push through a fifty–fifty profit sharing agreement that was more favorable than its earlier royalty arrangement.[47] Implementation was initially patchy. Saudi Arabia was short-changed with the posted price that was used for the royalty calculation, but ultimately pressed successfully for a revision.[48] With growing revenues, the Saudi state required greater institutionalization. Oil funds needed to be funneled in a more structured way into development projects than the highly personalized style of patrimonial rule allowed for. Since the family patriarch had grown old, there was also the need to give a new generation of aspiring princes a stake in the government. In terms of regime stability, the establishment of ministries and other institutions proved to be crucial. With family domination over the state, Saudi Arabia and other Gulf monarchies had a broader talent pool to draw from and could secure wider legitimacy via clientele networks than absolute monarchs like King Idriss of Libya or the Shah of Iran. The "dynastic monarchy" (Herb) did not rely solely on one personality. Instead, the royal family became an institution unto itself, one that was about to govern the emerging bureaucratic state of the oil era.[49]

Institution Building and Contradicting Subsidy Regimes

Ibn Saud had been adamant about not relinquishing discretionary spending power. He resisted any formal budgeting and development planning. Ruling directly via the personal distribution of royal largesse was regarded as an important prerogative of the ruler and an indispensable means of cementing his authority. Decision-making was highly informal and heavily influenced by "princely jealousies," which in turn influenced the nascent process of institution building.[50] Institution building was the number one priority during the 1950s. Then Crown Prince Faisal remarked in 1958 that without a "proper internal organization" and budget "outside assistance [would be] useless."[51] Finance and Foreign Affairs were the only ministries until Ibn Saud decreed the creation of the Ministry of Interior in 1951. After his death formal institutions proliferated. The Directorate of Agriculture, which had been part of the Ministry of Finance since its founding in 1947, became an independent

---

[47] Maugeri 2006: 56ff.

[48] Vitalis 2007: 134. The posted price of ARAMCO was initially kept so low that the effective profit share of Saudi Arabia was 22 percent and not 50 percent. The "Red Sheikh" Abdullah al-Tariki, who would later become the first Saudi oil minister, adamantly lobbied for a revision.

[49] Herb 1999.

[50] Jones to State, 13 October 1953, USRSA, Vol. 2; Hertog 2010: 45.

[51] Heath to State, Jidda, 21 August 1958, USRSA, Vol. 5, 496. For the rivalry between Faisal and Saud and its impact on institution building see Yizraeli 1997, 2012.

Ministry of Agriculture (MoA) under Prince Sultan in 1953. Sultan's brother Fahd took over the newly formed Ministry of Education. The bureaucratic differentiation did not mean the end of patrimonial rule, however. Princes ruled over personal fiefdoms in a system of "segmented clientelism" (Hertog).[52] They were eager to safeguard their respective interests. Cooperation between institutions was sparse and underdeveloped. Externally, this led to overlapping responsibilities. Internally, the lack of reporting and insufficient supervision hindered the implementation of decisions.[53]

Nevertheless, the new institutions increasingly influenced agricultural development. The US and international organizations conducted feasibility studies, but the implementation of actual projects was in the hands of the MoA. In 1965 the ministry was renamed the Ministry of Agriculture and Water (MoAW), which signaled the greater importance and responsibilities for the agricultural sector. Beginning in 1955, the ministry established Agricultural Units in the provinces. They played an important role in the years 1955–65 in initial attempts at a widespread mechanization of agriculture. Afterwards their influence declined. They provided agricultural services by veterinarians and agricultural engineers, advised on the usage of pesticides and seeds, and had a rental service for farm machinery that was subsidized to the tune of 50–70 percent.[54]

From 1960 to 1964, the first agricultural census was undertaken. It comprised all of Saudi Arabia except for Jazan. Half of the roughly 87,000 Saudi farms had fewer than 0.5 ha. Less than 20 percent had more than two ha. Mixed cultivation was prevalent in highly segmented plots of land, which were separated by mud walls and canals. Small peasants were poor and most did not even have the money to borrow the subsidized machinery from the Agricultural Units. Additionally, the effect of the machinery subsidy was neutralized by competition from subsidized imports of basic food items, which started in 1959. Debt forgiveness schemes and import tariffs on vegetables from 1962 were not able to counter this trend.[55]

Affordable food for an increasingly urbanized society was seen as imperative for political legitimacy, which was severely challenged by revolutionary leaders and movements in the Arab world. A memorandum by the erstwhile general secretary of the Egyptian Muslim Brothers Abdul Hakim Abidin to King Saud in 1958 warned in no uncertain terms about pervasive communist infiltration that would need to be countered by "well planned reforms covering all aspects of life." It recommended taxing the wealthy, reining in land

---

[52] Hertog 2010: 44.
[53] "The Administrative Reform Program, Kingdom of Saudi Arabia." Progress Report with Supporting Studies, confidential/for discussion only, January 1973, Ford Foundation Archive (73478).
[54] Philipp 1984: 33f.; Halbluetzl 1963.
[55] Philipp 1984: 35.

speculation, and constructing a summer resort in Taif to prevent the unnecessary spending of Saudis abroad.[56] To achieve a more equitable income distribution, it called for assistance to the "poor and have-nots." Food would need to be more affordable, especially fruits and vegetables, which remained out of reach for the lower classes. Import restrictions would need to be reduced, particularly for grains. Somewhat contradictorily, self-sufficiency was advocated at the same time. Also recommended was the build-up of a strategic reserve of one year, as King Saud's predecessor Ibn Saud had allegedly done during World War II. The latter idea was possibly motivated by supply disruptions to Jeddah in the wake of the Suez Crisis and the blockade of the Canal in 1956.[57]

Obviously, a number of the recommendations were mutually exclusive. Self-sufficiency in an arid country like Saudi Arabia was only achievable at high costs. Without producer subsidies, it would have jeopardized the goal of affordable foodstuffs for urban classes. Thanks to oil rents, these contradictions did not matter. Saudi Arabia ended up subsidizing consumers and producers alike (Table 3.1). The first Saudi oil minister, Abdullah al-Tariki, who had obtained better royalty agreements from ARAMCO and later had to go into exile after falling in disgrace with King Faisal, sounded a cautious note on Saudi agriculture. Saudi Arabia could never become an agricultural country. It would need to focus on processing industries for its raw materials instead. He discarded the idea of self-sufficiency. Saudi agriculture should be developed, he argued, but if imports were cheaper one should take recourse to such deliveries from abroad.[58]

Thus, Saudi Arabia gave mixed signals to the agricultural sector. Subsidies on 21 major food imports put farmers at a disadvantage.[59] But the government also put a support system in place that aimed at increasing agricultural

---

[56] Memorandum to King Saud about General Reports in the Kingdom from Abdul Hakim Abidin, 4 August 1958, USRSA, Vol. 5, 711–23. The issue of land speculation remains a controversial issue to this day. Abidin, a son-in-law of Hassan al-Banna, was exiled to Syria in 1954 by the new Egyptian Revolutionary Command Council (RCC). Mitchell 1993: 52, 141, 153. He was close to the Jordanian government and to an anti-Nasserist "Riyadh-Amman axis" that is described in an article about the history of the Jordanian Muslim Brotherhood. Al-Zaydi 2005. The memorandum does not state Abidin's background, yet his self-identification as a non-Saudi guest of the country and the circumstances described above make it likely that the memorandum is from the Egyptian Abdul Hakim Abidin in question.

[57] Jidda to State, 22 September and 20 November 1956, USRSA, Vol. 4, 402, 412. The blockade led to hoarding and temporary price hikes, especially for canned goods and luxury items, but not so much for staple foods, which arrived via Thailand, India, and East Asia. Perishable goods continued to come by ship from Asmara in Ethiopia, but shipments from Beirut and airfreight were interrupted.

[58] Interview with Al-Tariki in *Al-Bilad*, 10 July 1959, USRSA, Vol. 5, 131ff.

[59] The import subsidies were introduced after a Riyal devaluation in 1959 of 16.7 percent to make up for the loss in external purchasing power. They applied to twelve kinds of cereals, five kinds of oilseeds, sugar, milk products, and meat. Philipp 1984: 35.

Table 3.1. Timeline of agricultural subsidy regimes in Saudi Arabia

1928–30	Import tariffs on motor pumps and farming equipment abolished, introduction of an installment system for their purchase
1955	Machinery rental subsidy of 50–70% by Agricultural Units of MoA
1959	Subsidies on imports of 21 basic food items
1963	Preferential farm credits by SAAB
1966–9	Restriction of import subsidies to wheat, grain, rice, and meat and their gradual reduction towards 1969
1968	Public Lands Distribution Ordinance
1973–5	Input subsidies: fertilizer, machinery, diesel, well drilling, farm equipment, airfreight of cows, animal feed
1978	Wheat support price scheme
1984	40% reduction of wheat support price
1989	Further reduction of wheat support price for large companies, does not apply to small farmers. Two-tiered system
1989	Barley import subsidy ends to encourage domestic production
1993	Quotas for subsidized wheat introduced
1996	Saudi wheat exports end
2000	Temporary reinstatement of barley import subsidies. Flexible handling thereafter
2003	Barley producer subsidy ends
2008	Phase-out of the wheat subsidy until 2016
2007–09	Rice import subsidy
2011	Barley import subsidy raised

production. The Saudi Arabian Agricultural Bank (SAAB) was founded in 1963 and provided financing to farmers at preferential rates. By the mid-1960s, about half of all imported grain was in the form of milled flour that could not be stored. To enable an emergency storage facility of up to six months and to realize cost savings from bulk handling, the Ford Foundation recommended the import of untreated grains and the expansion of the local milling industry.[60]

In 1968, the Public Lands Distribution Ordinance allotted cultivable land to private persons for free.[61] The first population census in 1962–3 established that half of the 3.3 million Saudis were dependent on agriculture. Meanwhile, the agriculture's value added lagged behind other sectors. The dependence on food imports grew together with high birth rates, changing diets, and increased numbers of pilgrims and expatriates. By the 1970s, politicians in Saudi Arabia and elsewhere in the Middle East perceived the food gap as a significant problem.[62]

---

[60] Woolley, Riyadh to Bloom, Comments on "A Grain Storage and Milling Program for Saudi Arabia," Ford Foundation Archives, 20 August 1964 (69645).

[61] Private persons received 5–10 ha each and sometimes up to 20 ha. Institutions received up to 400 ha, but had to start using the land within two to three years or it would go back to the state. Philipp 1984: 41.

[62] Richards and Waterbury 2008: 147f.

The various credit programs stimulated agricultural production. Close to 300,000 ha. were cultivated by 1965. Beneficiaries were mostly medium-sized and large farms. Small farmers faced neglect. The large-scale Al-Hasa Irrigation and Drainage Project (IDP) was finished in 1971 and aimed at expanding the acreage of the Al-Hasa oasis that had suffered by desert encroachment and sinking water tables, possibly caused by water demand from oil installations.[63] In the west, several dams were built or rehabilitated, but most of the increase in water supplies came from motor pumps, which showed the fastest growth of all agricultural modernization devices.[64] Saudi Arabian Fertilizer Company (SAFCO) was the first petrochemical down-stream industry of Saudi Arabia. It was established in 1965, a decade before Saudi Basic Industries Corporation (SABIC), under whose umbrella it is incorporated today.[65] Nowadays Saudi Arabia has developed into a global fertilizer player, but in the 1960s, production was designed to serve its own emerging agricultural sector. Similar to financing, the increased usage of mineral fertilizer was concentrated on larger farms. The agricultural support structure that was put in place in the 1960s was enhanced by further subsidies in the 1970s and would lead to a massive, oil revenue fueled expansion at the beginning of the 1980s.[66]

3.4 SELF-SUFFICIENCY AND THE SAUDI WHEAT BONANZA 1970s–1990s

Producer subsidies in Saudi Arabia increased dramatically in the 1970s. At the heart of agricultural expansion were mechanization, hybrid seeds, mineral fertilizer application for wheat, and factory farms for livestock production. Fewer than 5 percent of Saudi farmers used fertilizers in the 1960s. The Mexipak high yield variety was first test planted in 1965 and an "Accelerated Wheat Production Program" began in 1971 under the auspices of the Ford Foundation.[67] It aimed at doubling yields on irrigated areas. A reduction in food import subsidies that started in 1966 helped domestic agricultural producers. Import subsidies were restricted to wheat, grain, rice, and meat and

---

[63] Jones 2010: chapter 4.

[64] Philipp 1984: 28, 45.

[65] See the company's website <http://www.safco.com.sa/> (accessed 9 April 2012). The government owns 70 percent of SABIC, which in turn owns 42.99 percent of SAFCO today.

[66] Philipp 1984: 44–8.

[67] "An Evaluation of the Economic Feasibility and Technical Requirements for an Accelerated Wheat Production Program in Saudi Arabia," March 1970, Ford Foundation Archive (77658); Kingdom of Saudi Arabia 1970: 258; Philipp 1984: 40–4; Lippman 2004: 195f.; El Mallakh 1982: 78–91.

were gradually reduced through 1969. The Ford Foundation recommended a complete abolition of wheat import subsidies, a generous fertilizer program, and a guaranteed minimum price for Mexipak wheat that would be administered by a central procurement agency. The government created such an agency in 1972 with the establishment of the Grain Silos and Flour Mills Organization (GSFMO).

The system of "segmented clientelism" that had been emerging since the 1950s resulted in uncoordinated agricultural policies during the oil boom of the 1970s. Responsibilities were divided with no lead agency. The increasingly well-endowed Agricultural Bank was under the remit of the Ministry of Finance, the Ministry of Labor and Social Affairs oversaw the rural cooperatives, and the Ministry of Commerce and Industry ran the GSFMO. The MoAW lacked important tools for policy-making. It shared responsibilities for water with the Ministry of Interior, the Water Desalination Organization, and the Ministry of Planning. The high level of institutional fragmentation and the overlapping responsibilities contributed to duplication of loans and subsidies. As the government was designed to redistribute rents instead of collecting taxes, its institutions lacked vital information about the population and did not have the bureaucratic capacities to penetrate various subsectors of the economy. To allocate resources effectively, the role of intermediaries like brokers and business people became indispensable. The allocation process favored large landholders over small-scale farmers. Only they were in a position to provide the feasibility studies and the capital that were necessary to implement the sort of large-scale farming that had become a strategic aim to raise food production.[68]

The MoAW and the SAAB administered subsidies for input factors that were introduced from 1973 to 1975. Fertilizers, pumps, well operation, agricultural machinery, and animal feed were subsidized to the tune of 50 percent, dairy and poultry equipment by 30 percent. The cost of importing cattle into the kingdom by air was borne in full by the government.[69] However, production expanded significantly only once the government launched a wheat price support program in 1978. By 1979, it guaranteed a purchasing price of $933 per ton of wheat, about six times the world market price at that time.[70] Whereas the Second Development Plan (1975–80) sought only to "minimize the Kingdom's dependence on imported food," the Third Development Plan (1980–85) made a "prudent level of self-sufficiency in food production" a major policy goal. Large-scale farming was set as a priority.[71] Interest-free loan

[68] Hertog 2010: 96f.; Chaudhry 1997: 179f.; Lackner 1978: 156; Kingdom of Saudi Arabia 1975: 114.

[69] Kingdom of Saudi Arabia 1980: 143; Whelan 1981: 107; Philipp 1984: 56.

[70] Nowshirvani 1987: 8; Kingdom of Saudi Arabia 2009c.

[71] Kingdom of Saudi Arabia 1975: 123, 1980: 149. For an account of Saudi Arabia's overall economic development that closely tracks the respective five year plans see Niblock (with Malik) 2007: 52ff.

provision by the Agricultural Development Bank and land distribution by the Public Lands Distribution Ordinance of 1968 had only risen modestly through the 1970s, but they began to soar in the early 1980s. If the effect of input subsidies was added to the wheat support price, the effective protection rate was close to 1,500 percent at the end of that decade. Loans to farmers rose from under $5 million in 1971 to over $1 billion in 1983. Subsidized barley imports for the expanding livestock industry grew dramatically. Wheat production skyrocketed from less than 3,300 tons in 1978 to over 3.9 million tons in 1992, making the desert kingdom the sixth largest wheat exporter worldwide at that time.[72] A farm lobby developed. Alongside import licenses, sponsorship schemes, government contracts, and land grants, subsidized agriculture was an important tool of the state to distribute oil rent and buy political acquiescence. Main benefactors were royals and associated businessmen.[73]

The Failure of the Wheat Program

The GSFMO acted as agent of the wheat price support program. Originally established as an importer and flour producer, it became the sole distributor and stockpiler on a national level and effectively a price setter by allocating subsidies via guaranteed prices and later quotas.[74] The resulting overproduction created a problem for the government. Storage capacity was not sufficient. Wheat rotted under the open sky or had to be given away as aid. All the while, farmers abandoned other crops in favor of subsidized wheat, which led to increased import requirements in items like vegetables.

The distorted price structure of grains provided an incentive for all kinds of fraudulent activities. Subsidized barley imports grew much more than what could have been justified by expanding livestock production, suggesting that there was vivid contraband to neighboring countries. On the other hand, Yemenis started to smuggle wheat from African food aid deliveries via the Empty Quarter. Then they sold the wheat for a profit to the GSFMO at the subsidized price with the help of accomplices among Saudi farmers.[75]

The most problematic issue was sinking water tables. There have been widely differing studies about groundwater resources in Saudi Arabia, some of them overtly optimistic, but the Ministry of Planning warned as early as 1975 about excessive water consumption of the wheat program.[76] Water strain showed in other areas as well. In the oases of Al-Qatif and Al-Hasa traditional communal water management systems were abandoned opening the way to a

[72] Richards and Waterbury 2008: 163.   [73] Luciani 2005.
[74] Shepherd 2010: 5.   [75] Nowshirvani 1987.
[76] *Saudi Gazette*, 20 December 2011.

true tragedy of the commons. Declining water tables led farmers to seek individual solutions by drilling deeper wells, thereby further aggravating the problem. A lack of water provision, poor water quality, inadequate sewage disposal, and the apparent ineptitude of government institutions to cope with the problem took on a political security dimension in their contribution to the Shiite uprisings in the Eastern Province in the fall and winter of 1979 and 1980.[77]

To counter overproduction and water waste, the wheat support price was lowered more than 40 percent in 1984, with a guarantee that it would remain on that level until 1989. When this did not achieve desired results, purchasing quotas were established but soon abolished after pressure from the farm lobby.[78] Only in 1993 were they successfully introduced.[79] The government resorted to payment delays in an attempt to curb production. In 1989, the support price was further reduced to $400 for large companies in a two-tiered price structure. The companies successfully circumvented it by selling wheat to small farmers who then sold it on to the GSFMO as their own production for which a higher price of $533 still applied.[80] In the 1990s, there were further reductions in wheat subsidies and a decline in production. Saudi wheat exports ceased in 1996.[81] The Fifth Development Plan (1990–95) promoted barley at the expense of wheat. Subsidies on barley imports were abolished in 1989 to encourage domestic production for the livestock industry.[82] Yet already one planning period later it was acknowledged that land requirements for barley self-sufficiency would have been excessive—70 percent of the total acreage.[83] Subsidies for barley production were effectively ended in 2003.[84] The support price of wheat had fallen from $933 per metric ton in 1981 to $267 in 2004.[85] By 2005, the cultivated area in Saudi Arabia was a quarter below that of 1992.[86] It became clear that the grandiose vision of large-scale agriculture found in the Third Development Plan would not be achieved. Concerns about water

---

[77] Other factors included political oppression and "willfulness on the part of Shi'a community leaders to express and practice their various ideological convictions" in the wake of the Islamic revolution in Iran. Jones 2006: 219–22. In 1993 the government struck a deal with Shiite leaders to refrain from protests in exchange for gradual reform, which became brittle again in the wake of the Arab Spring, when violent protests occurred in Saudi Arabia's east. *Reuters*, 23 July 2012.

[78] Nowshirvani 1987: 8; Okruhlik 1992: 297.

[79] Agriculture and Agro-Food Canada 2005. The quota for public companies was 200,000 tons and for individual farmers 65 tons.

[80] Okruhlik 1992: 297, 301.

[81] Kingdom of Saudi Arabia 1995: 218.

[82] Kingdom of Saudi Arabia 1990: 204; Okruhlik 1992: 298.

[83] Kingdom of Saudi Arabia 1995: 213.

[84] Agriculture and Agro-Food Canada 2005. For an overview of subsidy regimes in the early 2000s see Al-Nimri 2002: 185–205.

[85] Agriculture and Agro-Food Canada 2005, 2001.

[86] FAO 2008e: 1.

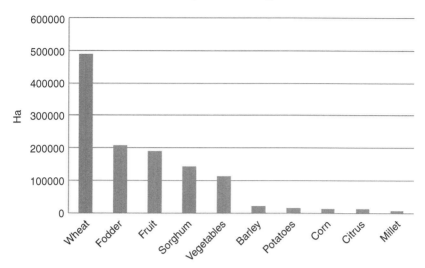

Fig. 3.1. Harvested crops in Saudi Arabia (2006)
Source: FAO 2008e

depletion and the lack of Saudi workforce participation crept into planning considerations.

In 2001, the Ministry of Water (MoW) was founded to improve efficiency of water usage. The former Ministry of Agriculture and Water was stripped of its responsibility for the latter and is now just the Ministry of Agriculture as it was before 1965. Electricity was added to the portfolio of the MoW in 2004 making it the MoWE, in order to guarantee optimal planning of power generation and desalination, which are intertwined.[87] Other institutional changes included a redefinition of the Irrigation and Sanitation Authority at Al-Hasa and the Al-Kharj Agricultural Project. The MoWE also acquired water and sewage discharge responsibilities from the Ministry of Municipal and Rural Affairs and other government agencies like the Water Desalination Organization. It has been entrusted with more efficient water management, collecting water revenues, and the possible introduction of market-based tariffs. It also licenses the digging of wells and determines which depth they can have. The MoA, which tends to represent the interest of the water guzzling agro-industry has been effectively demoted. The MoWE centralizes the formerly disparate responsibilities for water in one institution in order to "ensure a balance between water and food security."[88] "Our biggest challenge is the conflict between agriculture and other water users," admitted Mohammed al-Saud, the Deputy Minister for Water and Electricity in 2010.[89] In the Eighth Development Plan

---

[87] FAO 2008e: 11.   [88] Kingdom of Saudi Arabia 2000: 209.
[89] *Der Spiegel*, No. 11, 15 March 2010.

(2005–09), water conservation, rainwater collection with dams, and reclaimed wastewater usage ranked high alongside an emphasis on "small and medium high-value agriculture in rural areas."[90] Finally, in 2007 the Saudi government decided to phase out wheat production until 2016 by reducing guaranteed wheat quotas by 12.5 percent annually over the following eight years.[91] At that time, wheat made up the largest share of harvested area, followed by fodder crops like alfalfa, fruits—most of which were dates—sorghum, and vegetables. Barley, potatoes, corn, and citrus fruits only constituted a minor share of the total harvested area (Figure 3.1).[92]

Cui Bono? Motivations for the Wheat Program

The wheat program did not try to sedentarize Bedouins as did previous agricultural modernization programs. A widely stated goal was the promotion of rural development in order to prevent the flow of Saudis from the country-side to the cities, where they started to form shanty towns.[93] Job creation for young people in the villages and balanced economic development between urban and rural areas have been regarded as important for the preservation of moral values, social equitability, and cultural heritage by many Saudi observers.[94] By 1970, almost half of the Saudi population lived in cities, up from 21 percent in 1950 (Table 3.2).

Urbanization continued unabated after the 1970s. Saudis may still celebrate an idealized past of a Bedouin lifestyle with occasional camping trips into the desert, but they have become one of the most urbanized societies globally, with more than 80 percent city dwellers today. If rural development was a sincere goal of the wheat program, it failed abysmally. In the 1960s, investments had focused on the enhancement of productivity in traditional farming areas like date groves in the eastern oases, the Al-Kharj farms, or mountainous regions in the Asir where dams were built. In contrast, most of the new agricultural investments took place in uninhabited areas above fossil water aquifers, in the Najd and in the north where no farming had been practiced before. Only 11 percent of the distributed land between 1970 and 1984 was in regions with traditional farming communities: 3 percent in Asir and Hejaz and 8 percent in Al-Hasa.[95]

---

[90] Kingdom of Saudi Arabia 2005: 542.

[91] Mousa 2008b.

[92] For an account about the reduced importance of the MoA in the 2000s from the viewpoint of a Saudi agro-businessman see Al-Rasheed, Turki Faisal 2010: 123–36.

[93] Kingdom of Saudi Arabia 1985: 179, 1990: 194; Wilson and Graham 1994: 222.

[94] Al-Nimri 1995: Vol. 2, 59; Al-Rasheed, Turki Faisal 2010: 147–54.

[95] Chaudhry 1997: 177.

Table 3.2. Urbanization rate of Saudi Arabia

Year	1950	1960	1970	1980	1990	2000	2005	2015 (est.)	2030 (est.)
%	21.3	31.3	48.7	65.9	76.2	80	81	83.1	85.7

Source: United Nations 2011.

The distribution schemes had a clear bias towards royals and well-connected businessmen in the cities of Najd who had no prior farming experience. Their agro-companies were funded with state support. Job creation for locals was all but absent. Asian blue-collar workers took the agricultural jobs because the menial labor and the low pay were not appealing to Saudi nationals. The actual running of the farms was in the hands of Western management companies. By 2011 Saudi nationals represented only 1.8 percent of the agricultural workforce—8,800 out of nearly half a million.[96]

Geopolitical reasons have been cited as motivation for the wheat program and the Sudan bread-basket strategy of the 1970s that hoped to turn Sudan into a food exporter for the Arab world. The US politicized food trade in the 1970s and threatened a food embargo in retaliation to the Arab oil boycott. Self-sufficiency considerations ranked prominently in the Five Year Plans of the 1970s and there is convincing archival evidence that these factors were on the minds of Gulf rulers (see chapter 4). Elie Elhadj, a researcher from SOAS, downplays them a bit too much, yet he makes a convincing case that wealth distribution among royals and predominantly Najdi businessmen was the most important driving force of the wheat program.[97]

The Public Lands Distribution Ordinance of 1968 did not dramatically increase land distribution. Redistributed land from 1968–80 was only 7 percent of the size that was distributed during the height of the wheat boom from 1980 to 1992. If sedentarization and rural development had been the main motivation, land distribution could have been considerably higher after 1968. If geopolitical considerations were the main motivation, the massive distribution would presumably have begun earlier, immediately after the food embargo threats in 1973, rather than seven years later. The fact that wheat production was increased well beyond self-sufficiency levels by the beginning of the 1990s and the overrepresentation of absentee landlords also hint at the importance of wealth distribution and elite co-optation. The wheat program triggered a process that gained a momentum of its own and became very costly. Elhadj estimates that the direct costs of subsidies of the Saudi wheat program were $85 billion between 1984 and 2000, which was equivalent to 18 percent of the country's $485 billion in oil revenues during that period. These

---

[96] *Arab News*, 21 July 2011. In contrast the *Nitaqat* program for workforce nationalization in the private sector aims at 30 percent Saudization quota in the agricultural sector.
[97] Elhadj 2006, 2008.

costs would easily double if indirect costs like the involved bureaucracy, subsidized fuel and electricity inputs, soft loans, and the value of the distributed land were considered. The direct distribution of money and the import of foodstuffs from the world market would have been much cheaper.[98]

A cursory look at the main agricultural companies that were founded in the 1970s and 1980s demonstrates a characteristic pattern of state support for royals and associated businessmen who ran their projects with the help of Western joint venture partners. Many of these companies have been crucial players in the foreign agro-investment drive that started in 2008.

The National Agricultural Development Corporation (NADEC) was built on the remnants of the Haradh Agricultural and Animal Production Corporation, which had been initiated by King Faisal for the settlement of Bedouins but failed to attract them.[99] The state owned 20 percent of NADEC, private shareholders the rest. Farm management was granted to the US agricultural company FMC in cooperation with Saudi businessman Sulaiman Olayan. The latter also ran the Saudi Agricultural Development Corporation as a joint venture with Prince Khaled bin Abdullah. NADEC, over a quarter of which is today owned by the Al-Rajhi family, has served as a model for a number of other companies that were formed on the same principles of public–private cooperation with large royal shareholders. Prince Muqrin bin Abdulaziz chaired the Hail Agricultural Development Corporation (HADCO). It was the largest producer of wheat in the mid-1980s. Prince Abdul Majid bin Abdulaziz founded the Tabuk Agricultural Development Corporation (TADCO) in 1982. The Saudi Arabian Agricultural and Dairy Corporation was established as a joint venture between Prince Abdullah al-Faisal, who owned 75 percent, and the Swedish company Alfa Laval, which acted as manager and minority shareholder. Almarai was a joint venture between the Irish agro-businessman Alastair McGuckian and his brother Paddy, and Prince Sultan bin Mohammed bin Saud al-Kabeer. It would gain worldwide fame by building the world's largest integrated dairy farm with 35,000 cattle. Other notable companies included Al-Wataniyya Poultry of the businessman Sulaiman Abdulaziz al-Rajhi and the John Deere agency of the Al-Khorayef brothers, which supplied the new projects with machinery, seeds, fertilizer, and pesticides.[100] Later establishments were the Gassim Agricultural Co. (GACO) in Buraydah (1985), the Al-Sharqiyah Development Co. (SHADCO, 1986), the Al-Jouf Agricultural Development Co. (JADCO, 1988), and the Jazan Company for Agricultural Development (JAZADCO, 1993).[101]

[98] Elhadj 2006, 2008.

[99] Philipp 1984: 63, 77; Lippman 2004: 190.

[100] Nowshirvani 1987: 10.

[101] See <www.gaco-agri.com>, <www.asharqiyah.com.sa>, <www.aljouf.com.sa>, and <www.jazadco.com.sa> (accessed, 29 March 2011).

In sum, the major aim of the wheat program differed from earlier agricultural modernization. It was not about achieving control over nomads via sedentarization or asserting authority in existing farming communities like Al-Hasa, but distributing oil wealth among a regime-stabilizing elite.[102] The end of the wheat program for lack of water raises the question of what will happen with entrenched structures in the future and what can be offered to vested interests as a quid pro quo.

3.5 WHEAT OR WATER

Council of Ministers Resolution No. 335 of 19 November 2007 listed 21 procedures for more efficient water usage, among them the decision to phase out wheat production by 2016. Beside the wheat quota reduction, the resolution shifted consumption subsidies to imported grains and dismantled import tariffs. Plans for the privatization of the GSFMO were a visible sign of the end of the subsidy regime.[103] Tariffs on cereals, animal feed, and wheat flour were completely abolished, and the tariff rate for 75 other foodstuffs was reduced to 5 percent, the general external tariff rate of the GCC customs union.[104] This was also being done to comply with regulations of the WTO, which Saudi Arabia joined in 2005. Achieving WTO compliance has been used as a trailblazer for economic reform and became a fixture in the deliberations over the Ninth Development Plan (2010–14).[105]

Resolution No. 355 also issued bans on exporting wheat, fodder, and vegetables that are cultivated on open fields, including potatoes and melons. It paid particular attention to water-intensive fodder crops like alfalfa and barley and encouraged their imports through credit guarantees and tariff waivers. It also recommended promoting international agro-investments in order to cultivate such fodder crops abroad.[106]

At a conference planned for September 2009 in Zanzibar about Arab–African cooperation in agriculture, most of the scheduled speeches of Saudi and other Gulf participants centered around the procurement of green fodder like alfalfa from Africa.[107] The conference was canceled because the Tanzanian hosts were concerned about the participation of then OAU President Muammar Gaddafi and the costs required to meet his demands for security and pomp. The Saudis,

---

[102] Jones 2010: 232.
[103] Kingdom of Saudi Arabia 2010b: 553.
[104] Mousa 2008a.
[105] Hertog 2010: chapter 7; Kingdom of Saudi Arabia 2010b.
[106] Kingdom of Saudi Arabia 2010b: 549f.
[107] Conference program in my possession. The planned conference was organized by the Europe Southern African Development Community (SADC) States Bridge; see <www.essb.de> (accessed 18 June 2012).

who were going to put up part of the money, were also displeased about the prominent participation of someone with whom they had less than cordial relations.[108] The conference agenda showed that fodder is badly needed. Unlike cereal production, meat and dairy output continued to expand in the kingdom, particularly the latter, which grew 75 percent from 1998 to 2008.[109] While alfalfa is mostly fed to cows and camels, sheep consume the massive barley imports of the kingdom. The subsidies on barley imports incentivize the import of lamb rather than adult sheep, as it cheapens the subsequent fattening towards the Ramadan and Hajj season.[110] Feedstock supplies are also crucial to maintain sheep and camel herds of Bedouins and their loyalty to the government.

In Search of Agricultural Niches

Agriculture as a whole has hardly been eliminated in Saudi Arabia. According to the Ninth Development Plan, agriculture is only at the beginning of a "radical restructuring process" that will "subject . . . agricultural development to the constraints of water resources."[111] Only water-intensive crops like wheat, barley, and alfalfa have been targeted for a phase-out. Otherwise, officials hope to get "more crops for less drops" as the Minister of Agriculture Fahd Balghunaim put it.[112] Cultivation is to be shifted to more value added crops like fruits and vegetables. Efficiency gains are expected from greenhouses, wastewater recycling, and drip irrigation.[113] The Saudi Arabian Agricultural Bank was renamed the Agricultural Development Fund and its capital was increased to SAR20 billion, signaling a continued commitment to domestic agriculture.[114] The US–Saudi Arabian Business Council has pointed out that Saudi Arabia has earmarked over $28 billion for domestic agricultural projects through 2020.[115] As large-scale cereal farming is on its way out, there has been a shift of attention to smaller projects for fruit and vegetable

---

[108] Interview with one of the conference organizers, Dubai, 8 March 2010. Gaddafi had purportedly planned then Crown Prince Abdullah's assassination in 2003 who famously told him before the Iraq war: "Your lies precede you and your grave is in front of you." *Daily Mail*, 10 June 2004.

[109] *Saudi Gazette*, 26 March 2011. Between 2004 and 2008 production of chicken meat declined due to the impact of the avian flu, so did the number of sheep, goats, and camels, but the number of cows grew strongly with 6 percent on average. Kingdom of Saudi Arabia 2010b: 547.

[110] Interview, Saudi agro-businessman, Princeton, 27 September 2011.

[111] Kingdom of Saudi Arabia 2010b: 545.

[112] "Cultivating Sustainable Agriculture," advertising supplement promoting Saudi Arabia, *Foreign Affairs*, November–December 2007.

[113] Lippman 2010: 91; Kingdom of Saudi Arabia 2010b: 550; NCB Capital 2010.

[114] *Saudi Gazette*, 27 January 2009.

[115] Lippman 2010: 95; US–Saudi Arabian Business Council 2008: 1.

production, organic farming, and even bee keeping. During the eighth planning period (2005–09) a majority of credit allocation went to individual farmers rather than large corporations.[116] Instead of loans for big wheat in the Qassim and Al-Dawasir, it is now about olives in Jawf, tropical fruits in Jazan, and citruses in Najran.[117] Saudi Arabia is already one of the largest date producers in the world, and Saudis take great pride in the quality of their dates, which are processed by companies like Al-Bateel. One can get them with almonds and orange peel fillings or as date vinegar and non-alcoholic champagne. However, as fruit trees are perennial crops that require irrigation all year round, they may actually consume more water on the same area and on an annualized basis than wheat. Only reduced acreage or vegetable production in greenhouses would actually mitigate the water problem.[118]

The preponderance of niche sectors is also exemplified in the country's stated objective of becoming a large shrimp exporter.[119] North of Al-Leith on the Red Sea coast, the National Prawn Company (NPC) produces shrimp on 250 square kilometers.[120] The Al-Rajhi and Al-Sudairi families own NPC, with the Japanese trading house Sojitz holding a minority stake. The project is the second largest shrimp farm in the world with a production of 15,000 tons annually. Shrimp are not part of the traditional Saudi diet, even though the Hanbali School of jurisprudence that is predominant in the kingdom allows their consumption.[121] Hence, shrimp are produced primarily for export, with some flown to London for next-day sales. The main market is Asia, where customers appreciate the high quality of shrimp raised in the salty and less polluted Red Sea water.[122] NPC also experiments with planting algae in order to reduce its dependence on fishmeal as feedstock. It aims to establish further shrimp farms in the south of Al-Leith and possibly on the African Red Sea coast at a future point in time.[123] Together with the private sector arm of the Islamic Development Bank it announced large-scale shrimp projects in Mauritania in 2012.[124]

[116] Kingdom of Saudi Arabia 2010b.
[117] Kingdom of Saudi Arabia 2010b: 550f.
[118] FAO 2008e: 9.
[119] Lippman 2010: 95. Lippman mentions that Saudi Arabia wants to become the world's largest shrimp exporter. This is an overstatement given an annual production of 15,000 tons as compared to large producers like China (1.2 million tons in 2007), Thailand (500,000 tons), or Vietnam (377,000 tons). FAO 2011d.
[120] Gulf Research Center (GRC) 2009. The company's website is <http://www.robian.com.sa/home.html> (accessed 18 June 2012).
[121] Cook 1986: 237–40. All Sunni schools allow consumption of aquatic animals in general, except for the Hanafi School, which only allows fish. Shiite doctrine, which can be found on the east coast of the Gulf, is even stricter, only allowing fish with scales.
[122] Interview with Fumimasa Murakoshi, General Manager Sojitz Middle East in *GRC Economic Research Bulletin*, Vol. 2, October 2006.
[123] Interview with NPC management, Al-Leith, June 2008.
[124] *Arab News*, 26 December 2011.

The land needs of aquaculture have led to some opposition. Members of the local population have complained about excessive land allocation to the NPC project. They would like to see the project benefit local communities to a greater extent by providing jobs or access to some of the facilities on the fully integrated site, which has its own power station and supermarket. While competing land uses in the barren *sabkha* salt marshes in the form of agriculture or tourism are limited, such opposition hints at widespread discontent with land deals and a diffuse feeling in disadvantaged rural areas of being left behind by government policies. NPC has tried to placate opposition by highlighting job creation and training programs for locals, who make up 10 percent of its workforce of 2,400. It claims a low environmental impact because its low stocking density allows it to refrain from using antibiotics and because the onshore ponds limit the impact on other marine life.

Aquafarming is often sold by officials as an exercise in self-sufficiency and food security.[125] This is a charitable interpretation as saltwater fish are carnivorous and require imported fishmeal as feedstock. Their protein production is also less efficient than herbivorous fresh water fish like carp, tilapia, or catfish, which only play a limited role in the arid Gulf.[126] Yet, aquafarming does not entail the same consumption of water reserves as livestock industries and can play a role in relieving the region's waters from overfishing. While the Third Development Plan (1980–85) referred to an "abundance of fish . . . [that has] hardly been exploited," such abundance has disappeared.[127] Today, the coastlines of the Arabian Peninsula suffer from severe overfishing, particularly in territorial waters. The Jeddah coast will be depleted of fish within 15 years if current exploitation rates continue.[128] Fishing moratoriums were enacted in Saudi Arabia, the UAE, and Oman in 2011 to allow stocks to recover.[129] Ambitious plans remain. Saudi Arabia has launched a "fishery revolution." With a bold expansion of aquaculture along its west coast, it wants to become self-sufficient in fish by 2019.[130]

Enter the Agro-Lobby

While Saudi Arabia may successfully master a transformation from water-guzzling cereal production to water-saving high value agriculture, there is a

---

[125] *Trade Arabia*, 22 November 2010; interview with Saudi official, Cambridge, Mass., 4 May 2010.

[126] Brown 2009: 226f.

[127] Kingdom of Saudi Arabia 1980: 141.

[128] Gulf Research Center (GRC) 2009: 116.

[129] *The National*, 2 March 2011; *Gulf News*, 5 March and 15 August 2011; *Saudi Gazette*, 15 March 2011.

[130] *Al-Hayat*, 2 June 2012.

price to be paid for what Deputy Minister of Agriculture Abdulllah A. al-Obaid described as the "tough decisions to end the story" of wheat cultivation in Saudi Arabia.[131] The MoA has been charged with helping farmers overcome the negative impact of the reform process and is lobbying for their interests. Al-Obaid admitted that the MoA would have liked a slower pace of WTO-inspired trade liberalization and would have preferred to keep wheat production in the north where water consumption is less.[132] While the wheat schemes appear to be gone for good, meat and dairy production are not and the ministry has engaged in rearguard fights. The MoA opposed a 2010 motion by the Saudi Majlis al-Shura to ban dairy exports. The motion argued that dairy exports squandered declining water resources and that dairy production should be limited. This directly threatened the dairy industry, which grapples with overcapacities in fresh milk products and therefore needs export outlets.[133] Dairy company Almarai's stock price was negatively affected. The company signed an agreement in 2007 with the Saudi government to support the export of dairy products from Saudi Arabia and expected it to remain in effect. The Minister of Agriculture Fahd Balghunaim defended the current practice, stating, "The government's policy is to reduce the production of crops that use a lot of water. Dairy products do not use a lot of water. They use barley to feed cattle and barley is imported."[134] He did not mention the large water consumption of dairy production itself. Even the discussions about wheat production resurfaced at the end of 2011 when the influential Minister of Interior and then Crown Prince Nayef ordered a renewed study of the issue. A possible reconciliation of water sustainability and wheat production, concerns about import dependence, and a need for more "balanced results" in comparison to earlier studies were quoted as reasons.[135]

Interests are evidently vested and change will not come easily. This is also true for the widespread practice of switching to alfalfa production as the wheat subsidies are phased out. Alfalfa is planted all year round, not only over a period of four months in the winter like wheat. It typically uses five times more water than wheat, and even more in the hot summer months. Turki Faisal al-Rasheed, the chairman of Saudi agro-company Golden Grass Inc., readily acknowledges this as a problem, but he points to his need to amortize investments in tractors, irrigation equipment, and other fixed capital: "Better bad

---

[131] Kingdom of Saudi Arabia 2009c.

[132] *Le Monde Diplomatique*, English edition, 30 January 2010. For a similar Majlis al-Shura proposal and a feasibility study see *Al Eqtisadiah*, 24 January 2012.

[133] Kingdom of Saudi Arabia 2005: 536. The same is true for eggs. The overcapacity relates to fresh milk products. As Table 1.6 shows, overall self-sufficiency in milk and dairy products only stands at around a third, as other products such as dry milk are imported in huge quantities.

[134] *Saudi Economic Survey*, Vol. 44, No. 2158, 10 February 2010.

[135] *Saudi Gazette*, 20 December 2011.

profits than no profits."[136] Water consumption of agriculture has actually increased since 2008 as a result of wheat's substitution with alfalfa.[137] The end of the wheat program will thus not mean the end of excessive water consumption in Saudi Arabia unless solutions for other water-intensive sectors like dairy and fodder are found. The agro-business community has already lobbied for compensation, either in the form of cash payments or in the form of shares in a public investment company that would invest in agricultural projects abroad.[138]

The subsidized agricultural schemes in Saudi Arabia have proven to be economically unfeasible and ecologically unsustainable. Attaining food security via self-sufficiency has proven to be an illusion, as there is not enough water. Reliance on food trade will continue to grow. The larger the import dependence of Saudi Arabia and other Gulf countries, the more they will be worried about market failure and food export restrictions as in 2008. The drive towards international agro-investments is directly connected to this growing vulnerability. Another factor is the political economy of domestic agriculture, which aims at providing alternative business opportunities to an industry that is in a thorough transformation process due to a lack of water.

3.6 AGRICULTURAL DEVELOPMENT IN THE SMALLER GULF STATES

Agricultural developments in the smaller Gulf states were more limited than in Saudi Arabia. Their lack of water and arable land is more pronounced and agricultural traditions are less developed. Rain-fed farming like in Asir and Yemen is largely impossible along the Gulf coast. It has only been practiced in some areas of Oman and the Hajar Mountains in the northern Emirates. Dryness, flash floods, and slow soil formation under the prevalent climatic conditions are issues as in Saudi Arabia. The few suitable soils have high amounts of soluble salts and tend to incur salinity without proper drainage.[139] Agriculture was historically restricted to oases. Pastoralism focused on semi-sedentary herding of sheep and goats. Camel-based, long-distance nomadism as in Saudi Arabia was not common. Oil income led to a decline of traditional agriculture and pastoralism. Native populations moved to the booming towns of the oil era, and expatriate farmers took over the work of their landowning ex-farmers cum landlords. The residual farming in smaller Gulf states is not

---

[136] Interview with Turki Faisal al-Rasheed, Jeddah, 13 February 2010.
[137] *Al Eqtisadiah*, 20 September 2011.
[138] Riyadh Chamber of Commerce and Industry 2010. For details see chapter 7.
[139] Bowen-Jones 1980: 48.

predominantly undertaken for commercial purposes, even though it produces a not insignificant amount of dates, vegetables, and livestock. Its main purpose is to provide green countryside retreats for landlords and to keep emotional links to ancestral lands. The support for such farms must rather be seen "as a cultural obligation to communities in transition than as viable investment."[140] As in Saudi Arabia, reliance on the government has been extensive, whether in the form of indirect subsidies for inputs or via direct government funding of enterprises and joint venture projects. The advent of the motor pump also led to severe water wastage. Meanwhile, Gulf states pay at least lip service to more efficient water use and have enacted national strategies to this end.[141]

The amount of cultivated land in the smaller Gulf states clearly falls behind that of Saudi Arabia and cereal cultivation does not play a role. Only the UAE and Oman command a substantial cultivated acreage, particularly in the field of permanent crops, which are mainly date palms (Table 3.3). The UAE under Sheikh Zayed also developed water-intensive afforestation projects that bore some resemblances to the agricultural largesse of Saudi Arabia.

In contrast to Saudi Arabia, the UK, not the US, was the closest partner for technical cooperation in the smaller Gulf states after the war. The UK administered foreign policy until independence: 1961 in the case of Kuwait and 1971 in the case of the UAE, Oman, Bahrain, and Qatar. By their own admission, development was not a priority for the British. The British Government of India, which was in charge of the Trucial states, followed a policy of

Table 3.3. Cultivated area in the Gulf (ha, 000)

	Saudi Arabia	Kuwait	Bahrain	Qatar	UAE	Oman
Total area	214,969	1782	71	1100	8360	30,950
Cultivated area	1214	7	4	6	255	59
as % of the total area	0.6	0.4	6	0.6	3	0.2
Area under annual crops, temp. fallow and temp. meadows	1012	6	1	3	65	13
Area under permanent crops	202	1	3	3	190	46

Source: FAO 2008a–f.
Note: Data for Saudi Arabia (2005), Kuwait (2003), Bahrain (2000), Qatar (2004 and 2001 for breakdown), UAE (2003), Oman (2004).

[140] Bowen-Jones 1980: 52.

[141] A Royal Decree declared water resources in Oman a national resource in 1988 and a National Water Resources Master Plan for the period 2001–20 was later prepared. Qatar has a Permanent Water Resources Committee (PWRC) that is tasked with formulating a comprehensive National Water Resources Management and Development Strategy (NWRMDS) through the year 2050. The Abu Dhabi Water Resources Master Plan of 2009 aims to make water consumption rates more sustainable in the emirate.

"non-interference on land." It invested only few resources until 1953.[142] Apart from surveys, an agricultural development scheme for the Trucial states was only started in 1955. Until then agriculture was confined to dates, local tobacco, limes, and, in certain areas, wheat. Tomatoes, onions, eggplant, and white radishes were the four main vegetables grown. Lack of knowledge and mechanical equipment was widespread. A British document stated, "The few land-owners who had installed diesel-powere [sic] pumps at that time were more interested in swimming-pools than in agriculture."[143]

Kuwait

The Emir of Kuwait had visited the Al-Kharj farm together with Ibn Saud and was deeply impressed by the choice of fruits and vegetables that were at the disposal of the Saudi king thanks to his pet project. Returning to Kuwait in a plane loaded with watermelons and cantaloupes from Al-Kharj, he investigated whether similar projects would be possible in his country.[144] However, lack of water, competing urban uses, and poor soils impeded agricultural development. A government-owned experimental farm was established in 1953 on 40 ha near Sulaibiyya on the outskirts of today's city of Kuwait. Its prodigious water consumption with conventional irrigation illustrated the need for either more water or more efficient usage.[145] Between 1925 and 1950, Kuwait imported water by boat from the Shatt El Arab in Iraq in order to supplement scarce supplies from domestic wells.[146] A water pipeline was contemplated in 1953–4 and raised high hopes in the emirate.[147]

The British were less enthusiastic about the country's agricultural potential, although they conceded the project would have its benefits, "not least in increasing the amenities of their at present unlovely town."[148] Underground water reserves and a distillation plant for seawater were regarded as insufficient to develop the city-state. The British cautioned that the precious water from Iraq should only be used for residential supplies and some "market gardening." Plans for large-scale irrigation of cereals or cotton were discarded as Kuwait lacked water and had "practically no agriculturalist of any kind."[149] Worse, the import of Iraqi farm labor combined with Iraqi aspirations for Kuwaiti territory might have caused Kuwait a "Sudetan-German problem" in the future. Planting grains in Iraq itself and importing them from there was

---

[142] Wheatcroft 2005: 97, 105; Tuson 1990: Vol. 9, 25.
[143] Bahrain to Dubai, 19 February 1960, in Tuson 1990: Vol. 12, 506.
[144] Sanger 1954: 66.   [145] Bowen-Jones 1980.
[146] FAO 2008b: 7.
[147] Burrows, Bahrain to Eden, 23 May 1954, 3, in Burdett 1998: Vol. 2, 369.
[148] Burrows, Bahrain to Eden, 23 May 1954, 3, in Burdett 1998: Vol. 2, 369.
[149] Burrows, Bahrain to Eden, 23 May 1954, 3, in Burdett 1998: Vol. 2, 369.

regarded as more economical.[150] The construction of a model farm for fruits, vegetables, and dairy production was suggested at a site in Al-Jahra where suitable soils existed. Farther removed in the west of the city, the remoteness of the area promised to reduce the occurrence of water wastage for leisure projects.[151]

The Kuwait Development Board welcomed the model farm project in principle. However, the Board requested that the ruler declare all land outside the town itself state land in order to battle land speculation and prevent local sheikhs from "grabbing all land that was billed for development."[152] Sir Alexander Gibb & Partners undertook a feasibility study for the model farm for the Kuwait government, which was critically reviewed by a French agricultural expert.[153] British officials were concerned about the foreign policy implications of the water pipeline, given undefined border issues and known Iraqi irredentism towards Kuwait.[154] The British representative was surprised that the Kuwaitis were not too worried about dependence on Iraqi water supplies upon completion of the project. "They will have given a fairly large hostage to their neighbours," he remarked and speculated that they thought that a "combination of Arab brotherhood and the protection of Her Majesty's Government should be enough to avert any danger."[155] Ultimately, concerns about sovereignty led to the abandonment of the project.

Still, there was a rapid development of irrigated agriculture in the 1960s, partly spurred by small water discoveries in Al-Abdali close to the border with Iraq. Concerns for security of food supplies motivated the Kuwait Department of Agriculture to design a plan to expand vegetable, meat, and dairy production in the mid-1980s, which would be assisted by modern technologies like hydroponics.[156] Nowadays Kuwaiti agriculture is dominated by livestock production (67 percent of value) followed by plant production and fisheries. About 45 percent of harvested land is dedicated to vegetables. Kuwait does not

[150] Burrows, Bahrain to Eden, 23 May 1954, 3, in Burdett 1998: Vol. 2, 369.

[151] "Another great advantage is that it is far from the gardens of the Sheikhs, who will not be able to steal the water as it passes." W. F. Crawford, "A Sweet Water Supply from the Shatt El Arab for Kuwait," 21 December 1953, in Burdett 1998: Vol. 2, 386, 393f.

[152] W. F. Crawford, "A Sweet Water Supply from the Shatt El Arab for Kuwait," 21 December 1953, in Burdett 1998: Vol. 2, 386, 393f.

[153] Sir Alexander Gibbs & Partners, "Kuwait Water Supply. Final Report on the Shatt El Arab Scheme," London, September 1954; François Couprie, "Project de mise en valeur par l'eau d'irrigation en provenance du Shatt-El-Arab," attached to letter of Political Agency Kuwait, D. A. Logan to FO, 22 February 1955, in Burdett 1998: Vol. 2, 249–363 and 444–50.

[154] Iraq first claimed sovereignty over Kuwait in the 1930s under King Ghazi. After Kuwaiti independence in 1961, General Qassim who had toppled the Hashimite monarchy renewed Iraqi claims and only backed out after Britain sent troops to Kuwait as a deterrent. In 1963, Iraq recognized Kuwaiti sovereignty only to challenge it again with Saddam Hussein's invasion in 1990.

[155] Burrows, Bahrain to Eden, 23 May 1954, 4, in Burdett 1998: Vol. 2, 370.

[156] Bowen-Jones and Dutton 1983: 135.

have the preponderance of cereals like in Saudi Arabia or date palms like in UAE and Oman.[157]

Bahrain

From the mid-nineteenth century, the small island of Bahrain developed into a pre-eminent trading hub in the Gulf region under British protection.[158] It always had a more urban outlook and even less agricultural potential than other Gulf countries. After World War II, British authorities undertook some survey work for irrigated land expansion, but recommended that the country focus on urban, not rural, development.[159] Bahrain should become a business and holiday center. The land was deemed barren and without sufficient water supplies. Any agriculture needed extensive irrigation to leach the salty soils. The drilling results of submarine springs that were bubbling up off the coast from the central Arabian aquifers had proven disappointing. Nonetheless, there was widespread wastage of water. Some artesian wells ran all night long, and excessive watering damaged date plantations. Bahrain had already faced water shortages in the 1920s. By the 1970s, the water table sank two inches every year. The artesian onshore and offshore springs lost pressure. Neighboring Saudi Arabia was drawing more and more from the aquifer that also feeds Bahrain. Date palm cultivation had already gone into decline in the inter-war period. Agricultural development through the 1980s focused mainly on vegetables, meat, and poultry production.[160]

Qatar

Qatar was the best assessed country in the Gulf by the end of the 1970s due to extensive agricultural survey work by UN agencies. It had neither large oases nor a farming tradition. After 1948 the government embarked on a program to irrigate depressions in the south of the country, so called *rawdat* (sing. *rawda*), with the help of motor pumps and expatriate labor from southern Iran and Pakistan. This led to a short-lived boom in vegetable production. Qatar was an exporter of vegetables to the middle Gulf region at that time. The government tried to balance cereal imports with these export revenues, but overall Qatar remained a substantial net importer of food.[161] Like in Kuwait and Saudi

---

[157] FAO 2008b: 3.   [158] Onley 2007.
[159] Bahrain to FO, 22 March 1949; Bahrain to FO, 22 December 1953; brief by W. F. Crawford on dwindling supplies and problems, in Burdett 1998: Vol. 1, 363–6, 321–5.
[160] Bowen-Jones and Dutton 1983: 117–20.
[161] Bowen-Jones 1980: 57.

Arabia, land distribution and subsidized agriculture were used to allocate resources among regime stabilizing clients and royals.[162] Only 35 percent of the irrigation water was used for crop plant, indicating a high allocation for leisure gardens. Water wastage was rampant and diminishing water tables, groundwater quality, soil permeability, and drainage caused growing problems by the mid-1970s. Agriculture was upgraded in 1989 and organized in a separate ministry.[163] Today it is organized as a separate department within the Ministry of Environment alongside water, fisheries, and animal resources. By 2006, Qatar announced a National Water Resources Management and Development Strategy that would include the installation of meters at irrigation wells in order to curtail groundwater wastage.[164] Since 2008, the government has embarked on a unique vision of agricultural modernization. Bucking the general trend in the Gulf, Qatar wants to expand agriculture with the help of water-saving technologies and solar-based desalination. It aims to become 70 percent food self-sufficient by 2023, up from currently 10 percent (see chapter 7).

Trucial States

In the Trucial states agricultural interest of British development officers in the 1950s was concentrated in the mountainous areas of the northern Emirates and Oman. Rainfall and run-off water were more abundant there than in Abu Dhabi, which had only very limited reserves of brackish water. Agricultural development in Ras al-Khaima was deemed feasible by drilling shallow wells and renovating the system of *falaj* canals, which had fallen into disrepair with the advent of the motor pump.[165] Like in Bahrain, there were considerable problems with silt soils and water salinity. A program to advise local gardeners was established, and a number of agricultural trial stations were built, but the local population consisted largely of Bedouins who were used to a nomadic lifestyle and had limited interest in settled agricultural production.[166]

Sheikh Zayed, who would later become president of the UAE, started promoting agriculture and afforestation in his native Al-Ain in the 1950s and 1960s. Al-Ain was privileged in terms of water availability in comparison to Abu Dhabi and the Al-Liwa Oasis where water resources fluctuated heavily with rainfalls that could fail for years at a time.[167] Zayed renovated the *falaj* canals and distributed water for free. This astonished the British authorities.

---

[162] Crystal 1990: 148f.   [163] Crystal 1990: 184.   [164] FAO 2008d: 14.

[165] Iraq Petroleum Company to Chandler Brothers, Colwill and How, 5 May 1955; Resident (Bahrain) to FO, 18 March 1955; "Report on a preliminary investigation of water resources and their utilisation for agricultural development in the plains south of Ras al-Khaima in the Eastern Trucial States," no date, but *ca*.1960, in Burdett 1998: Vol. 1, 583–605.

[166] Dubai to FO, 29 May 1960, in Burdett 1998: Vol. 1, 612–15.

[167] Wheatcroft 2005: 20, 80–3.

They explained it as a general policy of Zayed "to improve the living of his people without costs to themselves."[168] Formerly, farmers had paid a proportionate tax in line with the number of hours for which their fields and groves were watered. Later, Sheikh Zayed would transplant the free of charge model to the town of Abu Dhabi and other emirates. As in Saudi Arabia, the free distribution of water and a mastery of natural resources generated loyalty. Promotion of agriculture became part of the ruling bargain of the allocation state. Stylizing the ruler as champion of the environment developed into a pillar of legitimacy.[169]

Oman

Agriculture in Oman has been concentrated in highly dispersed areas along the Batina coastal strip between Muscat and Sohar.[170] By Gulf standards, its agricultural potential is high. In the 1970s, when the population was only 750,000 people, an estimated half of Oman's cropped area would have been enough for self-sufficiency in vegetables, fruits, and forage products, if efficient agricultural technologies had been applied. Experts recommended that Oman focus development efforts on increasing productivity rather than acreage expansion.[171] Family farms with smaller than five ha dominate land tenure in Oman. They make up 91 percent of farm holdings and 52 percent of cropped land. Date palms and fodder constitute about half and a quarter of the harvested area respectively. Modern irrigation is widespread in the case of vegetables and fodder production, but underdeveloped in the case of dates and other fruits.[172]

The UAE under Sheikh Zayed

After Oman and Saudi Arabia, the UAE is the largest of the Gulf states. Its usage of fossil water aquifers for agriculture and afforestation most resembles Saudi Arabian largesse. Between 1965 and 1979, 800,000 trees were planted. This number grew to nine million by the end of the 1990s. In 1978, 65 percent of the Ministry of Agriculture's budget went into afforestation, much more than into food production and commercially viable agriculture. Public parks, gardens, and roadside landscaping were the priority.[173] Afforestation has been close to the heart of Emiratis and was part of the myth of Sheikh Zayed as a

---

[168] Henderson, Abu Dhabi to Lamb, Bahrain, 27 March 1960, in Tuson 1990: Vol. 12, 506.
[169] Davidson 2009: 128, 137; Jones 2010.   [170] Dutton 1980: 171.
[171] Dutton 1980: 175.   [172] FAO 2008c: 4.
[173] Bowen-Jones 1980. For the nine million tree figure see Al-Fahim 1998.

champion of the environment. Despite its association with "nature," the cultivation of trees in the desert was the very opposite. Far from being naturally obtainable, it was only possible through large inputs of money and energy in the form of pumped or desalinated water.

Howard Bowen-Jones reported in 1980 steep declines in cultivated area in the Gulf states for lack of water. Yet this cannot be corroborated by historical FAO statistics. The cultivated area grew in all smaller Gulf states since the 1970s, except for Bahrain where it has stagnated since the 1980s. In the UAE, it virtually exploded. The agricultural area more than tripled between 1994 and 2003.[174] In 1968, a Five Year Plan granted priority to agricultural development. A number of research stations were set up with the aim of developing locally adapted varieties of crops.[175] Striving for self-sufficiency became a "matter of principle" for Sheikh Zayed, according to an official portrayal of the ruler by the government-owned think tank, the Emirates Center for Strategic Studies and Research (ECSSR).[176] While never achieved, steps were taken to make major improvements in agricultural productivity. The FAO carried out a detailed survey of agricultural potential in 1973. Noting the resource constraints, it advised against a "massive effort to expand agriculture."[177]

This advice was not heeded. Agricultural development in the UAE evolved in two phases. In the 1970s, essential infrastructure was built up. Land was reclaimed, wells were dug, and a fishing fleet was commissioned. A second phase in the 1980s saw the implementation of actual production and marketing operations.[178] The government set up a model farm in 1983 and extensive research was undertaken in the period 1976–81.[179] The International Center for Biosaline Agriculture was established in Dubai in 1992 to research desert hardy and salt tolerant crops, but their dissemination has been limited.

As part of its generous welfare system, the UAE has granted land and subsidies for nationals to set up farms that are usually operated by expatriate labor. The government purchases dates directly at a subsidized price. In the emirate of Abu Dhabi this also applies to fodder. Only vegetable production is

---

[174] FAO 2008f, 2011c; Bowen-Jones 1980: 47. Bowen-Jones reported that Kuwait, Qatar, and Bahrain witnessed steep declines in cultivation of 50 percent and more in the mid-1970s. His numbers differ from historical FAOSTAT data in terms of absolute numbers and growth of cultivated area, even though he quotes contemporary FAO studies. He points out that at that time survey work was in many cases still rudimentary and data compilation in a state of flux. His numbers are much smaller than what FAOSTAT gives as the cultivated area at that time and way below the current cultivated area. The number that he gives for Kuwait's land suitable for irrigation appears particularly outsized in comparison to other smaller Gulf states.

[175] Wheatcroft 2005: 148f.

[176] Wheatcroft 2005: 204.

[177] Wheatcroft 2005: 204.

[178] Taryam 1987: 269ff.

[179] For an overview of state-run model farms see Bowen-Jones and Dutton 1983: 156.

market-based. Water provision for agricultural irrigation comes from ground-water and is free, while desalinated water provision for residential use, which is often used for landscaping and home gardens, is heavily subsidized. The first desalination plant was installed in Abu Dhabi in 1976 and capacity has been expanding since.

The declared goal of self-sufficiency remained distant at the end of the 1980s, with only 20 percent of consumption covered. The lack of water and arable land impeded greater production. Water usage for afforestation and gardens diverted water away from agriculture. The work of the research centers was neither centralized nor synchronized. The multitude of uncoordinated agencies with overlapping responsibilities created problems further aggravated by the federal structure of the UAE. The federal Ministry of Agriculture operated separately from the departments of agriculture in Abu Dhabi and Al-Ain. The municipalities in other emirates that were in charge of distributing land did not coordinate their activities with both of these institutions.[180]

In 2003, three-quarters of the UAE's 255,000 cultivated ha were used for permanent crops, mostly date palms. The remainder was used mainly for fodder crops and vegetables.[181] In contrast to Saudi Arabia, cereal production has been absent. Irrigated areas increased from 67,000 ha in 1994 to 226,600 ha in 2003.[182] In 2001, the Dubai Department of Economic Development boasted that self-sufficiency in vegetable and dairy products reached 80 percent.[183] This number is certainly too high. It is belied by the cosmopolitan merchandise on display in Dubai supermarkets. It is also unlikely that agricultural production has kept up with population growth in recent years. Population figures in the UAE have seen a massive upward revision to 8.26 million (Q2, 2010) from 4.1 million in 2005.[184] This can be attributed to statistical correction of flawed older data and new migrant workers who have been attracted by the economic boom of the country.

Water consumption has remained utterly inefficient. The UAE has the highest water footprint per capita in the world, more than double the world average.[185] The water footprint measures the amount of fresh water needed to produce the goods and services that a country consumes. Three-quarters of the UAE's footprint comes from imported goods, but the remaining quarter is a draw on local water resources. Irrigation accounts for 81 percent of groundwater abstraction and Rhodes grass accounts for 60 percent of the agricultural water use.[186] Like alfalfa in Saudi Arabia, this

---

[180] Taryam 1987: 269ff.   [181] FAO 2008f: 1, 4.
[182] FAO 2008f: 7.   [183] Davidson 2005: 129f.
[184] *The National*, 8 April 2011.
[185] <http://www.waterfootprint.org/?page=cal/waterfootprintcalculator_national> (accessed 10 July 2012).
[186] Dawoud 2007: 39; Government of Abu Dhabi 2009.

water-intensive crop has been targeted for a phase-out. Its lavish subsidization feeds a substantive livestock industry, whose feces constitute an additional threat to groundwater quality. At current rates, groundwater resources will be depleted within 20–40 years. Agriculture will fail unless water demand is reduced or substituted by expensive desalinated water. To a certain extent this is already practiced; officially, 11 percent of desalinated water production is directed to agriculture, but the actual figure is possibly higher.[187]

Conclusion

Several conclusions can be drawn for the smaller Gulf countries. They have no cereal production worth mentioning and they have not followed the grandiose agricultural designs of Saudi Arabia, with the partial exception of the UAE. Some of them have increased their cultivated area massively, but the focus has been mostly on date palms, fodder, gardens, and tree planting. The smaller Gulf countries have used water far above replenishment rates. The subsidization of agriculture and free provision of irrigation water have been used as a means to distribute wealth to the national population, buy legitimacy, and foster a notion of heritage and belonging to the land.

Like in Saudi Arabia, agriculture and energy are closely intertwined because water provision requires energy inputs for both pumping and desalination. As the aquifers run dry, desalination remains the only technically feasible solution for supplying water. But high energy prices and skyrocketing domestic demand highlight the massive opportunity costs. Energy spent on water production could instead be used for economic diversification or generating hydrocarbon export revenues. Qatar puts great hopes on new farming technologies and links its food security strategy closely to the development of solar energy applications for water desalination. At least for water-intensive cereals, food production from desalinated water will likely remain a chimera. If the vision of Saudi wheat self-sufficiency has been absent in the smaller Gulf states for lack of natural endowments, it has been fairly widespread elsewhere in the Middle East and has often been driven by strategic considerations.

3.7 CEREAL PROGRAMS ELSEWHERE: EGYPT, IRAN, SYRIA, AND SUDAN

The means of subsidizing agriculture with oil revenues were particular to Saudi Arabia, but the country's interest to promote wheat self-sufficiency

---

[187] Government of Abu Dhabi 2009.

was not unique in the Middle East. After the exploding food gap of the 1970s, governments in the Middle East have tried to foster cereal production after decades of neglect. Given consumption patterns and nutritional values, wheat and rice are crucial for food security around the globe. As staple foods, they are of greater importance than more luxurious food items like sugar, meat, dairy products, and oil seeds. Cereal production in the Middle East might not be competitive and is in some cases ecologically harmful due to groundwater depletion, but the strategic incentive to command a certain level of self-sufficiency has been strong. It is not without precedent as the Allied Middle East Supply Center promoted a shift of acreage from cotton to cereals during World War II. While motivations have been similar, actual implementation of cereal programs differed from one country to another.

Only Saudi Arabia, Libya, Jordan, and Morocco subsidized wheat production in the 1970s.[188] In other countries in the region, agricultural production was actually taxed. Import-substituting policies used agriculture in order to funnel capital into the expanding industrial sector. Two mechanisms changed relative prices between agricultural and industrial goods: (1) government purchasing monopolies paid farmers below world market prices, and (2) an overvalued exchange rate made exported crops like cotton more expensive and imported crops like cereals cheaper. Growth in agricultural production was discouraged.[189] The 1980s and 1990s saw a revision of such policies, most notably in Egypt and Syria.

Egypt

Cotton, wheat, rice, sugarcane, beans, and winter onions were all regulated in Egypt in the 1970s. Livestock production on the other hand was protected by tariffs and bureaucratic import hurdles until 1987. Only in fruit and vegetable markets did the government abstain from interference. Hence, a shift of acreage into horticulture and fodder production like clover (birsim) was encouraged. Alarmed by the widening food gap of the 1970s, Egypt began dismantling these policies in the 1980s. In the 1990s, this process accelerated and by 1995, only cotton and sugarcane remained under government regulation. Food subsidies had reached their peak in 1980 when they covered 20 commodities and constituted 15 percent of the government budget. By contrast, food subsidies made up only 6 percent of government spending in 1997 and encompassed four commodities (coarse "baladi" bread, coarse "baladi" flour, edible oil, and sugar).[190]

---

[188] Richards and Waterbury 2008: 162.
[189] Richards and Waterbury 2008: 160–5.   [190] Adams Jr. 2003.

On the supply side, the liberalization of prices encouraged a shift into wheat production. It grew dramatically and was further stimulated by the introduction of high yield varieties. From 1986 to 1998, wheat yields in Egypt increased by 50 percent and wheat production tripled on an acreage that had only doubled during the same period.[191] A considerable part of this growth has been attributed to previous underreporting by farmers who had an interest in hiding the true size of their harvests from the cooperatives that paid low prices.[192] Still, the magnitude of growth can hardly be ascribed to statistical underreporting alone. Egypt's self-sufficiency ratio in wheat increased from 21 percent in 1986 to 46 percent in 1998. A further increase of this ratio by price politics alone would have entailed exorbitant costs. Instead, studies recommended investments in agricultural research and extension.[193]

Egypt remained far from completely self-sufficient. As the largest wheat importer in the world, it ultimately realized food security by food imports. Economic diversification away from mere rent extraction, inclusive growth, and new sources of foreign exchange were most critical, not self-sufficiency in food production. Here the Mubarak regime like other countries in the region failed to provide a more even distribution of income. Economic growth existed side by side with increased marginalization during the liberalization era of the 1990s and 2000s. Ray Bush's verdict is scathing: "While Egypt developed Egyptians did not."[194]

The idea of self-sufficiency has gained new momentum after the Arab Spring. The new Egyptian government announced a program to achieve self-sufficiency in wheat and the revival of the cotton trade. At the heart of this program was an increase of wheat purchasing prices by 25 percent, which put them slightly above prevailing world market levels. Improved seeds and extension services aim at productivity increases, but expanding the wheat self-sufficiency ratio beyond the 60 percent level in 2011 would require expanding acreage. Egypt is short in arable land, and efforts to expand wheat acreage have faced challenges. Some of the land for the new wheat program is expected to come from the Toshka Valley land reclamation project to the west of Lake Nasser, where land was sequestered from Saudi Prince Al-Waleed's Kingdom Holding after an anti-corruption case against the former Egyptian Minister of Agriculture Yousef Wali. Wali was also Deputy Prime Minister and General Secretary of the ruling NDP before he was stripped of his official positions in 2004 under another corruption charge. As a large landowner he used to be a driving force of the Mubarak's regime policy of economic liberalization. The case against Kingdom Holding claimed inappropriate business dealings and a

---

[191] Kherallah, Minot, and Gruhn 2003.
[192] Mitchell 2002: 251f.; Bush 1999.
[193] Kherallah, Minot, and Gruhn 2003: 134, 157.
[194] Bush 2012. See also Bush 2002.

too low purchasing price at the time of land acquisition in 1998.[195] A group of Egyptian and Saudi investors in the US announced their support of the Egyptian wheat program and Kingdom Holding was able to keep part of its land after a settlement. It has also announced a new investment drive of $350 million in an agro-industrial project in Egypt. Thus, Saudi investors may well be part of a revamping of Egyptian agriculture. Yet the Toshka Valley project has been criticized because of diversion of water from the actual Nile Basin and salty soils. Its hot climate is hardly suitable for wheat cultivation.[196]

Iran

Iran is another country in the Middle East with an outspoken policy of food self-sufficiency. The beginning of food net imports in Iran dates back to 1970. Wheat and sugar imports expanded in particular. Some have attributed this expansion to an alleged decline in agriculture as a result of the Shah's White Revolution and neglect in the wake of the oil boom. This, in turn, is said to have led to urban migration and pauperization, which then provided the fertile ground of the Islamic revolution in 1979.[197] However, Ahmad Ashraf has pointed out that production of agricultural goods increased dramatically from 7 million tons in 1960 to 19 million tons in 1975. He blames population growth for accelerated migration and rising imports, since it outpaced the considerable growth of food production.[198] Still, development policy under the Shah stressed industry, construction, and urban services while agriculture received little investment in research and technology. The high yield varieties of the Green Revolution that were spreading elsewhere in the developing world were not commonly employed in Iran. Agricultural production expansion relied on increased acreage and was mostly static.[199]

The Islamic revolutionary government formally upgraded agriculture, making it a "major axis" of development in its official planning. Khomeini declared food self-sufficiency a political priority, terming it a "jihad" and likening it to the war effort against Iraq.[200] Food imports were severely hampered by the war. The strategic port of Khorramshahr in the Shatt El Arab was closed from late 1980 on. Sea-borne food transport was restricted to the ports of Bandar Abbas and Bandar Khomeini, which lay farther away from

---

[195] *New York Times*, 11 May 2011.
[196] *Gulf News*, 20 June 2011; *The National*, 12 April 2011; *Reuters*, 7 June 2011.
[197] Hooglund 1982; Ashraf 1991.
[198] Ashraf 1991: 289. The population increased from 19 million in 1956 to 34 million in 1976. Urban migration had already started in the 1940s, as traditional farming in mountainous regions was unable to provide for the rising number of people.
[199] McLachlan 1986.
[200] Haghayeghi 1990: 6.

combat operations. The decline in oil exports and a shortfall in foreign exchange compromised Iran's ability to purchase food items on international markets, and Iran's increasingly bellicose relationship with the US made relying on food imports a strategic vulnerability because embargoes were feared. Radical elements of the revolution favored extensive land reform that would have gone beyond the Shah's White Revolution. But they were unable to prevail over more conservative elements that represented the merchants, 'ulama', and landowning classes, who stressed the importance of property rights as guaranteed by Sharia law. By 1985, they succeeded in eliminating the hotly debated Clause C of the Land Reform Law, which stipulated upper ceilings of ownership. Efforts at land reform fizzled out during the following years.[201] Yet agricultural extension services and irrigation did expand. Immediately after the revolution, the regime raised wheat prices by 50 percent with regular increases thereafter. Production increased. The reason was once again static expansion of cultivated land, not productivity growth. By 1989, self-sufficiency in wheat and rice was 53 and 71 percent respectively.[202] In the 1990s, the regime changed gear and tried to engineer dynamic expansion and productivity growth with the help of large-scale farming, capital investments, and greater involvement of the private sector.

Beside economic independence, welfare for the poor ranked high on the regime's agenda and it established an extensive system of subsidies. Of course, restrictions on consumer prices went against the declared aim of stimulating agricultural production. These mutually exclusive policy goals put the regime in a dilemma that it tried to solve by subsidizing production and consumption alike, very much like in Saudi Arabia. While wheat prices were consistently raised, the prices for flour remained relatively constant as the government subsidized them.[203] The necessary funds came from redistribution of oil rent. Initial attempts to reform the system in the 1990s were largely unsuccessful. A reduction of subsidies proved politically too sensitive. Ayatollah Khamenei intervened directly in 2003 and rescinded previous flour price increases. By 2010, subsidies for fuel, electricity, and food reached more than 10 percent of GDP. Even with oil prices near all-time highs, the strain on the treasury was unsustainable. The Ahmadinejad administration launched a program of cutting subsidies while trying to ameliorate the impact on the lower and middle classes through direct cash payments.[204]

Iranian wheat production nearly doubled between 2000 and 2008 and the country came relatively close to its declared goal of self-sufficiency. But a

---

[201] Ashraf 1991: 297–304; University of London, Centre of Islamic and Middle Eastern Law 1995: 90–8; Alamdari 2005: 302–9; Shakoori 2001: 164f.
[202] Haghayeghi 1990: 17.   [203] Amid 2007: 541.
[204] *The Economist*, 13 January 2011.

drought in 2008 forced Iran to import almost half of its requirements, making it one of the largest wheat importers worldwide.[205] Throughout this period agriculture was exposed to mixed policy signals. The preferential treatment of wheat was an exception. An overvalued exchange rate and the abolition of tariffs had led to an import boom in many agricultural commodities other than wheat, including rice, sugar, cotton, and fruits.[206] Then, in September 2010, the government declared an import ban on agricultural products, among them rice and wheat, in order to stimulate domestic production.[207] This was not the end of the story, however, as in spring 2012 Iran appeared again as a large buyer on world markets against the backdrop of an escalating nuclear stand-off, fears that sanctions might disrupt food imports, and expectation of a lean harvest.[208] Beside arrangements with Pakistan and India for barter exchange and payments in non-convertible Indian rupees from oil sales, its arch nemesis, the US, of all things, was among its procurement sources. Food has been mostly excluded from US sanction regimes since the failed grain embargo against the Soviet Union in 1980. It remains to be seen how Iranian agriculture will fare amidst strategic consideration and mixed policy signals. The ongoing process of subsidy reform will undoubtedly be crucial and will entail a delicate balancing act between interests of urban consumers and an agricultural sector that has been supported by input subsidies.

Syria

An exceptional case in the region, Syria escaped the neglect of agriculture prevalent in most oil-exporting countries. It managed to avoid the Dutch disease focus on non-tradable items as a result of a boom in commodity exports and foreign exchange inflows. It fostered self-sufficiency for strategic reasons, while land reform and agricultural subsidies served to cultivate a political support base in rural areas. Agricultural production did not keep pace with increasing demand in the 1970s, so the government paid farmers above world market prices to encourage production during the 1980s and 1990s.[209] In the 1980s, income growth stagnated due to oil price corrections, but population growth and therefore demand growth showed no sign of abating. At the same time, supply was hampered by droughts and a lack of productivity increases during the 1980s. But Syria was able to smooth out yield variations by moving wheat production out of marginal into irrigated lands and by making greater use of drought-resistant seeds and dryland farming.[210] The government tried to

---

[205] *Financial Times*, 16 April 2009; USDA 2009, 2008.
[206] *PBS*, 20 February 2010.   [207] *MEED*, 13 September 2010.
[208] *Reuters*, 1 March, 2012.   [209] Richards and Waterbury 2008: 162.
[210] Richards 1991.

increase cereal production in the 1990s, by shifting acreage from cotton to wheat. One reason for this shift was the deterioration of Iraqi food security in the wake of a multilateral UN trade embargo, which served as a warning to concerned Syrian authorities. The irrigated area doubled between 1985 and 2000 and farming expanded into fragile steppe eco-systems. Syria became self-sufficient in wheat and barley by the mid 1990s. With a short drought induced interruption in 1999/2000 it remained so until 2008 when another drought wrought havoc in the north-east of the country.[211] Food security was affected by fluctuation in domestic harvests, which led to greatly varying import needs. In the wake of economic liberalization the Syrian state increasingly focused on smaller groups of regime supporting cronies at the expense of the rural popula-tion. Competing agencies of the segmented bureaucratic landscape shrouded water issues in strategic secrecy and were unable to implement more efficient water management practices. Oil production used to be a major source of foreign exchange, but it is in terminal decline. By 2008, net exports in crude oil were not able to pay for import needs in refined products and the overall petroleum balance turned negative for the first time. The Syrian uprising and an oil embargo by the EU against Syrian oil exports in December 2011 worsened the situation. Without economic diversification, financing food imports will be increasingly difficult for Syria.

Sudan

Sudan offers another example of a state-led cereal program. As in Egypt, the Sudanese government used to tax cotton via its marketing monopoly. This induced a switch to sorghum, peanuts, and wheat. It has been estimated that productivity levels of cotton remained 50 percent below their potential be-tween 1974 and 1980/1 due to such disincentives, even though a structural adjustment program in 1978 targeted the taxing of export crops.[212] In the wake of famines, droughts, and reduced food aid, the 1980s were a decade of encouraged wheat and sorghum production. In 1989, the new Islamist govern-ment launched a national campaign to achieve wheat self-sufficiency over three years. Production of staple crops on irrigated land increased at the expense of cotton, whose production declined by 40 percent from the mid-1980s until the turn of the century.[213] A short spike in wheat production in 1991–3 was short-lived. It was only achieved by an unsustainable increase in input factors. Increasingly isolated after its support of Iraq's Kuwait invasion the regime ran out of money and the self-sufficiency miracle faded. In the rain-

---

[211] Westlake 2000; Daoudy 2005: 81. Hinnebusch 2011.
[212] Richards and Waterbury 2008: 161.   [213] IFAD 2002: 3.

fed areas, increased acreage for sorghum was not accompanied by production growth due to ecological degradation and dysfunctional agricultural policies (see chapter 6). Proponents of a trade-based approach to food security discount strategic considerations, overstate the reliability of world markets, and overlook the importance of staple crops in Sudanese subsistence farming. Yet their criticism of diverging production incentives in Sudan offers interesting clues. It has been estimated that a 50 percent increase of wheat yields in the Gezira irrigation scheme would have been necessary to generate a similar foreign exchange return as cotton. For every hectare of cotton produced and exported, Sudan could have purchased 50 percent more wheat on world markets than the wheat it produced on the very same hectare in Sudan.[214]

3.8 CONCLUSION

The decades after World War II witnessed a steady rise in irrigation and the mechanization of agriculture, particularly in Saudi Arabia. Sedentarization, land distribution, and control of water were important tools of political power and nation-building. Lush gardens became markers of wealth, and the advent of the motor pump led to wasteful water consumption practices. The post-war decades also saw the gradual development of agricultural institutions. There was an interest in using agriculture for economic development and in achieving self-sufficiency, but many projects were in fact subsidized white elephants. Early pilot farms like the one in Al-Kharj were a precursor to the Saudi program of wheat self-sufficiency that took off in earnest in the 1980s. Agricultural modernization focused on a stratum of privileged royals and associated business families. Traditional farming populations and pastoralists were excluded and were instead swept up in the overwhelming process of urbanization in Saudi Arabia.

A US embassy cable in 2010 argued, "The Kingdom may be able to replicate its agribusiness model in Africa successfully, especially since it probably will be willing to pay above-market prices for the food produced."[215] Yet, the Saudi practice of importing large-scale farming operations lock, stock, and barrel and using foreign managers to run them gives reason for caveats. Saudi domestic agricultural development was used to reward privileged clients, neglected traditional agriculture, and showed disregard for ecological constraints. This reminds one of the current land grab debate and the criticisms leveled against Gulf agro-investments in foreign countries. One key difference is that displaced farming populations in target countries could not count on

---

[214] Hassan, Faki, and Byerlee 2000.
[215] WikiLeaks cable 10RIYADH102, US Embassy in Riyadh, 24 January 2010.

urban development and the redistribution of oil rent should they not get a fair share in such agro-projects.

In the smaller Gulf states agricultural ambitions were more subdued because of limited land and water resources. Still, aspirations were substantial, particularly in the UAE under Sheikh Zayed. Instead of cereal production as in Saudi Arabia, the other Gulf countries focused on date palms, fodder, tree planting, and gardens. Proponents of agricultural modernization in the Gulf have often shown a strong belief in technical fixes and blatant disregard for ecological constraints, not unlike the irrigation projects in the southwest of the US after which agricultural projects in the Gulf were modeled. As fossil water aquifers are rapidly being depleted, managing water demand has become an important policy goal, which has led Saudi Arabia to phase out wheat production by 2016. The substantial livestock sector, on the other hand, has resisted cutbacks in water consumption thus far. The agro-business community in Saudi Arabia has called for compensation to make up for the downsizing of agriculture, suggesting that this could be in the form of shares in agricultural investment vehicles abroad.

Agriculture in the Gulf countries will undergo a major transformation over the coming years towards the production of more value added crops like fruits and vegetables with the help of water-saving technologies like greenhouses, hydroponics, and drip irrigation. Some of the products like fresh milk, cut flowers, or shrimps are exported and would only contribute to food security as far as they generate income in disadvantaged rural areas. Cereals and livestock fodder will need to be increasingly imported. This food import dependence raises concerns about strategic vulnerabilities that are deeply rooted in the region. Fear of political embargoes motivates mistrust in normally open markets. The cereal programs in Saudi Arabia and other Middle Eastern countries like Iran, Egypt, Sudan, and Syria are products of this concern. Apart from the fragile supply situation during World War II, food security concerns have been raised on numerous occasions in the Middle East, particularly in the 1970s when the US used food trade as a foreign policy tool.

4

The Food Weapon: Geopolitics in the Middle East

The food weapon has left a similar imprint on the collective unconscious in the Arab world as the oil weapon has in the West. Food trade has been used to further geopolitical goals, which has prompted desires for self-sufficiency. With Saudi blessings, Washington withdrew food aid under the Food for Peace Program to entice Egyptian policy changes in the 1960s. The politicization of food trade reached its pinnacle in the 1970s. The US contemplated grain embargoes against the Arab world and a grain cartel. Afterwards food trade was depoliticized and commercial considerations prevailed; however, Iraq saw the most sweeping application of the food weapon when it was exposed to a multilateral UN embargo during the 1990s. Arab fears resurfaced in the wake of the global food crisis in 2008, when agro-exporters announced export restrictions out of concern for their domestic food security.

Middle Eastern countries have shown a persistent preference for some degree of self-sufficiency in cereals out of strategic concerns. Dependence on fragile trade links and volatile global markets is seen with suspicion. In a world of international market liberalization under the WTO umbrella it may appear as a distant memory, but food has been an important aspect of warfare and a foreign policy tool throughout history, ranging from Napoleon's Continental System to the German *Hungerplan* and the US naval blockade of Japanese-held territories in World War II.[1] The Middle East has not been an exception. In World War I Mount Lebanon was worst affected by the naval blockade of

---

[1] For an overview of pre-twentieth-century blockades and embargoes see Ellings 1985: chapter 1. For Napoleon's Continental System see Heckscher 1964. For an overview of economic sanctions in international politics since World War I see Hufbauer, Elliot, and Oegg 2008. For World War II examples see Tooze 2007: 476–85; Collingham 2011: chapters 4, 5, 16, and 17. The *Hungerplan* aimed to feed the German army off the land and envisaged the starvation to death of 30 million Russians with statistical sobriety. It was planned to cut off food supplies to the population of the newly founded cities of Stalin's industrialization drive. Realization of the plan remained partial due to changing war fortunes, but was epic enough, particularly during the siege of Leningrad. Sixty percent of Japanese casualties in World War II were caused by starvation, not military action, as supply lines in the Pacific were disrupted by the US Navy.

the Entente because its agriculture was export led and lacked cereal production. Ibn Saud and other rulers in the Gulf were painfully aware of their fragile dependence on food imports during World War II. When the US contemplated a food embargo in retaliation to the Arab oil boycott in 1973, Gulf countries were prompted to develop Sudan as an Arab bread-basket. It also informed the Saudi wheat program that took off in the 1980s. Apart from strategic considerations, a degree of self-sufficiency has been advocated to preserve local farming traditions as they foster a sense of community and play a role in livelihoods of smallholders, ecological landscaping, and culinary traditions.[2]

A trade-based approach to food security frowns upon this penchant for self-sufficiency and recommends specialization along comparative advantages instead. To make the best use of precious water resources the Middle East should focus on more value added crops like cotton, fruits, and vegetables, often for export. Water-intensive cereals on the other hand should be imported. As a lot of water is needed to produce them, they constitute "virtual water" that water scarce countries can access via food trade.[3] Food security and accessibility would then need to be ensured by inclusive growth policies. Yet, in the Middle East these policies have not materialized in the past as liberalization favored a few privileged cronies. Large-scale projects might lead to agricultural growth, while excluding rural poor from development at the same time. While logical on paper, the trade-based approach to food security tends to collide with these contradictions and the geopolitical threat perceptions that loom large in the region. Many Arab analysts have made the argument that the independent development of Arab states is only conceivable if vulnerability to food extortion can be eliminated.[4] Military vocabulary pervades the talk about food security. Authors have seen the food weapon at play whether it is the second Gulf War or Israeli politics in the occupied Palestinian territories.[5] Food self-sufficiency, Arab economic integration, and strategic storage have been regarded as means to cope with the dangers of a US-led grain cartel, the cut-off of preferential food aid, or an outright food boycott.[6] Turki Faisal al-Rasheed, a well-known Saudi agro-businessman and commentator, sums up widespread concerns when he pleads that the Arab region's staple crops should be produced with "Arab capital, Arab land, and Arab water," because food supplies can be threatened like oil supplies and "America's future weapon is wheat."[7]

[2] Zurayk 2011. For the blog of the author see <www.landandpeople.blogspot.com> (accessed 18 June 2012).

[3] Allan 2001; Richards and Waterbury 2008; Magnan et al. 2011; Devlin 2003.

[4] Al-Sayyid 1994: 197–201; Hafiz 1976: 175; Balba 1975: 175; Hanafi 1986: 43.

[5] Al-Sayyid 1994: 197–201; Kurzum 1997: 108.

[6] Al-Hindi 1981: 35–46.

[7] Al-Rasheed, Turki Faisal 2010: 142,160, 2008.

4.1 FOOD FOR PEACE AND GANGSTERISM BY COWBOYS: SAUDI ARABIA VS. NASSER'S EGYPT

Egypt from the 1950s to the 1970s offers a prime example of how a developing country was included in the post-war food regime of Western surplus disposal and how food trade was used by the US to further foreign policy goals. Saudi Arabia as a regional competitor of Egypt was part of this unfolding story. If the UK and industrialized countries in Europe had relied on grain deliveries from colonial settler states, Russia, and India between the 1870s and 1930s, the post-war years saw a change of the global food regime. Grain production in developed states rose with a concomitant need for surplus disposal in developing countries, which previously had been self-sufficient in staple crops, while exporting cash crops via colonial trade networks.[8] Dan Morgan has outlined how "grain became one of the foundations of the postwar American Empire." Wheat affected diets, diplomacy, and currency politics alike, rivaling oil in its importance as a strategic commodity.[9]

Growing mechanization, fertilizer input, and support programs took off in the wake of the Dust Bowl farm crisis of the 1930s, when ecological degradation of farmland in Oklahoma and other Mid-Western states forced farmers to abandon their land. After the push for increased food production in World War II, these technological changes led to structural grain surpluses in the US and Canada. In the 1950s, mineral fertilizer application tripled worldwide and agricultural productivity increased.[10] Food production in war-ravaged Europe recovered and was modernized. Once the old continent ceased to be an outlet for agricultural surpluses, North American grain producers faced slack demand. The end of the Korean War exacerbated this problem.[11]

P.L. 480 and the Post-War Food Regime

To counter farm price deterioration, surplus disposal in developing countries became declared US policy in 1954 with the enactment of Public Law (P.L.) 480, which allowed for subsidized exports of food aid. Under John F. Kennedy it was enhanced with a development assistance agenda and renamed the Food for Peace Program in 1961. It was repeatedly used for political ends. George Stanley McGovern, the first director of the program, believed that food aid was "a far better weapon than a bomber in our competition with the Communists for influence in the developing world."[12]

---

[8] Friedmann and McMichael 1989; McMichael 2009a, 2009b.
[9] Morgan 1979: VII. See also Weis' account of the "temperate grain-livestock complex," Weis 2007: chapter 2.
[10] Smil 2001: 116.   [11] Wallerstein 1980a: 4f.   [12] Burns 1985: 126.

The fate of P.L. 480 was also closely tied to the ups and downs of agricultural export markets. Because it was a considerable drain on the US Treasury, commercial considerations were introduced over time. Steps to reduce the US overhang in non-convertible foreign currency that resulted from P.L. 480 sales were taken in 1959 and in 1966 payments in dollars or other convertible currencies were stipulated in a gradual phase-out.[13] P.L. 480 politics thus played out in a triangle of farm lobbyism, foreign policy, and fiscal interests.[14]

With rising food prices in the 1970s, the need for surplus disposal all but vanished and the US Department of Agriculture lobbied for primacy of commercial deliveries at the expense of food aid. The disengagement on the foreign aid front coincided with a keen interest of the Nixon administration to withdraw from the Vietnam quagmire and reduce other costs of hegemony such as providing the anchor currency of the Bretton Woods system at a fixed exchange rate with gold. As for food aid, Secretary of Agriculture Earl Butz neatly summed up the new US position, "As we are not the world's policeman, neither are we the world's father-provider."[15]

Carrots and Sticks for Egypt and the Saudi Position

Gulf countries were not Food for Peace recipients. Due to rising oil revenues after World War II and their comfortable budgetary situation, they did not qualify and were supposed to purchase commercial deliveries on the open market. Yet, they witnessed first-hand how P.L. 480 food deliveries became utilized in a stick and carrot policy by the US towards Egypt, and Saudi Arabia was entangled in diplomatic considerations around this issue.

In September 1962, Nasserist officers staged a coup in Sana'a and deposed the autocratic ruler of North Yemen, Imam Muhammad al-Badr. The ensuing civil war between the rebels and royalist forces pitted Egypt against Saudi Arabia. The latter supported the royalists and the former sent 50,000 troops to help the Republican forces. Nasser and his increased popularity in the Arab world was a severe challenge to Saudi legitimacy. It took place against the backdrop of socio-political tensions at home. In 1945 and in the 1950s workers at ARAMCO had gone on strike protesting working conditions, limited career opportunities for Saudis, and an ethnically segmented system of privilege at the then US-owned company.[16] High-level technocrats like the future oil minister Abdullah al-Tariki and liberal minded royals criticized the mode of oil revenue appropriation. The Yemeni conflict exacerbated such challenges to authority. Several Saudi airforce crews defected to Egypt. Exiled Saudi labor leader Nasir al-Said proclaimed a Republican counter government out of

---

[13] Wallerstein 1980a: 37, 44.   [14] Wallerstein 1980b; Ruttan 1996.
[15] Rothschild 1976: 290.   [16] Vitalis 2007.

Yemen. Even one of the king's own brothers, Talal, temporarily joined the camp of dissidents by renouncing his royal titles and founding the Arab Liberation Front out of Cairo. He predicted the collapse of the Saudi monarchy and the establishment of a democratic republic.[17] In a bid to counter the ideological threat of Arab nationalism King Faisal reacted by creating a pan-Islamist narrative of legitimacy with Saudi Arabia at its core. Corresponding institutions like the Organization of the Islamic Conference (OIC) and the Islamic Development Bank (IsDB) were built up in the 1970s and doled out development aid to gather goodwill abroad.

The US tried to contain Nasser's regional ambitions and lent its support to Saudi Arabia. Yet, it was wary of betting on the wrong horse. The domestic opposition against the Saudi government signaled weakness while Nasser moved from strength to strength in the Arab world. Since the US was trying to prevent closer cooperation between Egypt and the Soviet Union, it was ready to give incentives to Egypt to lure it to the Western camp.

When the US offered inducements, food aid played a crucial role.[18] The Eisenhower administration had interrupted P.L. 480 supplies to Egypt for a "decent interval" in 1956 after it had grown disenchanted with Nasser's flirtations with the Soviets and his refusal to negotiate a settlement of the Arab–Israeli conflict. However, in 1958 the situation changed when the West lost Iraq as an important ally in the region. The Hashemite monarchy was toppled by General Abdul Karim Qassim who withdrew Iraq from the Baghdad Pact, opened diplomatic relations with the Soviet Union, and followed a non-aligned stance. The US started wooing Nasser again and resumed economic aid. It was entirely based on P.L. 480 and was gradually increased over 1959–60.[19] US foreign policy became more sophisticated by the 1960s. It was less mired in binary Cold War thinking than in the previous decade. Upon assuming the presidency, Kennedy granted Egypt a three-year P.L. 480 contract. Egypt was allowed to purchase wheat with Egyptian pounds, which were not internationally traded. Hence, they were largely useless for the US. The US embassy in Cairo was humming with deliberations about what to do with the surplus cash. Some of it could be spent on USAID projects within Egypt, but there were not enough projects to absorb all the money. A substantial part was used to purchase Arabic books for US libraries, identifiable to this day by a P.L. 480 marker in the front.[20]

---

[17] Vitalis 2007: 238f.; Burns 1985: 134–9.

[18] Other examples of politically motivated food aid shipments in the two post-war decades included Tito's Yugoslavia, Poland, Pakistan, South Korea, South Vietnam, Cambodia, Israel, Turkey, and Indonesia. The countries were either allies or relatively moderate regimes that the US hoped to draw away from the Soviet orbit. Morgan 1979: 258; Wallensteen 1976: 291.

[19] Burns 1985: 118f.

[20] Interview with Gary Sick, who worked at the US embassy in Cairo in the 1960s and was later a staff member of the US National Security Council under Presidents Ford and Carter, New York, 20 January 2010. See also Wallerstein 1980a: 37.

Between 1958 and 1965 Egypt was the largest per capita recipient of US food aid in the world. Nearly half of P.L. 480 deliveries in the Middle East between 1960 and 1973 went to Egypt and Israel. Morocco, Algeria, and Tunisia received a similar share. Less than 10 percent went to other countries in the region.[21] Egyptian wheat imports grew from 0.1 percent of total imports in 1955 to 18.6 percent in 1964. This "wheatification" of diets at the expense of traditional staple crops like rice, corn, beans, or cassava was observable all around the Third World in the 1960s and was actively promoted by US export interests. Iran was another country where the US and other wheat exporters competed vigorously for the expansion of market share.[22]

Food imports became a serious drain on foreign exchange for Egypt.[23] Securing food imports at preferential conditions developed into a high priority of foreign policy-making. The US was the only country that was able to provide such quantities. The share of P.L. 480 deliveries of total Egyptian grain imports rose from 24 percent in 1959 to 66 percent in 1960 and to 91 percent in 1964.[24] Yet, the US had come to realize that economic aid is not to be equated with political influence. The Soviets who had financed the High Dam at Aswan would go through the same experience when they were expelled by Sadat a few years later. Sometimes Egyptian politicians "acted as if aid was a donor obligation," remarked Hermann Frederick Eilts, a US Ambassador to Riyadh in the 1960s and to Egypt in the 1970s.[25] Nasser would rather accept risks to Egyptian food supplies than compromise on his international grandstanding, be it in the Yemen civil war, the Arab–Israeli conflict, or Congo's post-independence turmoil. The initial optimism of the Kennedy administration to use P.L. 480 food supplies as a means of foreign policy and development assistance faded and gave way to growing disenchantment with the Nasser regime. Congress lobbied against P.L. 480 deliveries to Egypt, and so did Saudi Arabia, which argued that they enabled Egypt to direct military resources to Yemen.[26]

When protesters against the US involvement in Congo burnt down the library of the United States Information Service in Cairo in November 1964 and Egyptian security personnel failed to step in, President Johnson decided that enough was enough. He put Egypt on a "short leash." Nasser reacted to the initial threats of the US ambassador with an incendiary speech in Port Said in which he unequivocally stated that Egyptians could tighten their belts. He was not willing "to sell Egypt's independence . . . [and] accept gangsterism by

---

[21] US Senate Committee on Foreign Relations, memorandum to all members by Carl Marcy, "PL 480 and other aid to NES 1960–73," 20 November 1973, McGovern Papers, Series 4c, Box 623: Middle East 1973, Near East Subcommittee (2) Folder (FRC).

[22] Morgan 1979: 229, 123ff.; Andræ and Beckman 1985.

[23] Burns 1985: 114.   [24] Burns 1985: 119, 150.

[25] See his foreword in Burns 1985: XV.   [26] Burns 1985: 144.

cowboys," he declared.[27] P.L. 480 deliveries were suspended shortly after at the beginning of 1965. When Nasser toned down his rhetoric they were briefly reinstated, but a shorter six-months agreement was not prolonged beyond summer 1966.[28] Henceforth, Egypt would have to take deliveries at market rates. P.L. 480 shipments only resumed in 1974 under the condition that Egypt would enter peace negotiations with Israel. By 1978 Egypt was again the largest recipient of food aid under P.L. 480 with 30 percent of the total.[29]

Saudi Arabia was careful not to be associated with openly lobbying for a stop of P.L. 480 supplies to Egypt. King Faisal instructed his ambassador in Washington accordingly.[30] But once the food deliveries were terminated, the Saudi stance was one of thinly disguised consent. Secretary of State Rusk informed King Faisal beforehand about the American decision not to extend the P.L. 480 agreement. He said that he expected Cairo's reaction to be a "violent one" and that Saudi Arabia and the US would be most likely "subjected to a fresh tirade of propaganda from Cairo." Although Faisal expressed that "as . . . a human being . . . [he found] it very difficult to actually suggest that people be deprived of food in any way," he was not too fazed by the food security concerns of his ideological rival in Cairo. He opined that "It was up to the giver to determine in his own best interest what to give, to whom, how much and when."[31]

However, Egyptian foreign policy did not demonstrate the kind of mellowing that had been hoped for. In a meeting on 6 January 1967 the US Ambassador in Riyadh, Eilts, told Saudi businessman Rashad Pharaon who used to be the personal physician and a close adviser to Saudi Arabia's founding King Ibn Saud that "contrary to widely-held belief in Saudi circles," the termination of P.L. 480 deliveries had not led to an Egyptian withdrawal from Yemen. Rather, it had strengthened Egyptian resolve and reduced the leverage of the US to influence the country's regional stance in a favorable way, especially after Egypt was able to obtain some wheat from the Soviet Union as a substitute.[32] The Saudis supported the sanctions against Nasser, but the Egyptian P.L. 480 episode also gave them a first-hand insight into what

---

[27] Burns 1985: 159f.

[28] US suspension of aid as a stick was used globally in the 1960s, albeit food aid was sometimes excluded from the sanction packages for humanitarian reasons. Examples included the Goulart and Allende governments in Brazil and Chile; Cuba, and North Korea (because of their leftist leanings); Pakistan, India, Malaysia, and Indonesia (to sanction inter-state belligerence); or Ceylon and Honduras (for attempted nationalization of US property). Wallensteen 1976: 292; Nelson 1968; Morgan 1979: 259f.

[29] Burns 1985: 192; Wallerstein 1980a: 46. Five years earlier the largest P.L. 480 recipients were still Vietnam and Cambodia, where half of P.L. 480 food aid went at that time.

[30] State to Jidda, 20 March 1965, FRUS 1964–68, Vol. XXI, 685.

[31] Memorandum of Conversation between King Faisal and Secretary of State Rusk, Washington, DC, 22 June 1966, FRUS 1964–68, Vol. XXI, 531.

[32] Jidda to State, 10 January 1967, FRUS 1964–68, Vol. XXI, 542.

dependence on food imports and a lack of hard currency to purchase supplies could mean. It must have rekindled memories of their strong dependence on Allied food aid during World War II. Indeed, shortly after, in the 1970s, they were targeted by the food weapon themselves.

4.2 WE FREEZE, THEY STARVE: COUNTER THREATS TO THE OIL EMBARGO

The politicization of the food trade grew in magnitude in the 1970s. On several occasions, the US government implemented export restrictions, either to further political goals or in an attempt to reduce food inflation at home. In 1973, a food embargo was contemplated as a retaliation to the Arab oil boycott. A general soybean export embargo in 1973 and a temporary moratorium of grain sales to the Soviet Union and Poland in 1975 were meant to protect American livestock producers against rising feedstock prices and to keep food prices at home in check. President Ford was against the use of food embargoes as an outright foreign policy tool, however. When pressed to enact a grain embargo against the Soviet Union for its entanglement in the Angola conflict in 1976, he stressed the role of the US as a reliable supplier and refused. His adversary and successor Jimmy Carter, on the other hand, endorsed such measures against the Middle East or the USSR and employed a grain embargo against the Soviets in 1980 shortly after their invasion of Afghanistan.[33]

The experience of food embargoes was sobering for the US. It was a story of redirected trade flows and lost market share for American farm products. Others like Australia, Argentina, or the European Economic Community happily picked up the slack and delivered food to the targeted countries. The latter chose to bear some negative consequences instead of changing their foreign policy.[34] Meanwhile, American farmers were up in arms over lost income and exerted political pressure to stop the embargoes. The food embargoes also prompted agricultural production elsewhere and could lead to a lasting loss of market share. Japan and some Western European countries reacted to the soybean embargo with investments in Brazil, which turned the country into a major soybean exporter and competitor in a field in which US farmers had previously enjoyed a "virtual monopoly."[35]

---

[33] Memorandum of Conversation, Ford, Kissinger, Scowcroft, 6 January 1976, Ford Library, available at: <http://www.ford.utexas.edu/library/document/memcons/1553331.pdf> and "Agriculture. America's Heritage," available at: <http://www.fordlibrarymuseum.gov/library/document/factbook/agricult.htm> (accessed 11 April 2012); *Washington Post*, 8 August 1976; *AP*, 7 August 1976.

[34] Paarlberg 1980.

[35] US Congress 1977: 35.

This is strikingly similar to the production cuts of Arab oil producers and their oil embargo against the US and the Netherlands in 1973. The price hikes of the 1970s finally spurred oil production in the North Sea, the Gulf of Mexico, and Alaska and led to a reduced market share of OPEC. The embargoed US and the Netherlands continued to receive deliveries via third countries. Barring prevention of delivery by military means, an embargo cannot prevent supply of a fungible commodity. Insofar as supply shortages occurred, they were caused by an allocation and price control system in the US. The effect of the oil embargo was in some ways more psychological than real, at least in hindsight.[36]

Still, it was a major foreign policy concern as long as it was in place. It prompted calls for use of the food weapon and was an important factor in the shuttle diplomacy of US Secretary of State Henry Kissinger in 1973–4 when he brokered the disengagement between Arab and Israeli forces. While the US was pushing for an early end to the embargo, the Arab stance was one of withdrawal to the 1967 demarcation lines. Kissinger has criticized perceived vacillations and stalling tactics on the Arab side. But despite all their differences, the tone of cables and exchanges between the US and Saudi Arabia was remarkably friendly. The Saudis stressed that it was not their sole decision to make. Hardliners like Syria and Libya effectively had veto power in what was essentially a pan-Arab affair.[37] The Saudis argued that an end to the embargo was only a matter of time. They were even ready to break the embargo when the US asked them to supply oil to the US navy. Their only condition was that it would not be made public.[38]

Not all exchanges were so conciliatory, however. "We freeze, they starve" became a widespread slogan in Washington.[39] On 21 November 1973, Kissinger spoke about possible "countermeasures" if the embargo was to continue "unreasonably and indefinitely." This prompted a reply from the Saudi oil minister, Zaki Yamani, on Danish television where he said that Saudi Arabia would cut oil production by 80 percent in such an event.[40] In a later interview with *Business Week*, Kissinger specified that military intervention in response to oil price hikes would be dangerous and inappropriate, but he

---

[36] Yergin 1991: 617. For an overview of the oil price controls in the 1970s that were largely abolished by the Carter administration in 1979 see Taylor and van Doren 2006: 8–11.

[37] See also Kissinger 1982: 664, 875.

[38] Remarks by Yamani to Ambassador Akins after consultation with King Faisal, 28 December 1973; Oil boycott timeline and "Oil deliveries to U.S. Fleets," Jidda to State, 13 February 1974; "Saudi Oil Deliveries to U.S. Military During the Oil Boycott," Jidda to State, 20 April 1974, Nixon Library, NSC Files, Country Files Middle East, Saudi Arabia Vol. V, January 1973–April 1974, Box 631. For an overview of events see Safran 1985: 152–67.

[39] Morgan 1979: 265.

[40] Safran 1985: 165. As a commoner, Yamani was only a technocrat and messenger; he did not belong to the inner power circle of royals. Kissinger 1982: 877–80, 1999: 672f.

would not rule it out in the case of "some actual strangulation of the industrialized world."[41]

The food weapon was contemplated as a possible retaliation. Congress enacted legislative changes that allowed for implementation of export controls if cooperative approaches failed.[42] Kissinger commissioned a classified study about the vulnerabilities of oil exporters to food embargoes and Congress debated a food boycott as one of several counter-measures to the Arab oil embargo.[43] However, like the most radical proposal of occupying Arab oil-fields, it was rejected as impractical. In case of an occupation, Saudi oil minister Yamani told the study mission that Saudi Arabia would destroy its oilfields and the vulnerability of the vast network of pipelines and oil instal-lations to sabotage was evident.[44] As for food, the leverage of the US was asymmetrically lower. It was a large consumer with limited supply alternatives in oil, while the Gulf countries with their modest population size were a small consumer with ample opportunities to substitute US food deliveries. The US report argued that only a multilateral approach by all OECD nations would have a chance of success, but it deemed such an approach improbable given the lack of unity among oil-consuming countries in the industrialized world. France was singled out as a likely breaker of a counter-embargo as it was on the Arab oil producers' "friendly list" and was exempted from cutbacks:

> To be effective, a counterembargo against the Arab oil states would have to be a multilateral effort involving a majority of the free world's industrialized nations. However, the current state of disorganization and lack of cooperation among the countries of Western Europe, particularly the NATO alliance, and Japan in face of the embargo and production cuts, makes immediate chance for such an action remote. France, as an example . . . appears unilaterally to be making every effort to keep its Arab oil imports flowing. The study mission was able to see, firsthand, evidence of French-supplied foodstuffs to Syrian forces during the October war.[45]

The Saudis were honestly astonished by threats of counter-measures to the Arab oil boycott. They felt that the US did not recognize their mediating efforts. At the height of the embargo Saudi Minister of State for Foreign Affairs Omar Saqqaf conveyed to the US ambassador that Saudi Arabia was disturbed by the "concerted" US campaign against the Arabs and a deliberate distortion

---

[41] Interview with Henry Kissinger, *Business Week*, 13 January 1975.

[42] Export Administration Act (H.R. 15264) and Report of the House-Senate conference on the Act (H Rept. No. 93-1412). Erb 1974: 81f.

[43] Morgan 1979: 263; Kissinger 1982: 880; US Congress 1973: 22–8.

[44] US Congress 1973: 27.

[45] US Congress 1973: 26. For the attempts of Europeans and Japan to dissociate themselves from the US in order to maintain access to Arab oil see Kissinger 1999: 682ff., 1982: 881. The US was "not a little paranoid after a year of nonstop confrontation with France" and pressed for a common stance of consumer countries that would later lead to the establishment of the International Energy Agency—in Paris.

of their position.[46] A few weeks later he complained to Kissinger about the "violence" of the American reaction when initial promises to lift the embargo against the US by year's end were not met and the OPEC summit in Tehran raised the posted oil price from $5.12 to an unprecedented $11.65.[47] Although ultimately not implemented, discussions about a counter-embargo raised eyebrows in the Gulf countries. They shaped their Sudan bread-basket plans in the 1970s and efforts to achieve food self-sufficiency in the 1980s.

The Australian Connection

The degree of concern is exemplified by Saudi overtures to Australia about mutually guaranteed oil and food supplies in 1974–5, which led to intense discussions in Australian ministries.[48] Abdullah Alireza, Acting Governor of Petromin, told the Australian ambassador that a renewed Arab war with Israel and a resumption of the oil embargo were "inevitable and imminent." Under such circumstances, Arab oil supplies would be only available on a government-to-government basis to ensure the efficiency of an embargo. Since the Saudis were concerned about retaliatory action against their food supplies, they sought Australian assurances. They were interested in long-term supply contracts for sugar, meat, and grains and offered guaranteed oil deliveries in return. They also asked whether storage facilities for animal feed could be converted to hold food for human consumption and whether Australia had its own means of transport to ensure that food supplies would reach their destination. It was the impression of the Australians that no similar oil-for-food deal had been offered to other grain exporters and that Alireza acted on behalf of Prince Fahd and the Saudi government.[49]

In fact similar offers were later put forward by Prince Fahd himself and by Mohammed Ibrahim al-Sheikh, the Director of Intelligence responsible for foreign surveillance.[50] Prince Fahd was Second Deputy Prime Minister and Chairman of the Higher Petroleum Committee. He was widely regarded as a likely successor to King Faisal. Fahd expressed his view that oil deals were too important to be left to anybody other than governments and that they should

[46] Jidda to State, "Subject: Saudi Views on U.S. Threats against Arabs," 22 November 1973, Nixon Library, National Security Council (NSC) Files, Country Files—Middle East, Saudi Arabia Vol. III, Box 630.

[47] Kissinger 1982: 891.

[48] "Oil and Food Arrangements with Saudi-Arabia," March 1975, Secret, National Archives of Australia (NAA), CL1417; "Saudi Arabia—Proposed Food for Oil Agreement, 1974–1975," Secret, NAA S938 Part 1.

[49] Jeddah to Canberra, 5 and 23 December 1974, NAA CL1417 and S938 Part1.

[50] Jeddah to Canberra, 21 December 1974 and 28 January 1975, NAA S938 Part 1.

be increasingly tied to offsetting agreements about economic and technical cooperation. In this context food supplies from and agricultural cooperation with Australia were mentioned in particular.

Australia finally decided against a specific oil-for-food deal, although some officials voted in favor of it.[51] The overriding concern was that it would alienate the US and other important allies. The major oil companies would have also looked unfavorably at an increase in government-to-government dealings, and the Australians felt less urgency, since their embassy in Tel Aviv deemed a resumption of Arab–Israeli military conflict unlikely. Meanwhile, time worked against the Saudis, as oil consumer solidarity strengthened. The united front of Arab oil producers, on the other hand, had weakened. US threats of military intervention pushed smaller Gulf states off balance and Saudi Arabia suspected that Abu Dhabi had entered a secret agreement with the US to supply oil in exchange for exemption from any military intervention the US might undertake. The Australian embassy in Jeddah considered Kuwait and Qatar also likely defectors in the event of a renewed oil embargo.[52] In sum, Australia was not ready to deliver guarantees beyond long-term supply agreements with a *force majeure* clause. Instead, it was suggested that the two countries enter into a "formal, but broadly worded, Trade Agreement" with a "confidential assurance" that both sides would use their "best endeavours" to maintain mutual trade ties, but without mentioning specific commodities.[53]

The Iranian Hostage Crisis and a Discarded Food Embargo

For all intents and purposes, Saudi fears were overblown. A food boycott against the Arab world was rejected by the US administration for the same reason for which the grain embargo against the Soviet Union would fail a few years later. Barring military coercion, there were no means to prevent trade flows of a fungible good on sufficiently open world markets. This also became apparent in the wake of the Islamic Revolution and the Iranian hostage crisis, when the Carter administration evaluated possible retaliatory measures. After the beginning of the crisis in November 1979, a ban on Iranian oil exports to the US was imposed and shortly afterwards US assets of the Iranian Central

---

[51] The Minister of Minerals and Energy and the Ambassador in Jeddah were in favor of an oil-for-food deal while the stalwarts of high politics (Prime Minister, Defense, and Foreign Affairs) were against it. The Minister of Agriculture took a neutral middle ground and cautioned about the feasibility of an all out guarantee.

[52] Jeddah to Canberra, 28 January 1975, NAA S938 Part 1.

[53] Draft Cable to Jeddah, 20 January 1975; "Record of Discussion Saudi-Arabian Oil/Australian Proteins," Confidential, 15 January 1975, NAA S938 Part 1; Ad-hoc Cabinet Minute, Decision No. 3371, "Proposed Oil/Food Arrangements with Saudi Arabia," Canberra, 11 March 1975, NAA A5925.

Bank were frozen. In January 1980, the US sponsored a UN Security Council resolution that called for sanctions on all exports to Iran except food and medical supplies, but it was vetoed by the Soviet Union. The US then approached other countries and asked them to apply the sanctions anyway. A US trade embargo against Iran was only enacted in April 1980 with Executive Order No. 12205. It also excluded food and medical supplies and was lifted after the end of the hostage crisis in January 1981.[54]

If a food embargo against Iran was not implemented it was not for a lack of consideration. The National Foreign Assessment Center analyzed Iran's food import dependence in detail by product category, trading partners, and possible substitution trade in the advent of an embargo.[55] Iran needed to import about 25 percent of its requirements on average. It was particularly vulnerable in the case of vegetable oils where the import dependence reached 80 percent, of which 70 percent was supplied by the US.[56] The US was also an important supplier of rice, wheat, feed grains, beef, and mutton. However, the memorandum estimated that Iran would be able to substitute about 50 percent of missing imports from other sources, even in the case of a collective embargo with friendly Western countries. It was noted that "Iran's oil is a powerful tool in finding alternative sources of supply for agricultural goods."[57] All that could be hoped for would be short-term supply problems in Iran and higher prices. Concerns about negative repercussions on the US in terms of lost farm income and its international reputation as a reliable food supplier also weighed in the balance. Thus, the question of a food embargo against Iran was discussed, but ultimately never seriously considered in the National Security Council of the Carter administration.[58]

At the same time, considerable pressure was put on Australia to cut its food exports to Iran, as Australian cabinet papers reveal. Australia resisted such pressures because it was not inclined to let go of its lucrative food trade business with Iran and it was anxious to preserve its reputation as a "reliable supplier of food" in the growing Middle East export market. It conveyed that it preferred not to receive a formal request from the US to cut food exports. Iran switched from the US to Australia as its major supplier of wheat in November

[54] Executive Order No. 12205—Prohibiting certain transactions with Iran, 7 April 1980, available at: <http://www.archives.gov/federal-register/codification/executive-order/12205.html> (accessed 12 April 2012). More extensive sanctions against Iran were only resumed from 1983 onwards and saw a comprehensive expansion under the Iran-Libya Sanctions Act in 1996. Franssen and Morton 2002.

[55] National Foreign Assessment Center, "Iranian–US Economic Sanctions: Impact and Reactions," Top Secret, 29 November 1979, Carter Library, NLC-25-43-2-1-4.

[56] National Foreign Assessment Center, "Iranian–US Economic Sanctions: Impact and Reactions." In the case of corn and feed grains the import dependence was 60 percent, for rice 40 percent, and for wheat 15–20 percent.

[57] "Contingency Paper re Trials of Hostages," Top Secret, 11, Carter Library, NLC-6-30-1-10-0, Brzezinski Material, Country File, 20 November 1979.

[58] Gary Sick interview.

1979, even though there was no formal embargo on US food exports to the Islamic Republic. Out of 6.5 million tons of total wheat consumption up to 1.5 million tons were imports, mostly from Australia, from where Iran also imported large quantities of meat. Like the assessment of the US National Foreign Assessment Center above, the Australian government argued that an embargo would only lead to trade diversion. Iran would find substitutes elsewhere, most notably in the Eastern bloc and via third party trade with Gulf countries. It also pointed to Iran's considerable oil and currency reserves and expected that the country could obtain "oil-for-food barter deals" easily. After much agonizing, the Australian government decided to put a "total embargo" on non-food items in unison with the European Community countries to comply with US requests. The export of "foodstuff suitable for human consumption" was excluded from the embargo, but not livestock fodder like hay or inedible agricultural goods like wool. Another restriction Australia imposed upon itself was that it declined Iranian overtures to enter into long-term supply contracts.[59]

4.3 US CURRENT ACCOUNT, INFLATION, AND FOOD POLITICS

The contemplated use of the food weapon against Arab oil exporters in 1973 and Iran in 1979 and the grain embargo against the Soviet Union in 1980 had a clear foreign policy motivation. Other US export restrictions in the 1970s were motivated by domestic US concerns such as food inflation and rising imbalances in the foreign trade position. Their implications for countries in the Middle East were equally important. Reduced availability of food aid potentially affected the poorer countries among them, while the oil-rich countries were drawn into a sophisticated game of international diplomacy around petrodollar recycling, food aid, and agricultural development. By the time of the second oil shock discussions went one step further, when a grain cartel was propagated as a means to counter the impact of oil imports on the US trade balance.

When the US lost its oil spare capacity at the beginning of the 1970s the power balance in global oil markets shifted to OPEC. The balance of payments

---

[59] *The Australian*, 1 January 2011; *Herald Sun*, 1 January 2011; Memorandum No. 686, Iran—food trade—Related to Decision No. 11262 (FAD), 29 April 1980; Memorandum No. 786: Impact on existing contracts of a full embargo on non-food trade with Iran—Related to Decision 11664 (FAD), 20 May 1980; Submission No. 3959, Measures against Iran—non-food trade—Related to Decision No. 11227 (FAD), 21 April 1980; Decision 11567 (FAD), Iran—possible food trade embargo—Without submission, 12 May 1980, NAA, available at: <http://recordsearch.naa.gov.au/SearchNRetrieve/Interface/SearchScreens/BasicSearch.aspx> (accessed 12 April 2011).

problem that had emerged with the crisis of the Bretton Woods system was aggravated. Food prices had risen alongside oil prices and had ushered in the world food crisis of 1974. To cope with the financial vulnerability, the dominant position of the US in global food trade was identified as a possible remedy. At the same time, rising inflation and domestic food price concerns influenced the discussion about food exports and the allocation of food aid.

Global Imbalances and Petrodollar Recycling

With the demise of the Bretton Woods system of fixed exchange rates in 1971 and the end of the dollar's gold convertibility, the status of the dollar as a global trade and reserve currency was called into question. The US started to accumulate intermittent trade deficits in the 1970s, and oil exporters contemplated using the IMF's Standard Drawing Rights[60] for pricing oil instead of the dollar. As the oil exporters' accumulated assets were affected by the dollar's devaluation, they also pondered "modest diversification" of currencies, as the CIA put it in a memo. The US exerted great efforts to prevent that from happening. In order to balance the current account disruptions that had been caused by the oil price shock, ways had to be found for the oil exporters to spend their newly earned petrodollars. Saudi Arabia, in particular, was courted by Washington to invest in US securities. The US gave Saudi Arabia special tranches of treasuries that did not go through the competitive auctioning process. After initial hesitation, it also supported a Saudi seat on the board of the IMF.[61]

Beside this financial shuttle diplomacy, US food exports played an important role in debates about how to reduce global imbalances that were induced by the oil price hike. On various occasions commercial oil-for-food links were made, sometimes arguably to justify farm subsidies. This started at the beginning of the 1970s, when oil prices began to creep upward.[62] In April 1973 a report to the Texas Department of Agriculture declared, "Our monetary drain into Arab Bloc Nations to buy oil is about to become such a torrent that it will terrify, if not bankrupt, the dollar. . . . The only hope of stemming that torrent is agriculture."[63] With the advent of the oil crisis Treasury Secretary George

---

[60] Members of the International Monetary Fund (IMF) have the right to acquire foreign currency from the IMF in exchange for their own, proportionate with the size of their quota. Standard Drawing Rights were extended after 1970 by the creation of Special Drawing Rights, which enabled members to obtain further amounts of foreign currency.

[61] Spiro 1999: 105–10, 124.

[62] Reisner 1993: 13; US Congress 1977: 43.

[63] Report to Texas Department of Agriculture in a letter of David A. Witts to Don Paarlberg, Director of Economics at USDA, 12 April 1973, NARA, Maryland, RG 166, Records of the Foreign Agricultural Service, Agricultural Attaché and Counselor Reports 1971–1984, Box 62.

Shultz also started looking at food exports as a means of redressing balance of payments deficits.[64] In a similar vein, the senator of North Dakota argued in a 1981 hearing that farmers should be supplied with petroleum products in a timely and, if necessary, privileged fashion in times of crisis. Keeping up agricultural production was not only necessary for food security, he said, but also to balance America's foreign account. US farm exports had been equivalent to oil imports in 1973, but by 1978 the latter had doubled to $80 billion, while farm exports had remained constant at $40 billion.[65]

The American Housewife vs. Food Aid

The second economic concern that affected food politics was inflation, which picked up markedly in the 1970s. The American dinner table and the interest of the "American housewife" were ever present when US politicians debated export restrictions like the soybean embargo of 1973 or export promotions like P.L. 480 deliveries to Egypt and Syria.[66] Large grain purchases by the USSR in 1972 were dubbed the "great grain robbery" and were blamed for domestic food price inflation. They prompted a mandatory reporting system for foreign grain sales under the Agriculture and Consumer Protection Act in 1973.[67]

The economic concerns and the advent of the world food crisis changed food politics within the US administration. The USDA started to favor commercial deliveries at the expense of food aid and other government stakeholders than USDA and USAID became interested in food aid politics. The State Department began to see food as a strategic concern and a bargaining chip. It claimed greater responsibility and muscled its appendage USAID aside, whose focus was predominantly developmental. As responsibilities for international food policy were increasingly stripped from the USDA and

---

[64] Gelb and Lake 1974: 179; Wallerstein 1980a: 199.

[65] US Congress 1981: 119. This gap has grown. Figures of net-trade allow a more accurate comparison as the US also imports food. In 2010, the US maintained a petroleum products deficit of $265 billion and a farm products surplus of only $16 billion. U.S. Census Bureau 2011. Yet, farm lobby groups praised the beneficial impact of food exports on the US current account as they did in the 1970s.

[66] Statement by John T. Dunlop, Director of the Cost of Living Council, US Congress 1977: 43; Morgan 1979: 242. Press Conference of Senator Hugh Scott and Congressman Gerald R. Ford, 10 July 1973, Ford Library, available at: <http://www.ford.utexas.edu/library/document/fordcong/4535873.pdf>; Memorandum of Conversation, Ford, Kissinger, Scowcroft, 17 September 1974, Ford Library, available at: <http://www.ford.utexas.edu/library/document/memcons/1552793.pdf> (accessed 12 April 2012).

[67] US Congress 1977: 45. This was extended to a prior approval system in October 1974 that also included soybeans. By March 1975 it was terminated, but the reporting system remained in place.

transferred to the State Department, Agriculture Secretary Earl Butz grew "tired of being treated like a cross-eyed step-child."[68] There was considerable rivalry between him and Kissinger.[69] Meanwhile, the specter of domestic inflation drew the attention of economic planners and technocrats at the Office of Management and Budget (OMB), the Council of Economic Advisers (CEA), the Council on International Economic Policy (CIEP), and the Treasury Department. They wanted to know how food aid and exports might affect domestic price levels.

With reduced need for surplus disposal, tight budgets, and rising inflation, food aid came with greatly increased opportunity costs. It developed into a bone of contention that was closely linked to the oil diplomacy of that time.[70] International food policy-making was very much driven by personalities, most notably Kissinger, Ford, and Butz. The latter was skeptical of the "grain power" crowd and the inflation skeptics in Washington who argued for export restrictions either for political or economic reasons.[71] Commercially, the world food crisis was a beacon for the American farmer after decades of depressed prices and a need for surplus disposal. As long as prices did not fall below certain target levels, Butz felt the Food for Peace outlet was no longer needed. For him it was simply a safety valve. He famously put a zero for P.L. 480 requirements in his 1973 USDA budget request and declared, "If Henry [Kissinger] needs it, let the money come out of his budget."[72]

For his part, Kissinger stressed the need for global food security and the use of food aid as a policy tool.[73] He made it a point to bring food-related issues and control over preparations for the World Food Conference in 1974 under the purview of the State Department. He claimed the commercially minded USDA did not have the necessary "imagination," while the fiscally conservative CIEP was not "constructive" enough.[74] Under Kissinger's guidance, two National Security Study Memoranda (NSSM) were dedicated to food-related issues. NSSM 187 was finished before the oil crisis and dealt with international cooperation in agriculture while the controversial NSSM

---

[68] Telcon Kissinger and Butz, 16 October 1975, 12:03 p.m., available at: <http://www.gwu.edu/~nsarchiv/NSAEBB/NSAEBB135/19751016.pdf> (accessed 2 June 2012).

[69] Morgan 1975.

[70] Gelb and Lake 1974: 177; Ruttan 1996: 149.

[71] Morgan 1979: 267.

[72] Ruttan 1996: 170.

[73] Initially Kissinger and Shultz thought about using the food problems of the developing world against OPEC, by blaming them on oil price hikes. Only in April 1974 did the "conversion" of Kissinger take place and he became an advocate of more food aid. Gelb and Lake 1974: 179ff.

[74] Memorandum to Kissinger by Charles A. Cooper, Secret, 16 August 1973, Nixon Library, Box H-200.

200 identified population growth in LDCs as a security risk and advocated contraceptive measures to restrict it.[75] NSSM 187 contributed to the agenda setting for the World Food Conference where cooperation with OPEC on food issues was sought.

The World Food Conference 1974 and OPEC

At the World Food Conference, the US position revolved around five major points: an increase in food exports by surplus countries, accelerated food production in developed countries, US assistance in this matter, improved financing for food imports, and internationally coordinated but nationally held food storage to fight emergency situations.[76] The US was opposed to an international grain reserve and wanted to keep storage under national sovereignty. Butz had wrested storage away from government control under the Nixon administration and was adamant that a market-oriented private sector approach should prevail in national storage.[77] This raised concerns in the Middle East. Hashim Awad, a former Minister of Commerce of Sudan argued that pan-Arab food security concerns were spurned after the US and other food exporters rejected a proposal of the FAO for an international food reserve.[78]

Kissinger was interested in food issues for three primary reasons. Firstly, food aid could be used strategically and was easier to push through Congress than other aid because of domestic farm interests. Nixon's "food for war" program had used food deliveries to further strategic goals since 1968 by allowing South Vietnam to make arms purchases with the proceeds from P.L. 480 Title I sales.[79] Now Kissinger used food aid promises to Egypt, Jordan, and Syria in his shuttle diplomacy to bring about a peace process in the Arab–Israeli conflict. Secondly, rising food prices were a security threat and were damaging relations between the US and developing countries. On the other hand, the fight against food inflation could be used to split the "unholy alliance" of LDCs and OPEC and isolate the latter. Thirdly, he also wanted to bring OPEC on board to finance agricultural development in the Third World. Food aid was under pressure from the inflation hawks within the administration and the USDA, which pressed for commercial deliveries. Kissinger hoped that oil funds could ameliorate the budget squeeze that was

---

[75] NSSM 187 led to extensive correspondence that argued for sole responsibility of the State Department. Nixon Library, Box H-200. It was completed on 5 September 1973, NSSM 200 on 24 April 1974.
[76] Kissinger 1999: 697.   [77] Shaw 2007: 157.
[78] Spiro 1989: 492.   [79] Morgan 1979: 258.

looming over food programs. This kicked off a process that led to the establishment of the International Fund for Agricultural Development (IFAD) in 1977.[80]

Kissinger's motivation was hardly humanitarian. For him food aid was "one of the few weapons we have to deal with oil prices." It could be used to reward friends and either punish adversaries or entice their cooperation. Kissinger wanted to have it as a foreign policy tool and admitted that he "[did not] give a damn about Bangladesh or humanitarian grounds."[81] For President Ford agriculture had played an important role in balancing the current account and withstanding the economic shock of quadrupling oil prices. It accounted for a quarter of US GNP at that time. Food was a US asset comparable to the oil asset on the other side and he intended to use food aid to encourage OPEC's cooperation on energy issues.[82] For Ford's speech in front of the UN General Assembly on 18 September 1974 Kissinger proposed talking points that linked an oil tax to promote energy conservation with high food aid. Only if the US showed willingness to expand food production in order to keep food prices in check could it expect the same from OPEC. Ford was enthusiastic, saying that he liked "the speech theme of relating food and oil prices." The final text of the speech made use of the notion of interdependence between oil and food producers and the need for cooperation. Ford declared, "It has not been our policy to use food as a political weapon, despite the oil embargo and recent oil price and production decisions."[83] The initial threat of a food counter embargo increasingly gave way to a more cooperative stance. It helped to alleviate fears of the food importing oil producers but also put considerable demands on them in terms of oil price moderation and participation in international development efforts. Yet, the economic repercussions of high oil prices intensified with the second oil price shock and led to renewed debates in the US about how food could be used to alleviate them.

---

[80] Shaw 2007: 121f.; Wallerstein 1980a: 198; Kissinger 1999: 678; Ruttan 1996: 170ff.

[81] Memorandum of Conversation on Food Policy, Ford, Kissinger, Butz, Ash, Greenspan, Scowcroft, 17 September 1974, Ford Library, available at: <http://www.ford.utexas.edu/library/document/memcons/1552792.pdf> (accessed 2 June 2012). The conversations between Ford and Kissinger have been described by the latter as "remarkable . . . for their lack of psychological undercurrents, complexes, or hidden motivations." Rodman 2009: 86.

[82] Memorandum of Conversation, Ceausescu, Macovescu, Ford, Kissinger, Scowcroft, Sinaia/Romania, 3 August 1975, Ford Library, available at: <http://www.ford.utexas.edu/library/document/memcons/1553195.pdf> (accessed 2 June 2012). For the share of agriculture in GNP see NSSM 187, 2, Nixon Library, Box H-200.

[83] Memorandum of Conversation, Ford, Kissinger, Scowcroft, 17 September 1974, Ford Library, available at: <http://www.ford.utexas.edu/library/document/memcons/1552793.pdf> (accessed 2 June 2012); Gelb and Lake 1974: 183. For the speech text see <http://www.fordlibrarymuseum.gov/library/speeches/740081.htm> (accessed 12 April 2012).

4.4 THE GRAIN OPEC

In the wake of the wheat export moratorium to the Soviet Union and Poland in 1975, the US tried to extract Russian oil deliveries at a discount to OPEC oil. For Kissinger wheat was a bargaining chip in the Cold War. He was also interested in the potential psychological impact of a grain-for-oil deal on OPEC countries if the US managed to come up with an alternative supplier of oil. The US had hitherto not received oil from the Soviet Union. President Ford, evidently warming up to the shrewd rationale of the barter deal, boasted in the press about perceived American negotiating prowess, "We are trying to be good hard-nosed Yankee traders. And when we end up with an agreement I can assure you that the U.S. will do as well in the areas where we want help as they will."[84] While the Soviets had an interest in saving hard currency by engaging in such a "barrels for bushels" deal, they were disturbed by the publicity that Kissinger gave to the negotiation in order to intimidate OPEC. They could not be seen as undermining OPEC and Third World nationalism in public, and the American expectation of a discount of 12 percent struck them as unfounded.[85] To act as a price breaker against OPEC in the oil market also would have gone against their long-term export interests. As a result, the Russians would not budge. They were unwilling to sacrifice sovereignty for fodder imports for their livestock program, even though the latter helped to literally beef up consumption standards and domestic legitimacy. Their position also strengthened as their business partners in international grain trading houses were scraping supplies together from other world regions. Foreign Trade Minister Nikolai Patolichev told Kissinger's emissary, Under Secretary of State Charles Robinson, that the Russians would rather "starve to death" than give in to political pressure, and the deal faded away towards the end of the year.[86]

One aspect of the bushels for barrels proposal to the Soviet Union was that it tried to tinker with market forces in order to beat OPEC at its own game. By the second oil crisis, others thought about a more systematic approach that would go beyond one isolated instance. The public mood was at a fever pitch. In a survey by the National Broadcasting Associated Press seven out of ten people supported food embargoes against OPEC countries, and country singer Bobby "So Fine" Butler sold half a million copies of his song "Cheaper Crude or No More Food."[87] If OPEC acted as an oligopolistic price setter in oil, why

---

[84] Morgan 1979: 275.

[85] Yergin 1991: 643f. Senator Humphrey's assessment was blunt: "[To tell the Russians] we will be nice to you and accept your oil at 5 percent less when all the world needs oil . . . is just stupid." US Congress 1979a: 27.

[86] Morgan 1979: 273–7.

[87] *Chicago Tribune*, 10 June 1979.

not try the same in wheat in order to put pressure on OPEC to lower oil prices or to increase farm prices to make up for the increased oil import bill?[88]

In 1979, Congressman Jim Weaver (D-OR) proposed a bill for the introduction of a National Grain Board in the US with some similarities to the Canadian Wheat Board. It would buy all grain headed for foreign markets, while leaving the domestic market open and competitive. He argued that grain markets were not free and dominated "by monopoly buyers . . . monopoly sellers and a few grain companies." To achieve better prices for US farm products, a level playing field was required.[89] The Grain Board would be in a position to set floor prices and reimburse the difference between the "free market domestic price and the minimum export price" to farmers on a pro rata basis. The Grain Board could also pass on potential windfall profits to farmers, which had hitherto been made by the big five grain trading companies, Weaver claimed, and went on to announce the formation of the grassroots based "National Barrel for a Bushel Committee" together with the American Agriculture Movement (AAM).[90]

As a next step, he suggested that the National Grain Board could coordinate its policies with Australia and Canada. Together they could use their dominant market position to raise grain prices on world markets and "get tough with OPEC."[91] On occasions, Argentina was included as a fourth possible member of such a cartel, which was proposed by Congressman Ron Mottl (D-OH) in bill H.R. 120 on 14 May 1979. Similar proposals were put forward by Daniel Moynihan (D-NY),[92] and Senators George McGovern (D-SD) and Henry Bellmon (R-OK) who floated the idea for such a cartel at the annual National Farmers Union (NFU) meeting of 1979. The NFU endorsed the plan.[93] Martin Palmer of the National Barrel for a Bushel Committee was optimistic. "We are the OPEC of grain . . . [and] the bread-basket of America is the Saudi Arabia of America," he exclaimed.[94]

The food industry, including grain traders like Cargill, and the National Association of Wheat Growers opposed a grain cartel at a hearing before the Senate Committee on Foreign Relations on 8 May 1979, arguing that it would not work and hurt their business interests.[95] At a subsequent hearing, the reactions were also predominantly negative. Objections pertained to different

[88] It is a matter of debate whether OPEC can be described as a cartel before its introduction of production quotas in 1982. Yergin 1991: 719.

[89] Morgan 1979: 246. See 96th Congress, H.R. 3042 and H.R. 4237, available at: <http://thomas.loc.gov/home/LegislativeData.php?&n=BSS&c=96> (accessed 14 November 2011). For Weaver's statement see US Congress 1979b.

[90] *Chicago Tribune*, 10 June 1979; *Washington Post*, 25 November 1981.

[91] *Boston Globe*, 5 August 1979.

[92] *New York Times*, 4 July 1979.

[93] *Chicago Tribune*, 24 March 1979.

[94] *ABC Evening News*, Special Assignment: Bushels for Barrels, 11 and 12 September 1979.

[95] Schmitz et al. 1981: 16f.

characteristics of oil and grain markets and the asymmetries between the relative position of the US and OPEC in these markets. Weaver's proposal was ridiculed. It was akin to "repair[ing] a broken arm by amputating a leg," the North American Export Grain Association argued.[96] The Carter administration initially flirted with the idea, but Secretary of Agriculture Bob Bergland changed course and Weaver's bill was overwhelmingly rejected in the House. It would have been impossible to implement the proposal and close all loopholes. At the same time, it would have caused welfare losses outside of OPEC and would have compromised the negotiating position of the US.[97] The Ford administration had used the World Food Conference to contrast its stance of increased food exports with OPEC's cartel-like collusion.[98] With a grain cartel the US would have given up this moral high ground as food import dependent developing countries would have been hurt the most.

Problems of Grain Cartel Implementation

The idea of the bushels for barrels slogan was to get back to the situation before the oil shock when one bushel of wheat cost approximately the same as a barrel of oil—two dollars. This would have balanced the negative impact of the oil price hikes on the US trade balance, so the argument went. However, restricting production in order to maximize price and profits only works for the short run, if at all. Cartels are inherently unstable. How fast a cartel unravels depends on available alternatives and how quickly non-cartel members can raise supply. This in turn depends on natural resource endowment and the elasticity of supply and demand in the respective product markets. Here, several asymmetries exist between oil and wheat.[99]

Global oil resources are geographically much more concentrated than areas that are cultivated or cultivable with wheat, and the Middle East's relative share of oil production is higher than North America's share of wheat production. Other staple crops can also substitute wheat, while oil substitution is still limited. Some petrochemical feedstock and thermal fuel oil applications can be replaced by natural gas, biomaterials, or coal. However, the role of oil products in these areas is less important than in the transport sector, where they are still without immediate substitute and command a virtual monopoly. While oil can be simply left in the ground, storage of grain is expensive and would put additional costs on any grain cartel. Modern agriculture uses a high level of hydrocarbon inputs like fertilizers and pesticides, but that snippet of

---

[96] US Congress 1979a: 37.
[97] *Wall Street Journal*, 31 August 1978; *Chicago Tribune*, 4 March 1977; *Baltimore Sun*, 12 May 1979; *Wall Street Journal*, 19 September 1979.
[98] Kissinger 1999: 697.   [99] For the following see Luttrell 1981.

information aside, grain, unlike oil, is not a finite good. Production in one year does not limit production potential in the next. Grain producers do not have the same incentives as oil producers to stretch production profiles over time. They would rather sell as much as possible in any given year. While 60 percent of global oil was traded in the 1970s, this was only true for 16 percent of grain. Therefore, considerable potential for increasing production in the wake of higher prices existed, and US farming interests were afraid of encouraging foreign competition with a grain cartel.[100]

Unless cartels organize all members of an industry, other producers will happily pick up the slack and will produce at full capacity in order to maximize their profits. Oil supplies are inelastic in the short run. New investments require high fixed capital investments and capacity additions require time to come online, but, barring global peak oil, they are eventually developed. OPEC countries had learned this lesson by the 1980s when additional supplies came on the market from the North Sea, the Gulf of Mexico, and Alaska. The US had similar experiences in agriculture with price support schemes like the cotton agreement of 1933, the wheat agreement between Canada, Australia, and Argentina in the same year, and the International Wheat Agreement that lasted from 1949 to 1965.[101] In a manner similar to OPEC, the US became the residual supplier of wheat and continuously lost market share.

Since demand and supply elasticities for grains were higher than for oil, the vulnerability of a grain cartel would have been greater than that of an oil cartel. Even if successful, increased prices would have mainly hurt the developing world, which had already borne the brunt of the oil price shock. Meanwhile, OPEC countries would have been able to afford higher prices and source alternative supplies. The incentives to break ranks within a cartel also increases with its success as rivalry arises over how to split reduced outputs and increased profits. OPEC and its sobering experience with poor quota discipline once again offers an instructive example that indicates the likely fate of a grain cartel.

Loopholes and weaknesses were not lost on academic proponents of a grain cartel, although they were deemed manageable. Andrew Schmitz et al. argued in favor of a grain cartel as it would provide members with a producer rent, not unlike the oil exporters.[102] To avoid undermining substitution effects they wanted to include coarse grains beside wheat in such a cartel. The impact of price hikes on poor countries they wanted to remedy with food aid, which

---

[100] *Chicago Tribune*, 10 June 1979; *Christian Science Monitor*, 12 October 1979. The asymmetries and the limited threat of a wheat embargo were not lost in the Gulf region itself, see Bahanshal 1990.

[101] Luttrell 1981: 19; Gleckler and Tweeten 1994: 2. The 15 percent acreage reduction of the attempted wheat cartel in 1933 was only honored by Australia; when Argentina exceeded its export quota the agreement broke down in 1934.

[102] Schmitz et al. 1981: 55f., 93f.

would have entailed controls that such aid deliveries were not sold on to non-eligible third parties. Other problems of cartel implementation, such as the free rider problem, cheating among cartel members, and public–private sector coordination also would have required administrative measures. Even if one agreed with the basic rationale of a grain cartel, overcoming these obstacles required excessive trust in bureaucratic capabilities. In the end, a grain cartel was not considered practical. Despite noted similarities, the oil and wheat markets were different. The relative position of the US and OPEC in each of them was not comparable. Furthermore, a cartel's success could only be temporary and would have hurt developing countries more than OPEC.[103]

With falling oil prices in the 1980s, the idea of a grain cartel faded. French Minister of Agriculture François Guillaume proposed it at the height of transatlantic farm wars over export subsidies, but the Reagan administration followed a course of trade liberalization and the proposal was a non-starter.[104] Nowadays, an occasional pundit might tout the idea in light of the recent hike in oil prices, but overall chances of success are slim.[105] Public sentiment in the US is much less responsive than in 1979. As Russia has regained its pre-World War II status as a major grain exporter, it has raised the idea of forming a grain cartel with Ukraine and Kazakhstan on several occasions since 2007. In 2009, it established the United Grain Company (UGC) for food trading. This led to international concerns that Russia might try to use the state company in the same way it has used Gazprom to leverage its influence in world gas markets. However, Russia's importance in world grain markets declined when it declared an export embargo in 2010 after droughts caused concerns about domestic food security. UGC itself was privatized in 2012. The Russian cartel plans did not really pick up and reactions by potential partners were subdued. The international community signaled that a grain OPEC might jeopardize Russia's ambitions of WTO accession, and the proposal fell by the wayside.[106]

4.5 THE REAGAN DOCTRINE OF AGRICULTURAL TRADE

If food trade was highly politicized in the 1970s, the 1980s saw a return to the strong export orientation of the heyday of P.L. 480 in the 1950s and 1960s. US agriculture faced again a severe crisis of overproduction. The spike in commodity prices in the 1970s had encouraged farmers to take out loans and

---

[103] Luttrell 1981.

[104] *Washington Post*, 5 December 1986.

[105] See op-eds by Raymond J. Learsy, *Huffington Post*, 27 February 2008 and 14 February 2010.

[106] *The Moscow Times*, 27 August 2007; *Financial Times*, 31 July 2008; *Bloomberg*, 9 October 2009; *Washington Post*, 8 June 2009; *Reuters*, 7 June 2009; Vassilieva and Smith 2009.

expand production. They were now confronted with the doubly deleterious effects of declining commodity prices and skyrocketing interest rates on their outstanding loans as the Fed embarked on a course of monetary tightening. The strength of the dollar also led to decreased demand for their products in foreign markets. More farms went into foreclosure than during the Great Depression. Political pressure on the Reagan administration to stabilize prices increased. The "Reagan Doctrine on agricultural trade"[107] focused on export promotion as a major pillar of such a support strategy, alongside acreage reduction, food stamp programs, and other subsidies. Despite the geopolitical grandstanding of the Reagan administration, the grain trade was not as politicized as in the preceding decade and mostly followed commercial imperatives. In a marked about-face from the policies of the 1970s, the doctrine identified three major pillars of food trade policy:

> (1) no export restrictions will be imposed on farm products as a result of rising domestic prices; (2) farm exports will not be used as an instrument of foreign policy except in an extreme situation, and then only as part of a broader embargo, supported by other nations; and (3) world markets, especially those for agricultural products, must be freed of trade barriers.[108]

According to John Block, the secretary of the US Department of Agriculture 1981–6, it was important to "reestablish the US as a reliable supplier of food" after the embargo-prone 1970s.[109] The wheat embargo against the USSR was terminated in April 1981, three months after Reagan assumed office and an agricultural embargo protection clause was included in the Agricultural and Food Act of 22 December 1981.[110]

Commercial priorities prevailed. Agitation against export subsidies of the EU and Brazil and competition over the Russian grain trade were major issues.[111] Export interests had "a key role in determining policy in the Department of Agriculture."[112] Apart from the Soviet Union, Japan ranked high on the list of targeted countries as it was the world's largest soybean importer at

---

[107] White House Memorandum for Edwin Meese III, "Key Issues for 1983 and 1984," 8 October 1982, Reagan Library, Leonard, Burleigh C.W.: Files 1982–1984, OA12162.

[108] Hews to Erickson, 17 September 1982, Reagan Library, AG003, ID 095395.

[109] Interview with John Block, Washington, DC, 14 January 2010. See also Letter of Congressman Cooper Evans to President Reagan, 5 February 1982, Reagan Library, AG004, ID059575.

[110] Alikhani 2000: 44. For details and a temporary reinstatement of sanctions after the declaration of martial law in Poland that did focus more on technology exports see De Mestral and Gruchalla-Wesierski 1990: 200f.

[111] Memorandum for Edwin Meese III, 12 July 1982 and John Block to Secretary of Treasury Donald Regan, 23 November 1982, Reagan Library, AG 003, ID 119338 and ID 119545; US Congress 1983.

[112] Interview of Richard Smith by Thad Lively, 14 November 1989, The Foreign Affairs Oral History Collection of the Association for Diplomatic Studies and Training at the Library of Congress, available at: <http://hdl.loc.gov/loc.mss/mfdip.2004smi08> (accessed 13 April 2012).

that time. According to John Block, the Middle East "was not a food trading priority" in comparison, not even Egypt with its substantial wheat imports.[113] Still, Middle Eastern countries were approached as well. P.L. 480 legislation underwent the most sweeping change since the Food for Peace Act in 1966 to increase exports to developing countries. The Food Security Act of 1985 reinstated the eligibility of payments in nonconvertible foreign currency, which had been discontinued in 1966. More importantly, P.L. 480 was superseded by a number of new exports subsidies like the Export Enhancement Program (EEP) that was used to counter equally subsidized grain exports of the European Union in the Middle East, North Africa, and Eastern Europe.[114]

In 1983, John Block headed a delegation of the USDA to Saudi Arabia and tried to convince his counterparts to give up their wheat self-sufficiency drive, which was taking off at that time. Planting water-intensive crops in the desert was "crazy," Block argued. Instead, the Saudis would be better off importing wheat from the US. It struck him as odd that billions of dollars were spent on agriculture in a hostile environment while the US idled prime land to stabilize prices. At the same time, he was aware that the reputation of the US as a reliable supplier of food had been compromised by its cavalier politicization of food trade in the preceding decade. He came with a unilateral no embargo pledge that President Reagan had personally approved. A reciprocal commitment of Saudi Arabia to refrain from politically motivated oil export restrictions was not discussed.[115]

Despite these assurances, Block did not receive more than courteous questions during his meetings. No serious matter was raised and talks remained general. Block did not have a concrete offer that would have guaranteed certain quantities, nor was he in a position to offer extended guarantees in terms of price and grades, as the US did not have a wheat board with centralized procurement like Canada and Australia. Their wheat boards with their national distribution monopoly were in a better position to offer long-term supply contracts and one-stop services, thus putting US exports at a disadvantage.[116] The embargo threats of the preceding decade still loomed large. The Saudis saw domestic self-sufficiency as a priority and received the US offer with suspicion. "They didn't trust us," says John Block.[117] Turki Faisal al-Rasheed, a Saudi agro-businessman who participated in talks with US delegations at that time, confirms this lack of confidence. The threats of a food embargo against the Arabs in 1973–4 did not worry the Saudis that much, they were perceived as mere "slogans," but the actual putting into practice of such

---

[113] John Block interview.   [114] Ruttan 1996: 177–80, 191.
[115] Lippman 1983.   [116] John Block interview; US Congress 2004: 28.
[117] John Block interview. See also Philipp 1984: 80.

an embargo against the Soviet Union in 1980 stirred deep anxieties, even though Saudi Arabia fervently opposed the Afghanistan invasion.[118] Block's proposed specialization along comparative advantages did not resonate well, and the Saudi self-sufficiency strategy continued unabated.

The depoliticization of US food trade has continued since the 1980s. Even under the extended sanction regime against Iran in the mid-1990s, food exports had a leniency period and were gradually phased out through February 1996. After pressure from the farm lobby, the Clinton administration made an about-face in April 1999 and lifted restrictions on the sale of food and medical equipment to Iran.[119] The abstention from unilateral food sanctions and their usage as a diplomatic weapon was also part of George W. Bush's program in the presidential election campaign 1999.[120] In 2008/9 and 2012, Iran appeared as a large buyer on international grain markets and also purchased from US suppliers.[121] Food embargoes are out of fashion; they have proven to be too blunt a tool in the 1970s and other issues have loomed larger in the foreign policy equation. Concerns such as domestic farm income, the reputation of the US as a reliable supplier of food, and humanitarian considerations have all helped to prevent the renewed use of food as a weapon.

If food is still used as a foreign policy tool, it is as a carrot. Nowadays the share of food aid in cross-border food shipments has diminished compared to the heyday of surplus disposal and more than half of it is distributed by the World Food Program rather than by bilateral government-to-government programs.[122] Yet, the latter still play a role. US food aid was offered to North Korea as a quid pro quo against a suspension of enrichment activity and a moratorium on nuclear and missile tests in 2012. Even though North Korea upended the deal with a missile launch in April 2012, Marcus Noland and Stephen Haggard of the Peterson Institute have shown a historic coincidence of American aid offers and North Korean diplomatic concessions.[123] Former US Presdient Bill Clinton suggested that the US should offer long-term grain delivery contracts to China and Saudi Arabia and linked the proposal somewhat cryptically to a long-term reduction of the US dependence on Chinese financing and Saudi oil.[124] When export restrictions returned in the wake of the global food crisis of 2008, they came from countries other than the US, like Vietnam, Russia, and India. They were also enacted out of concerns for domestic food security, not to achieve foreign policy goals. The only exception to this trend of depoliticization has been Iraq in the 1990s. Here, the food

---

[118] Interview with Turki Faisal al-Rasheed, Jeddah, 13 February 2010.
[119] Alikhani 2000: 208.   [120] *Slate*, 11 August 1999.
[121] *Wall Street Journal*, 27 March 2012; *Reuters*, 1 March 2012.
[122] Paarlberg 2010: 70ff.
[123] *The Economist*, 14 January 2012; Haggard and Noland 2007.
[124] Clinton 2011: 170.

weapon exerted a terrible toll in a multilateral sanction setting and showed Arab countries the possible implications of their food import vulnerability.

4.6 NO OIL, NO FOOD: IRAQ IN THE 1990s

Shortly after Iraq invaded Kuwait in August 1990, the United Nations Security Council imposed a near total trade and financial embargo on the country. Only imports of medical supplies and foodstuffs in the event of "humanitarian circumstances" were allowed. Iraq was shut off from international financial transactions and its foreign assets were frozen. Since it was not allowed to export anything, and since oil made up 95 percent of its export earnings, it was cut off from foreign currency revenues that could have paid for imports.[125] With modifications, the embargo continued until the Allied invasion and the fall of Saddam Hussein's government in May 2003. The initial raison d'être of the sanctions was to end the Iraqi occupation of Kuwait. After the Iraqi withdrawal, the stated purpose shifted to regime change, payment of war reparations, and disarmament of weapons of mass destruction. The sanctions regime thus entailed somewhat of a paradox, as it demanded compliance from a regime it aimed to abolish at the same time. Although the sanctions were unsuccessful in bringing about regime change or significantly altering Iraqi foreign policy, they were fairly successful in sealing Iraq off and allowing the import of supplies only selectively.[126]

Sanctions against Iraq were multilateral and entailed the military enforcement of the embargo by monitoring land, air, and maritime access points to the country. Unilateral embargoes like the ones of the US against Cuba or the Soviet Union had a largely symbolic effect and essentially only caused trade diversion via third parties. In contrast, alternative suppliers were off limits in the case of Iraq because of the multilateral nature of the embargo. Its effects were much more severe and in many ways comparable to a military siege. Assistant Secretary of State Thomas Enders had rejected plans for a food embargo against Arab oil exporters in the 1970s as futile "unless you have destroyers all the way around."[127] Now this necessary precondition for a successful embargo was actually being met in Iraq for the first time since World War II. Although the sanctions were multilateral, the driving force behind their continued maintenance was the US. It vigorously advocated them despite opposition at various stages from UN agencies, major powers like

---

[125] For cost calculations see Hufbauer, Elliot, and Oegg 2008: 105.
[126] Gordon 2010; Mazaheri 2010; Niblock 2001; Meyer and Califano 2006; Arnove 2003.
[127] Rothschild 1976: 301.

Russia, France, and China, and the majority of the UN Security Council and the UN General Assembly.

Iraq had once been a bread-basket of the Middle East and a major supplier of grains to other countries in the region during the reign of the Middle East Supply Center in World War II. As late as 1958 American officials pointed to the anxiety of the country to dispose of exportable grain surpluses and advised helping Iraq with marketing efforts, otherwise it would turn to the Soviets for help.[128] Yet, agriculture was neglected in the wake of the oil boom and productivity gains trailed behind population growth. By the 1970s, the country became a food net importer. On the eve of the Kuwait invasion, it imported about 70 percent of its supplies of cereals, legumes, oils, and sugar.[129] After the sanctions were installed, wheat and flour imports dropped from 3.4 million tons in 1989 to 797,000 tons in 1993.[130] Without food imports, daily food supplies diminished dramatically. By 1991 prices of some basic foodstuffs like rice and wheat flour had risen by 4,500 percent.[131] A UN mission in July 1991 raised alarm at the unfolding humanitarian crisis. It recommended allowing Iraq to export oil again, so it could import necessary civilian supplies and restore its infrastructure. The Iraqi government rejected this first oil-for-food proposal, because it regarded it as an infringement upon its sovereignty. Therefore, the only open door to legal imports of humanitarian goods were deliveries that the Iraq Sanction Committee of the UN approved on a case by case basis and for which Iraq had to pay with cash it had on hand from its limited reserves. Until the establishment of the Oil-for-Food Program in 1995 and its launch in December 1996, this was Iraq's only access to imported commodities apart from smuggling, mainly via Jordan and Turkey.

Food security deteriorated massively and there was an increase in child mortality, water-borne diseases, and malnutrition in the 1990s. The majority of estimates put the "excess mortality rate" of children who would not have died in the absence of sanctions at 500,000 or more for the period between 1990 and 2003.[132] The bombardments of the war in 1991 had destroyed public infrastructure. Water treatment facilities, telecommunication, and power plants were in disrepair. The sanctions and their narrow definition of dual-use goods made reconstruction all but impossible. The food distribution system was equally hampered by lack of trucks, spare parts, and tires. Even if food imports entered the country, it was difficult to make sure that they could reach their destination.

The rationing system that was installed by the Iraqi government thus relied mainly on domestically produced food. On the eve of the Oil-for-Food Program in 1996 it was only able to guarantee daily supplies of 1,100 calories

---

[128] Rountree to Dulles Washington, 27 December 1958, FRUS 1958–1960, Vol. XII, 203.
[129] Gordon 2010: 33.   [130] Ahmad 2002: 182.
[131] Gordon 2010: 22.   [132] Gordon 2010: 37.

per person, about half of what is regarded as a minimum for a healthy living. The Iraqi population with the means to do so had to procure food on the black market to make up for this shortfall. Real wages in the fairly urbanized Iraqi society declined by 56 percent on average between 1990 and 1996.[133] Food accessibility for lower and middle classes decreased dramatically. By the mid-1990s, Iraq was on the verge of widespread famine.

Without the rationing program, the food situation would have been worse. As in the two previous decades, the Baath regime showed concern for welfare measures and associated legitimacy gains, while maintaining a blatant disregard for human rights and civil liberties. The rationing system was also a powerful tool to control the population.[134] The government had a system of central procurement for cereals and oil seeds in place, and left the allocation of fruits and vegetables mostly to market forces.[135] It was stipulated that half of irrigated cropland had to be planted with cereals. Subsidized input factors like fertilizers were centrally provided to farmers. Thus, the government hoped to counter the problems of ambiguous land and water rights and the unavailability of credit.[136] The relative importance of agriculture in the overall economy increased after decades of neglect. There was a reverse flow of labor into the sector and the government encouraged a 70 percent expansion of acreage. However, production only increased by a much smaller margin. Yields remained even below the levels of the 1950s and 1960s when the large-scale mechanization measures of the 1980s had not yet been undertaken. Limited productivity could therefore not be entirely explained by sanctions on the import of machinery, quality seeds, fertilizers, and pesticides, at least in the case of cereals. Rather, expansion into marginal lands and a downward bias of official figures might have been the reason.[137] As the Oil-for-Food Program also allowed for the importation of agricultural input factors, the government tried to stimulate agricultural production after 1996 by encouraging more drip irrigation, tapping into groundwater resources, and applying center pivot irrigation in order to fight the prevalent problem of saline soils.

Child mortality did not increase in the semi-autonomous region of northern Iraq, where the UN administered the Oil-for-Food Program "on behalf of the Iraqi government," while it increased dramatically in southern and central Iraq, where Saddam Hussein continued to rule. Various US administrations therefore blamed the corruption and ineptitude of the Iraqi dictatorship for the food security malaise. Yet, the north received a higher per capita share of oil revenues, its agriculture was in better shape, and it was in a better position to avoid the embargo due to more porous borders.[138] Over time, opposition to the sanctions mounted within the UN apparatus, among NGOs, and among

---

[133] Gazdar and Hussain 2002: 46.   [134] Mazaheri 2010.
[135] Ahmad 2002: 184f.   [136] US Congress 2004: 17.
[137] Gazdar and Hussain 2002: 53ff.   [138] Gordon 2010: 26.

countries other than the US. There was widespread consensus that it was the sanction regime itself that caused the humanitarian crisis, and not just corruption of the Iraqi regime.

Initially, opposition by Arab governments to the plight of the Iraqis was limited. Many continued to endorse the sanctions at the beginning of the 1990s. The Gulf Arabs still felt threatened by Iraq and had not forgotten the Kuwait invasion. Syria had been a political rival since the 1960s, and the common border had been closed most of the time. However, throughout the 1990s, Arab public opinion was increasingly galvanized around the humanitarian plight in Iraq and new Arab media like *Al Jazeera* spurred widespread debates that Arab officialdom could not ignore. While sympathy for Saddam Hussein's regime was not common, compassion for the Iraqi people developed into a "defining quality of Arabness."[139] Arab politicians had to pay at least lip service to a reconsideration of the Iraqi sanction regime, and this pressure contributed to the eventual enactment of the Oil-for-Food Program. By the mid-1990s, only Kuwait and Saudi Arabia were still publicly supportive of US sanction policies, while others would approve of Iraqi containment only in private. By the end of the 1990s, most Arab leaders opposed the sanctions regime in public and the Kuwaiti hard-line stance was vilified in Arab public opinion.[140] Beside the twin challenges of emerging new media and increasingly autonomous public opinion, the Iraq sanctions and their successful implementation also entailed another lesson for Arab countries. Reliance on foreign food supplies was dangerous. In Syria, it spurred a program to increase wheat production and shift cultivated acreage from cotton to grains.[141]

The Oil-for-Food Program led to widespread corruption. The Australian Wheat Board conquered about 73 percent of the market for Iraqi wheat imports by paying illegal kickbacks to the Iraqi regime.[142] After the fall of Saddam Hussein, the US has tried to regain its market share in the country and rebuild its previous position as a major supplier to Iraq.[143] As part of an opaque and often mismanaged reconstruction effort, the Bush administration put an erstwhile Cargill executive, Daniel Amstutz, in charge of reviving the Iraqi farm sector. As a former representative of a large grain trader, Amstutz applied his view of US agriculture on Iraq. Inefficiency of small producers caused by a lack of free markets was his diagnosis. The Iraqi farm sector, which had been dependent on the government for subsidized input factors and

---

[139] Lynch 2006: 115.

[140] Lynch 2006: 14, 72, 92, 95, and 97–116.

[141] Westlake 2000; Daoudy 2005: 81. According to Daoudy, Syrian executives uniformly named the Iraq sanctions in interviews as a motivation for the Syrian grain program. Interview, Cambridge, Mass., 4 May 2010.

[142] Bartos, Australian Wheat Board, and United Nations Oil-for-Food Program 2006; Overington 2007.

[143] US Congress 2004; Schnepf 2003.

guaranteed prices, was opened to foreign competition. The legal protection of intellectual property rights of seed providers like Cargill received outsized attention compared to more pressing issues of agricultural development like extension services or credit facilitation.[144]

So far, Iraqi agriculture has remained in poor shape. It was badly hurt by drought at the end of the 2000s and by reduced water flows via the Euphrates and Tigris because of dam projects on the Turkish side.[145] Iraq not only continues to import most of its cereals, but also large quantities of fruits and vegetables, which are not produced domestically in sufficient quantities and quality. To protect the domestic market, the government temporarily banned imports from neighboring Iran, Turkey, and Syria in 2010. This benefited the farmers, but led to severe price hikes in the cities.[146]

To this day foreign agricultural investments have been limited. Imports of agricultural machinery for modernization have been slow, and suppliers of center pivot irrigation devices that could ameliorate the widespread problem of soil salinity in Iraq still hope for more business.[147] Although Gulf countries have been invited to invest by the Iraqi government, they have not announced a single agricultural project in Iraq, while they have otherwise scouted the globe for such projects. Apart from concerns about the security situation, there is a deeply situated mistrust about the Shiite-led government in Baghdad and its alleged ties to Iran. Saudi Arabia appointed a non-resident ambassador as late as 2012. It seems that Iraq remains quite distant from reconnecting with its past glory as a Middle Eastern bread-basket. Due to population growth and the decline of water flows through the Euphrates and Tigris, this might prove to be a daunting task. Still, Iraq, like Sudan, could prove to be a wild card in terms of agricultural production and water consumption in the Middle East, if agricultural development was fostered successfully.

4.7 CONCLUSION

The food weapon looms large in the collective unconscious of the Middle East. Like the oil weapon in the West, the threat perception informs policy-making. Since World War II, Gulf countries have been painfully aware of their food import dependence. In the 1960s, they not only saw first-hand how the US used food aid as a foreign policy tool against Egypt, they also actively encouraged the withdrawal of preferential food deliveries to their ideological rival in

---

[144] *The Guardian*, 28 April 2003; Naylor 2008: 413f.
[145] Chulov 2009. See also Zurayk 2011: chapter 2.
[146] *The National*, 12 June 2010.
[147] Interview with irrigation company executive, Dubai, 26 April 2009.

Cairo. Similarly, Gulf countries supported the most dramatic application of the food weapon in the Middle East, the multilateral UN embargo against Iraq in the 1990s. In the 1970s, they were targeted themselves by the food weapon. The US pondered a grain embargo in retaliation to the Arab oil boycott and rejected it only for reasons of impracticality. OPEC countries were much less dependent on US grain deliveries than the US was dependent on oil imports. Moreover, given Gulf countries' limited population size at that time, they would have easily found alternative suppliers. Still, the mere threat of a food embargo was enough to worry policy-makers. Like oil importers, Gulf countries were concerned about diversity of supply and transport security. They reached out to alternative suppliers like Australia, developed the vision of Sudan as an Arab bread-basket, and finally cast their lot with a massive expansion of subsidized domestic agriculture.

Fears of the food weapon subsided in the 1980s with the return of structural surpluses on world markets and an aggressive search for export outlets by the US and other grain producers. The US was careful to depoliticize the food trade out of concern for domestic farm interests. This policy stance lasts to this day. Yet, the suspicions of the 1970s are present. The export restrictions in the wake of the global food crisis of 2008 have reawakened existing concerns in the Gulf countries. This time, interference in the food trade did not come from the US and was not motivated by foreign policy goals. Instead, it arose out of domestic food security considerations in countries like Argentina, Vietnam, and Russia. As such, they showed some similarities with the concerns of the Ford administration about the effects of export demand on domestic food price levels.

Russia proposed a cartel-like cooperation with neighboring grain producers Ukraine and Kazakhstan at the end of the 2000s. Similar ideas had been en vogue in the US in the 1970s in the hope of enhancing food producer revenues and achieving parity between oil and wheat prices—a barrel for a bushel. Such plans were discarded for impracticality then. Their chances of realization are even slimmer now. Yet, for net food importers like the Gulf countries, such discussions are disconcerting. The food export restrictions of 2008 have informed a drive for privileged bilateral access to food production. The most publicized reaction has been the announcement of agricultural investments abroad, mainly in developing countries with food security issues of their own. As such it shows striking similarity with the unsuccessful Sudan bread-basket vision of the 1970s.

Part II

Gulf Food Security and International Agro-Investments

5

The Global Land Grab Phenomenon

If "land grab" was a forgotten expression in political dictionaries it has been all over the media since the eruption of the global food crisis in 2008. Food deficit countries in Asia and the Gulf and Western financial investors have embarked on a spree of land acquisitions around the globe. Motivations range from food security concerns to profit maximization and stable supplies of industrial inputs like cotton, rubber, or biofuels. For the Gulf countries the domestic political economy of food, their need to phase out water-intensive crops, and their experience of past geopolitical supply disruptions have been important aspects of the equation.

The global land grab has made headlines and been shrouded in secrecy at the same time. There is a lack of transparency. Investors and host countries release data only in a piecemeal fashion. Apart from some countries like Cambodia or Ethiopia, documents with contract details are not available. Data quality in many developing countries suffers from lack of bureaucratic capacities and overlapping responsibilities between different government agencies.

If there has been understatement on the one side, there have been exaggerations on the other. The economics of NGO funding and the blogosphere require purpose and sensationalism. Downsized newsrooms can afford neither on-site investigations nor letting slip a "hot" topic that is spreading elsewhere on the internet. Vague declarations of intent have been reported as realities and there has been a bias towards more colorful stories. Phil Heilberg, a swashbuckling investor from New York who is proud of his close relationship with South Sudanese warlord Paulino Matip and declares himself a "Mafia head," is likely to attract more attention than the investment of a bureaucratic pension fund in a developed and food secure country like Australia, even though Heilberg's project has not seen any implementation whatsoever.[1]

Media perception and actual project implementation on the ground have become two very different things. Media reports can give some indication of

---

[1] Funk 2010; Pearce 2012: 41–4.

trends and prevalent investor interests, though. The websites of the Barcelona based NGO GRAIN and the International Land Coalition (ILC) have aggregated such media reports in databases.[2] Announced land acquisitions started to rise in 2005, accelerated in 2008 and peaked in 2009.[3] The World Bank, the IIED together with FAO and IFAD, and some NGO reports have undertaken national inventories in target countries that drew on government sources, surveys, and third party interviews.[4] Where media reports tend to overstate, government sources might underreport, limit access to data, and exclude deals that are still under negotiation. Estimates about the size and scope of global land acquisitions vary according to chosen period, status of investments, and nature of investment, e.g. whether investments in mining, tourism, and forestry are included.[5]

The issue of reliability of media reports was highlighted in April 2012 when ILC, German consultancy GIZ, and research centers in Hamburg, Montpellier, and Bern released the Land Matrix. The Land Matrix was advertised as the world's largest and most detailed database about large-scale land acquisitions. It claimed to submit media reports to a rigorous verification process consisting of cross-checking of various sources and surveys in host countries. Based on this verification it assigned reliability codes to land acquisitions.[6] Only news items with some triangulation like research reports or press releases by investors and governments were included. However, the individual reliability codes for each project were not made public on the release of the website. There is also the possibility to declare projects as failed and remove them from the database, but it is unclear what is required for that to happen. The verification process is ongoing and as a work in progress there might be improvements over time, but at its release the Land Matrix gave a distorted image of international land acquisitions. It reported deals over millions of hectares as fact that never materialized such as announced projects by South Korean Daewoo in Madagascar and Chinese ZTE in the Republic of Congo. While South Sudan figured prominently with deals that have never made it beyond the announcement stage, the database did not mention any of the projects in North and Central Sudan, where some implementation has actually taken place. Thus, it involuntarily underlined the very problem it had set out to resolve: the unreliability of media reports.[7]

[2] <www.farmlandgrab.org> and <www.commercialpressuresonland.org> (accessed 2 May 2012).

[3] Anseeuw, Wily, et al. 2012: 6.

[4] Deininger et al. 2011; Cotula et al. 2009; Görgen et al. 2009; Horne et al. 2011; Baxter et al. 2011; Deng 2011; FIAN International Secretariat 2010; Deng and Mittal 2011; Mousseau, Mittal, and Phillips 2011; Baxter and Mousseau 2011.

[5] For a comparison of methodologies see Cotula 2012.

[6] Land Matrix 2012; Anseeuw, Boche, et al. 2012.

[7] Rural Modernity 2012d, 2012c, 2012a; Brautigam 2012b, 2012a.

The private sector arm of the World Bank, the International Finance Corporation (IFC), has been accused by advocacy groups of abetting large-scale land transactions.[8] Yet in 2011, the World Bank produced a report that was critical of land investments and apparently contested within the bank itself.[9] Based on data of the GRAIN website, it estimated that between October 2008 and August 2009 large-scale land deals over 56.6 million ha were announced globally. This was flabbergasting if compared to worldwide agricultural land expansion of 3.8 million ha annually before the global food crisis.[10] Two-thirds of the announced deals were in sub-Saharan Africa, where most of the land is formally owned by the state. While in Latin America and Eastern Europe purchases of land are possible, access to land in Africa is usually facilitated via long-term leases from governments.[11] Countries with "poorer records of formally recognized rural land tenure" attracted the most interest. This added to concerns about the transparency and equitability of such deals.[12]

Yet, implementation of projects in the World Bank study lagged behind; actual farming had started on only a fifth of the announced projects and on much smaller scales than originally intended. The implementation gap was particularly high for Gulf countries, India, the UK, and Libya, but also applied to China.[13] Bureaucratic procedures were marred with administrative gaps, many investors lacked the technical knowledge, and some of them may have acquired land only for the purpose of speculation. Another major finding was that the domestic investors were more numerous than the widely publicized foreign ones, even though in some cases they might have a foreign joint venture partner like the Sudanese agro-businessman Osama Daoud and his DAL Group, which is cooperating with Saudi investors.[14] The importance of domestic investors and the implementation gap has also been noticed by NGO reports that have been highly critical of the negative aspects of land investments.[15] The problem has not so much been a "foreignisation of space,"[16] but an agricultural expansion that could be to the detriment of smallholders and pastoralists regardless of investors' nationality. Shifting cultivation and customary land

[8] Daniel and Mittal 2010.

[9] Deininger et al. 2011. A draft of the report was leaked to the *Financial Times* (27 July 2010) "by a person who said they wanted to prevent the World Bank releasing the report in the middle of the summer holiday period." A first version of the report was then published in September 2010.

[10] Deininger et al. 2011: 51, 10. For the longer period between 2000 and April 2012 an 83.2 million ha estimate for announced deals has been given by Anseeuw, Wily, et al. 2012: VII.

[11] Cotula et al. 2009: 76.

[12] Deininger et al. 2011: XXXII.

[13] Deininger et al. 2011: 52f.; Brautigam 2012a.

[14] WikiLeaks cable, 08KHARTOUM1416, US Embassy in Khartoum, 18 September 2008.

[15] Horne et al. 2011; FIAN International Secretariat 2010.

[16] Zoomers 2010.

rights about grazing grounds, migratory routes, and access to water holes could be undermined.

The problems are numerous. Unrecognized land rights can lead to loss of livelihoods and can impede proper compensation. At times governments engage in outright expulsion of holders of customary land rights or lack the bureaucratic ability to process large-scale projects. A connection to the broader development planning of target countries is often not discernible. Investor proposals are insufficient or technically not viable. Projects have mostly been offered at nominal land leases. The interest of respective governments has not been so much in immediate revenues, but in the developmental impact of ensuing investments.[17] Yet, promised offsetting benefits such as the building of infrastructure, schools, and hospitals often have not materialized. A study by FAO, IFAD, and IIED pointed out that pledges are often vague and "tend to lack teeth."[18]

5.1 PATTERNS OF AGRICULTURAL EXPANSION

The agro-investment drive would be unlikely without the paradigm shift in food prices that has been described in chapter 1. On the supply side, productivity growth has flattened out and negative ecological backlash like water stress, soil erosion, and climate change is taking its toll. On the demand side, meatification of diets in emerging markets, population growth, biofuels, and the financial sector's discovery of commodities as an asset class have played crucial roles.

Agricultural production growth since World War II relied mainly on increased yields and happened on a relatively steady area of land. Between 1961 and 2005, expansion of cultivated area contributed less than a quarter to production growth and intensification of cropping intervals only 8 percent.[19] This begs the question what a future agricultural expansion may look like.

Currently, around 11 percent of the world's surface area—about 1.5 billion ha—is farmed with crops. This is less than half of the 3.65 billion ha that the IIASA assessment of 2011 estimates as the global land area with potential for rain-fed cultivation.[20] However, such biophysical surveys are theoretical figures. A lot of this land reserve is already in use for other important purposes. Forests cover 45 percent, 12 percent is in protected areas, and human settlements take up about 3 percent.[21] Pastoralists also use large swathes of land for

[17] Cotula 2011.   [18] Cotula et al. 2009: 101.
[19] Deininger et al. 2011: 10.   [20] HLPE 2011: 24; IIASA 2011.
[21] Bruinsma and FAO 2003: 40.

extensive livestock husbandry. The land might be underutilized, but it is hardly idle. Expansion of agricultural production into these areas comes with social and environmental costs. Much of the land reserve has characteristics that make farming difficult, such as hilly terrain, lack of infrastructure, humid climate, high variability of rainfall, dryness, cold temperatures, or low soil fertility. Due to the higher exposure to climatic risk factors, food production on marginal land shows greater variability from one year to another. Yet, it has become more attractive to put marginal land into production because food prices are high and already cultivated land has been lost to soil erosion and urban sprawl. Dryland farming also offers possibilities to remedy some of the associated challenges.

The World Bank report takes the proximity of transport infrastructure, ecological factors, and population density into consideration when assessing the suitability of land for rain-fed cultivation. It arrives at a lower figure of 446 million ha of land that is uncultivated and located in non-forested, unprotected areas with a population density of less than 25 persons per square kilometer.[22] This land reserve is heavily concentrated. Africa and Latin America account for over 70 percent and only seven countries for more than half of it: Sudan, Brazil, Australia, Russia, Argentina, Mozambique, and the Democratic Republic of Congo.[23] In contrast, rain-fed agriculture cannot expand anymore in the MENA region, South Asia, Central Asia, and to a certain extent East Asia. Arable land is a limiting factor in these regions.

Water is even more crucial. Nestlé Chairman Peter Brabeck-Letmathe has argued that the spate of international land deals is in reality a "water grab" for increasingly scarce water resources rather than a "land grab."[24]Agriculture uses 70 percent of global water supplies. Water withdrawal for 15–35 percent of global irrigation is deemed unsustainable and about 1.4 billion people live in basins with acute water stress. Water abstraction in the Middle East, Central Asia, Pakistan, Southern India, the southwest of the US, North China, and southeast Australia is over replenishment rates.[25]

Since the 1990s, there have been different modes of land expansion. In Latin America, forests were cleared for extensive livestock ranching. Technological advances and conservation tillage opened the acid soils of the Brazilian *cerrado* (savannah) for the cultivation of soybeans and other crops. Palm oil acreage in Indonesia doubled between 1997 and 2007. Malaysia also expanded this industry. In Vietnam and Thailand, government policies helped the expansion

---

[22] Deininger et al. 2011: 78ff.
[23] Deininger et al. 2011: 79f. See also Cotula et al. 2009: 60.
[24] Brabeck-Letmathe 2009.
[25] World Bank 2007: 182f.; Molden 2007: 11.

of rice production by smallholders. In Africa, smallholder farming expanded alongside population growth with no concomitant increase in productivity. Food production per capita declined between 1980 and 2000.[26] Policies until the late 1980s discriminated against agriculture via overvalued exchange rates, controlled procurement prices, and export taxes. Attempts at large-scale farming in Sudan, Tanzania, and Zambia were unsuccessful. Finally, in Eastern Europe and Central Asia, large-scale farms existed alongside a contraction of land use in the wake of the break-up of the Soviet Union.[27]

The World Bank has established a typology of four kinds of countries based on their availability of uncultivated land and so-called "yield gaps."[28] The latter describe suboptimal yields that trail behind the productivity that could be reasonably expected if improved technologies and management practices were applied on a given quality of land:

- Countries with a large land reserve and high yield gaps of 70 percent and more are mainly located in Africa. There are also some in Latin America like Bolivia and Peru.

- Countries with available land reserves but small yield gaps are primarily in Latin America (Brazil, Argentina, Uruguay) and Eastern Europe.

- Areas with large yield gaps, but small available land reserves comprise the majority of developing countries such as Rwanda, highland Ethiopia, Malawi, Kenya, the Philippines, Cambodia, and Central American countries, but also the Ukraine. Middle Eastern countries with limited water for rain-fed agriculture also fall into this bracket.

- Countries with a small land reserve and low yield gaps are found in Western Europe and in Asian countries with high population density like China, Vietnam, Malaysia, South Korea, and Japan. Middle Eastern countries with a large share of irrigated agriculture like Egypt and Jordan also belong to this category.

Two-thirds of agricultural expansion until 2030 will be in Africa and Latin America. Both continents are in the spotlight because of their available land and water reserves. Latin America's infrastructure is vastly better and its yield gaps lower. On the other hand, these advantages have been priced into land valuations, while African countries have offered investors very cheap lease agreements. Countries with limited land reserves but large yield gaps also offer the possibility of improving productivity with investments (e.g. Philippines, Cambodia). Yet, without formulas for mutual benefits, social conflict around land use is likely. This risk is even higher in countries with small land reserves and low yield gaps (e.g. Egypt, Vietnam). It is less

---

[26] Paarlberg 2010: 64.   [27] Deininger et al. 2011: XXXf., 26f.
[28] Deininger et al. 2011: 86–91.

obvious why they would need foreign investments. Mahendra Shah, who contributed to the IIASA and World Bank reports and was then a high-ranking executive at the Qatar National Food Security Programme, argued in 2010 that Gulf investments should focus on already cultivated areas with high yield gaps. He anticipated win-win situations if such gaps were closed by infusion of capital.[29]

The expansion patterns do not only happen in geographical areas with certain biophysical characteristics, but also in a political space. Tony Weis describes four types of countries that have diverging interests in the ongoing Doha round of the WTO about agricultural trade liberalization: (a) the heavily subsidized agro-industries of the grain–livestock complex in the northern temperate zones (US and Europe); (b) agro-exporters of the Cairns group that share the agenda of liberalization of the former group but lobby against its subsidies in order to improve the competitiveness of their own exports. The Cairns group mainly encompasses emerging market countries like Brazil, Argentina, Thailand, or South Africa, but also Canada and Australia; (c) China and India, which follow a policy of food self-sufficiency for strategic reasons. With 50 percent of the global rural population and a need to moderate rapid urbanization, they are anxious to protect their large class of small-scale farmers. As a result, they are reluctant to engage with full-fledged agricultural liberalization. Finally, there is (d), the marginals, which encompass large parts of the Third World. They are characterized by exports of cash crops from colonial times (e.g. cotton, coffee) and import dependence in staple foods which has developed since World War II.[30]

The agricultural expansion focuses on the marginals and the agro-exporters of the Cairns group. The marginals constitute a large bulk of the available global land reserve. Political instability and conflict hamper agricultural development in many of them. Yet cheap lease rates partially offset their lack of infrastructure and they offer the potential to increase yields significantly. The agro-industries in the northern hemisphere are less interesting from this point of view as they have largely utilized their potential yield, have a limited land reserve, and might come under pressure in the case of subsidy reductions. The Cairns group exporters on the other hand have an interest to do business with the food importers, but are not necessarily in need of their investments. Their agro-industries are already established. In fact, there is an interest to keep them national. Some of them like Brazil and Thailand have undertaken steps to limit foreign land ownership. Cooperation in these countries will rather take the form of joint ventures than outright land acquisitions.

---

[29] Shah 2010. [30] Weis 2007: 99–116.

5.2 ASIANS, ARABS, AND ASSET MANAGERS: THE DIFFERENT INVESTOR TYPES

Earlier agro-investments in the developing world focused on cash crops like tea, coffee, cocoa, palm oil, rubber, cotton, and tropical fruits. Staple foods and biofuels were absent. The latter were yet unknown, only taking off in earnest in the 2000s with supporting legislation and subsidies. The traditional grain exporters on the other hand produced staple foods in abundance. The investment case to expand staple crops production in the developing world was not there. The strong geographic focus on Africa and countries with weak records of recognized land rights is also new. Another peculiarity of the current investment drive is the new types of investors. In earlier times, the investments were the realm of food processing companies like Dole, Unilever, or Sime Darby. Now financial players and countries with strategic concerns have entered the fray.

Financial investors are driven by profit maximization. They have neither the need for nor the luxury of long-term strategic considerations. Their shareholders would not tolerate loss-making business endeavors over an extended period. Without the paradigm shift in food prices, their interest in agriculture would be zero. Investment banks like Morgan Stanley or Deutsche Bank and private equity companies like Black Rock have invested in farmland and food-related industries. They have also created corresponding investment products for pension funds and other institutional investors.[31]

Apart from exposure to agricultural commodities via derivatives and index funds, the focus of these investments has been on food processing, input provision, and trading. Most of the food-related TNCs are in these sectors. The existence of publicly listed companies is important for financial investors, as this constitutes tradability of acquired assets and a viable exit strategy in case of a private equity acquisition. In actual farming, TNCs are much rarer and focus on biofuels and tropical commodities like sugar cane, bananas, and cut flowers.[32] The global food system is an hourglass market that is segmented on the end of producers and consumers, but highly concentrated in the middle where procurement, processing, and distribution occur. A similar concentration exists on the side of input provision, where a few large companies control supplies of seeds, fertilizers, pesticides, and machinery. Profits accrue mostly on the end of corporations. In the US, the share of farmgate operations in the food system declined from 41 percent of accrued value in 1910 to 9 percent in 1990. At the same time, the relative shares of input provision, processing, and distribution grew.[33]

---

[31] GRAIN 2009; Pearce 2012: chapter 8.
[32] For an overview of food-related TNCs in the different subsectors see UNCTAD 2009: 29.
[33] Weis 2007: 82.

Actual farmland investments can be a viable option for financial investors in liquid land markets where land can be leased back to farmers or held for speculation. Australia, Eastern Europe, and the Americas have such markets, but not the developing world. Not every financial investor is suited to build up farming operations from scratch or turn around existing ones. There are examples of investment banks that have failed, while private equity funds are in a better position to assemble the necessary capacities and take a long-term view.[34] Beside the tropical commodities-producing TNCs there is evidence of some corporatization in staple food farming in Latin America and Eastern Europe. A company like Altima aims at acquiring and managing farm assets and wants to become the "first Exxon Mobil of the farming sector."[35] Such corporatization offers new avenues for financial investments. There are also examples of food processing companies like Lonhro that acquire farming operations in order to ensure feedstock supply, cut out middlemen, and facilitate benefits of vertical integration.[36]

Supply security is also a dominant motivation in food deficient nations in Asia and the Middle East, just on a much larger scale. Japan and South Korea are heavily dependent on food imports, like MENA countries. In calorie terms, net imports cover over 50 percent of their dietary intake. In China and India self-sufficiency is part of the state interest, but it is eroding. In the 1990s, productivity gains of the Green Revolution in India lagged behind population growth for the first time since the 1960s. Even before, productivity gains never really solved the problem of food accessibility for poor people. Lack of entitlements and distribution problems have threatened food security. Malnourishment of children has remained high at 46 percent according to UNICEF.[37] Every third malnourished child in the world lives in India. At the same time, the country faces an obesity epidemic among its middle and upper classes.[38] Overpumping of water for irrigation is widespread. India needs to anticipate a future where it will become a large food net importer again.

China faces the challenge to feed 20 percent of the world's population with only 9 percent of its arable land. The epic famine of the Great Leap Forward (1958–61) seems to betray a marked concern for food security.[39] Yet, self-sufficiency has always ranked high on China's agenda out of strategic considerations. Mao's famous dictum to "dig tunnels deep, store grain everywhere

---

[34] *Bloomberg Markets Magazine*, 5 October 2011.

[35] GRAIN 2009; interview with Altima executive, New York, 22 June 2009.

[36] Cotula et al. 2009: 57.

[37] <http://www.unicef.org/india/children_2356.htm> (accessed 3 September 2011).

[38] International Institute for Population Sciences 2006.

[39] The famine of the Great Leap Forward was the largest in history and killed as many as 30 to 45 million people. Forced collectivization, a misguided industrialization drive, government abuse, and bad weather conditions formed the backdrop of the famine. Becker 1996; Dikötter 2010.

and never seek hegemony," goes back to heightened tensions with the Soviet Union at the end of the 1960s.[40] Today, China holds 31 percent of global wheat stocks, followed by the US and India in the distance with 12 percent and 8 percent respectively. The Arab world holds only 10 percent of global stocks, although it is the largest wheat importer of the world.[41] China became a net food importer in 2004, despite strong production growth in the reform era since 1978.[42] Grain self-sufficiency continues to be high, but a surge in meat consumption has led to high import dependence in animal feedstock. In the case of soybeans, it is at 70 percent. Agricultural production will likely stagnate, as land is lost to urban expansion and ecological damage. Consumption will rise due to richer diets and some population growth. The latter is relatively small in comparison to many developing countries but very large in absolute terms because of the sheer size of the Chinese population. The government regards the current 95 percent self-sufficiency and a minimum of 120 million ha of cultivated land as a red line. In 2006, 122 million ha were remaining.[43]

The Chinese government has encouraged international agro-investments as part of its general "going global" policy, which it initiated in 1999. Incentives have focused on industrial input factors like rubber, palm oil, or cotton. Insofar as Chinese companies produce food crops in Africa, they do so for local markets, not for export to China. The long distance and underdeveloped infrastructure would make such exports prohibitively expensive.[44] After internal discussions about its future strategy of agricultural outsourcing, China reiterated the self-sufficiency goal in 2008. In its 20-year food security strategy, it suggested confining foreign agro-investments to commercial crops like cotton and plant staple crops domestically, with the possible exception of soybean imports from Brazil.[45] Thus, it is conceivable that China will increasingly outsource industrial crops in order to switch acreage to food crops at home.

State-owned companies have dominated China's foreign agro-investments. Advocacy groups have criticized their reliance on imported labor from China and the sheer size of announced projects. In 2006, the Forum on China–Africa Cooperation in Beijing evoked the spirit of "win-win cooperation" in the field of agriculture. China pledged to set up ten agricultural demonstration centers in Africa, a region it regards as a vital export market for corn and rice hybrid seeds. It has also used agro-investments as an instrument in its competition with Taiwan for diplomatic recognition and as an ancillary tool to soothe concerns about Chinese infrastructure and mining projects with high

---

[40] Oi 1989: 76.   [41] World Bank and FAO 2012: 13.
[42] Ash 2010; Ravallion 2009; Huang and Rozelle 1996.
[43] Brautigam 2009: 234.   [44] Brautigam 2009: 255ff.
[45] Cotula et al. 2009: 55.

environmental impacts.[46] Earlier rice projects in Africa that China had undertaken since the 1960s often fell into disrepair after the Chinese left. Relative complexity and labor intensity affected the continuity of projects despite their smallholder orientation. China has now tried to breathe new life into such schemes. However, in 2012 there were no signs of implemented Chinese projects above 10,000 ha in Africa and only a few above 5,000 ha. Media reports were often misleading exaggerations.[47]

One reason why China and India are so concerned with self-sufficiency and reluctant to engage fully with global liberalization of food trade, is that they are home to half of the world's rural population. Large-scale reliance on imports is an evidently larger vulnerability than for smaller countries.[48] Qatar, the UAE, and even Saudi Arabia have more discretion in managing food import dependence. They can feed all their population with imports if need be, which is clearly not an option for China and India. Insofar as they have had to take recourse to world markets for incremental deliveries, they have constituted a huge marginal demand on exports with ensuing price hikes. This was the case in 2010 and 2011 when China appeared as a large buyer of corn on world markets after a drought.[49]

South Korea has expanded its grain trading business beside farmland acquisitions. Chaebol conglomerates like Daewoo and Hyundai have led the investment drive. The country imports almost all its wheat and corn and is particularly interested in rice production, even though it is close to self-sufficiency because of high protectionist barriers. In India there is a larger participation of the private sector, which operates alongside the government-owned State Trading Company (STD). Companies like Karuturi or Emami Biotech have projects in Ethiopia ranging from flowers and biofuels to pulses, sugar cane, and oilseeds.[50] Other East African countries like Tanzania and Uganda are increasingly targeted. India is particularly interested to produce oilseeds, cotton, and pulses abroad.[51]

In Japan, five trading houses dominate food trade and processing: Mitsubishi, Itochu, Sumitomo, Mitsui, and Marubeni. Because of shrinking domestic markets they are expanding abroad to compete more efficiently with the large grain traders like ADM, Bunge, Cargill, Dreyfus, or Glencore. They have also moved upstream and purchased farmland in Brazil and Argentina.[52] In the 1970s, Japan invested in the expansion of soybean cultivation in Brazil after the US temporarily restricted exports in 1973. By 1996, the country relied on food production from 12 million ha of farmland overseas, about double the

---

[46] Brautigam 2009: 241. [47] Brautigam 2012a, 2009: 258; Cotula et al. 2009: 37.
[48] Weis 2007: 104–11. [49] *Financial Times*, 4 February 2011.
[50] Horne et al. 2011: 2. [51] GRAIN 2008: 6.
[52] *Bloomberg*, 17 November 2010; GRAIN 2008: 7.

size of the cultivated area at home.[53] Not all of this land was owned by Japanese; Japan has been anxious to foster multilateral approaches to land investments. It has not aimed at privileged bilateral access to food production. Rather it has tried to encourage multilateral initiatives at increasing global production levels in order to calm markets.[54]

In comparison, Gulf countries seek privileged bilateral access. Their sovereign wealth funds have played a strong role in investments and in Saudi Arabia government support for the private sector has been crucial. International agro-investments in Gulf countries are more state-driven than elsewhere. In Africa, private sector entities undertook about 90 percent of project announcements and government agencies only 10 percent.[55] In the Gulf countries, the role of the latter is more important.

5.3 LAND GRABS AND SOCIAL CONFLICT

There is a tendency in policy circles to discuss the availability of land as a technical challenge of matching available resources with superior management and technology. Yet, land availability is foremost a social issue. Land distribution is very inequitable in many countries of the world. In Brazil 3 percent of the population own 66 percent of the land, while about five million rural families are landless.[56] Access to land is crucial for improving agricultural production and rural livelihoods. Ownership patterns do not only influence income distribution. They also predetermine what is produced by whom for whom. If tenure security is weak, the incentive to invest is small. Small plot sizes and lack of access to credit and markets can lead to low productivity, especially if this is coupled with insufficient know-how and extension services. On the other hand large-scale agriculture can lead to productivity gains for certain crops, but can cause outright exclusion by concentration of landownership.

Historically, the expansion of commercial farming has not been kind to indigenous people and smallholders. In the US the former were deprived of their traditional livelihoods and ended up in reservations. The latter were a victim of Cochrane's "agricultural treadmill."[57] They vanished in great numbers if they failed to scale up and intensify operations in an environment of declining prices in real terms. Hence, the big question for any agricultural expansion is what happens to the smallholders and to indigenous people with

---

[53] Yamauchi 2002.
[54] *Financial Times*, 28 April 2009; *Asahi Shimbun*, 27 September 2010.
[55] Cotula et al. 2009; HLPE 2011: 20.   [56] Weis 2007: 113.
[57] Cochrane 1958. See chapter 1 for a discussion.

customary land rights if they have not disappeared already. A worst-case scenario of international agro-investments would entail expropriation of smallholders and pastoralists, followed by impoverishment or migration to the cities without encountering sufficient job opportunities. The respective countries might then produce more and cheaper agricultural goods, but they would do so for export, as many of its citizens could not afford them anymore.

Commodification of land is a young historical phenomenon. In many African countries, land cannot be bought and sold to this day. Originally, land concentration is not brought about by thrift and market transactions, as there is no market yet. In his account of the enclosure movement in England, Marx described it as an inherent aspect of capitalist development. The original accumulation (*ursprüngliche Akkumulation*)[58] introduces private property titles by force in settings were customary land rights and commons have prevailed. It establishes the rules of the game without following them. Its transaction currencies are violence, political intrigue, and glass beads. As a colonial practice, land grabbing of supposedly virgin lands was regarded as essential in expanding markets, procuring raw materials, and ridding mother countries of excess population. Cecil Rhodes, one of the architects of the British Empire, saw imperialism as a necessity to prevent civil war at home.[59] If the home country of the industrial revolution had problems in absorbing its rural migration flows at the height of its economic success it can be imagined what difficulties developing countries face nowadays.

There are concerns that the current agro-investments are a repetition of the past. Former FAO President Jacques Diouf warned about "neo-colonialist" aspects in foreign agro-investments that do not consider local stakeholders' interests. The fear is that they could lead to dispossession, compromise food security in target countries, and deprive them of development options.[60]

The vast majority of farmers worldwide are small-scale farmers. There is a controversial debate whether they can compete with large-scale farming. Paul Collier has derided a "middle–and upper-class love affair with peasant agriculture."[61] Romanticism for small-scale farming is misplaced, he argues, and growing urbanization inevitable. Even though he advises against the adaptation of Brazilian style "superfarms" in Africa, he sees the solution to the food

---

[58] The term is often translated as primitive accumulation, which is not entirely accurate as it fails to convey the notion of linearity. On the other hand, such linearity—industrialization and the rise of new urban classes that reproduce themselves on a capitalist basis—does not take place in Sudan and many developing countries. Primitive accumulation becomes a way of life rather than a stage of development. On a global level and adapting an earlier theorem of Rosa Luxemburg, David Harvey has argued that primitive accumulation or "accumulation by dispossession" is not a one-off event, but an infinite process that is used to cope with crises of overaccumulation. Harvey 2003. See also Hoffmann 2012.

[59] Weis 2007: 51.

[60] *Financial Times*, 28 April 2009; von Braun and Meinzen-Dick 2009.

[61] Collier 2008.

crisis in the growth of large-scale farming, contract farming by smallholders, and successful urbanization.[62] Doug Saunders has made a similar argument. In his view, pull factors and the promise of higher incomes cause urban migration. The "arrival city" on the outskirts of sprawling metropolises functions as a transitional incubator for the new migrants before they acquire urban equity and move up the social ladder. Continued links between the "arrival city" and the rural communities of origin enable a transfer of supplemental income to the countryside, which in turn allows for agricultural investments. Food security will improve as a result. Another major factor will be the diminishing birth rates that come with urbanization. Redundant small-scale farmers in the developing world will thus replicate the experience of today's developed countries in the nineteenth and twentieth centuries. They will urbanize and find jobs in the city.[63]

Yet, the absorption capacity of cities is in doubt. Growth momentum in the developed world has slowed since the 1970s. Expansion of markets has not compensated for the rationalization drive of the microelectronic revolution. Exploitability of labor has declined or only been simulated by credit bubbles that look increasingly tenuous.[64] The success of China and some other emerging markets has relied on consumer demand and outsourcing from the troubled developed world. The classic tale of urbanization and industrial development can be found there, but it is unclear whether it can be sustained or replicated in the vast majority of the developing world. Exclusion in post-industrial landscapes is widespread. Migration as a safety valve is not an option either. There is no second America around the corner and migration policies in the developed world are restrictive.

In his book *Planet of Slums* Mike Davis argues that urbanization in the developing world has disconnected from industrialization or even economic development per se. It is not job creation and the allure of the city that drive rural migration in his view, but push factors like structural adjustment, institutional decline, and civil wars.[65] Davis belittles the idea of leveraging micro-enterprises, which has been popularized by Hernan de Soto, as "an urban cargo cult amongst well-meaning NGOs."[66] For him the informal sectors of sprawling slums represent survival strategies with little chance of accumulation, dumping grounds for the permanent redundant, characterized by downward mobility. Collier and Saunders pride themselves on not being romantic about the traditional countryside and its hardships, but their optimistic view of urbanization includes a good deal of romanticism in reverse. Traditional

---

[62] Collier and Dercon 2009.

[63] Saunders 2010. For similarly optimistic views of urbanization see Glaeser 2011; Brugmann 2009.

[64] For the long downturn since the 1970s see Brenner 2006. For theories of over-accumulation see Harvey 2003; Kurz 1999.

[65] Davis 2006: 15f.   [66] Davis 2006: 184.

urbanization faces slack economic growth perspectives and needs more equitable and sustainable designs.[67] Even the Chinese leadership grapples with the migration flows to its cities and the needs of its vast rural population. Rural areas will not disappear anytime soon and are in need of sustainable development strategies.

The idea that productivity on large farms is necessarily higher than on small ones is a false dichotomy. Small-scale farmers are often locked into a state of low productivity. Yet, this is not primarily caused by a lack of scale but by lack of access to land, credit, markets, know-how, and extension services. Apart from cereal and sugar production, economies of scale in the agricultural sector are rather found on the supply and distribution sides.[68] Here the question arises whether cooperatives could attain them as easily as large agro-companies. Small- or medium-scale farming can actually offer productivity advantages as it leaves more room for proactive initiative and can leverage knowledge of local production factors. Vietnam has shown how land reform coupled with extension services to small-scale farmers can lead to productivity gains.[69] These advantages of small-scale farming are likely to grow with the need to adapt agriculture to ecological constraints. Modern centralized livestock production, for example, interrupts nitrogen and phosphorus nutrition cycles. Small operations are in a much better position to close these cycles by manuring practices and make agriculture more environmentally friendly.

Development debates have shunned the issue of land reform over the last decades. International donor institutions like the World Bank have preferred to concentrate on market reform instead of questioning unequal access to resources. Yet, market-based attempts at land redistribution have largely failed and there is a strong need for government-led land reform in places like Brazil, Colombia, the Philippines, and Indonesia.[70]

International agro-investments with their focus on large-scale plantations could thwart efforts at land reform without providing a development impetus for rural communities. Planned capital expenditures of such projects vary widely from very low for extensive livestock production to very high for sugar cane plantations. The job creation effect is often abysmally small as the World Bank points out. It ranged from 0.01 jobs per ha for a corn plantation to 0.351 jobs per ha on a sugar cane outgrower scheme in the Democratic Republic of Congo. In Ethiopia only 0.005 jobs per ha were created on investigated projects.[71] The Bank's assessment is scathing:

> Many investments... failed to live up to expectations and, instead of generating sustainable benefits, contributed to asset loss and left local people worse off than

---

[67] Cohen 2012.   [68] HLPE 2011; Wiggins, Kirsten, and Llamb 2010.
[69] HLPE 2011: 40.   [70] HLPE 2011: 29; Borras, Kay, and Lahiff 2007.
[71] Deininger et al. 2011: 64.

they would have been without the investment.... Case studies confirm that in many cases benefits were lower than anticipated or did not materialize at all.[72]

In most African countries land is formally owned by the state. Apart from cities and irrigation projects formal titling is rare. There is a severe danger that customary land rights are violated in the process of large-scale acquisitions. Local people often have only limited knowledge of the formal legal system and do not know how to affirm their rights. Even if transparency was ascertained, it is doubtful whether the logic of discounted cash flow calculations of a modern agro-project matches their livelihood priorities or would be understood by them in the same context.

Titling processes can establish tenure security. Yet, at the same time, exclusive private ownership of land goes against the nature of customary land rights where various rights to the same piece of land coexist. One family may use a plot for farming, leave it to village women for collection of firewood, and to migrant herders as grazing ground during fallow seasons. If community registration is chosen instead of individual plot-by-plot registration it can speed up the often slow bureaucratic procedures. At the same time, community registration carries the risk that local elites capture the titling process.[73] Thus, titling can increase tenure security of one customary land right holder and dispossess others, particularly vulnerable groups like women and herders. To make matters worse there is a plurality of rules and authorities that handle land rights ranging from local governments and village elders to central agencies.

UNCTAD's World Investment Report 2009 lays out the win-win case for international agro-investments. It argues that TNCs could help to raise earnings in rural areas and help a transition to an urbanized society by raising productivity, food safety standards, and food affordability.[74] A report by the Chicago Council on Global Affairs argues that TNCs could be trailblazers for agricultural development by linking small-scale farmers to global supply chains via contract farming.[75] FAO, World Bank, UNCTAD, and IFAD see a development potential of international agro-investments if done in a correct way. They have established a code of conduct on how "responsible agricultural investments" (RAI) should look.[76] RAI includes respect for customary land rights, strengthening of local food security, transparency, consultation, and social and environmental sustainability. The Voluntary Guidelines for Governance of Land Tenure that were finally endorsed by the FAO's Committee on World Food Security in May 2012 go beyond RAI. They command greater

---

[72] Deininger et al. 2011: 71.   [73] HLPE 2011: 28.
[74] UNCTAD 2009: 2.   [75] Hebebrand 2011.
[76] <http://www.responsibleagroinvestment.org/rai/node/232> (accessed 14 April 2012). See also von Braun and Meinzen-Dick 2009.

authority as they have been negotiated in a multilateral setting and make specific and binding reference to international human rights.[77]

The concept of Free Prior Informed Consent (FPIC) by local stakeholders is central in the debate about guidelines. To this end effective systems for grievance, redress, and mitigation must be in place.[78] Fully owned large-scale plantations meet with skepticism. Instead, collaborative business models like contract farming, joint ventures, management contracts, community leases, and new supply chain relationships are recommended.[79]

Advocacy groups come down firmly against any form of large-scale agro-investments, whether foreign or domestic. They regard the RAI debate as a publicity stunt to facilitate expansion of commercial farming. Any such expansion they see as a land grab and encroachment on rural livelihoods.[80] They point to the disruptive effect on traditional small-scale production and the lack of beneficial impacts like job creation, compensation, and infrastructure building. Advocacy groups are assisted by the UN Special Rapporteur on the right to food, Olivier de Schutter, who pleads for ecologically adapted small-scale farming. It might be less productive than large-scale farming on a cost basis, but more productive on a per hectare and a social basis. Additionally it renders important communal services and its environmental impact is much more sustainable, he argues.[81] A legitimate land transaction to the benefit of everybody involved essentially cannot happen from this viewpoint. Land deals are regarded as zero sum games that threaten food security in target countries.

Yet, this food security *is* already threatened. Many of the target countries are major recipients of WFP food aid. Subsistence farming is inherently unstable, often grapples with low productivity, and has problems in coping with exposure to sudden impacts like droughts. In a crisis, subsistence farming cannot feed its own people, not to mention the sprawling cities in developing countries. The question about alternatives often appears as a vague blank among advocacy groups, which tend to romanticize rural life. International institutions on the other hand are wont to underestimate the role of unequal development and the social dimension of land transactions. They are anxious to reflect a consensus of their constituting member countries. This was also apparent in the delayed publication of the World Bank land acquisition report and the political haggling behind the scenes about its contents.[82]

---

[77] FAO 2012b.
[78] For a discussion of FPIC see Cotula et al. 2009: 70f.
[79] Cotula and Leonard 2010; Vermeulen and Cotula 2010; Cotula 2010.
[80] FIAN International Secretariat 2010; Via Campesina, GRAIN et al. 2011.
[81] Schutter 2010b; UN Human Rights Council 2010.
[82] *Financial Times*, 27 July 2010; GRAIN 2010b.

5.4 CONCLUSION

The steep rise in announced international agro-investments since the global food crisis of 2008 has happened against the backdrop of a paradigm shift in food prices. Land expansion concentrates on Africa and Latin America and on countries that lack tenure security. Customary land rights and domestic food security interests are threatened. Whether there is room for mutually beneficial investments is a contested issue between investors, international organizations, and advocacy groups. They are only conceivable if a number of principles are adhered to that World Bank, FAO, UNCTAD, and IFAD have laid out in their RAI code of conduct. Yet, by their own admission, these principles have been disregarded on most of the projects where farming has started. Project implementation has lagged behind announcements so far, but conflicts about land tenure can be expected if more of these projects are realized. Earlier trends of international agro-investments focused on tropical cash crops by food processing TNCs. The new trend also comprises staple foods and biofuels. States with food security concerns in the Middle East and Asia and financial investors have appeared as new participants. With all these differences there are some striking similarities between today's agro-investments by Gulf countries and their Sudan bread-basket strategy in the 1970s. The latter failed for reasons of governance, lacking infrastructure, and global market developments. Yet, it informs today's endeavors by Gulf countries and functions as a precursor to them.

6

The Sudan Bread-Basket Dream

6.1 SURPLUS, STATEHOOD, AND DEVELOPMENT

"Sudan has a lot of potential and will always have." The exasperated quip by an FAO executive points to the great hopes that have been pinned on Sudan as a source of Middle East food security. With its huge land mass and irrigation potential, it has occupied the fantasies of pan-Arab development planners. The Arab League established the Arab Organization for Agricultural Development (AOAD) in Khartoum in 1970. In an article in 1976, John Waterbury quoted contemporary voices that compared Sudan to Brazil and the US west of the Mississippi—a mythical Arab new frontier for a region that became increasingly reliant on food imports in the 1970s.[1] The plan to develop Sudan into an Arab bread-basket did not materialize, yet this ambition is alive and well. It has been resuscitated in the wake of the global food crisis of 2008 when Gulf countries announced agro-investments in the country on a large scale. Ever cash starved, Sudanese politicians knew how to nourish such hopes. At an OAU summit in Libya in 2009, President Al-Bashir boasted that his food aid dependent country "is in a position to make a big contribution to . . . food security in Africa."[2] According to former Minister of Agriculture Abdullah Ahmed Abdullah, Sudan is even "one of three countries that can feed the world,"[3] and the Director General of the AOAD stated, "The whole Arab World's needs of cereal, sugar, fodder, and other essential foodstuffs could be met by Sudan alone."[4]

Now as then the northern elites of Sudan have used agricultural modernization to ensure regime survival, reward cronies, and attract foreign capital. Expansion of mechanized rain-fed farming in the 1970s and the dam program of the 2000s deeply affected customary land rights and led to resistance against the central government. Gulf countries' engagement in the 1970s remained behind expectations and they were hardly central to the plight of Sudanese agriculture. Still, their contribution to misguided agricultural policies and their

[1] Waterbury 1976a: 7.   [2] *Sudan Tribune*, 1 July 2009.
[3] Verhoeven 2012a.   [4] *Emirates Business 24/7*, 4 February 2009.

socio-ecological fall-out carries important implication for their investment initiatives today.

The Nile dominates Sudan's geography, a northern establishment its political system (see Map 6.1). Both factors have been a crucial backdrop for economic development and political conflict since the nineteenth century. Economic surplus is a prerequisite for statehood. In pre-colonial times, both were limited. The Funj Kingdom around Sennar in the east and the Sultanate of Darfur in the west relied on commerce along trade routes and exploitation of hinterlands. Slave trading was the linchpin of their political economy. Sudan was a periphery in comparison to Egypt and had a sparsely populated land mass. Nomadism, livestock breeding, and subsistence agriculture were prevalent. Weak statehood, low population density, and lack of economic centralization have resulted in a diverse ethnic segmentation of the populace.[5]

The Turkiyya

Egyptian ruler Muhammad Ali was on a quest for surplus when he invaded Sudan in 1821. He was not only after the slave, gold, and ivory trade of the Sudanese kingdoms, he wanted to push as far as he could to the sources of the Nile on which his ambitious development plans relied. Engineers of the Napoleonic mission to Egypt had spun the idea of all-year cultivation with the help of canals and irrigation, as a base for a centralized, powerful Egypt that could reconnect with its glorious past. Muhammad Ali pursued this vision ruthlessly during his reign (1805–48).[6] His ambition to become an international power in the Middle East needed armies and armies needed money. This money was to come from agriculture, the cotton trade, and rudimentary attempts at import substitution in arms and textiles. The state presided over the economy, owned the land, centralized irrigation, and exploited indentured labor and slaves. Muhammad Ali managed to increase agricultural production in Egypt at high human cost.

The reign of Egyptian rulers in Sudan, the Turkiyya, lasted until 1885. Although large irrigation projects like in Egypt were not undertaken, an agricultural mission and the traditional slave trade were combined in a painful mix. The state heavily taxed agricultural land along the Nile and imposed a tribute in the form of slaves. Thus, not only did the government undertake slave raids in the non-Muslim territories to the south, it also

---

[5] Waterbury 1976a: 2–5. For a map of Sudan's ethnic and linguistic segmentation see <http://gulf2000.columbia.edu/images/maps/Sudan_Ethnic_Linguistic_sm.jpg> (accessed 10 January 2010).

[6] Verhoeven 2012b: chapter 2.

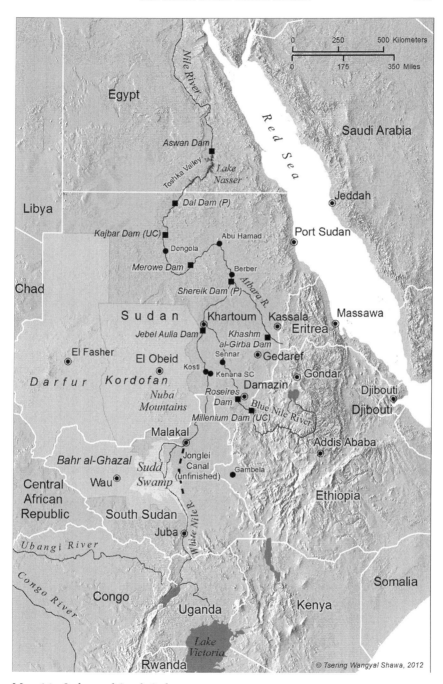

Map 6.1. Sudan and South Sudan

(P) = Planned
(UC) = Under Construction

encouraged such raids by tribes in the north and center, so they could pay for their tributes.[7] Khartoum superseded the old kingdoms as the new power center. Exploitation of the south and west and core–periphery relationships with racial and religious undertones have been characteristic of political conflict in Sudan ever since. The Turkiyya promoted centralization of production. A landed class developed in central Sudan and the Blue Nile province, albeit never on any scale like in Egypt, Syria, and Iraq during the nineteenth and early twentieth centuries. Otherwise, private landownership only existed along the Nile, where the inheritance rules of Sharia law led to highly fragmented holdings.[8] Beyond the riverain areas, collective utilization of land and tribal control prevailed.

British Rule

When the British came to power in Sudan after the intermezzo of Mahdi rule (1885–98), they inherited a system that managed its relations with the peripheries via patronage arrangements and punitive raids, and relied on riverain elites, agricultural taxation, and slave trading. While the British abolished the slave trade, they tried to expand agricultural production to pay for the administration of the country. Another factor was the increased competition that the British textile industry faced from the US, Germany, and even China. Increasingly pushed into the upper segments of the market, it needed fine, long-staple cotton, not the coarser short-staple varieties that prevailed in America and Asia. Lancashire needed a second supply source beside Egypt. Discussions to develop Sudan to this end started before World War I and the ambitious Gezira scheme south of Khartoum was launched in 1925.[9] It was a triple partnership of the state, the tenants, and two private management companies. It saw extensions in 1931 and 1937, developed into a major earner of foreign exchange, and attracted large armies of seasonal workers, bringing them into an expanding monetary economy. The British also encouraged private pumping schemes that were run by the elites of the two powerful religious sects, the Ansar and Khatmiyya. Sudan became one of the largest cotton producers in the world by 1930.[10] It already dominated the global market for gum arabic in 1904 with 70 percent.[11]

---

[7] Johnson 2003: 5.

[8] For the transformation from the matrilineal forms of inheritance and the feudal relations of land tenure of Christian Nubia see Awad 1971: 215.

[9] Barnett 1977: 5.

[10] Verhoeven 2011a, 2012b.

[11] Tignor 1987: 186.

Independence and the Nimeiri Regime

After independence in 1956, the new Sudanese government was keen to expand surplus generation and tax collection. The Gezira scheme fell to the Sudanese state after the expiration of the initial license in 1950. New irrigation projects like Managil, New Halfa, and Rahad were modeled after Gezira in the 1960s and 1970s.[12] Large-scale irrigation increased from 1.17 million ha in 1956 to more than 1.68 million ha in 1977.[13] Yet, increased mechanization and application of fertilizers and pesticides surprisingly did not lead to a growth in productivity. Production gains were only achieved by intensified land use and shortened fallow periods.[14] On average, 70 percent of Sudan's export earnings came from cotton, followed by gum arabic and groundnuts as distant seconds. Not surprisingly, the Sudanese state regarded control of the irrigation schemes as strategically important. They were major sources of revenue alongside the railways, the sugar monopoly, import tariffs, and export royalties.[15]

Export earnings did not keep pace with rising imports and unfavorable terms of trade. In the 1960s, an early easy phase of import substitution ended and the agricultural sector was in crisis. Critically short of capital, Sudan had to revert to standby credits of the IMF in 1966 and 1967. After a short flirtation with nationalizations and state-led socialism (1969–71), the Nimeiri regime (1969–85) made an about turn. It embarked on a conscious effort to attract foreign capital and increase exports. Sudanese land and natural resources were to be merged with Arab capital and Western expertise. The Development Act of 1972 and the Encouragement of Development Act of 1974 granted privileges like repatriation of profits after taxes and tariff protection against foreign imports. During a transition period from 1972–6 businesses were reprivatized and the state's role changed from direct interference to facilitation and infrastructure provision. The socialist rhetoric was kept, while trade unions and civil society organizations were crushed. In 1976, certain export and import monopolies were abolished and agricultural concessions were offered to foreign investors. This open door policy intensified until 1983.[16]

The Role of Mechanized Rain-Fed Farming

There have been four waves of agricultural modernization in Sudan. During colonial times and after independence irrigated agriculture and cash crops

---

[12] Wallach 1988; Davies 1991b: 344; Jansen and Koch 1982. For an overview of projects see: <http://www.worldbank.org/projects/search?lang=en&searchTerm=&countryshortname_exact=Sudan&src=> (accessed 15 April 2012).

[13] FAO 2005.   [14] O'Brien 1981.

[15] Waterbury 1976a: 20.   [16] Elnur 2009: chapter 3.

prevailed. The focus changed to mechanized agriculture in rain-fed areas and cereal cultivation in the late 1960s and 1970s. The 1980s saw a program of rehabilitation of the irrigated sector. Neglect of traditional forms of agriculture like pastoralism and shifting cultivation was a common denominator during all of these periods.[17] While irrigated cropland stagnated in the 1970s, the area used for traditional agriculture doubled by the mid-1980s and mechanized agriculture in rain-fed areas even increased fourfold.[18] Yet, irrigated agriculture continued to supply the majority of production and export revenues. At the end of the 1970s, the Gezira scheme alone produced 60 percent of Sudan's cotton, 75 percent of its wheat, and 35 percent of its groundnuts on merely 11 percent of the country's cultivated area. Only sorghum, Sudan's staple food, was predominantly produced in the rain-fed areas.[19]

Mechanized rain-fed agriculture in Sudan started in the 1940s in Gedaref close to Ethiopia, where the British produced sorghum to supply their troops.[20] By 1953, the government reduced its share in projects and began to lease out plots at nominal rates.[21] The focus of the private sector was still on the irrigated sector at that time. Apart from the large state-owned irrigation schemes, a nascent agrarian bourgeoisie invested in private pumping schemes in order to profit from the cotton boom in the wake of the Korean War. Only by the end of the 1960s did the investment preference move to the rain-fed sector. The Mechanized Farming Corporation was set up in 1968 in order to encourage private investments in large-scale farming. At the same time, the private pumping schemes were nationalized on generous reimbursement terms. This provided the private sector with capital to expand commercial farming in the rain-fed areas.[22] The hiatus of the Sudanese civil war (1955–72 and 1983–2005) and the improved political stability that came with it provided additional impetus.

With the Unregistered Land Act in 1970, the state declared formal ownership of unregistered tribal land outside the riverain areas and licensed large mechanized projects. Most of the tenants came from the cities and had no further attachment to the land; about 80 percent were urban merchants and the rest were mostly civil servants and military pensioners.[23] There was considerable concentration of project ownership; by 1985, just 4,000 investors who often lacked agricultural experience ran 40 percent of the cropped rainland. Most of the credits of the Agricultural Bank of Sudan went to large-scale projects. Only 0.5 percent went to small-scale farmers, who had to rely on the usury interest rates of informal moneylenders, the *shail* system.[24]

---

[17] Wohlmuth 1991: 442.   [18] Davies 1991a: 309.
[19] Kontos 1990: 652.   [20] Adam, Mohamed, and Hassan 1983: 57.
[21] Niblock 1987: 36–40.   [22] O'Brien 1983a: 19, 1981.   [23] O'Brien 1981: 25.
[24] Wohlmuth 1991: 438, 445; Davies 1991a: 315–19; Hansohm 1991: 119; Elnur 2009: 55.

Agricultural policies combined the worst of two worlds. The Soviet-inspired Five Year Plan 1970/1–1974/5 took a top-down approach, while the incentive structure for the private operators of the projects led to soil mining. With land relatively abundant but capital and labor scarce, the rational response of tenants was not to invest, but to get the maximum out of the soil and then move on. Relatively short lease periods of 25 years and lack of tenure security on illegal, undemarcated developments further motivated this quick money approach. Regulations to limit soil erosion by leaving 10 percent of the land to wind-breaking shelterbelts existed, but were not enforced and not heeded by most farmers.[25] Provision of extension services did not keep pace with expansion of cultivation and their quality was found wanting.[26] The environment deteriorated and agricultural productivity usually fell below profitable yields after five to seven years, but as long as new land was found at cheap lease rates business stayed good.[27]

Wastelands were produced on a continuous basis; mechanized farming was in fact "mechanized desertification."[28] It mainly expanded in the wetter zones in the south of central Sudan that had been difficult to clear with traditional farming methods. Insofar as it spread out to the sandy soils of the western part of the country, it proved particularly disastrous. The land was not suitable for this kind of agriculture and the erosion was reminiscent of the dust bowls that haunted the Mid-West of the US in the 1930s.[29]

Expansion of mechanized rain-fed agriculture in central Sudan was at the heart of the bread-basket strategy. Sorghum exports were to finance the import of wheat, which had become increasingly popular with city dwellers. This was accomplished during most years until the early 1980s, when the cereal foreign trade position showed a slight surplus.[30] Sorghum dominated rain-fed acreage at 80 percent and was particularly attractive because it was unregulated, unlike cotton, wheat, and groundnuts. As staple food, it was also used as in-kind payment for seasonal workers.[31]

Rain-fed areas were regarded as "empty land," but many of them were not. Pastoralists and shifting cultivators dwelt on them. Formal landownership of the state in the rain-fed areas has had a fragile coexistence with customary land rights and mechanized farms that were set up illegally in undemarcated

---

[25] Elnagheeb and Bromley 1992.

[26] After early beginnings on the Gezira scheme, a national extension service was established in 1958 with US funding and modeled after the US Land Grant College system. It largely relied on intermittent foreign funds and was understaffed. Politicians only paid lip service to its importance while its reputation among students and prospective employees was low. Doran 1980.

[27] Waterbury 1976b: 13; Elnagheeb and Bromley 1992; Oesterdiekhoff and Wohlmuth 1983a: 46; O'Brien 1981: 25.

[28] Catterson et al. 2003: 18.

[29] Oesterdiekhoff and Wohlmuth 1983a: 46, 48.   [30] Davies 1991a: 312ff.

[31] Kontos 1990: 654; Simpson and Simpson 1991: 262.

areas. Confusion about land tenure was exacerbated by competition between different ministries and ambiguity of responsibilities between local, regional, and national levels of government.[32]

Mechanized farming increasingly collided with customary land rights, as it expanded from 2 million ha in 1968 to 10.3 million ha in 2010.[33] Nomads lost grazing grounds and their migratory routes were cut by this expansion. Traditional shifting cultivation faced encroachment and shortened fallow periods. Deforestation not only caused erosion and declining soil fertility, it also compromised firewood collection and income generation via gum arabic production. Gum arabic was an important earner of foreign exchange before the advent of oil production in the late 1990s. Its decline affected the ability to import fuel. As a result, alternative charcoal consumption grew and added even greater pressure on forest cover.[34]

The impact of modern agriculture in Sudan has thus been varied. In the northeast and the center, irrigated and mechanized schemes have provided employment for a large army of seasonal laborers from western regions like South Kordofan. They caused ecological damage, but also added to livelihood options.[35] However, by the 1980s the poorly regulated expansion of mechanized farming led to growing disenfranchisement of customary land rights' holders. Their vulnerability to famine increased ahead of the drought of 1984–5.

Mechanized Farming and Political Conflict

Above all, mechanized farming was a political project of undermining local control over resources in the countryside and redirecting them towards export-oriented agriculture. It expanded most in opposition strongholds like the Blue Nile province. Nimeiri hoped to co-opt or break the old elite networks

---

[32] Elnagheeb and Bromley 1992: 361.

[33] Coalition for International Justice (CIJ) 2006: 53.

[34] Elnagheeb and Bromley 1992: 361. Oil in Sudan was discovered in the later 1970s. Because of the renewed eruption of civil war, foreign oil companies, mainly from the US and the UK, left in 1984. Production only kicked in in earnest at the end of the 1990s, this time under the leadership of Chinese oil companies.

[35] Jay O'Brien sees the emergence of a national labor market and corresponding remittances as instrumental in cushioning the impact of the Sahel drought from 1968 to 1973. O'Brien 1985: 26. As far as Darfur is concerned Alex de Waal disagrees. He argues that for seasonal labor migration Darfur was too far away from the rain-fed projects in Gedaref. Remittances were at best sporadic. Yet, he sees a fallback option in the form of the few commercial farming operations in Darfur itself. In the post-war decades, they were set up on virgin land and did not collide with traditional agriculture. Rather than increasing vulnerability to famine, the advent of seasonal wage labor provided small-scale farmers with an alternative income in case of crop failure from the 1950s to the 1970s. De Waal 2005: 69f.

of the Khatmiyya and Ansars and their control over the peripheries.[36] The state used formal ownership of land outside the riverain areas to reward cronies. Concomitant to the Unregistered Land Act of 1970 the government asserted its authority over peripheral regions by abolishing the Native Administration in the northern provinces that had been in place since the days of the British as a system of relatively loose indirect rule. Province councils that were dominated by merchants and bureaucrats from the riverain center replaced it.[37] Later in the 1980s, weak local governments were set up that relied on the central government for their budgets and lacked administrative autonomy. The modernist infatuation with large-scale projects was part of a strategy to build a new middle class of administrators and entrepreneurs loyal to the regime. The National Islamic Front (NIF) and its leader Hassan al-Turabi carried the logic of subjugation of the periphery to its extreme after it came to power in a joint coup with military officers under Omar al-Bashir in 1989. The Civil Transactions Act of 1990 explicitly forbade recognition of customary land rights by courts throughout the country. Mechanized farming dovetailed again with the political agenda. When the NIF launched jihad campaigns in the Nuba Mountains in 1992, brutal resettlements were used to break restive communities and empty the land for mechanized farming operations. Similar developments occurred in the provinces of southern Blue Nile, northern Upper Nile, and northern Bahr al-Ghazal.[38]

Violent conflict in Sudan has often been explained in religious and ethnic terms while socio-economic factors have been neglected.[39] The systematic underdevelopment of the south and the privileges of the riverain elites in the north formed an important backdrop of the Sudanese civil war. For a long time the equally underdeveloped west showed an inclination to opt in rather than opt out. It supported the Mahdi's army at the end of the nineteenth century, and rural migrants from the west formed an important base of the NIF in Khartoum and Omdurman when it came to power in 1989. Al-Turabi would try again to gather support from the western regions after his power struggle with Al-Bashir in 1999. Yet, by the 2000s violent conflict erupted in Darfur like in the South before. The systematic overrepresentation of northerners in crucial positions was among the grievances, as a popular clandestine publication, the Black Book pamphlet (*al-kitab al-aswad*), pointed out.[40]

Drought and climate change have also taken their toll on Sudanese agriculture. Desertification and increased conflicts between herdsmen and farmers

---

[36] Verhoeven 2012a, 2011b: 10.   [37] Johnson 2003: 130.

[38] Coalition for International Justice (CIJ) 2006: 50f; Keen 1994: 94; Verhoeven 2012b: chapter 7.

[39] For example Voll and Voll 1985.

[40] Justice and Equality Movement (JEM) May 2000 and August 2002; El-Tom 2003; Cobham 2005.

formed an important backdrop of the Darfur conflict. "Failed nomads" were an ample recruiting ground for militias that the regime used to fight opposition forces with a strategy of "counterinsurgency on the cheap" as Alex de Waal and Julie Flint put it.[41] Still, it would be misplaced to see the Darfur conflict in crude Malthusian terms as an inevitable struggle over scarce resources. Like ethnic and religious differences, the ruling elites have used the scarcity argument to divert attention from their politics of power preservation, land allocation to preferred clients, and under-development of disadvantaged regions. Alternative outcomes would have been possible. The environment is not an independent variable that exists apart from political and social relations. They quintessentially shape it.[42]

Agricultural expansion in Sudan since Nimeiri has thus generated lots of conflict but little surplus. Migrant remittances from the Gulf countries became Sudan's main source of foreign exchange by the 1980s. Livestock replaced cotton as the most important export good, with Saudi Arabia taking 80–90 percent of all Sudanese sheep exports. Sorghum production remained stagnant over the 1990s. Wheat production sank.[43] The state shrank and was privatized at an accelerated rate to satisfy clientele networks.

The foreign policy blunders of the NIF severely hampered external rent acquisition. It sided with Iraq during the Kuwait occupation, hosted Osama bin Laden, and was involved in the assassination attempt on Egyptian President Mubarak while he was on a state visit to Ethiopia in 1995. Gulf countries, the West, and international institutions dramatically reduced their development commitments. Financial inflows by Islamist groups were no match for this loss. The start of Sudan's own oil production in 1999 gave the regime a new lease on life. However, three-quarters of the oil production is in the south and not available anymore with the partition of the country in 2011. The north's benefit henceforth mainly consists of the transit fees of the pipeline to Port Sudan, but the pipeline was shut down in 2012 after north and south could not agree on the costs of transit and renewed violence erupted between them. Hence, surplus will need to come again from agriculture. The regime has realized this early. It has launched a dam program in the 2000s and has called for an "agricultural revival" (*al-nahda al-zira'iyya*).[44] The parallels with the 1970s are striking. In both cases, the regime tried to attract Gulf capital for agricultural investments against the backdrop of tight budgets and a global food crisis.

---

[41] Flint and De Waal 2005: 24, 46. See also Johnson 2003; Prunier 2007: 47.

[42] Verhoeven 2011b.

[43] Elnur 2009: 62; Coalition for International Justice (CIJ) 2006: 70f.; Keen and Lee 2007: S13.

[44] Government of Sudan 2008. The official translation is "revival," although at times "renaissance" is used as well, which carries great symbolic value with its allusion to the nineteenth-century *nahda* in the Arab world.

6.2 THE GULF AND THE SUDAN BREAD-BASKET VISION

The bread-basket strategy was formulated in three major documents: The Six Year Plan of Economic and Social Development (1977/8–1982/3) (SYP), the Food Investment Strategy (FIS) of the Ministry of Agriculture (1977), and the "Basic Programme for Agricultural Development 1976–1985" by the Kuwait-based Arab Fund for Economic and Social Development (AFESD).[45] All of them shared the assumption that there were vast swathes of idle land in Sudan that could be put into production economically without causing social disruption and environmental damage. An often quoted number was 200 million acres of arable land of which only 15 million acres were supposedly cultivated. All the three documents focused on the modern irrigated sector and mechanized rain-fed farming. They did not consider traditional agriculture, which an ILO report at that time had identified for parallel expansion and possible complementarities with the modern sectors.[46] As rationale for the Basic Programme the AFESD gave the rising Arab food gap, which could be "exploited" and "threaten the freedom of Arab decision-making."[47]

Both Sudanese programs drew heavily on the comprehensive approach of the AFESD. The pan-Arab fund dispatched a mission to Sudan in 1974, to conduct a field study of the country's agricultural potential. It came up with a detailed ten-year development plan that partly followed earlier recommendations of an FAO delegation in 1973. It envisaged the investment of $5.5 billion over the period 1976–85.[48] More than half of the funding was to come from foreign loans and grants arranged by AFESD. The proposal envisaged the establishment of an authority based in Khartoum that would administer the funds and would guarantee adequate returns. The organization was to be shielded from Sudanese sovereign decision-making by guarantees against nationalization and rights for tax-free repatriation of profits. The summit of the Ministers of Finance of the Arab League in Rabat decided in 1976 to create the Arab Authority for Agricultural Investment and Development (AAAID). However, pledges by Arab governments were only about a tenth of the initial AFESD proposal.

The fund allocation of the AFESD proposal had geographical preferences that are telling about the agricultural potential of different regions, divergences in infrastructure development, and political preferences in Sudan. The north and east of the country were to receive 60 percent of the funds, the west 24 percent, and the south only 16 percent.[49] The northern dominance that the Black Book would later deplore was discernible. The south was also wary

---

[45] Oesterdiekhoff and Wohlmuth 1983a: 44–8.   [46] ILO and UNDP 1976.
[47] Spiro 1989: 494.
[48] Waterbury 1976b: 8. For a different estimate of $6.6 billion see Kaikati 1980: 100.
[49] Waterbury 1976b: 9.

about Sudanese policies towards Arab integration.[50] It feared that an influx of Arab investors and possibly Egyptian settlers could be to its detriment. The Jonglei Canal project faced resistance for these reasons. It would have reduced evaporation in the southern *sudd* swamps and increased flow to the north. Work started in 1978, but was aborted after the renewed outbreak of civil war in 1983.[51]

However, the investment case for the northeast was not mere political preference; it was also backed by hard economic facts. The northeast has rich alluvial soils of fine heavy clay that are particularly suited for irrigation. Yields on irrigated land in Sudan have been on average four to five times higher than in rain-fed agriculture. The triangle south of Khartoum that is formed by the junction of the Blue and White Nile is home to Sudan's large irrigation schemes. Three-quarters of its wheat and half of its rice were cultivated in this area. The proximity to Port Sudan and relatively good railway connections were another plus for foreign investors with export interests in mind.

In contrast, nomadism and semi-sedentary subsistence farming have characterized the west. The importance of livestock as a social status symbol, savings instrument, and currency for dowry payments encouraged large herds over commercial optimization. Only a relatively small share of each herd was slaughtered or sold each year and exports to Khartoum were hampered by insufficient transport connections. Due to population growth, traditional pastoralism outstripped carrying capacity and overgrazing developed into a major problem by the 1970s, especially in north Darfur. South Sudan on the other hand struggled with producing enough for subsistence, not to mention exporting surplus. Marred by poorer soils, the repercussions of the civil war, bad infrastructure, and the tsetse fly, production was low.

The AFESD plan envisaged that Sudan would be able to supply 42 percent of the Arab world's imports in edible oils by 1985, 20 percent of its sugar, and 15 percent of its wheat.[52] Planned production growth ranged between 100 and 150 percent; for wheat it was even 470 percent and for sugar 640 percent. Exports of oilseeds would double. Meat and fish exports were to increase tenfold, sorghum and millet exports eightfold. Sudan would turn from an importer of sugar and wheat into a substantial exporter. Cotton exports would remain more or less unchanged. The plan was to reduce reliance on cotton and shift acreage to cereals.[53] The real take-off of wheat production was planned for the time after 1985, with an increase from 1.2 million tons to 8.8 million tons by 2000. Together with the self-sufficiency programs in Libya and Saudi

---

[50] Ottaway 1987: 902.　　[51] Waterbury 1976b: 26; Howell, Lock, and Cobb 1988: 3.
[52] Elnur 2009: 46.　　[53] AFESD 1976: 21; Government of Sudan 1977: 9.

Arabia that were expected to mature in 1983 and 1990 respectively, the Arab project of food independence seemed within reach.[54]

Visions of Economic Union with Sudan: Saudi Arabia vs. Egypt

Optimism about Sudan's agricultural potential was high in the 1970s, regardless of poor infrastructure, shortcomings in the labor force, and rampant corruption. In a conversation with the US ambassador, Saudi Minister of State for Planning Hisham Nazer claimed in 1974 that Saudi Arabia was planning for an "economic union" with Egypt and Sudan. Such a union would be an ideal combination of Egyptian labor, Sudanese land, and Saudi capital, he hoped. He argued that the development of Sudan as a bread-basket would be much better than laborious experiments in Saudi Arabia on infertile land. A Red Sea economic union would be also more advantageous than integration with other countries in the Gulf or with Jordan. US embassy personnel suspected that the idea of such a Red Sea economic union was a "private project" of the minister that may or may not have been backed by Egyptian and Sudanese partners. They also speculated that Nazer's origin from the Hejaz and the proximity of this region to the Red Sea might have informed his stance in this question. The project could not be verified by other Saudi sources and the security adviser of the Saudi king ridiculed it.[55]

Yet, Nazer was not the only one harboring the idea of a Red Sea economic union. The Sudanese Prime Minister Abdullah Bey Khalil had proposed a variant of it to King Saud in 1957 already. The relationship between Saudi Arabia and Egypt was deteriorating at that time and King Saud had visited Ethiopia shortly before. Against this backdrop the Sudanese prime minister proposed a close association of Sudan and Saudi Arabia, this time with Ethiopia as a third party. However, King Saud made no promises and only showed polite interest.[56]

The Gulf countries were not alone in their interest in Sudan in the 1970s. Egypt looked at the agricultural potential of Sudan, Iraq, and Morocco to import cereals, sugar, and meat from there. Population growth in Egypt had outstripped its agricultural resource base and it was worried about its rising food gap.[57] Egypt's longstanding ties with Sudan go back to the Turkiyya (1821–85). During the Anglo-Egyptian Condominium over Sudan (1899–1955) Egyptian influence was in name only. Yet, the idea of a "unity of the

---

[54] Kiss 1977: 43f.

[55] Jeddah to State, 10 January 1974, Nixon Library, National Security Council (NSC) Files, Box 631, Saudi Arabia Vol. V January 1974–April 1974.

[56] Addis Ababa to State, 26 July 1957 and Khartoum to State, 15 August 1957, USRSA, Vol. 5, 336f.

[57] Waterbury 1983: 415.

Nile valley" loomed large in Egyptian and Sudanese struggles for decolonization. Sudanese independence in 1956 thwarted such hopes, but they resurfaced
in the 1970s.[58]

The Federation of Arab Republics (FAR) was a project of the late Nasser era
that aimed to unite Libya, Egypt, Sudan, and Syria at various stages. Consensus
about the details of a merger was never achieved and Sudan dropped out in
1971. Sudanese membership in the FAR would have endangered a peace
settlement in the south, which was Nimeiri's priority at that time.[59] Yet,
Sudanese–Egyptian rapprochement picked up again. Sadat pinned his hopes
on a friendly Sudan as a potential bread-basket for Egypt and an outlet for its
rapidly growing population.[60] He and Nimeiri signed the "Programs for
Political Action and Economic Integration" in February 1974. One year later
three joint ventures were founded: the Egypto-Sudanese Company for Agricultural Integration, the Egypto-Sudanese Company for Irrigation and Construction, and the Nile Valley Authority for River Navigation. The Jonglei
Canal which had been contemplated since the 1930s was pushed forward in
order to increase available water for future irrigation projects. In the Damazin
area south of Roseires it was planned to cultivate one million feddans with oil
seeds, cattle, and fodder by 1985.[61]

The competition with projects of Gulf countries was obvious. Egypt was at a
clear disadvantage. Like Sudan, it was lacking surplus and foreign exchange.
As a remedy, barter deals were proposed. A large Egyptian ministerial delegation traveled to Khartoum in May 1977 to activate projects that had been
approved in principle. In October 1977, bilateral parliamentary meetings were
held at the "conference of the Nile Valley people."[62] Border controls and trade
movements were eased, but implementation remained spotty. Egypt lacked
the capital to bring the envisaged projects to life.

6.3 GULF CAPITAL BUYING IN

Apart from official institutions like the AFESD and AAAID, there were private
and semi-private capital-holders from the Gulf investing in Sudanese agriculture. An early driving force of Gulf investments in Sudan was Khalil Osman, a
Sudanese national who had made his fortune in Kuwait. A veterinarian by

---

[58] Waterbury 1979: chapter 2.

[59] Bechtold 1973. Formally the FAR ended in 1977, at that time it comprised Egypt and Syria.

[60] Testimony of George Henry Mayer Schuler before the Special Committee to Investigate
Individuals Representing the Interests of Foreign Governments, Washington, DC, 4 August
1980, 24f., Carter Library, NLC-21-39-1-3-2.

[61] Waterbury 1979: 59–62.

[62] *Middle East News Economic Weekly*, 10 February 1979.

profession, he had earned the confidence of the ruling family after saving one of the royal cows.[63] With some initial loans, he built up the world's largest shrimping fleet at that time, which exported from the Gulf to overseas markets. Thereafter he ventured into a vast array of business activities ranging from textiles, paints, and pharmaceuticals to hotels and matches. His 45 companies were scattered all over the globe and bundled under the conglomerate of Gulf International (GI). He owned 25 percent of the company, the Kuwaiti royal and Minister of Foreign Affairs, Sheikh Sabah al-Ahmad al-Jaber, held the remaining 75 percent. Sudan developed into a focus of activity for GI. By 1975 Khalil Osman had established close relationships with President Nimeiri and commanded ten companies in various sectors, among them insecticide manufacturing and crop spraying services. With the spirit of the time, expectations were high. Khalil Osman saw Sudan "taking the American route" with imminent mass availability of Wimpy Burgers, blue jeans, and popcorn.[64]

Another large Kuwaiti investor was the 80 percent state-owned Kuwait Foreign Trading Contracting and Investment Co. (KFTCIC). It had an interest in cattle farming via the Sudanese–Kuwait Investment Co., a 50–50 joint venture with the Sudanese government. Given the Kuwaiti dominance, other Gulf investors faced challenges in breaking into the Sudanese market. The Saudi business mogul Adnan Khashoggi gained the trust of the impressionable Nimeiri with trips on his luxury yacht and by virtue of his Rolodex of international A-list contacts. By circumventing due institutional process of Sudan's government bureaucracy, he arranged for a number of large loans at high interest rates that Sudan could ill afford. Among them was a $200 million Eurodollar loan with a guarantee from the Saudi Arabian Monetary Authority (SAMA), the largest single loan to a developing country ever made at that time.[65] For his company Triad Natural Resources, Khashoggi acquired a license for a $100 million cattle-breeding project in the Damazin area, but Triad never used the 500,000 feddans to which it had acquired the rights; neither did American Tenneco Inc., which had leased 250,000 feddans.[66]

A signature project of that time was the Kenana sugar plantation. It exemplified the vision of a triangular success story of Sudanese land, Arab capital, and Western expertise. To this day, it is advertised as an example to attract Gulf investors.[67] Kenana was the brainchild of R.W. "Tiny" Rowland, an illustrious and controversial entrepreneur personality. Of German origin and born in India he made his fortune in Rhodesia when he developed his

---

[63] Vicker 1975.

[64] Vicker 1975; Waterbury 1976b: 3; Hoagland 1975b.

[65] Collins 2008: 126; Waterbury 1976b: 3; Tignor 1987: 208; Hoagland 1975a.

[66] Waterbury 1976b; Kontos 1990.

[67] Government of Sudan 2010: 4f.; interview with AOAD executive, Muscat, 2 March 2010.

company Lonhro from humble origins in mining into a globally operating conglomerate.[68] His individualistic and forceful style impressed Arab business partners but also created enemies. British Prime Minister Edward Heath referred to Lonhro as "the unpleasant and unacceptable face of capitalism" when Rowland was embroiled in a High Court case in 1973 in which eight directors of Lonhro sought his dismissal based on his temper and allegations of financial misconduct.

By that time, GI subsidiary Gulf Fisheries held 22 percent of Lonrho. Beside Khalil Osman there were two Gulf Arabs on the board of the company: Sheikh Nasser Sabah al-Ahmad of Kuwait and Mohammed al-Fayed of the UAE. Apart from their other differences Rowland's enemies found this Arab connection inappropriate and his Sudanese sugar plans unwise. Kenana's design was massive. It aimed to turn Sudan from a sugar importer to an exporter. When Rowland first proposed it to President Nimeiri he argued that Sudan had the potential to "take over first place from Cuba" in global sugar production.[69] Implementation of the project started in 1975 close to Kosti on the White Nile, 270 kilometers southwest of Khartoum. Later it expanded from 80,000 feddans to 300,000 feddans. Financing came jointly from the Sudanese government and Gulf investors. Lonhro had the management contract and 12 percent of the company, but disgruntled Kuwaiti shareholders pushed it out in 1977 after cost overruns.[70] After restructurings and dilutions, the major shareholders of the company today are the Sudanese government (35 percent), the Kuwait Investment Authority (KIA) (31 percent), and the Saudi government (11 percent). The Riyadh-based Arab Investment Corporation (AIC) still holds 7 percent and the AAAID 6 percent, but Gulf Fisheries nowadays only has a minor stake of 0.16 percent and Lonhro none at all.[71]

While the ambitious AFESD bread-basket plan got stuck because of Arab infighting there was substantial disbursement of bilateral Arab aid. By far the largest donor between 1972 and 1979 was Saudi Arabia followed by Kuwait (see Table 6.1).[72] Help for Sudan was not restricted to Gulf countries, Western and international donors played a major role, too. The US regarded Nimeiri as a strategic asset who in turn needed its protection against external threats. His support of Egypt's peace process with Israel, a potential role of the OAU in intra-African conflict resolution (e.g. Horn of Africa, Chad, and Western

---

[68] The original name was London and Rhodesian Mining and Land Company.

[69] Waterbury 1976b: 4.   [70] Tignor 1987: 206.

[71] <http://www.kenana.com/pagecontents.aspx?pageid=7> (accessed 16 February 2012).

[72] An earlier assessment of the National Security Council estimated total Arab disbursements from 1974–7 at $375 million and thus lower than in Table 6.1. It ascribed most of Arab investments between 1974 and 1977 to Saudi Arabia, with UAE and Iraq as distant second and third. It did not rank Kuwait high at all. NSA: Staff Material, International Economics, "Sudan: Arab Largess [sic] Breeds Financial Problems," Secret, 2 November 1978, Carter Library, NLC-29-44-1-8-3.

Table 6.1. Net disbursement of economic aid to Sudan from major donors, 1972–9 (million US$)

	1972	1973	1974	1975	1976	1977	1978	1979
Arab states total	–	–	86	50	263	118	244	–
Bilateral	–	–	49	36	231	102	228	367
Of which Saudi Arabia	–	–	9	25	165	67	125	298
Of which Kuwait	–	–	–	7	22	13	88	63
Multilateral	–	–	37	14	32	16	16	–
Western states total	37	43	54	110	114	109	172	–
Bilateral	10	17	33	60	54	56	112	–
Multilateral (mainly IMF, WB, UN)	27	26	21	50	60	53	60	–

Source: Interagency Intelligence Memorandum, Sudan, "The Nimeiri Regime Under Pressure," Secret, 1 March 1980, 16, Carter Library, NLC-6-73-3-8-4.

Sahara), his conflict with Libya's Gaddafi, and the situation in Eritrea, which fought for independence from the USSR-backed Mengistu regime in Ethiopia, were common points of interest.[73]

Sudan's Balance of Payments Crisis

The large inflow of funds for infrastructure projects such as roads and ports paradoxically contributed to a balance of payments crisis that was in full swing due to Nimeiri's politically motivated project megalomania. Sudan usually had to match foreign aid and investment inflows. To acquire the foreign currency for its share, it borrowed from oil exporters and international donors. As a result foreign debt rose from $375 million in 1973 to $1.5 billion in 1978.[74] A growing budget deficit was largely covered by borrowing from domestic banks, which led to inflation and decreased competitiveness of exports. The share of domestic banks in financing increased from 12 percent in fiscal year 1975 to 83 percent in 1977.[75]

The increasing balance of payments problems worried Arab donors. Their contributions more than halved in 1977 as Table 6.1 shows. Iraq and Kuwait even withheld oil deliveries to Sudan to make their point, after Nimeiri failed

---

[73] "Memorandum for the President by Cyrus Vance re Visit of OAU chairman Nimeiri of Sudan," 18 September 1978, Carter Library, NLC-15-49-5-10-6.

[74] "Sudan: Arab Largess [*sic*] Breeds Financial Problems," Secret, Carter Library, NLC-29-44-1-8-3.

[75] "Sudan: Arab Largess [*sic*] Breeds Financial Problems," Secret, Carter Library, NLC-29-44-1-8-3 and Interagency Intelligence Memorandum, "Sudan: The Nimeiri Regime Under Pressure," Secret, 1 March 1980, 16, Carter Library, NLC-6-73-3-8-4. The practice of excessive domestic borrowing continued in the 1980s. Elnur 2009: 60.

to curb mounting arrears.[76] Arab pressure finally pushed Sudan to accept an IMF program in 1978. Apart from the usual austerity and devaluation measures, the program required a reduction of development expenditure and a reversal of the government's policy of agricultural import substitution. The preference for staple foods like wheat over export crops like cotton had to be abandoned. The IMF accord reopened the way for extensive commitments of bilateral and international assistance. Once again Saudi Arabia led the field with a share of about 60 percent, most of it for oil purchases on a soft loan basis and some balance of payments support.[77]

Camp David and Foreign Aid

Sudan lost sympathies in the Arab world when the Nimeiri government sided with Egypt in the wake of its peace process with Israel. This raised concerns about financial flows from the Gulf countries. A US intelligence report warned that threats to regime survival would come mainly from the economic side. It proposed that the US should help Sudan with food aid, as full shelves ahead of the lean summer months would beef up Nimeiri's legitimacy. However, it also stated that neither the US nor Egypt could meet all of Sudan's financial needs. Sudan would be almost completely dependent on an Arab "dole." In this situation, a common theme in Sudanese opposition circles was "that Sudan could be saved by the rich Arabs," if only Nimeiri's alliance with Sadat did not prevent such salvation.[78]

Yet, the effect of Camp David on Gulf flows to Sudan has been overstated. Gurdon speaks of a collapse of Arab funding to Sudan by 90 percent after 1978.[79] This is a correct interpretation as far as planned AAAID projects were concerned, but other aid continued to flow and the reasons for the reduced AAAID commitments were motivated by a lack of commercial viability and reduced geopolitical threat perception as much as Sudan's support of the Camp David accord. Opposition to Camp David by Saudi Arabia and other Gulf countries was to a certain extent superficial. Not all bridges were burnt. Gulf countries feared that a failure of Sadat could lead to a left turn of Egypt and renewed Saudi–Egyptian rivalry as in the 1960s. Labor migration from and private Gulf investments to Egypt continued; only aid payments and trade

---

[76] "Sudan: Arab Largess [*sic*] Breeds Financial Problems," Secret, Carter Library, NLC-29-44-1-8-3.

[77] "Sudan: Arab Largess [*sic*] Breeds Financial Problems," Secret, Carter Library, NLC-29-44-1-8-3.

[78] Interagency Intelligence Memorandum, "Sudan: The Nimeiri Regime Under Pressure," Secret, 1 March 1980, 13, Carter Library, NLC-6-73-3-8-4.

[79] Gurdon 1991: 156.

were cut.[80] Similarly, Gulf funds continued to flow into Sudan, just not into projects associated with the bread-basket strategy. Assistance focused on balance of payments support and on non-agricultural projects that were linked to IMF conditionality.[81] Inflows in 1979 were higher than in any year before as Table 6.1 shows and in the early 1980s Saudi business tycoon and arms trader Adnan Khashoggi flew into Khartoum on a regular basis, bringing in money for the Nimeiri regime. In doing so, he purportedly did not act solely on his own, but functioned as a conduit for Saudi royals.[82] The Sudanese government made a renewed push in 1982 and tried to lure foreign capital to the rain-fed areas specifically.[83] In its Strategy for Development of Rain-fed Agriculture of 1986, it reiterated the importance of this sector for achieving self-sufficiency and regional food security. However, at that time Gulf interest in Sudan agriculture had already faded.[84]

6.4 THE BASKET CASE

The bread-basket strategy of the 1970s failed. Between 1975 and 1985 over $2 billion of foreign investments were poured into the agricultural sector of Sudan, but still its farm productivity stagnated and export earnings declined over the same period. The anarchic free-for-all expansion of cultivated land in rain-fed areas victimized traditional agriculture, its productivity was low, and yields did not justify the high costs of fertilizer and other input factors. Government regulation and extension services were insufficient. Irrigated agriculture remained the mainstay of Sudanese agriculture despite the relative neglect in the 1970s at the expense of the rain-fed areas.[85]

The AAAID was conspicuously absent in Arab spending efforts of the 1970s, although it was at the heart of the initial AFESD bread-basket proposal.

---

[80] Carter Library NLC-15-68-11-10-8; Waterbury 1983: 417–20. For an overview of Arab aid payments to Egypt in the 1970s see Hussain 1982: 79–85.

[81] Spiro 1989: 505.

[82] Interview with David Spiro, Princeton, 20 October 2011. Yahia Abdel Mageed, Minister of Irrigation and Water Resources under Nimeiri, says that Khashoggi brought in "a lot of money that was not properly used" and that he "could not put the finger on a single project" that Khashoggi actually implemented in Sudan. He dates declines in Gulf aid to the last two years of Nimeiri's rule that ended in 1985, not to Camp David. Interview, Khartoum, 21 November 2011.

[83] Davies 1991a: 318f.

[84] Wohlmuth 1991: 437, 441.

[85] Kontos 1990. Ayoub attributes the lack of fertilizer application in the rain-fed areas less to economics than to insufficient knowledge. He argues that a more widespread application could be achieved by awareness and media campaigns. Ayoub 1999: 498. The regional Ministry of Agriculture in Gedaref argues that its recommendations for fertilizer usage are not followed because farmers lack the finance and are afraid that the investment is in vain in case rainfalls fail. Interviews, Gedaref, 23 November 2011.

It was established with the idea of contributing a large proportion of the financing of agricultural projects of the Sudanese Six Year Plan (SYP, 1977/8–1982/3). However, at its inception in 1976 it only received a tenth of the initially envisaged funding and was hampered by Arab infighting. A Three Year Plan (1978–81) with a more conservative spending profile replaced the ambitious SYP in the wake of the IMF accord of 1978. Gulf donors supported this change despite a disproportionately high reduction of spending for planned AAAID projects. Thus, the AAAID did not start to implement projects before 1980 and its scale was watered down from the earlier ambitious plans. There were internal problems resulting from Kuwaiti skepticism towards the bread-basket strategy and legitimacy problems of the Egyptian AAAID president in the wake of the Camp David accord. His controversial management style alienated Sudanese officials and Gulf donors alike. The latter became increasingly disillusioned with the corruption of the Nimeiri regime, which led to inefficient and costly implementation of projects.[86] The urge for the bread-basket strategy also diminished as the Arab oil boycott and the ensuing confrontation with Western states were short-lived and Saudi Arabia massively increased its wheat production.

Despite this botched start, the AAAID developed some modest impact. Contrary to its pan-Arab name, it has essentially been a vehicle to spend Gulf capital on agricultural projects in Sudan. About 65 percent of its paid-up capital has come from the Gulf, while 71 percent of all funded projects have been in Sudan. Iraq and Sudan each contributed another 15 percent of the capital.[87]

Compared to the magnitude of the food gap in the Arab world, the AAAID's Sudanese projects remained limited and had often only the character of pilot projects. They remained far behind the agricultural developments in the GCC countries themselves, most notably Saudi Arabia, where subsidized wheat production exploded. A decisive contribution to Gulf food security or that of Sudan was not achieved. In its strategic outlook and assessment of 2002, the AAAID itself admitted that "the implemented projects so far are not of the anticipated scale and strategic dimension."[88]

Large-scale commercial agriculture in Sudan fell on hard times even before the famine of 1984–5, when a combination of political turmoil, economic crisis, and adverse weather conditions took a grim toll on the country's

[86] Spiro 1989: chapter 11; Al-Sayyid 1994: 208f. Spiro mentions the Arab Investment Company, the Kuwait–Sudan Investment Company, and the Kenana Sugar Company as negative examples. The establishment of a regional AAAID office in Dubai was partly motivated by facilitating better commercial control of projects in Sudan. Interview with AAAID executive, Dubai, 11 March 2009. For corruption as an intrinsic part of Sudan's political economy under Nimeiri see Kameir and Kursany 1985.
[87] AAAID 2002.   [88] AAAID 2002.

development.[89] Yields steadily deteriorated by up to 50 percent from 1961–96.[90] A modest expansion of production of sorghum and millet by 14 percent was only achieved by horizontal expansion of cultivated area. At the same time harvests increasingly fluctuated from one year to another. Variability of rainfalls grew, while their overall level declined.[91] Expansion of mechanized agriculture rested on the assumption that the relatively ample rainfalls of the 1950s and 1960s were the norm, but they were not. Instead, the Sahel has witnessed increased occurrence of droughts since the mid-1960s. The capacity of soils to absorb and retain moisture declined and possibly reinforced droughts.

Explaining the Failure: Macro-Developments

Jay O'Brien traces the failure of the bread-basket strategy back to the 1960s and Sudan's specific development model. Sudan was relatively unaffected by the Sahelian drought of 1968–73. O'Brien attributes this to its prevalent mode of accumulation at that time, which was peculiar in comparison to other African countries. The recession in cotton prices in the late 1950s diverted attention of private business interests from the irrigated areas to rain-fed farming, which required less tie-up of fixed capital in expensive equipment. Expansion of mechanized farming in rain-fed areas in the 1960s was geared towards the domestic market. A famine would have been bad for business and the interests of the agrarian bourgeoisie. Ordinary peasants had supplemental seasonal wage labor and subsistence production to fall back on.[92]

This system faced a crisis by the 1980s. The expansion and soil mining of mechanized farming in the rain-fed areas increasingly collided with traditional small-scale farming and pastoralism. The existing land reserve was not able to accommodate both of them anymore. The coping strategies of the traditional rural population aggravated the economic and ecological crisis. Pushed into ever more marginal land, which they had to use in unsustainable ways, yields declined and the need for cash income rose.

Cooperation between farmers and pastoralists gave way to conflict over land. Where herds used to graze and fertilize the land with their manure, nomads now faced enclosures. Sustainable crop rotation with millet and multiple species herds were given up either to maximize profits in the case of commercial farming or to maintain badly needed food production in the case of subsistence farming. As more and more land was cleared, humidity and

---

[89] Kontos 1990.   [90] Ayoub 1999: 493.

[91] Ayoub 1999: 493; Walsh, Hulme, and Campbell 1988.

[92] O'Brien 1983a, 1983b, 1985.

cloud formation declined, while soil salinity and desertification increased. As forests and scrubs vanished, people needed to buy charcoal and building materials to replace missing wood. Rising cash needs forced them to join a growing army of wage laborers while purchasing power eroded in the wake of the IMF structural adjustment program. The value of the Sudanese Pound declined from $2.87 in 1978 to $0.5 in 1984.

Meanwhile, the state taxed irrigated farming and the export sector to maintain itself, but due to negligence, exports only grew modestly throughout the 1960s. Between 1970 and 1976, the situation was aggravated. Annually, exports fell by 9 percent while imports rose by 7.8 percent. Increased import needs for infrastructure and development projects did not create accompanying export returns.[93] Within the structural heterogeneity of the Sudanese economy, domestic labor did not constitute sufficient demand for domestic production, which in turn was critically dependent on imported input factors. The lack of dynamic linkages within the economy prevented integration of the domestic economy via intermediate industries. The resulting "export compulsion" had to rely on cheap labor to maintain competitiveness which in turn led to insufficient domestic demand. A vicious cycle was established which Oesterdiekhoff and Wohlmuth suggested curing in the spirit of the time with a "delinking" of the Sudanese economy.[94]

Faced with structural constraints of the existing model, acute shortage of foreign exchange, and external pressure by donors like the World Bank and the Gulf states, Sudan attempted the transformation to a more export-oriented model in the 1970s. At the same time, it retained some of the old policies like the acreage shift from cotton to wheat. Nimeiri pushed back his earlier nationalization policies after 1972 and a commercial bourgeoisie gained in influence over the agrarian bourgeoisie and its commercial interests in the rain-fed areas.

O'Brien sees the Gulf countries as allies of this commercial bourgeoisie, instrumental in assisting the export-led turn of the Nimeiri regime and accomplices of the land grab scenario that was playing out in the rain-fed areas:

> The grandly vague breadbasket notion and the associated fanfare provides a distracting ideological disguise for the renewed exploitation of Sudan's resources and labor power, this time with Arab oil-producers in a prominent role. A basic premise, that 185 million feddans are lying unused, is false. Not only is this land in use, but it is shrinking at an alarming rate through desertification, a consequence of the predatory style of "breadbasket" expansion. People are dying in conflicts over access to what remains unclaimed by capital or the desert.[95]

---

[93] O'Brien 1983a, 1983b, 1985.
[94] Oesterdiekhoff and Wohlmuth 1983a: 43.
[95] O'Brien 1981: 26.

Land use conflicts in Sudan are widespread, but the central role that O'Brien attributes to Gulf investors is questionable. He fails to explain why they invested so little in the country, why the AAAID once it started timid operations in the 1980s was only a pale shadow of the earlier ambitious plans of the AFESD, and why many private Gulf investors like Khashoggi never implemented projects on the land they had leased.

Explaining the Failure: Projects

Gulf capital invested in rain-fed farming in the Blue Nile province. The Agadi scheme was a joint venture between the Sudanese government and the AAAID, while the Faisal scheme was a direct Saudi investment.[96] At its height in the early 1980s, expansion on the Agadi scheme led indeed to displacement of traditional farmers and pastoralists.[97] Yet, nowadays about two-thirds of plots lie idle with uneasy prospects of rehabilitation; the Faisal scheme is completely abandoned.[98] The projects suffered from bad management and their sustainability was compromised after the soil was mined. Displaced farmers and pastoralists paid a terrible price, but the projects were a disappointment for the government and businessmen as well.[99] At the end of the day, profit margins in rain-fed areas depended on unsustainable soil mining and were not high enough to entice international investors with global options of asset allocation. After massive price increases, Sudan imposed a meat export ban in 1975, which was also hardly encouraging for investment monies that had entered Sudan on the promise of its potential as an agricultural export hub for the Arab world.[100]

Agriculture was challenging in Sudan. Stephen Kontos was a representative for the Sahara Agricultural Venture (SAV) of US multinational Tenneco in the north of Sudan from 1982 to 1986. SAV aimed at producing fruits and vegetables for export to Saudi Arabia. Kontos argues that poor soils and lack of incentives for local farmers were at the heart of the problem.[101] The viability of the bread-basket dream hinged on the availability of irrigated land, but the most valuable land on the Nile was already occupied by small segmented plots. Large-scale projects had to be established on marginal land or in remote areas.

---

[96] Kontos 1990: 649. Their full names are Arab Sudanese Blue Nile Company and Faisal Agricultural Corporation respectively.

[97] Verhoeven 2012b.

[98] Interviews, Abd Ulgabar Hussein Osman, General Secretary, the High Council for Agricultural Revival, Khartoum, 20 November 2011 and Omer Marzoug, General Manager Agadi Scheme, Khartoum, 21 November 2011.

[99] Verhoeven 2012b: 6.

[100] Waterbury 1976a: 16.

[101] Kontos 1990.

Alternatively, collaboration with existing farms and cooperatives had to be found. SAV tried to introduce a system of contract farming around a corporate core and offered incentives like profit sharing and management participation. Yet it was unable to achieve consensus on a revenue split that would have paid for the investments in equipment. Farmers were deeply suspicious of outside interference. The cooperatives had been placed under direct government control in 1973 and increasing restrictions on what farmers could and could not plant had alienated them from the state. At the same time, traditional forms of land cultivation within extended families had disintegrated and weakened the bond of trust and kinship solidarity within the co-ops. Beside dysfunctional cooperation with tenants, insufficient infrastructure and unfavorable global market developments prevented success. A trend to migrate to the cities or to the oil-rich Gulf countries contributed to the disincentives aligned against agricultural projects.[102] In other cases projects failed at overcoming the preference for livestock production among recently or partially sedentarized people. As "reluctant cultivators" they did not have a problem with seasonal farm work, but resented all year round cultivation.[103]

The Gezira scheme was not a project of the bread-basket era, but constituted an important, if brittle backbone for the regime, because it provided a majority of agricultural production and export revenues. Its marked top-down approach alienated tenants who were highly dependent on production guidelines, input procurement, credit arrangements, and marketing by the Gezira Board and private businessmen.[104] This power distance grew further as original tenants who came mainly from the north migrated to the cities and consequentially sublet their plots to farmers from predominantly western regions. This landlordism decreased the motivation on the part of actual cultivators. As the Gezira tenants needed sorghum as quasi money to pay sharecroppers, they resisted the guidelines of the Gezira Board, which gave preference to cotton and allowed sorghum production only for subsistence needs.[105] A highly fluctuating migrant workforce often lacked necessary skills while the increased need for technocratic management positions could not be satisfied because of a brain drain to the Gulf countries in the wake of the oil boom.[106]

While Sudanese agricultural policies left small-scale farmers and tenants of state-owned irrigation schemes estranged, incentives for investors in the large-scale projects of the 1970s were substantial. The investors of the Kenana sugar company received extremely favorable conditions. The Sudanese government renounced most of its rights to levy taxes on the project and guaranteed sales

---

[102] Kontos 1990.   [103] O'Brien 1983a: 26; Briggs 1978: 470.
[104] Barnett and Abdelkarim 1991: 168–80.   [105] Kontos 1990: 665.
[106] Davies 1991b: 344–7, 355f.

prices in hard currency.[107] In the 1970s and 1980s, some investors did not mean to farm projects for real. The leases were only acquired to obtain tax advantages and other concessions, which were then used to finance other economic activities in Sudan.[108]

Technically Kenana was deemed successful, after all it managed to build one of the largest sugar factories of the world in the middle of nowhere, but it suffered from deteriorating terms of trade. Prices for input factors rose while tropical commodities suffered price declines in the 1980s and 1990s. Politics distorted economic decision-making, funds were siphoned off, and the huge size of the project complicated management. Awarding of contracts was notoriously delayed. Lack of infrastructure and skilled labor hampered implementation. The long distance from the next port (1,200 km) and insufficient roads constituted a problem. Shortly after its incorporation, Kenana announced a tripling of the initial cost estimates.[109] Sudanese sugar production rose since the 1980s, but Kenana fell short of its goal to turn the country into a major sugar exporter. It never exported sugar to the Gulf countries, a fact that is not lost on opponents of Saudi Arabia's current foreign agro-investment drive. Saudi Arabia's former WTO chief negotiator Fawaz al-Alami portrays Kenana for this reason as a failure and rather advocates deals with established food exporters.[110] The verdict of the Kuwaiti shareholders has been equally dismissive: "We haven't gotten our money out of that for 30-years," argues a Kuwaiti official in a WikiLeaks cable.[111]

Sudanese officials on the other hand describe the current state of the company uniformly as "very efficient" and "successful." The company is profitable and pays regular dividends.[112] Yet, these profits are made possible by input subsidies and taxation of consumers—sugar prices in Sudan are far above world market level. Kenana is the node of Sudan's "sugar system" that allows regime clients to prosper in a "messy patchwork of cartels, protected niches and liberalised spaces."[113]

With all its faults, Kenana is a surviving signature project of the bread-basket era. About half of its capital comes from the Gulf and with its pivotal position in Sudanese development politics it hopes to function as a conduit for renewed Gulf agro-investments in the country, albeit Gulf investors have only shown polite interest so far. The company originally considered an IPO of its shares in the UAE, like Sudanese telecom company SUDATEL has done,[114]

---

[107] Oesterdiekhoff 1982: 53.   [108] Davies 1991a: 319.

[109] Oesterdiekhoff 1982: 53; Spiro 1989: 503ff.

[110] Lippman 2010: 96.

[111] WikiLeaks cable 09KUWAIT1170, US Embassy in Kuwait, 15 December 2009.

[112] Interviews, Kenana and AAAID executives, Khartoum and Kenana factory, 21, 24, and 28 November 2011.

[113] Verhoeven 2012b: 199, 237.

[114] Interview, Kenana executive, Khartoum 28 November 2011.

but then it declared to list a quarter of its shares at the Hong Kong stock exchange by December 2012.[115]

The Faisal Islamic Bank, Food Trade, and the Famine of 1984–5

In sum, the impact of Gulf countries via agricultural investments was limited during the bread-basket era. However, their influence via financial operations and food trade was more substantial. The Sudanese government granted economic privileges as a strategy of overcoming cash shortages and fostering alliances with cronies. Private commercial banks were legalized in 1978, at the time of the IMF program. Saudi Prince Muhammad al-Faisal and other shareholders founded the Faisal Islamic Bank (FIB). After 1979, there was a rapprochement of the Nimeiri regime with Islamist groups. Hassan al-Turabi who would take over power in 1989 became general attorney in 1979 and Sharia law was introduced in 1983. Islamic banks were treated as religious institutions. As such, they were exempted from taxation and central bank oversight and were granted special privileges like preferred access to licenses and export credits.[116]

FIB developed into Sudan's largest exporter of sorghum, which was predominantly planted in the rain-fed areas. The government promoted sorghum exports to balance the disastrous trade balance and to finance the import of wheat, which had become the staple crop of city dwellers.[117] Sorghum exports soared between 1979 and 1983. An alternative policy proposal of building up food storage was not adopted. It would have helped to alleviate the famine of 1984–5.[118] Sorghum exports in 1981 and 1982 were particularly high because Saudi Arabia offered a special subsidy for imports of sorghum from Sudan.

Via the link of food trade Saudi Arabia was effectively underwriting the socio-ecological disaster of the horizontal expansion of mechanized rain-fed agriculture, even without being directly invested in it. Sorghum deliveries were hardly crucial for Saudi Arabia in comparison to its overall food imports, but they reduced Sudanese food security ahead of the famine. A lack of food entitlements of vulnerable segments of the population was at the heart of the problem, not so much a decline in food availability. There were similarities with other big famines in history in this respect (e.g. Bengal 1943, Wollo 1973, Bangladesh 1974).[119] The five-year average of per capita availability of food

---

[115] *Reuters*, 18 March 2012.   [116] O'Brien and Gruenbaum 1991: 199.
[117] Davies 1991a: 312ff.   [118] Shepherd 1988: 61ff.
[119] Locke and Ahmadi-Esfahani 1993. For the concept of entitlements and empirical examples see Sen 1981.

between 1980/1 and 1984/5 in Sudan was higher than in the 1960s and 1970s. With proper storage and distribution, the famine could have been avoided.[120]

Having said that, sorghum exports in the boom years of 1981 and 1982 constituted about 10 percent of production and must be seen in proportion. Gulf countries engaged in Sudanese agriculture, but they were hardly central to its plight and the crowding out of traditional farmers and pastoralists in the rain-fed areas. They never invested large quantities and Sudan never developed meaningful importance as a food exporter to the Gulf. Oesterdiek-hoff and Wohlmuth trace this back to pronounced risk aversion. Arab donors were never ready to follow up on the grandiose vision of the bread-basket plans. They demanded sumptuous guarantees from the Sudanese government for any investment they might undertake and closely trailed the IMF and its recommendations. Kenana was the only larger project where they really invested after securing extensive assurances like guaranteed off-take agreements in hard currency. Otherwise, they were stuck in feasibility considerations and never ventured beyond pilot plants. An inter-regional integration of food security as envisaged by the bread-basket plan failed. Gulf Arabs were not willing to pay a higher price than the world market at least for a transition period, to facilitate a long run adjustment towards regional self-sufficiency. They also did not support cooperation for the production of intermediate goods (fertilizer, machinery, irrigation equipment), which might have given the project a degree of depth and sustainability.[121]

6.5 THE AFTERMATH OF A FAILURE: 1980s AND 1990s

The famine contributed to the downfall of the Nimeiri regime (1969–85). After a brief period of parliamentary democracy, the NIF under Al-Turabi took over power in 1989 together with military officers under Omar al-Bashir. Al-Turabi was preoccupied with foreign policy and Islamization, and gave Abdelrahim Hamdi the new Minister of Finance leeway for the regime's Economic Salvation Programme (ESP). Hamdi believed that Sudan's planned economy was the root cause of its economic malaise. Yet the ESP was an idiosyncratic mix of liberalization, old command and control elements, and money printing.[122] At its heart was a program of wheat self-sufficiency, which the regime regarded as crucial for proving the material benefits of its new rule. It was achieved by an unsustainable increase in input factors in irrigated areas like the Gezira. In 1992, Al-Turabi announced wheat self-sufficiency and a

[120] Shepherd 1988: 61.
[121] Oesterdiekhoff and Wohlmuth 1983a, 1983b.
[122] Verhoeven 2012b: 142–7.

surplus of 100,000 tons that was exported to Kenya. Shortly after, production and productivity fell back to pre-ESP levels. The self-sufficiency push was fiscally not sustainable, especially after foreign aid payment declined dramatically in the 1990s.

The dependence of Sudan on foreign aid had been crucial for Nimeiri. Sudan found itself in a bind when it tried to reduce its reliance on US and Egyptian assistance after the end of his regime. Arab funds would have made the south suspicious, US aid the Islamists, and Egypt had financial problems of its own. Libya made an about turn in 1985, stopped funding the southern insurgents, and allied itself with Khartoum.[123] However, its aid and investment flows were limited, while those of the Gulf countries plummeted in the 1990s after Sudan sided with Iraq in the wake of the Kuwait occupation.[124] Depressed oil prices also limited the fiscal space of Gulf donors. Sudan's share of Arab official development assistance was only 0.5 percent in the 1990s, whereas it averaged about 5 percent in the preceding and following decades.[125] Commitments by Western and international donors all but vanished, too. The World Bank stopped loans in 1993 and the IMF expelled Sudan as a member. The US put Sudan on its list of states sponsoring terrorism in 1994.[126]

Stripped of his Saudi citizenship Osama bin Laden spent four and a half years in Sudan until 1996. He also pursued agricultural ventures during that time. In the Blue Nile province and in the Beja areas close to the Eritrean border he ran rain-fed farms that served as training and recruiting grounds for militant groups. As such, they were not only part of Khartoum's campaigns for subjugation of the respective peripheries, but also supported its intrusive foreign policy towards neighbors like Eritrea, Ethiopia, and Egypt.[127] Bin Laden also underwrote urgently needed wheat imports for the cash-strapped Sudanese government and was awarded agricultural export monopolies. At one point, he brokered a deal for Russian arms against Sudan's entire sesame harvest.[128] His construction company built modern roads to Port Sudan and to Damazin and started to raise the height of the Roseires Dam, before the project had to be abandoned for lack of funds. When he fell out of favor with the Sudanese government and had to leave the country, he complained bitterly that he had not been paid for his efforts and that the NIF was "a mixture of religion and organized crime."[129] He would continue to harbor his personal bread-basket dream. In an evident attempt to portray himself as a statesman, whose interests would go beyond his usual line of activities, he chastised Sudan in an audiotape in 2010 for leaving vast swathes of land idle. The Muslim

---

[123] Ottaway 1987: 904.   [124] Kepel 2002: 184.
[125] World Bank 2010a: 72.   [126] Collins 2008: 235.
[127] Johnson 2003: 137; Verhoeven 2012b: chapter 7.
[128] Johnson 2003: 137; Lesch 2002: 204.
[129] Collins 2008: 221.

world should invest more in agriculture and should take climate change seriously, he said.[130] Yet, he only invested an estimated $170 million during his stay in the 1990s.[131] His contributions, those of other Islamists, and some support from Iraq and Iran were no match for Sudan's loss of foreign aid from Gulf and Western donors.

The enforcement of Islamic banking throughout Sudan had a deleterious effect on agriculture. The NIF regime used Islamic banks and relief organizations to further its interests in the 1990s, building on the privileges for these institutions that Nimeiri had introduced earlier. The product array of the Islamic banks was ill suited for the producers of primary products and offered unfavorable conditions for forward sales. Instead of repayment in cash, farmers had to serve their loans in kind by delivering their harvest at a previously agreed upon price to the Islamic banks. In the prevalent high inflation environment, farmers were often unable to cover the cost of input factors by the time of harvest and went bankrupt. The banks compromised food security further by cornering food markets and bidding up prices. They held up to 40 percent of the country's sorghum stocks at times.[132]

The value of production in the mechanized rain-fed sector continued to fall throughout the 1980s and 1990s. Sorghum production was stagnant between 1994 and 2003 and wheat production declined.[133] Irrigated agriculture continued to be the mainstay of agriculture. Improvements of rain-fed agriculture were regarded as crucial to improve food security by IFAD and the Sudanese government's food security strategy.[134] Ayoub identified integrated land management, better extension services, and increased fertilizer application as necessary to establish some semblance of sustainability in rain-fed agriculture.[135] While rising costs for oil imports took a heavy toll on the Sudanese economy and its agriculture in the 1970s, the onset of oil production within the country by the end of the 1990s did not bring relief either. The rising oil income contributed to Dutch disease and relative neglect of agriculture and other sectors producing tradable goods.[136]

6.6 THE BREAD-BASKET RELOADED: A DAM PROGRAM AND AN "AGRICULTURAL REVIVAL" IN THE 2000s

Shortly after Al-Turabi had lost his power struggle against Al-Bashir in 1999 there was a speedy recovery of relations with Egypt and Gulf countries. Both

---

[130] *Der Spiegel*, 1 October 2010.   [131] Elnur 2009: 72.
[132] O'Brien and Gruenbaum 1991: 199; Elnur 2009: 79f.; Ali 1998.
[133] Keen and Lee 2007: S13.   [134] IFAD 2002.
[135] Ayoub 1999.   [136] IFAD 2002.

expected an end of Khartoum's Islamist adventurisms and both were crucial for the massive dam program that Sudan launched in the 2000s that would go far beyond its existing dams at Roseires, Sennar, Khashm al-Girba, and Jebel Aulia. The Nile is a vital interest of Egypt. Without its green light for the dams, the Gulf countries would have never provided their funding. Egypt has traditionally opposed dam projects south of its border, but it was ready to concede as Sudan's dams would prevent increased sedimentation of its High Dam at Aswan and prolong its life span. A widely rumored quid pro quo was the settlement of Egyptian farmers, so Egypt would benefit indirectly from the dams. Egypt also had an interest in bringing Sudan on its side to improve its negotiation position in the multilateral Nile Basin Initiative that was launched in 1999. Ethiopia and other upstream riparians have questioned the status quo of the Nile Waters Agreement of 1959 which allots three-quarters of the water to Egypt and a quarter to Sudan, while leaving the other riparians empty handed.

Parallel to Egypt, Khartoum was reaching out to Gulf countries to secure funding. Abdelrahim Hamdi, the architect of the Economic Salvation Program of 1989–91 and its short-lived wheat boom, was brought back by the regime to raise funds from the Gulf. He represented a technocratic spirit of economic liberalism that went down well with the ideological preferences of Gulf elites. He also had excellent contacts to the Kuwaiti head of the AFESD, Abdellatif Youssef al-Hamad, who in turn was close to the Kuwaiti Emir.[137] The Sudanese roadshow yielded impressive results. The Gulf countries committed to fund the heightening of the Roseires Dam and half of the $2.6 billion Merowe Dam alongside the Sudanese government and the Chinese. Credible unofficial cost estimates gauge the real costs of Merowe and the relative share of Gulf countries up to double the official figure.[138] Merowe was finished in 2009; completion of Roseires is expected by 2013–14. Further dams are to come online in 2015 at Burdana and Rumela on the Setait and upper Atbara Rivers, 80 kilometers south of the Khashm al-Girba Dam, whose storage capacity has decreased because of sedimentation. The Kajbar Dam at the third cataract is scheduled for 2016 and dams at Dal and Shereik at the second and fifth cataract are in the planning stage.[139] Once the dams are finished, Sudan will reach its allotment quota of the 1959 agreement for the first time.

The Comprehensive Peace Agreement (CPA) with the South was signed in 2005. Secession and a loss of oil revenues became a distinct possibility. With the dam program, the regime stuck to its old ideology of big is beautiful. For

---

[137] Verhoeven 2012b: 230.

[138] Verhoeven 2012b: 231.

[139] For an overview of the status of dam projects in Sudan and Ethiopia see Verhoeven 2011a: 18–22. See also website of the Dam Implementation Unit, <http://www.diu.gov.sd/en/setait .htm> (accessed 3 June 2012).

the first time since the failed bread-basket episode and the abandoned construction of the Jonglei Canal in 1983 it had the funds and the foreign policy leeway to embark on a hydraulic mission of epic proportions. The dam program also provided the country with an alternative development narrative ahead of the breakaway of the south. Legitimacy discourse switched from Islamist radicalism to the image of a responsible technocratic provider.

In 2006/7, the regime launched the Agricultural Revival Programme (ARP, *al-nahda al-zira'iyya*) and tried to woo Gulf investors once again. ARP was to capitalize on the dam program and Sudan's traditional natural resources. The successor to the NIF, the ruling National Congress Party (NCP), discussed ARP at a conference in 2005. Hamdi presented an unusually frank paper at the request of Al-Bashir. It outlined a strategy of regime survival over the following 10–15 years and how investments would need to be used to that end. Hamdi argued that the 25 million people in the triangle between Dongola, Kordofan, and Sennar are the political and economic base of the regime, because of superior education, infrastructure endowments, and ethno-religious homogeneity. The regime would need to focus on this "Northern Axis," which would be a viable entity even after a breakaway of the South or of Darfur. The peripheries would be expendable. Funds were needed, "very big and very fast," to develop the Northern Axis, and they would need to come from the Arab and Islamic world, as Western and international funds would not be as plentiful and tied to conditions:

> They will be late; Will be far less than promised; They will be surrounded by rules and bureaucracy of the donors ... Investment fund[s] will go to areas that are already predetermined in the Peace Agreement; that is, to the geographical south with its defined borders, Nuba Mountains[,] Southern Blue Nile. Moreover, these investment funds will be supervised by certain Commissions which ensure that they go to the specified zones only. Due to these facts, foreign investment will remain out of our hands and will not benefit the North much. In a sharp contrast to that, Arab and Islamic investment, both official and private will go to the Geographical North—as before.[140]

ARP was going to do the trick of capital acquisition. Personal and official connections to the Arab world were expected to help. The dams and ARP became a number one priority for the regime, which established new institutions to this end. It gave special authorities to the Dam Implementation Unit (DIU) and the Supreme Council for ARP and manned them with confidants of Vice President Taha who report directly to him. The DIU was further upgraded by becoming the Ministry of Electricity and Water. The Ministry of Irrigation and Water Resources (MoIWR) was sidelined. Dual responsibilities

---

[140] Hamdi 2005.

and estranged technocrats in the MoIWR have led to bureaucratic confusion since.

ARP reads in many ways as a repetition of the bread-basket strategy with a taste of awareness for the environmental damage that has been caused since then. Combating desertification and restoring vegetative cover are acknowledged as important; otherwise, ARP harps on the themes of the 1970s: food import substitution to save foreign exchange, agricultural export promotion to gain it; attraction of foreign capital and international strategic partnerships.[141] Agriculture and related industries are promoted as the core of the economy. With the looming separation of South Sudan it was not wise anymore to bank solely on oil. Sudan's hot climate is not conducive to wheat cultivation, but self-sufficiency was to be achieved by 2011, a task that was missed by a wide margin of 70 percent. Wheat cultivation in central Sudan did not pick up, because the plots there are too small according to Abdulgabar Hussein Osman, the Secretary General of ARP.[142]

Hence, the new plan is to cultivate wheat with center pivot irrigation in the desert of the north, where larger plots are available and the colder winter climate is more suitable for wheat. Water is to come not only from the Nile, but also from the Nubian Sandstone Aquifer, whose waters are not of fossil origin, but renewable as Sudanese officials would allege with steadfast conviction.[143] The International Atomic Energy Agency (IAEA), UNDP, and the Global Environment Facility (GEF), which have conducted a research project on the aquifer system since 2006, would beg to differ.[144] The plan is eerily reminiscent of the groundwater mining of Saudi Arabia's failed wheat program, while soils in northern Sudan are less suitable than the ones in Saudi Arabia. Still, the cultivation of a flabbergasting 1.5 million ha with the help of Gulf capital is "our main dream," says Osman.

Another priority axis of ARP is the creation of a "sugar belt" between the White and Blue Nile. Kenana, the surviving signature project of the bread-basket era and node of the Sudanese "sugar system," has been given a pivotal role. It has branched out into new fields like dairy farming and fodder production. It makes ethanol from the molasses by-products of sugar production since 2009 and its subsidiary Kenana Engineering and Technical Services (KETS) has put together the Sudanese Grand Sugar Plan, which aims to increase sugar production of Sudan from 750,000 tons to 10 million tons by 2020. As part of the plan, Kenana is a shareholder in the newly launched White Nile Sugar Company. In the wake of the government's privatization

---

[141] Government of Sudan 2008.

[142] Interview, Khartoum, 20 November, 2011.

[143] Osman interview, Khartoum, 20 November, 2011 and interviews in Wad Madani/Al-Gezira, 22 November 2011.

[144] <http://www-naweb.iaea.org/napc/ih/IHS_projects_nubian.html> (accessed 15 April 2012).

drive, it has been asked to run the Rahad and Suki schemes, even though it does not have experience in the cultivation of groundnuts, sunflowers, cotton, corn, and soybeans that are grown there. Experts describe the two projects overwhelmingly as a failure, with steep decreases in yields and tenants revolting against the Kenana management.[145] The export imperative of ARP can also be seen in the plans for the rain-fed areas where the focus is on cotton and oil seeds and the rehabilitation of gum arabic production.

Interest of Gulf investors picked up in the 2000s. Kingdom Holding of Saudi Prince Al-Waleed acquired the monopoly of meat exports to Arab countries, but the Sudanese government had to backtrack after protests of competing Sudanese traders and Saudi importers.[146] The Al-Rajhi group launched a project for wheat cultivation at Berber in 2005. Then announcements of projects proliferated after 2008 in the wake of the global food crisis. The Sudan bread-basket dream seemed to be coming true at last. Yet an understanding of the socio-ecological intricacies of Sudanese agriculture had not developed over time and project implementation remained spotty.

6.7 CONCLUSION

The world food crisis and the politicization of food trade in the 1970s prompted Gulf countries to develop Sudan as a bread-basket. Their investments were either undertaken with a strategic rationale of food security or with a commercial interest of profit maximization. In both cases they failed. The bread-basket plans of the AFESD and its brainchild AAAID and the various private Gulf investors never ventured much beyond pilot projects and feasibility studies. Commercial projects were not successful because of structural limitations such as lacking infrastructure, governance issues, and political instability. Global food markets corrected in the second half of the 1970s, threats of food embargoes were much less virulent in the 1980s, and Saudi Arabia embarked on its program of wheat self-sufficiency. This reduced the urgency of the bread-basket plan. The 1970s saw the launch of GCC development funds, but the steep rise in Arab development aid was broad-based and did not have the strategic and commercial thrust of the bread-basket vision. This thrust would only return in 2008, this time on a global scale.

Horizontal agricultural expansion in rain-fed areas of the Sudan had negative socio-economic and ecological effects. It disenfranchised holders of customary land rights, was used to reward cronies, and served to further the

[145] Verhoeven 2012b: 237. Interviews with former Minister and Undersecretary of MoIWR, Khartoum, 21 November 2011.
[146] Coalition for International Justice (CIJ) 2006: 73.

political agenda of consecutive Sudanese regimes. The Gulf countries' role in this process was more limited than often portrayed. Yet, Saudi Arabia was underwriting it to a certain extent with its imports of sorghum in the run-up to the famine of 1984–5. Saudi royals and businessmen were also associated with the networks of a rising Islamist trading bourgeoisie whose policies had a deleterious effect on Sudanese agriculture.

In sum, the bread-basket strategy not only failed to prevent the famine of 1984–5, it contributed to it to no small extent. It did not manage to practice a sustainable and balanced expansion of modern agriculture and reconcile it with traditional farming and pastoralism. The basic premise that large swathes of Sudanese land are idle was wrong. Yet, the Sudanese government, Gulf countries, and the IMF repeated this mantra in the wake of the global food crisis of 2008 when a new wave of agro-investments was announced.[147]

---

[147] The IMF is evidently unfazed by the rich literature about land use conflicts in Sudan. In its Chapter IV report on Sudan in 2010 it reiterates the tale of vast swathes of idle land, which it puts at 80–85 percent of total arable land. IMF 2010: 9.

7

Return to the Future: Current Gulf Agro-investments

The global food crisis rang alarm bells in the Gulf countries. Rising food prices were a concern, but with ample oil revenues they were more like a nuisance. The real issue was the food export restrictions that countries like Argentina, Russia, India, and Vietnam temporarily enacted. These restrictions triggered a deeply ingrained sense of vulnerability and evoked memories of threatened food supplies in World War II and the 1970s.

Affordable food is an important part of the social contract and such failure of markets reinforced the perception that food security is too important to be left to them. At home, governments reacted by subsidizing and controlling food prices while augmenting strategic storage of food items. Their most publicized reaction was the announcement of international agro-investments, which aim at privileged bilateral access to food production. Announced projects have often been beyond 100,000 ha and one feels reminded of the gigantic AFESD vision of the Sudan bread-basket in the 1970s. While Sudan has been again in focus, this time Gulf countries have been scouting the globe for possible projects, including Australia, Cambodia, Ukraine, or Uruguay.

There has been resistance in local communities to land investments, but governments in target countries have been eager to attract Gulf capital to modernize their agricultural sectors, build up infrastructure, and improve their sources of revenues. High oil prices have taken a grim toll on global balances of payments. Many developing countries have been most affected, as in the 1970s. Oil exporters and Asian manufacturers like China are the countries with major current account surpluses worldwide. As the food crisis coincided with the global financial crisis, there has been no lack of solicitors for Gulf capital. Cash-strapped Western banks and governments have vied for it alongside countries that have offered their land for investments. Presidents and ministers from the Philippines and all over Africa have visited the Gulf to promote agricultural investments in their countries, just to mention a few.[1] Even war-torn and land-locked Afghanistan has recommended itself as a "Food Basket for Gulf Countries."[2]

The plethora of announced agro-investments created a separate media reality that suggested that GCC countries would produce food in foreign countries on a large scale and export it back to the Gulf. Yet, five years after the wave of agro-investments started rolling this was not the case. Announcements have not been accompanied by widespread implementations on the ground. There has been a lack of data other than simple press releases and newspaper reports. Details of leasing agreements and contracts are rarely published by official institutions and companies involved. Only vague ballpark figures about projects and their size have been released, sometimes with the pomp and inclination towards superlatives that were characteristic of announcing Dubai real estate deals.

The lack of data and research has not only been attributable to the recent nature of the phenomenon, but also to a general lack of transparency in the region. The Gulf countries are "rentier states"; while in advanced "production states," i.e. industrialized countries, society supports the state via tax revenues, rentier states support themselves and their societies via distribution of oil rent. In exchange for supply of welfare services and job guarantees in the public sector, the state expects political acquiescence—no taxation and no representation.[3] Major transmission mechanisms of transparency are therefore missing.

There is no accountability of companies towards the taxman and of democratically elected governments towards their constituencies. Accountability of companies to shareholders is also limited as many companies are either owned by the government (e.g. the national oil companies) or by members of the royal family. Others are non-listed family enterprises. Even among the listed companies, most of the larger ones have the state as a majority shareholder.[4] A culture of corporate social responsibility that would engage with non-company stakeholders is only at a nascent stage. The scarcity of information also applies to the targeted countries, where governments divulge data only reluctantly or do not have the bureaucratic capacities to collect information in the first place.

---

[1] See the lists of participants of the Gulf-Africa Conferences that were held in Riyadh on 4–5 December 2010 and in Cape Town on 24–5 February 2009 at <www.grc.net> (accessed 18 June 2012); *The National*, 28 February 2011; *Saudi Gazette*, 13 September 2009; *Guardian*, 4 September 2008.

[2] E-mail invitation of the Afghan Business Council (ABC) in the UAE, 13 May 2009 for a conference about agricultural investments in Afghanistan that was later canceled. The First Afghanistan International Investment Conference was then held in Dubai on 1 December 2010 with participation of President Hamid Karzai. *Gulf News*, 30 November 2010.

[3] Luciani 1987.

[4] Woertz 2007.

7.1 TARGETED COUNTRIES AND CROPS

Figure 7.1 uses data from the farmlandgrab blog of the NGO GRAIN that collects global media reports about land investments. The figure is compiled from the announcement of concrete projects and high profile Memorandums of Understanding (MoUs) by Gulf countries. Mere delegation visits and vague declarations of intent were not included and the figure does not include all countries, only the most frequently cited ones. It gives an indication of preferred investment targets, but not of relative project size or status of implementation.

In terms of number of projects, Sudan is again leading the field, followed by Pakistan, the Philippines, and Ethiopia. Egypt, Turkey, Tanzania, and Asian countries like Cambodia and Indonesia also attracted considerable attention. Established food exporters like Australia, Argentina, Brazil, Vietnam, Ukraine, Kazakhstan, and Thailand have trailed in importance. At the end of the scale, there has been interest in countries including Morocco, Kenya, Mali, Senegal, and India. The Ph.D. thesis of Saudi agro-businessman Turki Faisal al-Rasheed includes a survey of 1,156 Saudi decision-makers about the most suitable countries for Saudi foreign agro-investments. Sudan again tops the list. Other preferred target countries include, in order, Egypt,

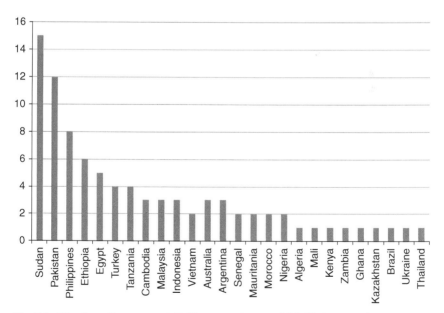

Fig. 7.1. Number of announced Gulf agro-projects and MoUs (2008–11)
Source: GRAIN 2012.

Ethiopia, India, Turkey, Pakistan, Mauritania, Australia, Brazil, South Africa, and the Philippines.[5]

Preferred target countries are food net importers and some of them struggle with limited water resources like the Gulf countries (e.g. Pakistan or Central Asia). None of them is a substantial food exporter to the Gulf countries at this stage, with the exception of Pakistan, which is an important supplier of rice. Fruit exports from the Philippines and Egypt and live animals from Sudan play a role in Gulf countries' imports, but are hardly crucial for their food security. Sudan, Pakistan, and Ethiopia are outright food insecure and were the three largest recipients of food aid from the World Food Program (WFP) in 2010.[6] After a drought in 2009, Pakistan fell victim to an epic flood in 2010, which exacerbated the social inequalities and corruption of its agricultural system.[7] Parts of Ethiopia, Somalia, and Kenya were hit by a major drought and the UN declared a state of famine in 2011 for the first time since the 1980s. Many target countries also have rapidly growing populations and will need to make up for this increase before developing any export capacity.

The choice of investment destinations is therefore counter-intuitive and controversial. Advocacy groups have accused Gulf countries of engaging in land grabbing on a large scale. A worst-case scenario would entail expropriation of smallholders and pastoralists and their migration to the cities without finding sufficient job opportunities. Capital-intensive agro-investments might then achieve production increases, but the produced food would be for export as many people in the respective countries would be unable to afford it. They would not have any benefits from such projects. In defense, Gulf officials have claimed that a win-win situation is possible. The triangular cooperation vision of the Sudan bread-basket strategy has been evoked with developing countries supplying the land and Gulf countries the capital to bring in know-how from developed countries.

With the global food crisis, the improvement of agricultural productivity in developing countries has moved to center stage of international debates, similar to the discussions during the time of the World Food Conference 1974. Sub-Saharan Africa in particular has occupied the fantasies of development planners, as it has not undergone a Green Revolution. Unlike MENA countries, large parts of it do not have a physical, but an economic water shortage. The Rockefeller and Gates Foundations launched the Alliance for a Green Revolution in Africa (AGRA) in 2006 and African politicians hope that productivity gains could be achieved via proliferation of commercial farming,

---

[5] Al-Rasheed 2012: 128ff. Countries that follow are Canada, Senegal, USA, Somalia, Argentina, Ukraine, Madagascar, Kenya, Tanzania, Vietnam, Ghana, Thailand, Mozambique, Zambia, Poland, Cambodia, Cameroon, Congo, and Kazakhstan.

[6] WFP 2011: 27. Together they received 56 percent of all WFP emergency food aid in 2010. Ethiopia's share was 27 percent, Pakistan's 18 percent, and Sudan's 11 percent.

[7] Hooper 2010.

which currently is confined to a few export crops like coffee, tea, or cocoa, apart from South Africa.[8]

In this sense, Gulf countries are just following international investment trends, but there are also strategic considerations that are peculiar to them. The geographical proximity of Sudan, Pakistan, and Ethiopia has the potential of offering logistic advantages and reduced fuel costs for transportation. The ports of Port Sudan, Gwadar in Pakistan, and Djibouti are nearby, even though their feeder infrastructure like railway lines and roads are in need of improvement.[9] Export considerations are the reason why the Abu Dhabi Fund for Development (ADFD) prefers projects in northern Sudan to those in the south,[10] while Abu Dhabi-based Al-Qudra Agriculture does not consider investments that are more than 600 kilometers away from a port.[11]

Sudan

Well-established political, economic, and cultural ties are another reason for investment preferences. Whether it is the IsDB, agro-businessmen, or academics, executives from the Gulf have identified Sudan as a priority axis for agricultural investments. They are interested in its land and water resources, even though they reckon serious shortfalls in governance.[12] Sudan has been an important recipient of Gulf development funds in the 1970s and 1980s and there are residual projects of the Sudan bread-basket strategy like the Kenana sugar company. Khartoum is also host to AAAID, AOAD, and the Arab Bank for Economic Development in Africa (BADEA). Sudan is a member of the Arab League and politicians from both sides are used to interacting with each other. Gulf countries have a vital interest in the stability of the country. Qatar's mediation in the Darfur conflict led to the signing of a peace accord between the government of Sudan and the Liberation and Justice Movement in Doha in July 2011.

Gulf countries have been traditionally close to the north and have been wary of a partition of Sudan, but they endorsed it when it finally happened in July 2011. Saudi Minister of Agriculture Fahd Balghunaim said his country could imagine investing in agricultural projects in South Sudan. The Saudi Prince Badr bin Sultan purportedly holds a lease of 105,000 ha of land in Unity State and the UAE's Al-Ain National Wildlife has acquired land for a tourism

---

[8] See <www.agra-alliance.org> (accessed 18 April 2012); interview with the ambassador of Uganda to the UAE, Dubai, 10 June 2010. For a critique of AGRA see Oakland Institute 2009.

[9] Saudi Arabia invests in expanding port facilities in Djibouti and Jeddah. WikiLeaks cable, 09RIYADH1447, US Embassy Riyadh, 11 January 2009.

[10] Interview with ADFD executive, Abu Dhabi, 19 April 2009.

[11] Interview with Al-Qudra Agriculture executive, Abu Dhabi, 20 April 2009.

[12] *Arab News*, 26 June 2011; Al-Rasheed, Turki Faisal 2010: 171–8; Al-Qahtani 2009: 11.

project.[13] Yet, the overall preference is with the north as in the 1970s. The head of the food security committee of the Riyadh Chamber of Commerce and Industry said that it would take a long time before Saudi Arabia could invest in South Sudan.[14]

Gulf investors have led talks for contract farming arrangements on the Gezira scheme, whose privatization has started in earnest in 2009 after initial legislation in 2005.[15] Qatar's Hassad Food, UAE's Amtar, and Al-Rajhi International and HADCO from Saudi Arabia have projects for wheat and alfalfa cultivation in Abu Hamad, the Northern State, Berber and in the north of Khartoum respectively.[16] This preference for the north coincides with the Sudanese government's push for the Agricultural Revival Programme (ARP) and its preoccupation with wheat self-sufficiency that has been described above.

Pakistan

Pakistan is also close to the Gulf region, geographically, politically, and culturally. Oman used to entertain a triangular trade empire in the northern Indian Ocean, connecting the Arabian Peninsula with East Africa and South Asia. Up to 300,000 Omanis are of Baluchi heritage.[17] Pakistanis are one of the largest migrant communities in the Gulf and Pakistanis have been recruited to serve in Gulf police and military forces as Gulf rulers doubted either the loyalties or technical skills of their own subjects.[18] Pakistani officers used to train the Saudi airforce and intelligence cooperation has been close since the Soviet occupation of Afghanistan. The former Presidents Nawaz Sharif and Benazir Bhutto took refuge in Saudi Arabia and UAE respectively when the going got tough for them in Pakistan.

Some Gulf investment decisions are not solely determined by pondering of feasibility studies, but by considerations that are more mundane. Personal guarantees and preferences are important for long-term projects in world regions where institutions are underdeveloped. Countries like Pakistan or Morocco are popular holiday destinations for Gulf royals and elites. Asked

---

[13] Deng 2011; Deng and Mittal 2011.
[14] *Al-Sahafa*, 9 March 2011.
[15] Interview with director of the board of the Gezira scheme, 22 November 2011.
[16] Interview with ARP Secretary General, Khartoum, 20 November 2012; *The Peninsula*, 17 February 2009; *Financial Times*, 24 May 2009; interview with Minister of Agriculture Balghunaim, *Al-Riyadh*, 12 January 2011; for a presentation of Al-Rajhi's project for wheat cultivation in Sudan see <http://raii.net/sudannews.pdf> (accessed 4 April 2012).
[17] In this triangular trade, East Africa supplied spices, slaves, precious stones, and ivory, Oman frankincense and dates, and Pakistan/South Asia manufactured articles and textiles. Al Ameeri 2003; Valeri 2009; Peterson 1978; Nicolini and Watson 2004.
[18] *Al Jazeera*, 20 July 2011; Riedel 2011; Strobl 2011.

about the reasons why UAE companies have chosen Morocco as a destination for agricultural investments one businessman shrugged his shoulders and said that Sheikha Fatima, the favorite wife of the late ruler Sheikh Zayed and "Mother of the Nation" likes to go there. Another offered anecdotes of a falcon hunting party dashing to a potential project site in Pakistan and driving off with its four wheel drives after a short look around in order to follow more entertaining pursuits.[19]

After India, Pakistan is the largest supplier of basmati rice to the Gulf. In contrast to most African countries, private land ownership by foreigners is technically possible, though controversial. Pakistan has high inequality of land ownership. Large swathes of land are held by quasi-feudal landlords, who preside over a system of land tenure and bonded labor that still embodies vestiges of the old *zamindar* system.[20] The rigid rules of Sharia inheritance law have led to widespread shareholding within landowning families. Frequently occurring quarrels about exact allotments can make lease arrangements difficult.[21] The fact that Pakistan has offered Gulf countries a security force of 100,000 men to protect farm assets should they invest is an indication of intricate socio-economic conflicts that any large-scale land transaction would involve.[22] In a WikiLeaks cable, then Saudi Minister of Industry and Commerce Abdullah Zainal Alireza conveyed to US diplomats that an agricultural project in the country fell by the wayside "because the Saudi Government and its companies did not believe they could manage the security issues involved."[23]

Ethiopia

Ethiopia offers a similar geographical proximity like Sudan and Pakistan and ranks high on the investment agenda of Saudi Arabia. Both countries are growing increasingly close. When Ethiopian President Girma Wolde-Giorgis left a Riyadh hospital after treatment, he made two announcements that are telling of the mutual relationship. He stressed the importance of Saudi agro-investments for his country and promised to send Ethiopian housemaids to replace those from Indonesia and the Philippines whose hiring was stopped after a spat with the respective governments about minimum wages and treatment of migrant workers. The maid shortage made newspaper headlines for months and was no minor issue in a nation that is heavily dependent on foreigners for menial labor.[24]

---

[19] Interviews, Dubai, March and April 2009. [20] Khan 1981; Martin 2009.
[21] Interview with agricultural company executive, Dubai, 26 April 2009.
[22] *The Economist*, 23 May 2009.
[23] WikiLeaks cable, 09RIYADH1447, US Embassy in Riyadh, 11 January 2009.
[24] *Arab News*, 2 August 2011.

Ethiopia intends to lease three million ha, an area the size of Belgium, to private investors until the end of 2015 as part of its strategy of agriculture-led industrialization.[25] Saudi billionaire Mohammed Hussein al-Amoudi has an Ethiopian mother and has diverse business interests in the country ranging from construction to gold mining and agriculture.[26] A WikiLeaks cable in 2009 remarked that he "enjoys a special relationship with the [Government of Ethiopia] and reportedly deals directly with Prime Minister Meles."[27] Al-Amoudi owns Elfora Agro-Industries in the Oromia region, which is the largest livestock company in Ethiopia and his company Saudi Star has started to build a farm for rice in Gambela in the southwest of the country. It has leased 10,000 ha of land for 50 years for an annual payment of 300,000 Ethiopian Birr (*ca.* $17,000) with no stipulation for an adjustment for infla-tion.[28] Al-Amoudi plans to rent an additional 290,000 ha from the Ethiopian government. Expansion work and land clearing is progressing, often in con-flict with the local population.[29] Gunmen attacked the Saudi Star farm in April 2012 and killed several Pakistani and Ethiopian workers.[30]

Al-Amoudi is actively lobbying for Ethiopia as an investment destination within Saudi circles. The first feasibility study that the King Saud University (KSU) has contributed to KAISAIA was about Ethiopia and it recommended the country as a starting point for foreign agro-investments.[31] Political risk in Ethiopia is regarded as more favorable than in Sudan.[32] The high-level Saudi East African Forum in Addis Ababa in November 2009 gathered Saudi ministers and their counterparts from the region.[33] A number of other Gulf investors have announced projects in Ethiopia like Dubai World Trading Company, IFFCO, and Saudi consortium Al-Jenat, a joint venture of Almarai, TADCO, and JADCO.[34] However, in 2012, Saudi Star was the only Gulf investor holding an actual land lease according to a database of the Ethiopian government.[35]

---

[25] *Bloomberg*, 26 October 2010.
[26] See his personal website: <http://www.sheikhmohammedalamoudi.info> (accessed 15 April 2012).
[27] WikiLeaks cable 09ADDISABABA2900, US Embassy in Addis Ababa, 12 December 2009.
[28] Lease price and period in press reports differ from Saudi Star's lease agreement of 29 September 2009, whose numbers are given in Federal Government of Ethiopia 2009.
[29] Horne et al. 2011; Rice 2009.
[30] *AP*, 29 April 2012; Solidarity Movement for a New Ethiopia (SMNE) 2012.
[31] *Muntadayat al-Waha*, 15 December 2009.
[32] Interviews with members of the KAISAIA initiative, Dubai, 16 April 2009, Doha 14 November 2011.
[33] See <http://www.saudieastafricanforum.org/> (accessed 25 July 2011) and the ARTE documentary "Planète à vendre" which was aired on 19 April 2011.
[34] *Saudi Gazette*, 29 March 2009; *Reuters*, 11 April 2009; *Gulf News*, 24 June 2011.
[35] <http://www.eap.gov.et/?q=node/835> (accessed 20 April 2012).

The Philippines

The case for the Philippines as a Gulf agro-investment destination is less obvious. Far away from the Gulf, it does not offer the geographical advantages of closeness like Sudan, Ethiopia, and Pakistan. It also is a food net importer like these other countries. Yet it has ranked high in Gulf investment plans. Interest has focused on the southern island of Mindanao, which is less affected by floods and typhoons. It is also less densely populated than the northern islands. This has led to internal migration movements since the Marcos era and social conflict between Christian migrants and the original Muslim population.

Banana traders from the Gulf like Abdullah Abbar & Ahmed Zainy Co. from Saudi Arabia or Nader & Ebrahim S/O Hassan (NEH) from Bahrain have been present for a long time and have purchased bananas from local plantations and cooperatives. Business dealings have focused on the provinces around the island's capital Davao, not on the rebel areas in the northwest, even though a banana plantation project there brought together Saudi investors, Israeli irrigation specialists, and Muslim rebels at the beginning of the 2000s.[36] The Gulf traders have only engaged in contract farming insofar as it relates to their banana trade. However, NEH has now announced deals that also involve land acquisitions and other crops like rice. The banana traders might also help other Arab investors with their local experience as intermediaries.[37] The Saudi Al-Rajhi family has established the Far East Agricultural Investment Corporation (FEAICO) and plans to make the Philippines its food production and distribution hub in the Far East. It signed an MoU with its local partner Agrinuture Industries for corn and rice production on 50,000 ha in May 2010.[38] Cargill acquired a 28 percent stake in Agrinuture in October 2011. Bahrain has also shown a special interest in the Philippines and has announced projects for rice, fisheries, and bananas.

The Philippines hosts the International Rice Research Institute (IRRI), which is one of the institutes of the Consultative Group on International Agricultural Research (CGIAR) that are dispersed around the globe.[39] Yet Kuwaiti officials have pointed out that land in East Asia is not suitable for basmati rice that is preferred in the Gulf.[40] According to other Gulf investors, Vietnam and Thailand are better suited for rice cultivation because their climate is cooler and the days are longer. The Philippines would be better

---

[36] Solomon 2002.
[37] Interview with banana plantation manager, Davao, Philippines, 16 August 2010.
[38] Press release of Agrinuture to the Philippine Stock Exchange, 4 May 2010; Salerno 2010.
[39] Shaw 2009.
[40] WikiLeaks cable 09KUWAIT1170, US Embassy in Kuwait, 15 December 2009.

off focusing on corn, they argue.[41] The Philippines is not known for its export capacity. It is one of the largest rice importers in the world alongside Nigeria, Iran, Iraq, and Saudi Arabia. Like the Gulf countries, the Philippines was shocked by the export restrictions of agro-exporters in 2008. It has embarked on an ambitious self-sufficiency program for staple crops.[42] Yet, the USDA expects it to be the largest rice importer of the world in 2021 together with Indonesia.[43]

Other Countries

The group of countries that has attracted medium-sized interest also comprises geographically close countries like Turkey, Egypt, and Tanzania. Turkey has a sizable export sector for fruits and vegetables. It is the only Middle Eastern country that is a food net exporter in value terms, albeit it is a net importer in terms of dietary energy as it relies on imports of oil seeds and some cereals. It is more or less self-sufficient in wheat, but its production is hampered by seasonality and volatility of rainfall. Its reputation in the region has increased substantially under the Erdogan administration, not only because of political initiatives, but also because it is perceived as a role model in a region that is mired in economic stasis.

Egypt on the other hand might be geographically close, but is the largest wheat importer in the world. Apart from fruits and vegetables, it is an unlikely candidate to develop into a major food exporter to the Gulf. Yet, improvements of its agricultural sector and reduced wastage in its processing sectors could help to mitigate pan-Arab food security concerns. Gulf investors like Kingdom Holding and Al-Dahra have taken part in the Toshka Valley project that is built on reclaimed land in the southern desert, west of Lake Nasser. The project has been criticized for diversion of water from the Nile basin, high evaporation rates, and saline soils.

Other countries in the intermediate group include Asian countries that are not prominent exporters of staple foods like Indonesia, Cambodia, or Malaysia. The established Asian food exporters like Thailand or Vietnam trail behind. The same is true for export powerhouses in other world regions like Australia, Ukraine, Brazil, Argentina, and Kazakhstan. However, with time progressing there has been a shift of focus as investment challenges in developing countries have become apparent. Gulf countries are increasingly eyeing more mature markets where they face less political resistance and can count on developed infrastructure, markets, and legal frameworks. Three years

---

[41] Interview with Saudi agro-businessman, Princeton, 27 September 2011.
[42] *The Economist*, 19 November 2009.
[43] USDA 2012a: 29.

after the international agro-investment drive started, Qatar chose to invest in countries like Australia, Brazil, Argentina, or Ukraine for these reasons, said Mahendra Shah who was a director at the Qatar National Food Security Programme (QNFSP) at that time.[44]

West Africa has not ranked particularly high in terms of announcements, but Mali, Mauretania, and Senegal are host to relatively advanced pilot projects for rice production by the Foras International Investment Company. Foras has formulated far-reaching visions of cultivating 700,000 ha in Mali and Senegal and reached out to the International Rice Research Institute for technical support.[45] The company is the investment arm of the Jeddah-based Organization of the Islamic Conference (OIC). It was established in 2008 as a joint closed stock company on the initiative of the Islamic Chamber of Commerce and Industry. Beside the Islamic Development Bank (IsDB) it has a number of private investors from Saudi Arabia and other Gulf countries as shareholders such as the owner of Americana Group, Nasser Kharafi of Kuwait, the Saudi Binladin Group, or Saleh Kamel, the founder of the Dalla Albarakah Group and Chairman of the Islamic Chamber of Commerce and Industry.[46]

Should these pilot projects expand, they would tie in with the financing contribution of Gulf donors in the 1970s and 1980s to the Senegal River Development Organization (SRDO).[47] SRDO funded controversial irrigation projects along the Senegal River that flows through Mali, Mauretania, and Senegal. It was established in 1972 to jointly manage the river among the three major riparians. By smoothing out the flood cycles, parts of the river were made navigable for ocean-going ships and constant electricity production was possible. The river basin was converted from traditional flood irrigation of sorghum and millet to cultivation of rice, the staple food of urban classes. As the annual floods diminished, local communities had to give up their traditional forms of agriculture, which were integrated with fishing and livestock production. Wetlands and pastures receded, while farmers faced growing problems in financing the capital-intensive rice production which required fuel for the irrigation pumps, specific seeds, and fertilizers. Rice cultivation became less and less competitive in the 1980s and 1990s. Structural adjustment programs enforced a reduction of input subsidies and extension services. A devaluation of the domestic currency made input factors even more expensive while rice imports were liberalized and subsidized out of consideration for the urban population. The hope that irrigated agriculture would be a remedy

---

[44] *Reuters*, 13 October 2010.

[45] International Rice Research Institute (IRRI) 2009.

[46] <http://forasinvest.com/v2/index.php?lang=en> (accessed 4 June 2012); GRAIN 2010a.

[47] The original name is Organisation pour la mise en valeur de la vallée du fleuve Sénégal (OMVS).

for increased droughts in the Sahel has not materialized. Food security for rural dwellers has decreased instead of increasing.[48] The renewed push by Gulf investors for rice cultivation along the Senegal would need to address these past failures and its underlying socio-economic problems.

Targeted Crops

Gulf projects are motivated by domestic food security considerations and target staple crops like rice, wheat, and sugar. Animal feedstock like alfalfa, barley, corn, and soybeans are of great importance for the livestock industry in the Gulf, particularly in Saudi Arabia and the UAE. Saudi Arabia needs seven million tons of green animal feed per year, while it produces less than half of that amount.[49] Alfalfa is increasingly traded globally, either as hay or as pellets. The UAE is the fifth largest importer of alfalfa from the US, after Japan, South Korea, Taiwan, and Canada.[50] Saudi Arabia imported 45 percent of the worldwide traded barley in 2008. For other crops, its shares in global trade are only in the lower single digits.[51]

Announced projects by Abu Dhabi-based Al-Qudra for olive oil in Morocco and by Dubai World Trading Company for tea in Ethiopia are examples of commercially driven investments where food security considerations are not the primary motivation. Some Gulf projects also aim at more luxurious food items like meat, poultry, or fruits, but projects for biofuels, cut flowers, or industrial agricultural feedstock have been absent. The Kenana sugar company's production of ethanol for European markets is an outlier. It is meant to enhance the value of molasses by-products; it is not a core activity in its own right.[52] This abstention from biofuel projects is a major difference to other international investors, as such projects constitute a whopping 58 percent of announced international land acquisitions as based on media reports. Foodstuffs and forestry represent only 18 and 13 percent respectively.[53] As large oil producers, Gulf countries have sought to downplay the environmental impact of their main export product and are wary of potential competition. In the past, the Saudi oil minister has slammed biofuels for unfavorable economics and dubious environmental claims, promoting solar energy for electricity production instead.[54] Gulf countries have invested in mine sites abroad in

---

[48] Koopman 2004, 2009; Vick 2006; Spiro 1989: 478.

[49] Kingdom of Saudi Arabia 2009b.

[50] National Alfalfa & Forage Alliance (NAFA) 2008.

[51] Kingdom of Saudi Arabia 2009a, 2009b, 2010a.

[52] Interview, Kenana executive, 28 November 2011.

[53] Anseeuw, Wily, et al. 2012: 24. The remaining 11 percent are shared by tourism, mineral extraction, industry, non-food agricultural commodities, and livestock.

[54] *Gulf News*, 15 April 2008.

order to secure resources for their thriving heavy industries. Dubai Aluminum (DUBAL) has invested in alumina refineries in Guinea and the Indian state of Orissa, while Qatar Steel Company (QASCO) acquired rights for iron ore mining in Mauretania.[55] Similar investments in agricultural crops such as cotton or timber are unlikely as they serve as feedstock for industries that Gulf countries do not have at this stage.

South East Asia and Pakistan have been mainly targeted for rice production. Wheat production ranks less prominently and has been planned for Turkey, Kazakhstan, Australia, Sudan, and Pakistan. Predominant crops in East African countries differ from those demanded in Gulf countries.[56] Cassava is the most important staple food. Wheat is not common for climatic reasons and rice often needs to be introduced as in the mentioned Saudi Star venture in Ethiopia. Livestock production, oil seeds, and alfalfa are important to Gulf investors when looking towards Sudan.[57] The government of Sudan also classifies them as priority crops for export to the Arab world, beside wheat and pulses.[58]

7.2 THE STATE AS FACILITATOR: DIFFERENCES BETWEEN GCC COUNTRIES

The role of the state is dominant in the economies of the Gulf, be it via state-owned enterprises and funds, education, health care, or subsidies. The economies of the region are still characterized to a varying extent by allocation mechanisms of the rentier state, which has redistributed the oil rent among the business class via import licenses, sponsorship schemes, government contracts, land grants, and agricultural subsidies.[59] Differentiation between the public and private sectors can be difficult as major private enterprises (e.g. Dubai Holding, Kingdom Holding, Almarai, Al-Dahra) are held by members of the respective royal families.

The strong role of the state in agro-investments has manifested itself in three major ways: it has lent political support for land leases and negotiated framework agreements in target countries, it has undertaken direct investments via sovereign wealth funds (SWFs) or state-owned companies, and it

---

[55] Interview with Husein Murrar, Business Development Manager of Qatar Steel, *GRC Economic Research Bulletin* No. 6, June 2008; Woertz 2006.

[56] For a list of predominant crops in African and Central Asian target countries see Woertz et al. 2008: Appendix I.

[57] Interview with ADFD executive, Abu Dhabi, 19 April 2009.

[58] Government of Sudan 2010: 24–31.

[59] Luciani 2005. For a discussion of the changing nature of the rentier state and its interaction with the private sector see the introduction in Niblock (with Malik) 2007.

has provided concessionary finance to private sector companies. Framework agreements and land leases are usually not public and corresponding announcements not always clear. In one of the few cases where a contract about a land lease is available, the Special Agricultural Investment Agreement between Syria and Sudan of 2002, the Syrian government is the actual owner of the 50-year land lease.[60] In the case of the Gulf countries, land leases are rather held by the respective SWFs and companies.

There are notable differences between GCC countries in terms of targeted countries, investment activity, and structural set-ups. Saudi Arabia, UAE, and Qatar have been the most active investors, while Kuwait, Bahrain, and Oman have trailed behind. Saudi Arabia has focused on Sudan, Ethiopia, and other countries in East Africa, which are located close to its long coastline along the Red Sea. The UAE has shown a preference for Pakistan for similar reasons of geographic proximity. Qatar's interests have been widely spread ranging from Australia to Vietnam and Kenya. Saudi Arabia is the only country with a strong domestic agro-business class that has the wherewithal to expand abroad. Other GCC countries need to rely more on the state and on capacity building. Qatar and Saudi Arabia have the most institutionalized approach with the Qatar National Food Security Programme (QNFSP) and the King Abdullah Initiative for Saudi Agricultural Investment Abroad (KAISAIA).

The Qatar National Food Security Programme (QNFSP)

QNFSP aims to address Qatar's food security concerns in a comprehensive way by coordinating government agencies, international partner institutions, and companies like Hassad Food that engage in foreign agro-investments. QNFSP is part of the office of the heir apparent Sheikh Tamim bin Hamad al-Thani and international agro-investments are only one aspect of its coordinating role. At the heart of its work is a Master Plan for food security that it wants to finalize by the end of 2012. Right at a time when Saudi Arabia is phasing out wheat production the Master Plan revives the self-sufficiency strategy with the help of technological means like hydroponics and greenhouses that are run with solar-based desalination. With such technologies Qatar wants to produce up to 70 percent of its food needs by 2023—up from 10 percent today.[61] Back-up capacities for cereal production in case of a crisis are planned, but otherwise, cereals are slated for import, while more value added products like poultry and vegetables could be produced locally.[62] In the deplorable absence of regional coordination of grain procurement, limited

---

[60] Cotula et al. 2009: 33.   [61] *Gulf Times*, 20 February 2011.

[62] Interview with Fahad al-Attiya, Chairman and Vice-Chairman of QNFSP, Doha, 15 November 2011.

quantities of cereal production could also improve import efficiency. Qatar is a small country and its demand does not always allow for import diversification and the import of large and cost-efficient shiploads.[63]

The Master Plan implies a complete overhaul of the Qatari farm sector and its inefficient water consumption. In line with the penchant towards real estate in the Gulf some of the production will move downtown into vertical farming units in a newly built Food City.[64] As Qatar's aquifers are running dry, the water needs to come from desalination. Desalination is expensive and natural gas is needed for Qatar's electricity production and its industrialization drive into heavy industries like aluminum, petrochemicals, and fertilizers. Its export also fetches handsome foreign exchange revenues. In the other GCC countries that are short of natural gas, firing diesel, fuel oil, and crude oil in power and desalination plants is a recourse widely taken, but it comes with opportunity costs as the oil could be sold on international markets for a high price. Renewable energy is one of the four key sectors that the Master Plan deems crucial for attaining partial food self-sufficiency beside desalination and water management, agricultural production, and food processing.[65] Hence, agriculture ties directly into the debate about rising domestic energy consumption in the GCC, conflicting export interests, and alternatives to hydrocarbons, like renewables and nuclear energy.[66]

On the international stage, Qatar has trod carefully and has addressed its food security concerns in an international context. To pre-empt criticism of land investments it claims that it has put foreign agro-projects on hold until land rights issues have been sorted out in a mutually beneficial way and stresses adherence to international standards. State-owned Hassad Food announced that it would aim at investing in existing agro-companies rather than acquiring land rights and building up farming operations from scratch.[67]

Qatar has proposed the Global Dry Land Alliance (GDLA) at the United Nations, which hopes to organize 45–60 nations with arid or semi-arid environments, a framework that includes around two billion people.[68] GDLA aims at improving agricultural productivity in these countries by research and development and knowledge transfer. The response of other nations to the inter-governmental initiative is yet to be entirely clear, but Qatar plans to

---

[63] Interview with member of QNFSP, Washington, DC, 25 January 2010; Raboy et al. 2011: 2f.

[64] *The Peninsula*, 24 March 2011.

[65] See <http://www.qnfsp.gov.qa/home> (accessed 7 April 2012).

[66] Hertog and Luciani 2009; Aissaoui 2010; Kombargi et al. 2010; Supersberger et al. 2009; Lahn and Stevens 2011.

[67] Remarks of QNFSP Chairman Fahad al-Attiya at the Middle East Institute, Washington, DC, 25 January 2010; WikiLeaks cable, 09DOHA552, US Embassy Doha, 3 September 2009.

[68] Statement by the Deputy Secretary-General, DSG/SM/524, available at: <http://www.un.org/News/Press/docs//2010/dsgsm524.doc.htm> (accessed 2 August 2011); *Saudi Gazette*, 25 September 2010.

bring the initiative firmly on track by 2013.[69] It is anxious to align itself with international concerns and avoids portraying its agricultural initiatives as narrowly focused on national food security. This fits in with Qatar's other efforts to gain an international profile since the current ruler Hamad bin Khalifa al-Thani toppled his more traditionally minded father in 1995. Qatar is home of the satellite network *Al Jazeera*, has engaged in a flurry of international conflict mediations, and will host the world soccer championship in 2022. Some in the Gulf, and especially in Saudi Arabia, feel that Qatar is punching above its weight. Yet, its international activism has left an imprint on its food security initiative as well.

The King Abdullah Initiative for Saudi Agricultural Investment Abroad (KAISAIA)

The King Abdullah Initiative for Saudi Agricultural Investment Abroad (KAISAIA) was launched in January 2009 to coordinate Saudi overseas investments between different segments of the bureaucracy and the private sector. Compared to QNFSP, which has its own YouTube channel, and Facebook and Twitter accounts, KAISAIA does not even have a website. Involved ministries release occasional information via press releases and conference presentations, but a low profile dominates. While QNFSP is eager to attract international attention, Saudi Arabia prefers discreet decision-making, and shuns the limelight. Its food security plans are shaped by the fact that it has a large agrobusiness community. Contrary to other Gulf countries it also needs to cater to a vastly more populous constituency and has a substantial segment of poor among its domestic population, especially in rural areas.

There is a direct link between the political economy of Saudi Arabia's domestic agriculture and its planned agro-investments abroad. Cynics argue that they serve to open up new avenues for redistribution of oil rent as the old playground of domestic agriculture is downsized for lack of water. A reaction in a lively commentary blog below an article about KAISAIA alluded to Saudi Arabia's rich history in land speculation and crony capitalism arguing, "There will be two classes [in this initiative]: the merchants and the poor."[70] An op-ed in *Al-Ru'ya al-Iqtisadiyya* quipped that some Gulf officials give the impression that the Gulf countries were "Bangladesh or Chad." It warned that food security concerns should not be used to hand out subsidies to the private sector via foreign agro-investments. Any investment would need to be strictly commercial. Instead, it argued that the only viable food security strategy would be the improvement of incomes, like water-scarce Singapore has

---

[69] Al-Attiya interview; GDLA brochure by QNFSP, Doha, 2011.
[70] *Al-Riyadh*, 17 July 2009.

done. Food would be always obtainable on world markets, the op-ed maintained, albeit possibly at higher prices.[71]

The agro-business community has indeed lobbied for support. Saudi businessmen have argued that extensive state guarantees in the form of off-take agreements and soft loans would be necessary to achieve sustainable profits with agro-investments abroad.[72] The Riyadh Chamber for Commerce and Industry has proposed three different alternatives as to how farmers can be compensated for the phasing out of wheat production by 2016. Beside direct payments and government purchases of idled land it has suggested that 60 percent of such purchases could be paid with shares of a public investment company that would invest in agricultural projects abroad.[73] The Saudi Company for Agricultural Investment and Animal Production (SCAIAP) has been launched in April 2009 as part of KAISAIA with a capital of $800 million and could be used for such a purpose. Public offerings of state companies at attractive prices have been used as means to distribute oil wealth among the population. This contributed to the stock market hype in the GCC countries in the mid-2000s. Foreign agro-investments might be used for similar redistribution ends. The CEO of state-owned Hassad Food in Qatar has already mulled a future IPO of his company.[74]

KAISAIA is conceptualized as a public–private partnership. The government only wants to be a facilitator while actual project implementation and ownership should be left to the private sector. With political support and co-financing KAISAIA wants to encourage foreign investments by the companies that have grown with the help of subsidized domestic agriculture since the 1970s. The leadership of the initiative is with the Ministry of Commerce and Industry (MoCI), which purportedly is anxious that projects will make ends meet without too many subsidies.[75] SCAIAP is owned by the Public Investment Fund (PIF), which in turn is in the domain of the equally budget conscious Ministry of Finance. The Ministry of Agriculture as stalwart of the domestic agro-lobby has a deputy role in the initiative, but is less influential in the overall Saudi bureaucratic framework. The Ministries of Finance and Foreign Affairs are represented by undersecretaries. The Saudi Cabinet gave the final green light for KAISAIA projects in June 2012, specifying a maximum government share of 60 percent in the financing of projects. It also stipulated that target countries must allow at least 50 percent of the crops for export back

---

[71] Al-Sultan 2010.

[72] *Al-Jazirah*, 12 January 2011; interview with member of KAISAIA initiative, Dubai, 16 April 2009.

[73] Riyadh Chamber of Commerce and Industry 2010.

[74] *Reuters*, 28 May 2010; Woertz 2007.

[75] Interviews with FAO executive Abu Dhabi, 1 March 2010, banker, Jeddah, February 2010, and international consultant, Dubai, March 2011.

to the Kingdom.[76] Earlier, plans circulated to move the lead role in KAISAIA from MoCI to MoA, given its closeness to private agro-investors.[77] Then Minister of Agriculture Balghunaim announced plans to hand over the KAISAIA file from the ministries to SCAIAP in order to streamline procedures.[78] This would mean a major upgrade of the latter's role, which had not yet disbursed funds by 2012 to the great dismay of the business community.

KAISAIA aims at investments in countries with agricultural potential, low-cost labor, good administrative governance, investor protection, and tax relaxation for input factors. In an interview with the daily *Al-Riyadh* Balghunaim identified financial framework conditions as the largest threat to agro-investments such as unfavorable property rights and taxation laws, hampered repatriation of profits, and exchange rate devaluation. Legal changes after project implementation are of particular concern.[79] Other goals of KAISAIA are low-cost transport of food to the Kingdom, free choice of crops, and extended rights to the land either via ownership or via long-term lease contracts. The Saudi Cabinet has drafted a model agreement to safeguard private sector investments via Bilateral Investment Treaties (BIT). The first of this kind was signed in February 2010 with the Philippines.[80] KAISAIA acknowledges interests of stakeholders in target countries by addressing issues such as export quotas and local food security.[81]

KAISAIA builds on cooperation between the public and private sectors in Saudi Arabia. The Chambers of Commerce and Industry have functioned as a transmission belt to convey the goals of the initiative and take stock of the suggestions of the private sector. At the end of 2008, the business community stressed at a workshop at the Chamber in Jeddah that agro-investments would only be viable with extensive government support such as soft loans with long maturities, guaranteed off-take agreements, and build-up of infrastructure in the targeted countries. It was recommended to export only 25–40 percent to Saudi Arabia and 40–60 percent to international markets. The targeted countries were regarded as less attractive markets as their recommended allocation share was only 0–30 percent.[82]

Recommendations that have emanated from such workshops are telling as they show the inner antagonism of the Saudi agro-business community. On the one hand they see the foreign agro-investments as a new state-sponsored business opportunity, on the other hand they are afraid that domestic agriculture could be rolled back too much, be there lack of water or not: production abroad should focus on crops that cannot be planted locally like rice, sugar,

---

[76] *Saudi Gazette*, 12 June, 2012.   [77] *Al Eqtisadiah*, 24 January 2012.
[78] *Arab News*, 8 May 2012.
[79] Interview with Minister of Agriculture Balghunaim, *Al-Riyadh*, 12 January 2011. The risk of exchange rate devaluation has materialized in Sudan since 2010.
[80] *Arab News*, 16 January 2011.   [81] Kingdom of Saudi Arabia 2009a, 2009b.
[82] Al-Qahtani 2009: 34f.

and oilseeds. Wheat production on small plots that are cultivated by their owners should be preserved. Domestic agriculture that relies on renewable water resources should receive continued government support and subsidies.[83] Agro-businessmen have also cautioned that 100 percent reliance on foreign countries for food security would be imprudent and suggested maintenance of domestic wheat production to the tune of 50 percent of consumption.[84] Abdullah al-Obaid, the Saudi Deputy Minister of Agriculture, was careful to disperse fears that KAISAIA might lead to an abandonment of domestic agriculture. Rather it would offer complementarities; while water-intensive grain and fodder crops would be outsourced, the domestic agricultural sector should concentrate on crops that consume less water and are more adapted to Saudi Arabia's climate like fruits and vegetables.[85]

Other GCC Countries and the Issue of Strategic Storage

In the UAE arrangements have been more informal. It does not have a centralized task force with comparable authority like QNFSP. Its efforts to bridge bureaucratic divides and negotiate between different fiefdoms are more limited than in the case of KAISAIA. Its federal structure complicates a unified stance. Real power is not vested in the respective ministries, but with influential royals, their advisers, and associated institutions like the Supreme Petroleum Council. Control by individual emirates can be observed in areas like customs, the police force, transport, and utility companies. The federal budget is small and common policy implementation difficult. At its inception in the 1970s, the UAE resembled a confederation more than a federation in many ways. A consensus about further unification steps had to be delicately balanced. Individual emirates were reluctant to cede authority and revenues to a central government that still had to assert itself amidst tribal allegiances and unresolved border issues. Federal funding today still depends very much on oil-rich Abu Dhabi, which might press for more centralization in the wake of its bail-out of Dubai since 2009.[86] Notable players in the UAE are formally private companies like Al-Qudra or Al-Dahra that have members of the royal family as shareholders. The state-owned ADFD has been assigned a role to develop a large project in Sudan, but still needs to build up management capacities for agricultural projects or will need to find partners for such an endeavor.

Kuwait has a top-down approach with the ministries of finance and agriculture and the Kuwait Investment Authority (KIA) taking the lead. The KIA

---

[83] Al-Qahtani 2009: 37; Al-Rasheed interview.
[84] *Al-Jazirah*, 12 January 2011; *Al-Riyadh*, 21 September 2010.
[85] *Al-Riyadh*, 17 July 2009.   [86] Davidson 2008, 2005; Woertz 2012c.

considers agriculture as part of its overall investment interest in Asia, where it has good standing investment relations. Kuwait has the most pronounced rentier state structure in the Gulf with little diversification effort and a strong emphasis on redistribution policies. The parliament has a reputation of petty fights and procrastination. This can prolong decision-making processes or jeopardize projects altogether.[87] Bahrain has also shown a characteristic mixture of government support and private sector involvement. Its ability to engage in overseas investments is more limited because it does not command large oil revenues like Saudi Arabia, UAE, Qatar, and Kuwait. Bahrain's interest has been particularly pronounced on the Philippines with which it signed a bilateral investment agreement in 2001.[88]

Oman has abstained from the Gulf drive into agro-investments, apart from a small contribution to the Merowe Dam in Sudan. It has focused its food security strategy instead on the most developed system of strategic storage in the GCC. Storage was already extensive before the global food crisis and covered 3–4 months of the needs in staple foods.[89] By 2010 storage capacity was increased to 1 year for rice, 6 months for edible oils, milk, and sugar, and to 3–5 months for wheat.[90] Further expansion of wheat storage up to 17 months is planned, which includes the handling capacities at the ports of Sohar and Salalah.[91]

Oman has traditionally the closest relationship with East Africa and South Asia; the very regions other GCC countries target most. Zanzibar became the capital of the Omani empire in 1832 and the Omani Busaidi dynasty there lasted until 1964. A substantial minority of Omani citizens hails from Baluchistan from where mercenaries were recruited since the sixteenth and seventeenth centuries. Hence, Oman's lack of activity in foreign agro-investments comes somewhat as a surprise. One possible explanation is that Oman simply does not have the money as it is not as endowed with oil income as its richer neighbors. In fact, its oil production has peaked in 2001 and Oman is in urgent need of economic diversification. An after-oil age is not a mere academic discussion for the country. Still, the same is true for Bahrain where oil production peaked in 1977 already, and it has announced a number of foreign agro-investments.

---

[87] *MEED*, 19 March 2009. For Kuwait's political system see Herb 1999, 2009; Tétreault 2009.
[88] The text of the agreement is available at: <http://www.mof.gov.bh/topiclist.asp?ctype=agree&id=113> (accessed 5 March 2012).
[89] Interview with executive of Sites & Warehousing Affairs, Ministry of Commerce and Industry of Oman, Muscat, 24 November 2008.
[90] Interview with member of the Oman Food Security Strategy, Muscat, 3 March 2010. Purportedly the ruler wanted to increase rice storage to even two years.
[91] World Bank and FAO 2012: 14; *Oman Daily Observer*, 31 July 2011.

Other GCC governments have also increased strategic food storage. Kuwait has eyed storage of staple foods up to one year.[92] Currently the Saudi GSFMO has capacity of over ten months and holds ending stocks of at least six months of domestic wheat consumption, which it wants to increase to one year by 2016.[93] This would be comparable to the 1980s, when the Third Five Year Plan (1980–5) aimed at a capacity of twelve months, up from the six months in the plans of the 1970s.[94] Like in Oman, handling facilities in the largest ports are expanded (Jeddah, Yanbu, Dammam, Jubail). Management of this storage could pass on to the private sector if plans to privatize the GSFMO go ahead. The UAE decided to build up a strategic food reserve in 2008. It has shown a somewhat reduced degree of urgency in comparison with Oman or Saudi Arabia. By 2010, a plan by the federal Ministry of Economy was given the green light, and by early 2012, there were indications that a storage scheme would be implemented with a prominent role for the private sector in its management.[95]

Offered Deals

The NGO GRAIN has reported that Gulf countries would provide oil delivery contracts in exchange for access to farmland and food export guarantees. Academic articles then repeated this claim, yet it cannot be corroborated.[96] In the tumultuous 1970s, Saudi Arabia offered preferred bilateral barter relationships to Australia, but even then, they were never put into practice. As oil is a global and fungible commodity, such market segmentation would be difficult and expensive to achieve. Gulf countries are inclined to give supply assurances to Asian joint venture partners in refining and storage projects as they value the oil demand security that comes with such bilateral relationships. That they would offer special oil deals to countries that are not established food exporters like Sudan or the Philippines while their oil finds ample takers on world markets is unlikely. Oil pricing has also changed fundamentally since the 1970s from an intransparent system of posted prices to globally traded benchmarks. Barter deals would go against the common practice of Gulf countries to price their oil against such benchmarks like WTI, Brent, or a sour crude basket of Argus

---

[92] WikiLeaks cable 09KUWAIT1170, US Embassy in Kuwait, 15 December 2009.

[93] Mousa 2012; World Bank and FAO 2012: 14.

[94] Philipp 1984: 80f.

[95] *Gulf News*, 26 April 2010; interview, executive of agro-company, Abu Dhabi, 27 March 2012.

[96] GRAIN 2008: 4; Zurayk, Chaaban, and Sabra 2011.

in the case of Saudi Aramco. Barter arrangements do not play a role in discussions about reform of the current pricing system.[97]

Still, Gulf governments seek guarantees from host countries and they are ready to give them, just not in the form of oil. On numerous occasions, proposed farmland deals have been associated with offsetting investments in infrastructure and loan guarantees for target countries. This also matches the practice of the 1970s when oil exporters gave balance of payments support to LDCs that were affected by the oil price hikes. Institutions that have given such support have been the respective ministries, the Arab Monetary Fund (AMF), BADEA, ADFD, and the Special Arab Aid Fund for Africa (SAAFA) facility, which merged with BADEA in 1976.[98] It has also been suggested that Gulf countries could provide agricultural input factors like fertilizer and diesel at subsidized rates, thus mimicking practices of domestic agriculture.[99]

Gulf countries have offered offsetting agreements for farmland deals on numerous occasions. Kuwait's prime minister reportedly offered hydropower projects and $600 million in loans in exchange for lease arrangements for rice production while visiting Cambodia in August 2008.[100] Qatar has signed up for bilateral investment funds with Vietnam and Indonesia that include agriculture beside other areas of cooperation like energy. In another deal, it offered Kenya to fund a new port in Lamu in exchange for leasing 40,000 ha of land in the fertile Tana River delta. Lamu would be a second port beside Mombasa and could serve the hinterland of Kenya, Ethiopia, Somalia, and Sudan.[101] According to a WikiLeaks cable, Qatar was later pushed aside by China, which wrested the port contract away from it.[102] Meanwhile, the Tana River project shows no signs of implementation.[103]

Offsetting agreements are important for host countries, as the actual land leases are nominal at best. Saudi Star's lease payment is about $17,000 per annum according to the lease agreement. That is not a lot for a nation of 90 million people. Additionally, Saudi Star accesses tax holidays. Without investments in infrastructure, rural development, and job creation benefits would be limited. On a global level, the World Bank has deplored that promises of offsetting agreements in farmland deals are vague and often not followed

---

[97] For the historical emergence of today's benchmark pricing system see Yergin 1991: Parts IV and V. For the reduced attractiveness of WTI as a benchmark in recent years, see *Oxford Energy Forum*, Issue 87, February 2012. As an alternative to benchmark pricing Luciani has suggested an open auctioning system of physical barrels. Luciani 2010.

[98] World Bank 2010a: 22f.

[99] Interview, Saudi agro-businessman, Princeton, 27 September 2011; *Emirates 24/7*, 5 March 2011.

[100] *Phnom Penh Post*, 13 March 2009.

[101] *Daily Nation*, 31 December 2008.

[102] *Daily Nation*, 10 December 2010.

[103] FIAN International Secretariat 2010: 19; interview, Kenyan diplomat, Doha, 13 November 2011.

through.[104] Gulf investors on the other hand are wary that initially favorable investment conditions are unilaterally altered once projects start running and there is no way back. In Sudan, Gulf projects have been affected by tax increases after project implementation that impacted upon initial business plans.[105] Whether Argentina changes its tax code frequently or Egypt raises the rents for reclaimed land after tenants have achieved the cumbersome task of plot development, Saudi businessmen take notice.[106]

One goal of GCC countries is to attain privileged bilateral access to food production. To this end, they have tried to circumvent countervailing domestic legislation if needed. While negotiating agro-investments in Pakistan, the UAE tried to get "a blanket exemption" from Pakistani export restrictions, which the country had implemented for reasons of domestic food security.[107] The UAE wanted to have exemption for all possible projects, but the Pakistani side was only willing to give such privileges for specifically proposed agricultural free zones. Philippine regulations bar foreigners from owning land, producing on existing agricultural land, and exporting more than 40 percent of produced staple crops. Saudi Arabia managed to sign agreements that address these issues. Saudi companies can lease land via joint venture partners, they are allowed to produce in areas of Mindanao that are deemed "unproductive," and by targeting basmati rice rather than the prevalent white rice varieties they can get around the staple food requirement. Thus, these agreements give Saudi Arabia access to land and food production that would be closed to other foreign investors.[108]

7.3 THE INVESTORS: SOVEREIGN WEALTH FUNDS, STATE-OWNED COMPANIES, AND THE PRIVATE SECTOR

If the Gulf governments are active in negotiating favorable framework conditions, the actual implementation of agro-investments is in the hands of sovereign wealth funds, state-owned companies, or the private sector. They have varying degrees of independence from the respective governments. Sometimes new bespoke institutions for agro-investments like Qatar's Hassad Food have been founded. In other cases existing institutions have changed their business approach to agro-investments. Some of the funds that have been

---

[104] Deininger et al. 2011: 68ff.
[105] Interview with Saudi agro-expert, Muscat, 3 March 2010.
[106] Al-Rasheed, Turki Faisal 2010: 163–70; Al-Rasheed interview.
[107] *The National*, 8 June 2008; *Arab Build*, 12 May 2008.
[108] Salerno 2010: 23.

around since the 1970s have moved beyond debt financing via soft loans. Either they have taken a more equity-oriented strategic approach like the ADFD or they have ventured out of their natural realm of portfolio invest-ments into a field where they have formerly not been present, like the Kuwait Investment Authority (KIA). In Saudi Arabia with its agro-business commu-nity, public–private partnership arrangements dominate.

SWFs and State-owned Companies

Andrew Rozanov first coined the term "sovereign wealth fund" (SWF) in an article in the *Central Banking Journal* in 2005.[109] It has gained widespread usage since then against the backdrop of global financial imbalances. Even though SWFs are still minor players compared to banks, pension funds, and insurance companies the growing amount of assets at their disposal has led to Western fears that they might use investments to leverage political objectives. However, without proper differentiation of the term SWF, its explanatory power is limited. Sole focus on the trait of state ownership can be misleading.

Rozanov has proposed a liability-based approach to SWFs that categorizes them according to the sources of their funds and their intended usage.[110] A commodity fund in the Gulf essentially represents equity-financed offshore assets without immediate liability standing against them. This gives the owning state considerable discretion in decision-making. Non-commodity funds of export-oriented nations in Asia (e.g. the China Investment Corpor-ation) on the other hand can be debt-based as a result of sterilizing foreign exchange inflows. The central bank buys foreign currency to avoid an appre-ciation of the domestic currency. To counter an ensuing increase of money supply and inflation, it then mops up the excess liquidity by issuing domestic debt instruments. This local debt stands against the accumulated foreign assets and constitutes an important liability for the non-commodity SWFs. Their foreign assets are hardly able to earn the interest of domestic liabilities and cover the secular appreciation trend of an undervalued domestic currency. Hence, strictly financially, this asset allocation does not make sense. It can only be properly understood as a function of an export-led industrialization strat-egy and its development priorities, which might change in the future and focus more on growth driven by domestic demand.[111]

The usage of funds affects asset allocation as well. It makes a big difference whether SWFs are held for a contingent liability (e.g. buffer stocks, stabiliza-tion funds), a fixed liability (e.g. pension reserve funds), a mixed liability

---

[109] Rozanov 2005: 52–7.
[110] Rozanov 2008. See also Castelli and Scacciavillani 2012: 97ff.
[111] Woertz 2012a, 2012b.

(e.g. endowment funds with a spending rule), or whether they have open-ended liabilities like the portfolio SWFs of the smaller Gulf states (KIA, ADIA, QIA). The latter do not need to fund current expenditure as oil revenues are sufficient in comparison to population size and required budgets. Investment horizons can be long and equity exposure high. Capital income to finance domestic budgets would only be needed in case of sustainably falling oil revenues caused by declining oil production or depressed prices. In this case, the SWFs with open-ended liabilities would increasingly acquire the characteristics of endowment-type mixed liability funds. Compared to the portfolio SWFs of the smaller Gulf states Saudi Arabia has to cater to a much larger population. In the wake of the global financial crisis and oil price corrections in the second half of 2008 it had to repatriate over \$60 billion of its foreign assets to finance counter-cyclical spending at home. Not surprisingly, it does not have a proper SWF for international portfolio investments, but holds most of its assets in liquid fixed income instruments with the Saudi Arabian Monetary Agency (SAMA), the country's central bank.

Beside funding source and liability profile, the asset allocation of SWFs is affected by the political systems of their respective owners.[112] Whether it is a ruling party as in China, a monarchy as in the UAE, or a democracy as in Norway can make a difference in terms of accountability and transparency. This is also apparent in the Gulf itself, where the KIA is relatively transparent and under a certain degree of supervision of the parliament, while QIA and ADIA are relatively opaque.[113] They are more geared towards being discretionary tools of the respective rulers.

Gulf SWFs have traditionally kept a low profile. They have been oriented towards portfolio investments and have not acquired more than 5 percent in any given company to avoid disclosure requirements. Despite fears to the contrary, they have not used investment allocation for political ends since the 1970s. They need to provide income and investments for an after-oil age and their asset accumulation does not result from an export-led industrialization strategy and associated benefits. Hence, capital preservation and achievement of risk-adjusted returns are of greater importance for them than for Asian non-commodity funds.[114] The latter already got something for their dollars and euros indirectly, i.e. a capital stock and industrialization, while the Gulf countries still want to buy something with theirs. In this context Gulf investments increasingly focus on companies that can benefit economic diversification at home. This has led to the establishment of SWFs with a more strategic private equity orientation in the 2000s (e.g. Mubadala). At the same time, state-owned companies like SABIC or Borouge have successfully

[112] Woertz 2012a.
[113] For a SWF transparency scoreboard see Truman 2010: chapter 5.
[114] Woertz 2012b.

matured and have shown an interest in strategic international acquisition like any other company of their size would do.

One can differentiate between six types of sovereign wealth in the GCC countries. Some of it is not relevant for agro-investments, some of it very much so, some of it increasingly so:

- Central bank reserves (e.g. SAMA)
- Portfolio SWFs (e.g. ADIA, KIA, QIA)
- Funds with a private equity nature (e.g. Hassad Food, Mubadala)
- International development funds (e.g. ADFD, SDF, KFAED, AFESD)
- Domestic development funds (e.g. SIDF, PIF, Mumtalakat)
- State-owned companies (e.g. Zad Holding, SABIC, Borouge)

Until the 2000s the international development funds were the sole vehicles for state-led agro-investments (see Figure 7.2). They invested in agricultural development in LDCs without taking equity stakes and left project implementation to the respective companies and governments in host countries. Agricultural projects made up mostly 15 to 18 percent of their spending.[115]

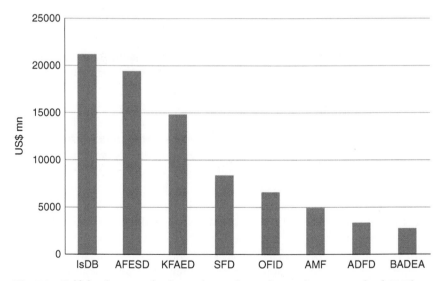

Fig. 7.2. Gulf development funds: total cumulative financial assistance (end 2007)
Source: World Bank 2010a.

---

[115] World Bank 2010a: 17, 46, 78. Only the IsDB has a smaller share of 6.7 percent and the AMF does not finance any agricultural projects at all as a purely financial institution. BADEA on the other hand has made agriculture a priority issue and allotted 25 percent to it in its Fifth Five Year Plan 2005–09. IsDB itself gives a higher share for its agro-projects of 10.2 percent. IsDB 2011: 12.

Their primary aim was developmental. The strategic leadership role of the AFESD in creating the Sudan bread-basket vision was an outlier.

The development funds are an offspring of the oil boom. The Kuwait Fund for Arab Economic Development (KFAED) was a pioneer and already established in 1961. It widened its mandate in 1974 to developing countries beyond the Arab world and increased its capital fivefold. The Saudi Fund for Development (SFD) was established in 1974 and the Abu Dhabi Fund for Development (ADFD) in 1971. Qatar, Bahrain, and Oman do not have comparable national development funds. Beside these funds, GCC countries have distributed aid via a number of regional and multilateral institutions like the Kuwait-based AFESD (est. 1971), the Khartoum-based Arab Bank for Economic Development in Africa (BADEA, est. 1974), the Jeddah-based Islamic Development Bank (IsDB, est. 1975), the Vienna-based OPEC Fund for International Development (OFID, est. 1976), the Abu Dhabi-based Arab Monetary Fund (AMF, est. 1976), and the Riyadh-based Arab Gulf Programme for United Nations Development Organizations (AGFUND, est. 1980), which finances technical cooperation and humanitarian assistance by supporting specialized UN agencies. OFID and IsDB are not strictly Arab organizations, but Gulf countries provide a large share of their funding: Saudi Arabia contributes 25 percent of IsDB's and 30 percent of OFID's financing, while Kuwait's shares are 8 percent and 7 percent respectively. All national and multilateral funds coordinate their activities via the Coordination Secretariat of Arab National and Regional Development Institutions, which is hosted by the AFESD in Kuwait.

In addition to the development funds, a large part of Arab official development assistance has been distributed as direct bilateral aid to beneficiary countries. Distribution channels were usually different ministries like foreign affairs or finance. Agenda-setting in the fragmented bureaucratic landscape has often been murky and unified policy has not always been discernible. In Saudi Arabia, the Ministry of Foreign Affairs is formally in charge of individual bilateral relations, but its influence is limited as it is a weak and disorganized body in the overall bureaucratic framework. The Ministry of Interior is very powerful and controls private financial aid flows and individual relief campaigns, but it has no comprehensive strategy. The equally influential Ministry of Finance is in charge of government-to-government grants, but largely acts according to ad hoc requests of the Royal Court. To complicate things further, private relief organizations often have royals as patrons and are in fact para-statal institutions.[116] The UAE has established the Office for the Coordination of Foreign Aid in 2008 in order to facilitate better

---

[116] Correspondence with Steffen Hertog, 30 June 2011.

coordination, evaluation, and international visibility of UAE development efforts and the involved institutions.[117]

The strong preference for bilateral relations is reflected in a low level of disbursement via multilateral institutions compared to OECD–DAC countries.[118] Gulf donors have also distributed sector-specific development aid via the International Fund for Agricultural Development (IFAD). Conceived at the World Food Conference in 1974, IFAD was launched in 1977 with joint funding from OECD (58 percent) and OPEC countries (42 percent). They and the developing countries have a third of the voting rights each. OPEC has been prominent in IFAD's administration. Four of the fund's hitherto five presidents have been from OPEC countries (Saudi Arabia, Algeria, Kuwait, and Nigeria).[119]

Gulf development funds adopted a more strategic orientation in the 2000s. They have underwritten the Sudanese dam program that is central to the renewed push of the Sudanese government towards agricultural mega projects. Even though the Merowe Dam is primarily for electricity generation, there have been persistent rumors that Sudan promised Gulf countries and Egypt land and irrigation projects as a quid pro quo for the dam deals.[120]

Since 2008, there has been a proliferation of governmental players in Gulf agro-investments. All of them share the common motivation to move beyond dispersed loan financing. They are seeking to acquire strategic equity stakes in agricultural production. When the Gulf states started to formulate their food security strategies in 2008, they often lacked the appropriate institutions and expertise. On occasion, unlikely candidates were equipped with the task; in other cases, mission purposes were modified or new organizations were established.

The KIA has appeared as an agro-investor, although it has traditionally been a portfolio investor and has no prior experience in running such projects. The ADFD was instructed by its chairman Sheikh Mansour al-Nahyan to manage a Sudanese agro-project even it did not have experience in taking an active project management role and did not have a single agro-engineer among its ranks at that time.[121] The QIA on the other hand has established a subsidiary, Hassad Food, to acquire and manage agricultural projects. Similarly, the government-controlled conglomerate Dubai World created a

---

[117] World Bank 2010a: 4.

[118] Between 1973 and 2008, it was 13 percent versus a 30 percent average in the OECD. The main multilateral distribution channels were Arab Financial Institutions (4 percent of total), the World Bank (4 percent), UN agencies (2 percent) and the African Development Bank (1 percent). World Bank 2010a: XIV and 1.

[119] Shaw 2009: 63ff.

[120] Verhoeven 2012b: 235f.; interview with author, 14 January 2012.

[121] Interview with ADFD executive, Abu Dhabi, 19 April 2009; *Financial Times*, 3 June 2008.

subsidiary for global investments in energy, mining, and agriculture, even though the debt crisis of the emirate impeded project implementation.[122]

In other cases, state-owned companies rather than sovereign wealth funds have been following agro-investments overseas. Zad Holding Company (formerly Qatar Flour Mills) established a joint holding company in Sudan and eyed exports to Arab food markets.[123] Qatari livestock company Mawashi announced an investment of $1 billion in corporate farms in Pakistan. It operates already a small livestock farm in southern Kordofan, where it also plants corn and sunflowers for the local market.[124] The government owns more than 8 percent of Mawashi. It announced its intention for a complete take-over in an opaque maneuver in February 2011, asking the stock exchange to suspend trading of the Mawashi stock without bothering to inform the company. Allegedly, Mawashi's management was not trusted in reliably supplying Qatari markets with livestock products, which the government subsidizes.[125]

The take-over story fits into the efforts at centralization of food security policies in Qatar. It confirms the supremacy of the state in sectors of the economy that are regarded as strategic. Compared to state-owned Hassad Food that resides in a slick office tower close to the Corniche, Mawashi's operation could not have been more different. Taxi drivers had difficulties finding the single-storey buildings on the outskirts of Doha that sit on an unpaved plot amidst ruminating livestock from Australia, Syria, and Somalia.[126] The place conveyed the tranquillity of a small Gulf town before the breakneck development of the recent oil boom. It was hard to imagine that these were the commanding heights for a planned one billion dollar investment in Pakistan. So far, the possible government take-over is still pending, but whether it remains private or not, Mawashi in its old form will possibly undergo a process of reform to fit into Qatar's ambitious food security strategies.

GCC countries lack expertise in overseas agricultural projects. To acquire know-how about corresponding crops, farm management, and investment environments Gulf institutions increasingly cooperate with international organizations like the FAO, which has opened an office in Abu Dhabi.[127] Saudi Arabia has approached the World Bank and the IRRI to connect it with countries in Africa and Central Asia in order to facilitate investments in food

---

[122] *Reuters*, 6 October 2008.

[123] *Sudan Tribune*, 22 July 2008; *Gulf Times*, 22 July 2008.

[124] Interview with executives of Mawashi, Doha, 15 October 2009.

[125] *The Peninsula*, 20 February 2011; *The National*, 15 February 2011.

[126] Mawashi gets 85 percent of its sheep from Australia, the rest mostly from Syria. Only a few animals come from Sudan, Somalia, India, and Pakistan. Interview with Mawashi executives, Doha, 15 October 2009.

[127] Interview with FAO executive, Abu Dhabi, 1 March 2010.

production.[128] QNFSP on the other hand has cooperation agreements with the International Center for Agricultural Research in the Dry Areas (ICARDA) and the Texas A&M University.[129]

Private Sector with Varying Government Support

Zad Holding and Mawashi are examples of food processing companies that aim at vertical integration abroad in order to enhance their value chain and secure feedstock. It remains to be seen whether this can develop into a broader trend in an industry that is dominated by the private sector. Savola and Almarai from Saudi Arabia and Kuwait Food Company (Americana) are by far the three largest food processers in the GCC.[130] The latter is specialized in frozen and packaged food and is less of a candidate, but Almarai has already agro-projects via its subsidiary HADCO, which it acquired in 2009, and it has invested in corn and soybean production in Argentina as feedstock for its dairy and poultry operations in Saudi Arabia.[131] Savola is also investigating opportunities in Sudan. Yet, on the sidelines of the Gulfood conference 2011 in Dubai the food processing industry of the region was mostly skeptical of foreign agro-investments. Lack of funds, limited domestic market size, and political instability in target countries were cited as risk factors. Without extensive government guarantees the incentive for upward integration to secure feedstock was not deemed too pressing.[132]

In Saudi Arabia, private sector interest in KAISAIA is intense. There is the hope that support for agricultural investments overseas might mimic subsidies for domestic agriculture from which companies have benefited greatly since the 1970s.[133] The SCAIAP fund has three members from the private sector on its board of directors.[134] However, its funds have been slow in coming. By 2011, it had not financed a single project and the business community started to complain about it. Only in 2012 were there signs that it had finally started moving. Still, there were public–private partnerships via other institutions. HADCO received 60 percent of the funding of a 10,000 ha wheat and corn project in Sudan from the Saudi Industrial Development Fund (SIDF), which usually focuses on domestic development. HADCO also insured up to 90 percent of its investment in the project through a pan-Arab, government-owned insurance company.[135]

[128] *Phnom Penh Post*, 13 March 2009; International Rice Research Institute (IRRI) 2009.
[129] See <http://www.qnfsp.gov.qa/home> (accessed 21 April 2012).
[130] Alpen Capital 2011: 25.   [131] *Reuters*, 21 December 2011.
[132] *Gulf News*, 28 February 2011.
[133] Interview with member of KAISAIA initiative, Dubai, 16 April 2009.
[134] *Financial Times*, 14 April 2009.
[135] *The Peninsula*, 17 February 2009; *Financial Times*, 24 May 2009.

government and private demand are of greater importance than they used to be. Yet, indirectly this private demand is still generated by government salaries and other forms of government spending.[31] Anti-cyclical government spending has proven to be crucial to cope with the global financial crisis. Thus, the private sector's capacities continue to be dependent on the state, even though transmission channels of rent distribution have changed and relative autonomy has increased. Gulf countries' fiscal position is privileged if compared with indebted OECD and developing countries, but their fiscal space for agricultural experiments became more limited with the global financial crisis and increased spending profiles. It only recovered in 2011 with rising oil prices and historically high production rates in Saudi Arabia.

8.3 FRAMEWORK CONDITIONS, WATER STRESS, AND CLIMATE CHANGE

Apart from some regional preferences and the focus on food crops, interests of Gulf countries are not very much different from other international investors when it comes to agro-investments: natural endowments and a favorable business environment are regarded as essential. During the Sudan breadbasket strategy in the 1970s Gulf countries were anxious not to forgo commercial considerations and endorsed the tough love that the IMF imposed upon the Sudanese government. Now as then there is interest in Saudi circles to team up with investors and institutions from OECD countries as they feel that they alone do not have the legal muscle to protect their investments.[32]

One reason for the project implementation gap might simply be that many target countries do not match these criteria. Challenges range from underdeveloped infrastructure to corruption, political unrest, and lack of skilled labor. Impediments such as these were the reason why the plan for Sudan as Arab bread-basket fell by the wayside shortly after its announcement in the mid-1970s. Furthermore, some of the target countries have serious water issues of their own and will be disproportionately affected by climate change, very much like the Middle East.

Business Environment, Political Stability, and Infrastructure

Unfavorable business environments rank top of the list of complaints of Gulf agro-investors. In a WikiLeaks cable of 2009, Kuwaiti officials dismissed press

---

[31] Hertog 2011.   [32] Correspondence with Saudi agro-businessman, 10 September 2011.

reports that any tangible agro-deals would have come out of their Asia trip. They identified lacking infrastructure and corruption as a problem. Investments in countries that are not established food exporters with a proven track record of delivering struck them as too risky. In times of crisis, the host government could be toppled if it allowed food exports and "we do not have an army to get it" remarked a Kuwaiti official dryly. Kuwait was rather interested in countries like the US, Australia, and Brazil and saw strategic storage as another option.[33]

Saudi agro-businessman Turki Faisal al-Rasheed is principally in favor of agro-investments in Sudan, but he points to an array of shortcomings like political unrest, unclear land rights, and lack of infrastructure. Apart from smallholder ownership along the Nile most of the land in Sudan is nominally owned by the state. It can only be leased by foreigners, but not purchased. For Al-Rasheed this is a deal breaker. The payment of compensation to previous users of land that is slated for investment should be borne by the Sudanese government, he argues. Other shortcomings in his view include high government fees and lack of clarity as to which level of government investors need to negotiate with.[34] When influential Saudi businessman Saleh Kamel unveiled a grand plan for cultivation of two million feddans in north Sudan by Saudi investors after discussions with Sudanese officials, it was important for him to stress that the farms would be "Saudi property in a free zone, unhindered by Sudanese laws and without obligation to pay fees or taxes." The benefits for the country would be in the form of hundreds of thousands of jobs, he argued.[35] Statehood requires money, which in the absence of rents means taxes. There is a certain contradiction when the Saudi business community demands regulatory activity from a functioning government and wants to have certain conditions on a silver platter, but otherwise prefers the hosting state as far away as possible.

Gulf governments have a fairly strong belief in orthodox metrics of efficiency as promoted by international organizations and Western consultancy companies. They commission consultancy reports of such institutions frequently and often twice for the same problem in order to weigh different opinions. As donors, Gulf countries have closely followed recommendations of the Bretton Woods institutions as the Sudan bread-basket episode has shown. They wanted to see implementation of standards, while trying to stay out of the limelight and avoid confrontation. It is worth taking a closer look at such internationally promoted standards as Gulf countries weigh the potential of their agro-investments in light of them.[36]

---

[33] WikiLeaks cable 09KUWAIT1170, US Embassy in Kuwait, 15 December 2009.
[34] Al-Rasheed, Turki Faisal 2010: 171–8.
[35] *Al Arabiya*, 7 April 2012.
[36] For an assessment based on the World Bank's EDBI see Al-Qahtani 2009: 11.

Table 8.1 gauges the business environment in target countries with the help of several indices. Against the backdrop of economic liberalization and globalization, prevalent development paradigms have stressed the importance of foreign direct investments since the 1980s. FDI is needed to acquire know-how and move up the production ladder, so the argument goes. To attract it, one needs "good governance." The World Bank introduced the concept in the 1990s at a time when the empirical track record of orthodox structural adjustment was questioned and reasons for failures were debated.[37] In 1996, the Bank commenced its rating and conceptualization of governance performance for the first time. Since then there has been a virtual proliferation of comparative governance rankings by public and private organizations.[38] Two of the most widely quoted rankings are the Ease of Doing Business Index (EDBI) by the World Bank and its subsidiary International Finance Corporation (IFC), which was launched in 2001, and the Global Competitiveness Report (GCR) of the World Economic Forum (WEF), which was first published in 1979.[39]

The concept of governance is fairly vague and can mean different things to different people. It includes transparent regulatory frameworks, effective administration, control of corruption, fair and responsive legal systems, and political stability. It shuns the word "democracy," replacing it with the more

Table 8.1. Governance rankings of selected target countries

	EDBI 2012 rank (out of 183)	GCR 2011–12 rank (out of 142)	HDI 2011 rank (out of 187)	CPI 2011 rank (out of 182)	FSI 2012 rank (out of 60)
Sudan	135	n/a	169	177	3
Pakistan	105	118	145	134	13
Philippines	136	75	112	129	56
Ethiopia	111	106	174	120	17
Egypt	110	94	113	112	31
Turkey	71	59	92	61	–
Indonesia	129	46	124	100	–
Australia	15	20	2	8	–
Kazakhstan	47	72	68	120	–
Brazil	126	53	84	73	–
Ukraine	152	82	76	152	–

Source: World Bank and International Finance Corporation (IFC) 2012; World Economic Forum 2011; UNDP 2011; Transparency International 2011; Foreign Policy Magazine and the Fund for Peace 2012.

---

[37] Nanda 2006.   [38] Springborg 2012.

[39] Other indices that measure aspects of governance and attractiveness for FDI comprise the Heritage Foundation's Index of Economic Freedom, the Milken Capital Access Index, and the Bertelsmann Stiftung's Transformation Index. For a discussion of various indicators and their application to the Middle East see Henry and Springborg 2010: 20–30.

technocratic "accountability." The EDBI's focus is on doing business specifically, not so much on broader aspects of governance and provision of services. It is geared towards larger international corporations and their investment interests. Needs of SMEs or poorer segments of the population are not as well reflected, if at all. At times, polls in a given country (e.g. Egypt) have revealed grossly differing opinions about the state of governance if compared with the EDBI and other leading indices like the Heritage Foundation's Index of Economic Freedom.[40] Similarly, most subindicators of the WEF's GCR have been identified by a survey among business executives. It likely reflects the universe as viewed from Davos. One might perceive this as a shortcoming, but it fits our purpose of gauging the attractiveness of a country for Gulf foreign agro-investments.

Still, there are problems of measuring that need to be kept in mind. The EDBI comprises ten different categories: starting a business, dealing with construction permits, getting electricity, registering property, getting credit, investor protection, paying tax, trading across borders, contract enforcement, and resolving insolvency. The rankings of a single country can vary widely from one category to another, making the average ranking less representative. Most importantly, the EDBI measures rules and procedures, not their implementation and realities on the ground like the GCR. This gives an incentive for countries to "game" the indicators in order to look attractive to FDI. Saudi Arabia has a bespoke department at the Saudi Arabian Government Investment Authority (SAGIA) where World Bank personnel are drafting reform measures to satisfy formal requirements of the EDBI.[41] Thus, Saudi Arabia has constantly moved up the EDBI ladder to rank 12 in 2012, a result that has struck practitioners as out of touch, given the at times cumbersome bureaucratic procedures in the country. Similarly, the EDBI called Egypt the world's leading reformer in 2008. In 2010, the country had been among the top ten reformers of the EDBI for a record four consecutive years. Robert Springborg suspects that this might have been attributable to manipulation of indicators as well.[42] In light of the consecutive developments of the Arab Spring, it surely puts into question the ability of the EDBI to indicate political stability.

The Human Development Index (HDI) of UNDP on the other hand gauges broader aspects of governance, welfare, and service provision, like health, education, equality, and life expectancy. The Failed States Index (FSI) by the Foreign Policy Magazine and the Fund for Peace also aims directly at measuring the stability of a state, its legitimacy, and its ability to forge consensus and control its territory. The FSI is based on indicators like quality of public services, refugees, security apparatus, factionalized elites, human rights, economic development, and demographic pressures. For comparison purposes,

[40] Springborg 2012.   [41] Hertog 2010: 175–9.   [42] Springborg 2012.

these two indices are included in Table 8.1 alongside the Corruption Perception Index of Transparency International. The latter is particularly relevant for setting up and running a farm with consecutive export of food, given the frequent contact with official institutions that such procedures require.

The most popular target countries of Gulf agro-investments occupy low ranks in all governance indices. Sudan comes in at the very end of the scale and is deemed one of the most corrupt countries according to the CPI. Only in the EDBI subindices for property registration (41), resolving insolvency (81), and paying taxes (103) does it perform considerably better. Pakistan is ranked very low by the GCR and HDI, while scoring slightly better in the EDBI. Its EDBI subranking for investor protection is high (29), but it performs badly in contract enforcement (154), property registration (125), and getting electricity (166). As in Sudan, corruption is endemic in the country. The GCR indentifies it as the major impediment for business after political instability. The Philippines is performing nearly as badly as Sudan in the EDBI, with the subindices for trading across borders (51) and getting electricity (54) as positive outliers. Yet, it manages to occupy a middle rank in the GCR, which regards the macroeconomic environment and relatively big and sophisticated markets as a plus. Corruption, inefficient bureaucracy, and infrastructure on the other hand are recorded on the negative side of the ledger for the Philippines.

Ethiopia's ranking in the EDBI is considerably better than in the HDI. Corruption is regarded as less widespread than in Sudan and its subindex ranking for institutions is relatively high in the GCR (58). Access to finance, foreign currency regulations, and inflation are identified as major impediments and not so much corruption and bureaucratic inefficiencies. Ukraine is performing very badly in the EDBI and CPI compared to its middle rankings in the HDI and the GCR. Brazil, Turkey, and Kazakhstan also occupy middle ranks, while Australia is the only OECD country among target countries with corresponding high governance ratings. The only index where the most popular target countries for Gulf agro-investments rank high is the one for Failed States. Sudan comes in third right after Somalia and Congo. Ethiopia and Pakistan are also part of the top 20, as are Nigeria (14) and Kenya (16). Many other target countries occupy ranks down to 60, like Egypt (31), Zambia (44), the Philippines (56), Madagascar (58), or Mozambique (59). Kazakhstan is not present on the FSI, but surrounded by states that occupy middle to lower ranks on the index like Uzbekistan, Tajikistan, and Kyrgyzstan.

Problematic governance in target countries can be an inhibiting factor for Gulf agro-investments. Yet, it might change over time. The ability of Gulf countries to reduce transaction costs via established channels in business and politics should also not be underestimated. Natural endowments on the other hand cannot be changed. Here, a number of target countries face a critical water situation, limited export capacities, and disproportionate exposure to climate change.

Water Stress and Export Capacity

Water, not arable land is the reason why agriculture is downsized in Saudi Arabia and other Gulf countries. It is a limiting factor elsewhere in the world as well, to the extent that the specter of "peak water" has been raised.[43] Table 8.2 shows the renewable water reserves in target countries, their virtual water trade, their food net trade position, and their current fertility rate that is influencing its population growth over the coming decades. The table shows country level data and does not accurately reflect regional water shortages, for example in southeast Australia or southern Kazakhstan. Furthermore, it is important to note that green or soil water is not part of total renewable water reserves, which only comprise surface and groundwater. Green water is contained in the soil and contributes to its moisture. It is the basis of rain-fed agriculture and about 70 percent of global food is produced with it, not with blue water, i.e. with surface or groundwater irrigation, which can also come from non-renewable groundwater sources as in Saudi Arabia. Green water cannot be metered, bottled, or shipped by pipeline. It is invisible, but it is contained in crops as "virtual water" and can be transported via food trade. It is the very essence of the Gulf countries' future food security.

Between 70 and 90 percent of the global trade in staple food commodities is undertaken by a few food trading houses, mainly the "ABCDs": ADM, Bunge, Cargill, and Dreyfus.[44] The trade in crops and derived products constitute 76 percent of global virtual water trade and 68 percent of this total comes from green water. Blue and grey (waste) water only contribute 13 percent and 19 percent respectively.[45] Currently global virtual water net exports focus on North America (40 percent), Australia and New Zealand (40 percent), and South America (20 percent). Given available water reserves, the share of Australia will likely decrease while that of Brazil is expected to increase.[46]

It is striking that some of the countries that Gulf investors have targeted have water issues of their own. Egypt uses water above its total renewable water reserves. The withdrawal rates for Pakistan and Sudan are high and for Kazakhstan significant. More importantly all four countries have low internal water reserves compared to total reserves.[47] A large part of their renewable

---

[43] Gleick and Palaniappan 2010. Peak water denotes the full usage of renewable water reserves, the depletion of non-renewable water resources, and "peak ecological water," i.e. when ecological disruptions of water abstraction outpace its benefits.

[44] Sojamo et al. 2012: 175.

[45] Mekonnen and Hoekstra 2011: 20.

[46] Allan 2011: 42, 85. For water footprints by country see Mekonnen and Hoekstra 2011; Hoekstra and Mekonnen 2012; Hoekstra and Chapagain 2007.

[47] Internal freshwater resources per capita are internal renewable resources, which include flows of rivers and groundwater from rainfall in the country but exclude river flows from other countries, divided by midyear population. (Definition by Food and Agriculture Organization, World Resources Institute, and World Bank.)

Table 8.2. Water resources, virtual water trade, and net food trade in selected target countries

	Total renewable water reserves per capita (m³/yr), 2008	Total internal renewable water reserves per capita (m³/yr), 2008	Water withdrawal of total renewable reserves in %[a]	Virtual water imports (Mm³/yr)[b] 1996–2005	Role of food net trade in total food consumption, %[c] 2006–08	Total Fertility Rate 2005–10
Sudan	1560	726	57.6	−3401	0 to−25	4.6
Pakistan	1304	311	79.5 (2008)	−41736	0 to−25	3.7
Philippines	5302	5302	17	−4297	0 to−25	3.3
Ethiopia	1512	1512	4.6	−1070	0 to−25	4.6
Egypt	703	22	119	9048	−50 to less	2.9
Turkey	2890	3071	18.8 (2007)	5786	0 to−25	2.2
Indonesia	8881	8881	5.6	−36923	25 to 50	2.2
Australia	23346	23346	4.6	−77192	50 to over	1.9
Kazakhstan	7061	4859	28.9	−22519	50 to over	2.5
Brazil	42886	28223	0.7 (2007)	−76948	50 to over	1.9
Ukraine	3035	1155	27.6	−16407	50 to over	1.4
Saudi Arabia	95	95	943 (2007)	17652	−50 to less	3

(a) Total actual renewable freshwater resources withdrawn (%), 2002 unless otherwise indicated.
(b) Is based on blue, green, and grey water.
(c) FAO definition: "The net-trade is obtained by subtracting the amount of food imports from the amount of food exports. Data on net-trade are converted in kilocalories using conversion factors by commodities in order to calculate the share of net-trade in the total Dietary Energy Supply."

Source: FAO 2011a; Mekonnen and Hoekstra 2011; FAO 2012a; United Nations 2010.

water reserves has been generated externally and reaches them via the Indus, the Nile, the Syr Darya, and other rivers. This points to delicate hydropolitics in the respective regions.

Nile riparians have tried to sort out the cross-border sharing of water resources in the Nile Basin Initiative. Pakistan and India agreed on reserved inflows to Pakistan in the Indus Water Treaty (1960). The five riparian states of the Aral Sea region—Kazakhstan, Kyrgyzstan, Tajikistan, Turkmenistan, and Uzbekistan—formed the Interstate Commission for Water Coordination of Central Asia (ICWC) in 1992. Under its remit are the coordination of water allocation and mitigation of the environmental problems that have been caused by excessive irrigation and the drying up of the Aral Sea. Lack of water is one reason why international agro-investors have preferred Ukraine or Russia to Kazakhstan.[48] There are also water issues between Turkey and the downstream riparians of the Euphrates and Tigris, Syria and Iraq. Turkey's total water reserves are lower than its internal ones because it has unilaterally guaranteed annual flows to Syria of 15.75 km^3. Tensions over water have subsided since they led to military mobilization at the time when Turkey started to fill up the dams of its Anatolian GAP irrigation project in 1990. But water sharing remains a sensitive issue between the three countries. Like in the Nile and Jordan basins, the situation is characterized by domination strategies of one hydro-hegemonic power and low intensity conflict.[49] Egypt, Israel, and Turkey are anxious to maintain their relative strength in the respective river basins. Apart from stretched renewable water resources, Egypt, Pakistan, or northern Sudan have limited green water reserves due to arid climate zones. Rain-fed agriculture is only possible in some regions of the respective countries and not at all in Egypt.

On a per capita basis, the available water reserves in the most popular target countries are relatively low in comparison to water-rich countries like Brazil; only in the Philippines are they higher. Like Saudi Arabia, Egypt and Turkey are importers of virtual water. Sudan and Ethiopia export a small quantity. Australia, Brazil, Indonesia, Ukraine, and Kazakhstan are substantial exporters, mainly from green water sources. Pakistan is a large exporter as well, but from stressed blue water resources that will be affected by climate change. Increased rainfall will be unable to counter the effect of melting Himalaya glaciers. Water flows of the Indus will be reduced. This will affect Pakistan's bread-basket, the Punjab. Without adaptation measures and productivity growth, the number of people that can be fed with food from the Indus basin might decrease by about 26 million by 2050.[50] Because of their physical water shortage, Pakistan and many Central Asian countries face problems

[48] Interview with CEO of agro-company, New York, June 2009.
[49] Zeitoun and Warner 2006.
[50] Immerzeel, van Beek, and Bierkens 2010; Knox et al. 2011.

similar to countries in the Middle East. Their ability to provide solutions to Gulf food security is limited. Many countries in sub-Saharan Africa, on the other hand, only have an economic water shortage at this stage. Increases in agricultural production are conceivable once large-scale investments in infra-structure and irrigation have been undertaken.[51]

The most popular target countries are all net food importers in calorie terms. In Sudan, Ethiopia, the Philippines, and Turkey 0–25 percent of calorie needs are covered by net imports. In Egypt, like in Saudi Arabia, this stands at over 50 percent. Indonesia appears as a food net exporter because of its palm oil production. In terms of cereals, the country is a large importer though, especially of wheat and rice. Australia, Brazil, Kazakhstan, and Ukraine are export heavyweights in the crops required by GCC countries like wheat, barley, and soybeans, but they rank less prominently as investment targets.

The limited export potential of many target countries will further decrease because of population growth; it is one reason why the World Bank doubts that Sudan could become an Arab bread-basket.[52] Yet the world at large and many Middle Eastern countries are amidst a demographic transition. On a global level, population growth rates will level out from 2050 onwards. Birth rates in Turkey and Indonesia are close to the replacement fertility rate of 2.1 children per woman. In Australia, Brazil, and Ukraine they are already below that level. This will lead to declining population growth rates after a transition period. In Ukraine the population is already shrinking. Birth rates in Ethiopia, Sudan, Pakistan, and the Philippines have started to decline as well since the 1980s, but they still remain well above the replacement rate and population growth will only level out towards the end of the century. More people in these countries will need to be fed; the likelihood that they could become food net exporters is slim, especially if water stress and climate change are taken into consideration.[53]

Climate Change

Gulf officials have on occasion denied the scientific evidence for manmade climate change out of fear for their oil exports, but representatives of KAISAIA have acknowledged it as a contributing factor to future global food supply problems and so have the Saudi MoWE, QNFSP, and the Islamic Development

---

[51] Molden 2007; World Bank 2007.

[52] World Bank, FAO, and IFAD 2009: 20.

[53] The UN expects global population growth rate to decrease to 0.36 percent in 2050–5. In Ukraine, the population peaked in 1990. In Ethiopia, the peak is expected in 2075, in Pakistan in 2070, in Indonesia in 2050, in Saudi Arabia in 2065, in the Philippines in 2090, in Brazil in 2040. Australia's population growth would level out in 2045 and in Sudan and South Sudan in 2090. United Nations 2010.

Bank.[54] Climate change will increase the risk of crop failure and yield declines. Developing countries will be affected in particular because they have warmer climates on average and have heightened exposure to extreme events such as droughts, storms, and floods. The impact is aggravated further as agriculture dominates their economies and capital for adaptation measures is scarce. IFPRI has estimated that $7 billion additional annual investments in adaptation programs like drought resistant crops and irrigation programs would be necessary globally.[55]

The range of projected impacts of climate change on agricultural production varies greatly depending on the chosen time horizon and crops, the methodology, and the underlying assumptions. Most studies only look at the direct impact of climate change and not at indirect effects such as cropland inundation, erosion, salinization due to sea-level rise, and increased weeds and pests. Estimates about precipitation patterns vary more than those about temperature increases. Increased variability of temperature and rainfall might be more damaging than their average change. The impact of a carbon fertilization effect is by far the largest uncertainty for agricultural production.[56] Africa, the Middle East, and South Asia will be severely affected by drought-based yield reduction, while North America and Russia will benefit from prolonged vegetation periods.[57] There are great differences between countries across Africa. The north and south will likely become drier and hotter while precipitation in the east and parts of central Africa will increase.[58] Wheat yields will see sharp declines in Africa and South Asia, while corn yields will at least hold up in East and Central Africa. Rice and wheat yields will be severely affected in India and Pakistan, with some studies estimating productivity decreases of a third and more by 2080.[59]

Climate change has already affected yield growth negatively since 1980, particularly in sub-Saharan Africa,[60] but the most dramatic changes will likely occur after 2050. Until 2030–40, there could be an aggregate positive effect of climate change on global agricultural output potential. Prolonged vegetation periods in temperate zones could offset capacity declines in tropical and subtropical regions of Asia, Africa, and Latin America. As oceans function as CO_2 sinks, that could lead to an ocean thermal lag for about two to three decades. Food trade could mediate the impact until then, provided the unrealistic assumption that predominantly agricultural developing countries find alternative exports and sources of foreign exchange to finance food imports.

---

[54] *The Peninsula*, 2 August 2011; Kingdom of Saudi Arabia 2009b.
[55] Nelson et al. 2009.   [56] Müller et al. 2009.
[57] Müller et al. 2011; Fischer et al. 2005; IPCC 2007; Knox et al. 2011.
[58] Collier, Conway, and Venables 2008.
[59] Knox et al. 2011: 61ff.; Cline 2007: 69f.
[60] Lobell, Schlenker, and Costa-Roberts 2011; Barrios, Ouattara, and Strobl 2008.

However, towards 2050 there will be aggregate declines in output capacity, particularly if the effect of carbon fertilization should not materialize.[61]

Carbon fertilization describes yield improvement as a result of increased concentration of carbon dioxide in the atmosphere. Carbon dioxide is an input factor for photosynthesis. Solar energy and CO_2 create carbohydrates with oxygen as a waste product. Increased CO_2 availability will lead to a reduction in pore density and openings of plants, which will reduce water loss from transpiration.[62] The effect of carbon fertilization on different plant species varies. C3 crops like rice, wheat, soybeans, fine grains, legumes, and most trees benefit from additional CO_2 in the atmosphere. The gains for C4 crops like corn, millet, sorghum, and sugarcane are much more limited.[63] This carries important implications for countries where these crops are prevalent as in Sudan.

As global warming increases temperature and precipitation in many regions, the race between these two effects will decide the outcome for soil moisture. Increased irrigation could offset negative effects, which will be observable for dryland farming. Global irrigation needs could increase by 20 percent by 2080.[64] Theoretically, Egypt might be able to ward off the impact of climate change by increased irrigation, while steep yield declines in Sudan would be attributable entirely to its dependence on rain-fed farming, not the irrigation sector. Yet, this begs the question whether models accurately reflect the costs of irrigation infrastructure and the availability of water. One of the studies incorporated by Cline argues that "Egypt may be atypical because of the massive availability of irrigation from the Nile."[65] This assumption looks weak given unfolding hydropolitics of the Nile. Egypt has maxed out its allocation of Nile water resources under the agreement of 1959 and Ethiopia has questioned this very agreement.

Climate change will disproportionately affect the favorite target countries of Gulf agro-investments. While the gravest effects will only materialize after 2050, there have been disturbing signs of things to come. Pakistan was hit by a devastating flood in 2010 and the following year the UN declared a state of famine in the Horn of Africa after a drought. The Gulf countries financed WFP food aid to the very countries they eyed for future provision of food imports. After the initial wave of project announcements in 2008, actually implemented projects focused more on developed markets like Australia or Brazil a few years later. Beside problems of governance and insufficient infrastructure it is conceivable that water stress and climatic risks contributed to hesitancy on part of Gulf countries.

---

[61] Cline 2007.   [62] *Science Daily*, 4 May 2011.   [63] Gornall et al. 2010: 2983ff.

[64] Hanjra and Qureshi 2010. Precipitation will mostly increase in the tropics and high latitude areas, yet these are not the areas where prime agricultural land is mostly situated.

[65] Cline 2007: 53.

8.4 RESOURCE NATIONALISM, NGOs, AND HYDROPOLITICS

Resource Nationalism

A formidable challenge to Gulf agro-investments has arisen in the form of political resistance. Selling land to foreigners is a touchy subject anywhere. Gulf countries know this first-hand. They forbid foreign landownership at home, apart from a few freehold zones in the UAE and Qatar. They nationalized their oil business in the 1970s because they regarded it as an important strategic asset. In a similar vein, some established agro-exporters have taken steps to limit landownership by foreigners. Agriculture is an export cash-cow for them which they want to keep national, not unlike oil for the Gulf countries. The largest rice exporter of the world, Thailand, announced via its Deputy Commerce Minister that foreigners could not acquire land but would be welcome to invest in joint ventures with a Thai-majority partner.[66] This bears some similarity to the obligatory sponsorship arrangements in the Gulf region, but it precludes the direct access to land that ranks high on the agenda of Saudi agro-businessmen. Mainly out of fear of Chinese acquisitions, Brazil, the world's biggest soybean exporter, has established legislation that limits large-scale landownership by foreigners.[67] Like Thailand, Brazil is interested in doing business with the Gulf countries and other food importers, but on its own terms. Australia has relatively loose oversight of foreign land acquisitions via its Foreign Investment Review Framework,[68] but a Liberal Senator, Bill Heffernan, has lobbied for a tightening of regulations. Other limitations were in place long before 2008. Saskatchewan province in Canada has had limits on foreign ownership since the 1980s. At that time, it enacted them out of concern over European, mainly German, buyers.[69]

Bolivia and Ecuador have also enacted legislation to limit foreign land-ownership,[70] but generally, politicians in less developed countries have been more receptive to capital inflows from abroad than the established agro-exporters. Ethiopia and other African countries lobby for agro-investment with bespoke investment agencies that provide one-stop solutions for investors. By giving away long-term land leases at nominal rates, they hope to get infrastructure support, employment creation, and agricultural development in exchange.[71] In contrast to Latin America or Eastern Europe, government-

---

[66] *Reuters*, 23 June 2009.   [67] *Reuters*, 19 April 2011; Sauer and Leite 2011.

[68] <http://www.firb.gov.au> (accessed 6 June 2012).

[69] Interview with executive of the Canadian government, Ottawa, 25 January 2011.

[70] HLPE 2011: 17.

[71] Land leases in Ethiopia are available for diverse durations usually up to 50 years. The lease of Saudi Star has 50 years. In Tanzania leases of up to 99 years are available. Cotula et al. 2009: 57ff.

allocated land leases are the norm in Africa, not outright purchases of land, as only 2–10 percent of the land is held under formal land tenure according to World Bank estimates.[72]

In Pakistan private large estate ownership makes land deals on the surface easier than in Africa, but the semi-feudal *zamindar* system is a bone of political contention and Gulf investors could become part of related political struggles or possible inheritance issues between various members of land-owning families. Landownership in Pakistan is extremely concentrated with about 2 percent of Pakistani households controlling more than 45 percent of the land.[73] In Turkey, on the other hand, land holdings are fragmented. Vision 3, an alliance of Bahrain-based Gulf Finance House (GFH) and Ithmaar Bank and UAE's Abu Dhabi Investment House (ADIH), signed an MoU for a $6 billion agricultural investment in the country in 2008, but ran into problems while pursuing land consolidation strategies.[74]

Whether it is Sudan, Pakistan, or Turkey, these examples show that politics of land acquisitions involve a broader public and go beyond bilateral government relations and mere deals between private contract parties. Gulf countries highlight the importance of personal relations and investments in countries with friendly governments. Yet, this is no substitute for stable legal frameworks and can backfire if the government in the host country changes. Saudi Kingdom Holding had to relinquish a large part of its agricultural project in the Egyptian Toshka valley in the wake of the Arab Spring as the new Egyptian government questioned whether business proceedings had been legitimate at the time of Kingdom's land acquisition in 1998.[75]

NGOs and Grassroots Resistance

Basic forms of traditional agriculture might underutilize what international organizations, investors, and governments describe as uncultivated "empty" lands, but these lands are hardly unused: small-scale farmers and pastoralists dwell on them. They have customary land rights and it is unclear whether they can get a fair deal out of large projects in the form of compensation, jobs, and business opportunities.

NGOs like GRAIN and grassroots movements like La Via Campesina have embarked on efficient advocacy campaigns. They have questioned the legitimacy of land deals right from the first announcements. This can lead to

---

[72] Cotula et al. 2009: 75f.; Deininger 2003.

[73] <http://go.worldbank.org/KQ3CN5O0J0> (accessed 22 April 2012).

[74] Interview with businessman from Turkey, Barcelona, 23 May 2012; *Arab News*, 2 November 2008.

[75] *The National*, 12 April 2011.

considerable pressure from below even if a government is receptive towards agro-investments. In Madagascar, a disputed large-scale land deal with South Korean Daewoo contributed to the downfall of the entire government. In the Philippines, the government had to cancel a large-scale land deal with China after public protests.

Planned projects of Gulf investors in Mauretania and Mali have met with resistance. After protests, the regional government of Baluchistan blocked direct deals between UAE investors and Pakistani farmers. The central government of Pakistan reacted by stipulating that outside investors have to share half of their crop with local growers.[76] Qatar's announcement of a 40,000 ha project in Kenya's Tana River delta faced opposition from pastoralists and the Eastern Africa Farmers Federation Union. It came at a time when Kenyan food security was stressed. Corn flour prices doubled in 2008 and the government had to introduce subsidies and price controls.[77] On Indonesian Irian Jaya, there is an ongoing government policy to encourage migration from Java and Sumatra to relieve population pressures and to out-populate restive indigenous people. They are non-Muslim, ethnically different, and increasingly oppose this influx. Protests have occurred against unequal deals and their environmental impact. Gulf countries would be part of such socio-economic conflict should they proceed with currently suspended investment projects. The Philippines has a legacy of large-scale plantation estates for colonial export crops like bananas and sugar. As in Brazil and Pakistan, concentration of landownership is high. A longstanding government policy and movements for land reform have had varying degrees of success. The issue of landownership is highly contentious. NGOs and left leaning parties have protested what they called a "secret agricultural pact" between the Philippine government and Bahrain.[78]

The plight of housemaids and migrant workers in the Gulf who come from the Philippines and Indonesia is another reason why Gulf agro-investments in these countries can be delicate. Human Rights Watch has highlighted widespread mistreatment ranging from excessive work hours and unpaid wages to physical abuse. The case of an Indonesian maid who was beheaded in Saudi Arabia for killing her employer in what she claimed was self-defense developed into a cause célèbre in Indonesia. In a nationally televised address Indonesia's president accused Riyadh of breaking the "norms and manners" of international relations and announced a moratorium on Indonesian labor migration to Saudi Arabia.[79] Similarly, the Philippines has demanded just

---

[76] *Reuters*, 18 May 2009.

[77] *Daily Nation*, 31 December 2008; FIAN International Secretariat 2010.

[78] Pamalakaya and KMP, joint press release, 24 June 2009, available at: <http://farmlandgrab.org/post/view/5766> (accessed 22 April 2012).

[79] *The Economist*, 3 July 2011.

treatment of its migrant workers and higher wages from Gulf governments. In August 2011, the government considered banning its citizens from signing on as domestic workers in Kuwait, Qatar, and the UAE unless these countries improved labor protection.[80] To pre-empt such initiatives Saudi Arabia temporarily halted recruitment of maids from the Philippines and Indonesia in 2011 and tried to replace them with personnel from Ethiopia, Kenya, and other African countries.

Negative perceptions of labor rights in the Gulf countries could spill over to the area of agro-investments. They may trump the importance of religious commonality that Saudi Arabia and the IsDB have highlighted in the field of international investments since the 1970s. On the Philippine island of Mindanao, Islam is an important ingredient of local identity, yet people would disapprove of a person by saying, "He is a Muslim, but has a bad Arab character."[81] Similarly, Egyptians, ever proud of their Pharaonic past, sometimes use the term "Arab" only for people from the Arabian Peninsula, whom they regard as nouveaux riches and slightly below the level of Egyptian accomplishments. When Saudi Arabia withdrew its ambassador from Cairo in 2012 after protests in front of its embassy, the new ruling party, the Muslim Brotherhood's Freedom and Justice Party, defended the demonstrators. In a statement on its website, it said they were "merely expressing the Egyptian people's aspiration to preserve the dignity of their fellow citizens who visit, live or work in Arab countries."[82]

Gulf countries are aware of the problem of labor rights to varying extents. They have reacted to criticism and wildcat strikes by improving labor regulations or enforcing their implementation. They have also engaged with the UN and other international organizations.[83] Still, the prevalent sponsorship system that keeps employees in a state of high dependency is likely to remain, even though Bahrain has started to reform it. The nature of labor migration in the Gulf and pronounced segmentation between locals and the blue-collar expatriate workforce provide little civil society bonds that could be capitalized on for the purpose of investments. At best, it will not prove detrimental for Gulf agro-investments.

In Ethiopia, the state has combined licenses for large-scale projects with forced resettlements. "Villagization" programs in Ethiopia in the mid-1980s were highly controversial. The state as formal owner of land embarked on a course of social engineering and resettled 4.6 million people from the populated highlands to the less developed, water-rich, but malaria infested lowlands in the west. By developing these areas, it was hoped to improve food production and food security in the country. New villages were created and existing

[80] *The National*, 5 September 2011.
[81] Interview with banana plantation manager, Davao, Philippines, August 2010.
[82] *Bloomberg*, 29 April 2012.   [83] Janardhan 2011: chapter 4.

ones unified in order to create a centralized infrastructure and allow for political control. In the 2000s villagization programs have resumed and have been combined with efforts of the Ethiopian government to attract foreign agro-investments. By giving away land leases, the government hopes to spur agriculture-led industrialization. Such projects have caused displacement of holders of customary land rights, not only on the widely publicized farm of Indian firm Karuturi and on the Saudi Star project site.[84] In April 2012, violent resistance became more frequent in Gambela. Gunmen attacked the Saudi Star farm and killed five workers.[85]

Protest against the Gulf-financed Merowe Dam in Sudan has also turned lethal since 2006. The dam required resettlement of over 50,000 people.[86] Violent protests also occurred against the planned Kajbar and Dal Dams in the north, where the local Nubian population fears that the necessary resettlements will undermine their livelihoods and culture. They see them as "part of an official plan of demographic engineering . . . to enhance the Arabization of the Nubians by resettling them far from their homeland."[87] Other protests in Sudan occurred at Egyptian and Qatari project sites in Sennar, where locals complained about lacking job opportunities in the capital-intensive projects.[88] A deal by Saudi businessmen in the same state collapsed after protests and in North Kordofan pastoralists threatened violence against a Saudi cattle ranching project on their ancestral land. The Kuwaiti-financed heightening of the Roseires Dam will lead to the displacement of 75,000 people in the Blue Nile province, which was a frontline state during Sudan's second civil war (1983–2005). The expansion of mechanized farming and land distribution to cronies trailed the ideological and military agenda of the regime. Resentment towards Khartoum still looms large. The benefits of the dam will not accrue to Blue Nile province; the electricity will be for the capital and other urban centers in the north, while its irrigation water will serve agricultural projects in Sennar. Civil war in the province resumed in August 2011 and conflict around the dam is likely.[89]

The GCC countries try to alleviate fears and balance potentially conflicting interests with stakeholders in target countries by pointing to job creation and stipulating that certain percentages of planted crops should remain in the host country to contribute to domestic food security.[90] To pre-empt criticism Qatar claimed to put foreign agro-projects on hold until land rights issues have been

---

[84] Horne et al. 2011; Pearce 2012: chapter 1. For a more benign view of the Karuturi project see Rural Modernity 2012b.

[85] *AP* and *Bloomberg*, 29 April 2012.

[86] *Financial Times*, 9 March 2007; Verhoeven 2012a.

[87] The Committe of Anti-Dal Kajbar Dams 2011.

[88] For the following see Verhoeven 2012a, 2012b: chapter 7.

[89] Verhoeven 2012a, 2012b: chapter 7.

[90] Kingdom of Saudi Arabia 2009a.

sorted out in a mutually beneficial way.[91] State-owned Hassad Food announced that it would aim at investing in existing agro-companies rather than acquiring land rights and building up farming operations from scratch. The AAAID chose a similar approach when it launched a $2 billion fund in October 2009.[92]

Gulf countries often evoke a win-win situation where they provide the capital and target countries the land and labor. Yet positive outcomes would likely be different from Gulf-owned large-scale plantations. Especially for labor-intensive crops, smallholder farmers may be as or more productive than large farm operations if they get access to input factors, credit, and markets. Contract farming and cooperatives might offer better and more equitable ways of project implementation.[93]

Saudi Arabia has acknowledged the problem by contacting groups that could sort out potential problems of project implementation on a community level.[94] Some form of diplomacy on levels below the respective central governments is required. Yet, it is unclear whether the Gulf states have fully realized the problem and whether they have the administrative capacities and non-governmental links to effectively engage with civil society groups on a local level. At this stage, Gulf countries have managed to become poster child villains of global advocacy groups without actually investing much.

Hydropolitics and International Relations

Agro-investments can also affect the international relations of Gulf countries, if they become party in controversial hydropolitics about cross-border sharing of water resources. Successful completion of agro-investments by Gulf countries in Ethiopia could pit them against the interests of Egypt.[95] The Nile water sharing agreement of 1959 allots 75 percent of the water flow to Egypt and 25 percent to Sudan, while Ethiopia and the other sub-Saharan riparians do not have any quota at all. They are supposed to make ends meet with rain-fed agriculture and green water. Historically, Egypt and Sudan have formed an alliance to defend this status quo against Ethiopia, with Egypt as a hegemon and Sudan as a junior partner. This alliance could become fragile if Sudan developed its water and agricultural resources and used its water quota under the agreement, which it has never done so far. As a result Egypt was able to

---

[91] Remarks of QNFSP Chairman Fahad al-Attiya at the Middle East Institute, Washington, DC, 25 January 2010.

[92] *Reuters*, 11 October 2009.

[93] HLPE 2011; Cotula 2010.

[94] Interview with executive of the European-SADC States Bridge, Dubai, 8 March 2010.

[95] Horne et al. 2011: 51; Brown 2011.

extract more than its quota in the past.[96] On the other hand, Egypt could participate in agricultural investments in Sudan and it needs to compromise with Khartoum in order to keep it in its camp against the other riparians in the south. Egypt and Sudanese officials indeed discussed wheat production in north Sudan on two million feddans in 2011.[97]

Ethiopia has been against the logic of the 1959 agreement and openly questioned it in 2010 together with Uganda, Tanzania, and Rwanda.[98] Contrary to earlier times, it might have the political stability and access to funding to develop hydro projects of its own like the recently launched Millenium Dam close to the border with Sudan. Sudanese agro-businessman and chairman of the DAL group, Osama Daoud, ominously warned US embassy officials that "Sudan will find out very soon that it does not have the (Nile River) water supply it thinks it does."[99]

There could be synergy effects of hydropolitical cooperation, however. Planned Ethiopian dams for electricity generation have evaporation rates seven times smaller than in north Sudan. Ethiopia has assured critics that it only intends to withdraw limited water supplies for irrigation from such dams. Because of Ethiopia's hilly topography, its irrigation potential is indeed more limited than in Sudan, which could expand cultivation along the Blue Nile all the way down to the Gezira scheme. A key adviser to the Ethiopian president summed the idea up poignantly: "Ethiopia provides the power, Sudan grows the food and Egypt brings the cash."[100] Additionally, South Sudan's oil production could be part of such a regional energy and food cooperation.

With military conflict re-erupting between north and south Sudan in 2012, this scenario looked unlikely. South Sudan's positioning in the regional hydropolitics is of crucial importance. The Blue Nile does not flow through its territory. It is dominated by the White Nile, which only contributes 14 percent to Nile water flows, but its land mass constitutes a third of Sudan's share of the Nile Basin. If South Sudan chose succession to the 1959 treaty this would imply an agreement with the north over relative allotments of water quota. It would also require discussions about water conservation projects in the south that the 1959 agreement stipulates, i.e. a resumption of the abandoned Jonglei Canal project, which is unpopular in the south. Such a stance would undermine South Sudan's ambition to grow closer with its southern neighbors and become a member of the East African Community (EAC). If South Sudan chose to disavow the 1959 agreement this would please Ethiopia and the EAC countries, but would mean open defiance of Egypt and Sudan. In the run-up to

---

[96] Waterbury 2002: chapter 6; Kliot 1994: 59; Zeitoun and Warner 2006.

[97] *Al-Sharq al-Awsat*, 28 March 2011.

[98] *Financial Times*, 15 May 2010; Salman 2011.

[99] WikiLeaks cable, 08KHARTOUM1416, US Embassy in Khartoum, 18 September 2008.

[100] Verhoeven 2011a. For earlier Sudanese-Ethiopian cooperation plans see Waterbury 2002: 137f.

independence, South Sudan has not prioritized the Nile file. Territorial disputes and oil transit fees have preoccupied it. Hence it might also choose a wait and see approach without forcing a decision for the time being.[101]

The Ethiopian dam projects could also undermine the rationale of existing dams in Sudan. This would challenge the narrative of legitimacy and development that the ruling National Congress Party (NCP) has built around its dam program of the 2000s. Some claim that one purpose of this program is to fully use Sudan's share of the 1959 treaty and establish acquired rights based on the principle of "prior appropriation."[102] Sudanese officials are also weary of electricity dependence on Ethiopia. Hence, cooperation with its southeastern neighbor is less likely than a continuance of its alliance with Egypt.

Egypt is concerned about the status quo and has been willing to compromise to keep Sudan in its camp. It gave the green light for Sudan's dam program and its subsequent financing by Gulf funds. This has come as a surprise to many, as Egypt has opposed World Bank funding for dam projects south of its borders before and has pressed Gulf countries and China on this point. Its opposition to Nile water abstraction by Ethiopia and riparians other than Sudan remains firm.

The Egyptian Council for Foreign Affairs, a think tank of diplomats, generals, and other public figures, raised alarm at its annual conference in 2010 over the water situation along the Nile. It warned explicitly about projects financed by Gulf donors and the World Bank and claimed that there is an indirect cooperation of Gulf countries, Israel, and the USA against Egyptian interests. A split of southern Sudan was equated in no uncertain terms with the *nakba* of 1948, the lost war against Israel, which marks a low point in the collective Arab memory.[103] There are very real concerns at stake and Nile Basin issues will have a high priority for Egyptian foreign policy in the years ahead. After the resignation of President Mubarak, the first country that the new Prime Minister Issam Sharaf visited was Sudan. In 2011, Egypt announced a program for self-sufficiency in wheat and a reinvigoration of the cotton trade, for which sufficient irrigation water would be crucial.[104]

In Egypt, Gulf countries have already been named as a party in a hydropolitical conflict. In other target countries, this seems further off, but is not unlikely. The Indus Water Treaty of 1960 resolved water issues between India and Pakistan and allowed the latter to develop its Punjabi bread-basket with the help of the Indus Basin Project. Yet, disagreements flared up in the 2000s

---

[101] Salman 2011: 164f.; Granit et al. 2010: 35.
[102] Interview with UNDP executive, Khartoum, November 2011. For the legal concept and that of "appreciable or significant harm" see Waterbury 2002: 28.
[103] Al-Ahrar 2010.
[104] *New York Times*, 11 May 2011.

when Pakistan objected to Indian hydropower projects on the Chenab and Jhelum rivers.[105] Turkey's Southeastern Anatolia Project (GAP) has been a bone of contention with Syria and Iraq. In 1990, it even led to a mobilization of troops. To fill the reservoir of the Atatürk Dam, Ankara temporarily reduced the Euphrates water flows to Syria and Iraq by 75 percent. Iraq threatened to bomb the dam and Turkey replied that it could cut off water supplies to Syria and Iraq completely. Differences have subsided since then and have given way to more cooperative approaches. Turkey has unilaterally guaranteed a certain flow of water to the downstream riparians. In 2009 all three parties negotiated how best to deal with a drought in Syria and Iraq. Yet, beyond a temporary increase of flows from Turkey, no agreement was reached. Like along the Nile and Jordan, hegemonic approaches to water management prevail.[106]

In 1987, Turkish President Turgut Ozal proposed a "Peace Pipeline" which would have brought water from the Ceyhan and Seyhan rivers to the Arabian Peninsula via Syria and Jordan. A parallel pipeline would have pumped oil to Turkey as payment.[107] Such water transport schemes were propagated by Turkish officials as late as the 2000s.[108] They have not seen the light of day, even though a pre-feasibility study by US-based Brown & Root Company found that the Peace Pipeline would have provided cheaper water supplies than desalination. Gulf countries were wary about the dependence. Syria would have had obvious reservations, even though the two rivers do not cross into its territory. Gulf agro-investments in Turkey and export of food to the Gulf could constitute a similar draw on Anatolian water resources in the form of virtual water exports.

Water wars have often been predicted but have never happened. War is not a promising tool to sort out water issues, as water cannot be as easily taken possession of as other commodities. More likely are various forms of low intensity conflict and jockeying for positions at international organizations and donor institutions, but also diplomacy and cooperation.[109] Risks of political conflict around water will likely increase beyond 2020, however.[110] When engaging in agro-investments, Gulf countries will be part of hydro-politics in target countries.

---

[105] FAO 2010a.

[106] Zeitoun and Warner 2006.

[107] *MEED*, 7 February 1992; Wilson and Graham 1994: 227. An Iranian proposal in 1992 to pump water to Qatar was not pursued either.

[108] Rende 2007.

[109] Verhoeven 2011b: 3–6; Waterbury 2002: 9ff.; Zeitoun and Warner 2006. The only exception was in 1964–6, when Syria tried to divert the Jordan headwaters in retaliation to Israel's diversion of Jordan waters to its coastal zones and the Negev. Israel bombarded the Syrian construction sites and the events that were set in motion played a role in the run-up to the 1967 war.

[110] Intelligence Community Assessment 2012.

8.5 CONCLUSION

The most popular target countries of Gulf investments are food net importers and have high population growth rates like Sudan, Pakistan, the Philippines, and Ethiopia. Their agricultural output potential will be disproportionately affected by climate change. Pakistan already faces a physical water shortage, while Ethiopia, Sudan, and Egypt are part of delicate hydropolitics along the Nile. The argument for these countries is that they have development potential, are geographically close, and have established ties with the Gulf countries. Projects have remained controversial. Alienated customary land rights holders have protested against planned Gulf projects on multiple occasions. At the same time, the fiscal space of Gulf countries has shrunk in the wake of the global financial crisis before recovering since 2010. There is a huge implementation gap and media reports about widespread land grabs are misleading. Most of the projects are mere announcements or at a preliminary stage. They would require improved diplomacy on part of Gulf countries, not only on an inter-state level, but also with the public and NGOs in target countries. Other shortcomings range from governance to infrastructure and natural endowments. Three years after the initial announcements Gulf countries turned their focus to more developed agro-producers like Australia or Brazil and eyed alternative approaches like strategic storage and food trading houses. This raises the question of what future food security policies of Gulf countries may look like.

9

Oil-for-Food Policies?

Gulf countries have to adapt to a global environment that is characterized by a paradigm shift in global food prices, renewed politicization of food trade, and increased need for virtual water trade in the form of crops. Domestic agriculture will not be at the heart of food security policies, as its role in food provision will face a relative decline, with the possible exception of Qatar's plan for futuristic self-sufficiency. Other factors like oil politics, economic diversification, asset management, social equitability, and international relations will be more important. Food security policies in the Gulf will be formulated in three major areas: domestic policies, multilateral regimes, and bilateral relations.

9.1 DOMESTIC POLICIES: OIL, DIVERSIFICATION, WATER

Safeguarding oil revenues is a necessary precondition for Gulf food security as long as they continue to dominate GDP, budgets, and export earnings. The ability of Gulf countries to keep oil prices high via OPEC is somewhat overstated. Only Saudi Arabia is holder of a significant spare capacity and as such, it is an important balancer of global markets in case of sudden supply shortfalls elsewhere. Spare capacity is not just maintained to keep prices high.[1] Three other levers are more important for Gulf countries to maintain their purchasing power: curbing domestic energy consumption, economic diversification, and keeping their overseas assets intact amidst financial turmoil.

Domestic energy consumption is skyrocketing in the Gulf countries and all of them now face a natural gas shortage, except for Qatar. The alternative, which is to fire diesel, fuel oil, or even crude oil in power stations, is expensive. When oil prices were low in the 1980s and 1990s this might have been an

---

[1] Mabro 2006.

option as there were shut in capacities and the production of additional barrels came essentially at no marginal cost. Nowadays burning oil in power plants comes with real opportunity costs: it would fetch a good price on world markets, especially if it was processed in deep conversion refineries to more value added products like diesel.[2]

Hence, the strategy of Gulf countries is to introduce new energy sources like nuclear power and renewables for the production of electricity and desalinated water to save natural gas for the petrochemical industry and peak load generation, while keeping oil for exports. They also pay lip service to more energy efficiency, although for reasons of political legitimacy they are reluctant to reform a system of cheaply priced energy that encourages wasteful consumption.

Economic diversification has become the holy grail of economic policies in the Gulf. Speeches of politicians and presentations by consultancy companies cannot do without it. Economic diversification is supposed to reduce dependence on volatile oil revenues and create jobs for a burgeoning youth population. In the long run it should provide income for an after-oil age. The record of diversification in the Gulf is mixed. The share of oil revenues continues to run supreme, even in the UAE, which has a thriving services and logistics industry. Its relatively high share of non-oil exports is somewhat overstated because it functions as a re-export hub for the region. There is a booming petrochemical industry in the Gulf, but it is not labor intensive. Hence, the transition to a "knowledge economy" and job creation in the service sector is now the *dernier cri* in Gulf capitals. Investments in education are certainly warranted as Gulf countries trail behind in international rankings. Yet, the concept of a "knowledge economy" is vague and capitalism not as dematerialized as new-age economists tend to fancy. Countries that rely on traditional forms of labor utilization like China or on exploitation of natural resources like Brazil have a stronger growth record than the OECD countries with their high share of knowledge intensive sectors. If knowledge goes into rationalizing production processes, it destroys jobs instead of creating them. If a "knowledge economy" truly creates new markets, the products it is selling are often intangible intellectual property rights (e.g. software) that require a lot of unproductive lawyers and policemen to protect them. The likelihood of the Gulf successfully competing in these sectors with established producers from Asia and the OECD countries is also slim. Yet for all the faults of the concept, economic diversification would be an important aspect of food security in the Gulf if qualification measures realized a sufficiently broad-based participation in economic development.

Gulf overseas assets are an attempt at conserving today's oil revenues for the future, but as the global financial crisis is firmly entrenched, Gulf countries are worried about the stability of such assets. They are major financers of the US

---

[2] Luciani 2012a, 2012c.
[3] Hertog and Luciani 2009; Supersberger et al. 2009; Lahn and Stevens 2011.

current account deficit. As in the 1970s, there has been a financial shuttle diplomacy by the US in the region. The Treasury Secretaries Henry Paulson and Timothy Geithner both passed through on various occasions. The portfolio management of SWFs has become more conservative after the large losses of 2008. There is an interest in reduced transaction costs (e.g. index funds) and investment alternatives in emerging markets and the commodities sector. There is also continued interest in strategic equity stakes in companies that can benefit the diversification of Gulf economies in fields such as petrochemicals, logistics, aviation, and renewable energies. Agricultural investments are part of these trends.

The phasing out of water-intensive agriculture might increase perceived vulnerability to import dependence. Yet, it also safeguards water security, which is an indispensable aspect of food security. Close to total dependence on desalination for potable water is already a reality in the smaller Gulf countries, but it is costly and difficult to manage, especially for a large country like Saudi Arabia. Riyadh is supplied by pipeline from the Gulf coast 400 kilometers away. Water loss to leakage is estimated to be 30–40 percent; inside Riyadh the losses even reach 60 percent, which the National Water Company (NWC) wants to bring down to a more sustainable 20 percent.[4] Disposal of the brine is ecologically harmful. Desalination infrastructure is also liable to oil spills or sabotage. In case of an interruption, many cities would run dry within a day or two. For this reason, Abu Dhabi has decided to build up a strategic water reserve in suitable geological formations.[5] If desalinated water is produced from renewable energies its storage can provide solutions for the problem of intermittency of these energy sources and ease their integration into existing energy mixes. Qatar intends to run its future agricultural expansion solely on solar-based desalination, so aquifers can recover and be refilled for use as strategic storage.[6]

Better water management and the ongoing reorientation of domestic agriculture are of crucial importance and could free water resources for industrial and residential use. Water subsidies that encourage wasteful consumption and precipitate the choice of water-intensive crops need to be examined. Wastewater recycling, drought resistant seed variants, and water saving technologies like drip irrigation and greenhouses can improve water efficiency. Richards and Waterbury point to the example of Israel, where such technologies managed to produce double the output with half of the water. However, this does not necessarily mean a reduction of water consumption, if such efficiency gains are used for expanding agricultural production. There is also scope for reuse of excessive irrigation water if it ends up in aquifers again. The effects of such reuse are not fully understood and efficiency gains might not be comparable to a finite resource.[7]

---

[4] *Al-Riyadh*, 7 April 2012; *Saudi Gazette*, 9 March 2010.
[5] *The National*, 6 December 2010; GIZ 2012.
[6] Interview, Fahad al-Attiya, Chairman QNFSP, Doha, 14 November 2011.
[7] Richards and Waterbury 2008: 170.

Population policies like in Iran have been recommended by IFPRI as an ingredient of food security policies in the Middle East.[8] So far, none of the Gulf states follows such a policy. Yet, the smaller Gulf states are already well advanced in a demographic transition. Their population growth will be increasingly driven by migration patterns, which are in turn dependent on development policies. Gulf countries may pause and think whether their plans to build large metropolises in the middle of the desert can be maintained sustainably and indefinitely at an affordable price. Population growth in Saudi Arabia is still very much driven by natural increases, although birth rates have come down as well. So far, there is no program in place to speed up the demographic transition. In Islamic theology, there is no comparable resistance against birth control like in Catholicism and some other Christian denominations. Still, family planning campaigns would be hard to sell in the deeply conservative kingdom. That said, near total urbanization and the trend towards nuclear families and female education are helping the ongoing transition like anywhere else in the world. The UN expects the Saudi population to peak in 2065 at 46.4 million in its reference scenario.[9]

Too many calories, not their lack, constitute a challenge to food security in the Gulf. In a global food system that is organized around the poles of obesity and hunger with an increase of packaged foods, food miles, and meat and sugar consumption, Gulf countries come down firmly on the pole of affluence. They have some of the highest per capita ratios of obesity and diabetes worldwide. This is a considerable drain on GDP with incalculable long-term risks. Gulf governments have started to launch awareness campaigns and promote physical exercise in schools and communities, but in the end, robust legal measures are required. Taxation of fast food and unhealthy diets and better product information that allows consumers to make informed choices are contentious among food industry representatives. Yet, Gulf countries might consider them like similarly affected OECD countries.

In sum, the Gulf countries have considerable domestic levers at hand to preserve their purchasing power, maintain water security, and manage food demand. Which international market conditions they encounter is an entirely different question and requires their interaction with states, companies, and institutions on an international level.

9.2 MULTILATERAL REGIMES: WTO, G20, INTERNATIONAL STORAGE, AND CLIMATE CHANGE

Gulf monarchs' rule is autocratic and they are used to a high degree of personal discretion in decision-making. There is a preference for personal

---

[8] Breisinger et al. 2010: 36.   [9] United Nations 2010.

relationships. Gulf bureaucracies are top heavy and their capacities to communicate at an institutional level are underdeveloped. The interaction of Gulf countries with international organizations has been limited for economic and political reasons. They never had to resort to the IMF or the World Bank for financing. They either enjoyed surpluses or were able to finance budget deficits by domestic borrowing. If they engaged with the Bretton Woods institutions, it was on par, as paid consultants, but never hat-in-hand and with the need to subordinate to conditionality clauses. Politically and militarily, Gulf states are relatively weak. They have to rely on Western security guarantees in an unstable region. As a result, they have preferred an approach of silent diplomacy and have not been very vocal in international and regional comparison. Apart from the Iranian nuclear file and the Arab–Israeli conflict there have been three exceptions to this relative absentia on the stage of international organizations: the WTO process, climate change negotiations, and global food security.

Saudi Arabia was the last GCC country to join the WTO in 2005. GCC countries have a high degree of trade openness compared internationally. They have never followed policies of import-substituting industrialization like Egypt or Syria. On the one hand, participation in the WTO process promises increased market access for their expanding diversification sectors such as petrochemicals, aluminum, and airlines. On the other hand, Gulf countries have tried to use WTO regulations to support ongoing reforms of their domestic economies.[10]

Saudi Arabia's process of WTO accession showed a lack of coordination and a high degree of institutional autonomy. Various ministries had little inclination to follow the negotiation agenda of the Ministry of Commerce and thwarted any progress at the end of the 1990s. In the case of the Ministry of Agriculture this meant an insistence on agricultural subsides.[11] To effectively engage with institutions like the WTO, Gulf countries would need to upgrade their often segmented bureaucratic capacities.

Traditionally the WTO has been preoccupied with trade liberalization and the reduction of import barriers. Export barriers are unusual and have not been on its radar screen. In the case of food it actually allows such restrictions on the grounds of domestic food security considerations. Such restrictions were implemented before the global food crisis of 2008 as well. Australia banned barley exports after a drought in 2004 and Indonesia, Malaysia, and the Philippines curbed food exports in the wake of the Asian crisis of 1997 to bring down domestic prices. For this reason the former WTO chief negotiator for Saudi Arabia, Fawaz al-Alami, has argued against foreign agro-investments, saying that they would not guarantee food security in times

---

[10] Hertog 2010: chapter 7.

[11] Hertog 2010: 235. The MoC became the Ministry of Commerce and Industry (MoCI) only in 2003.

of crisis. He recommends the build-up of strategic food reserves in the Arab world instead.[12]

Such programs are now being realized in the Gulf countries. However, IFPRI has contended that national approaches could lead to unnecessary and expensive storage, an inefficient global production system, and tighter markets if practiced widely on a global level. They could cause the very problem they want to mitigate in the first place. Instead, IFPRI has suggested an international food reserve not unlike the Global Strategic Petroleum Reserves that are coordinated by the IEA. Such a multilateral storage and information system could reduce volatility of markets by improving their transparency and predictability. Furthermore, a fund for market intervention could act as a "virtual storage" and prevent speculative overshooting of prices of agricultural commodities, which are widely traded on international futures exchanges. IFPRI hopes that with such an international reserve export restrictions like those in 2008 could be avoided.[13] In fact, increased transparency via the establishment of the Agricultural Market Information System (AMIS) by the G20 in 2011 has already helped to moderate market reactions during renewed food price rises in 2012.[14]

The idea of an international food reserve is an evergreen of development debates. It is not without critics.[15] In the 1970s, food exporters like the US were reluctant to give up sovereignty in this matter. The international bureaucracy that would administer such a program would face questions about its legitimacy and would need to overcome problems of collective action. It would need to establish trading bands for intervention and large bureaucracies do not have a proven track record of effective second-guessing of markets. Still, large institutional investors and hedge funds certainly did no better during the global financial crisis. Widespread market failure has led to a reconsideration of former heresies. An international system of food storage and market information could help to make food imports more predictable. It would help to mitigate supply and price risks for Gulf countries. At least a regional pooling of reserves could make storage less extensive and costly as the Middle East Supply Center has shown during World War II. Such a reserve would give GCC countries critical lead-time to look for alternative suppliers in times of crisis, while allowing them to optimize import strategies along the supply chain, especially for smaller countries, whose demand alone does not justify delivery by large vessels and whose storage costs are higher.[16]

---

[12] Al-Alami 2009.
[13] von Braun and Torero 2009; von Braun, Lin, and Torero 2009.
[14] <http://www.amis-outlook.org> (accessed 15 July 2012).
[15] OECD-FAO 2010: 67. For an overview of the historical debate since 1945 see Shaw 2007.
[16] World Bank and FAO 2012: 15; ESCWA and IFPRI mimeo 2012.

The importance of trade-related issues and market intelligence is also exemplified by Gulf countries' strategy to get a foothold in international food trading, which is dominated by a few large trading companies like ADM, Bunge, Cargill, or Dreyfus. The end of the marketing monopolies of the Australian Wheat Board in 2008 and of the Canadian Wheat Board in August 2012 has increased their importance. Abu Dhabi announced the establishment of a food trading house and was a major investor in the IPO of international commodity trader Glencore in 2011 alongside other Gulf investors like Saudi Prince Al-Waleed's Kingdom Holding. Glencore went on to aggressively push into the grain market by acquiring Viterra in 2012, the largest wheat handler in Canada and South Australia.[17] While privileged bilateral access to food production and national storage exemplify mistrust in the reliability of markets, Gulf countries also try to muscle their way into the controversial institutional set-ups of such markets and the virtual water trade that they represent.[18]

Gulf countries have engaged with global food policy debates, as Qatar's launch of the Global DryLand Alliance at the United Nations has shown. The Qatari President of the 66th UN General Assembly, Nassir Abdulaziz al-Nasser, has tried to fill this ceremonial post with more life than is commonly usual and raised issues like the impact of financial speculation on food prices, the Syrian crisis, and disaster relief.[19] With $500 million, Saudi Arabia gave the largest one-off donation ever to the WFP at the height of the global food crisis in 2008. It also participated in the FAO consultations about Responsible Agricultural Investments (RAI), even though it only sent the representative of a hired consultancy, Maxwell-Stamp, not a decision-maker of a company or ministry.[20]

More engagement with international organizations could open avenues for Gulf countries actively to raise their food security concerns. During the Uruguay round of trade liberalization the Net Food Importing Developing Countries (NFIDC) formed an interest group within the GATT that lobbied for affordable food imports. They had been beneficiaries of subsidized food exports from the US and the EU and their need for surplus disposal. Now they were afraid that trade liberalization and subsidy reduction might lead to a higher food import bill for them.[21] It could be an option for food importing countries today to organize themselves around the issue of export restrictions like the NFIDC did around the issue of subsidy reductions in exporter nations. Saudi Arabia could raise the issue also as a G20 member. Yet, it has not appeared to be vocal in that matter, even though France put global food

---

[17] *New York Times*, 11 March 2012.   [18] Sojamo et al. 2012.
[19] The website of his presidency is <www.un.org/en/ga/president/66/> (accessed 22 June 2012).
[20] FAO 2011b.   [21] Wolfe 1998: 122f.; Kaufmann and Heri 2007; Narlikar 2003: 186.

security on the agenda of the G20 during its presidency of the organization in 2011.

Climate change is a major threat to global agricultural production. As hydrocarbon exporters Gulf countries have played a rather obstructive role in the international climate change debate alongside large consumer nations like the US and China. As food importers, they may want to reconsider this stance. When the Intergovernmental Panel on Climate Change (IPCC) identified climate change as definitely manmade in its 1995 report, Saudi Arabia and Kuwait immediately opposed the findings.[22] Saudi Arabia has also lobbied against curbs on emissions. It has argued that it should receive financial compensation for revenue losses that might be caused by constraints on emissions and corresponding falls in oil sales. Its lead climate negotiator at the Copenhagen summit, Muhammad al-Sabban, has argued that climate change is not manmade, but rather a result of natural variability. Restrictions on greenhouse gases, therefore, were not warranted he said. A US embassy cable from February 2010 described him as a "rogue negotiator," but also pointed to more moderate Saudi voices like oil minister Al-Naimi and the former WTO chief negotiator Fawaz al-Alami. It saw signs of a more open-minded approach and remarked that "Saudi officials have suggested that they need to find a way to climb down gracefully from the country's tough negotiating position."[23]

In fact, Gulf countries have a stake in the global climate change debate. At the Cancun conference in 2010, they had a keen interest to qualify Carbon Capture and Storage (CCS) for carbon credits as they have ideal conditions for an application of the technology. Power plants, petrochemical complexes, and heavy industries are in close vicinity to oilfields, where associated natural gas has hitherto been reinjected in order to keep up reservoir pressure. A replacement with CO_2 injections would not only save scarce natural gas for the Gulf countries' industrialization drive, it would also earn them carbon credits under the Clean Development Mechanism (CDM) of the Kyoto Protocol or any other cap and trade system that might evolve in the future.[24]

Gulf countries are in need of know-how transfer for their food processing industries, their foreign agro-investments, and their redirection of domestic agriculture towards more water efficiency. Interaction with international institutions will be necessary and more frequent. First encounters have revealed mutual misunderstandings. At times, there has been the impression in international consultancy circles that Gulf countries were only interested in window

---

[22] Oreskes and Conway 2010: 204f.

[23] WikiLeaks cable RIYADH000184, US Embassy in Riyadh, 12 February 2010.

[24] The motion to include CCS into the CDM mechanism and not only renewable energies and landfills was put forward by Qatar. It was endorsed by other Gulf countries and other hydrocarbon producers like Norway and Australia. *The National*, 6 and 12 December 2010.

shopping and getting a carte blanche for their agricultural investment activities. After a visit to Saudi Arabia, Robert Zeigler, the head of the International Rice Research Institute, complained in the *New York Times* that the Saudis were only interested in the quantities of land acquisitions, not investing in urgently needed agricultural research and development.[25] The unusual choice of a public platform for such criticism would hint to a major irritation. A more refined knowledge of international institutions and their agendas would be required for a successful management of strategic partnerships.

Gulf countries have also shown an interest in breathing new life into pan-Arab institutions like the AAAID or the AOAD. Increased pan-Arab cooperation would be unable to achieve self-sufficiency because of a lack of water resources, but it could ameliorate food security and promote development in the wider Arab world. Gulf countries have mainly cast their eyes on allegedly virgin lands in Sudan and other sub-Saharan countries, but there is considerable potential in the traditional producer countries of the Middle East like Morocco, Egypt, Syria, and Iraq, not only in terms of increasing productivity but also in terms of reducing wastage in food processing and distribution. Aleppo houses the International Center for Agricultural Research in the Dry Areas (ICARDA) that belongs to the CGIAR network and has a long history of developing improved farming methods that are more sustainable. Yet, it is not a mere technical challenge but also one of adaptation to prevalent systems of land tenure as the problematic introduction of Australian methods of dryland farming in the Middle East showed in the 1970s and 1980s.[26]

Finally, Gulf countries need to manage their public image and address human rights violations as part of their multilateral efforts. They perceive food security too much as a strategic practice of states without taking the human security dimension in target countries into consideration.[27] The bad press around housemaid abuse and the plight of migrant workers has not helped their intention to launch agro-investments in the Philippines and Indonesia for example. Gulf countries have been at loggerheads with international NGOs like Human Rights Watch and the World Wildlife Fund over issues of labor rights and environmental standards. Their international agro-investments have propelled them into the crosshairs of NGO campaigns as well.

As authoritarian states they only allow limited participation at home, even though there have been cautious steps towards liberalization since the 1990s, with Kuwait and Bahrain at the helm of reform measures.[28] However, there has been a backlash in the wake of the Arab Spring and even before Gulf countries were hardly used to NGO politics. There is no established due process for association from below. At the end of the day NGOs require the rulers' explicit approval. Apart from crackdowns on potential NGO activities,

---

[25] Rice 2009.   [26] Springborg 1986.   [27] Shepherd 2012.
[28] Ehteshami and Wright 2008; Herb 1999; Khalaf and Luciani 2006; Teitelbaum 2009.

a widespread practice is to pre-empt concerns by establishing loyal Government Organized NGOs (GONGOs). Not surprisingly, as far as domestic NGOs exist their activities are rarely controversial. Beyond the Gulf's borders this is different and outlawing or cutting off internet connections not an option.

NGOs have developed into intricate players of a "global legitimacy game."[29] Multinational corporations have to engage with them, otherwise their reputation might be tarnished and their bottom line hurt. NGOs also serve as cooperation partners for international organizations and recruiting grounds for governments.[30] For Gulf countries this is new and unusual. NGOs did not have that reach during the first wave of petrodollar investments in the 1970s. Gulf governments still operate in a mindset that feels more comfortable with confidential handshake deals between statesmen and corporate leaders. They do not have sufficient capacities to engage in a public dialogue with NGOs and their constituencies. This can amount to a serious handicap in an increasingly globalized legitimacy discourse.

9.3 BILATERAL RELATIONS

With many target countries relationships are not too intense. The Gulf countries' trading relations are mainly with manufacturing nations in the OECD and some emerging markets like China or India. South–South relations with developing nations in Africa and Asia are less mature. Flight connections to countries that do not send labor migrants to the Gulf are limited; although they have grown with the success of international airlines in the Gulf region. Embassy representation of Gulf countries outside the OECD and the Arab world focuses on a few countries. Only Saudi Arabia has a larger embassy network.[31] Apart from Sudan and Pakistan, agro-investments in many target countries do not start off from a point of deep, broad-based trading relationships and established political dialogue.

With OECD nations this is different. The US in particular has close strategic relations with the region. It has military bases in Kuwait, Qatar, and Bahrain and it uses ports and military installations in the UAE and Oman frequently. It does not have a troop presence in Saudi Arabia anymore in order to placate public sentiment, but holds biannual strategic consultations with the Saudi leadership. There is a considerable convergence of strategic interests. The platform to discuss food security concerns with food exporting OECD

---

[29] Van Rooy 2004.   [30] DeMars 2005: 1.
[31] For a list of worldwide embassy representations see <http://embassyinformation.com> and <http://embassy-finder.com> (accessed 22 April 2011).

countries exists. The confrontational stance of the 1970s is absent and a renewed oil boycott with counter threats of a food embargo is unlikely. There is also a vivid interest on part of Gulf countries to use international institutions and standards or Western joint venture partners to safeguard commercial interests. This has been discernible during the Sudan bread-basket episode. A prevalent impression is that they alone could not guarantee their interests or that it would put them into unnecessary confrontation with recipient countries.

As Gulf countries venture abroad, they will become part of ongoing socio-economic conflicts in target countries, whether it is customary land rights in Africa, struggles for land reform in the Philippines, or resistance in Irian Jaya against settlers from the Indonesian population centers. Gulf countries could also become party to the delicate hydropolitics along the Indus, the Euphrates and Tigris, in Central Asia, and in the Nile Valley. International agro-investments can affect their international relations considerably.[32]

Oil-for-food policies constitute a formidable challenge for the bureaucratic capacities of the Gulf states. They will need to engage with governments, institutions, NGOs, and the general public more efficiently, more frequently, and often in a different fashion than at home. In their ongoing diversification drive, Gulf countries have used offset deals in an attempt to condition the sale of oil to the concomitant purchase of processed goods and implementation of projects. Yet outright oil-for-food barter agreements that were pondered with Australia in the 1970s are not very likely. They would be only conceivable in a situation of profound failure of international trading regimes. If they happen, the Gulf countries would seek such deals not from food net importers in the developing world but from established exporters with the track record and the institutional capability to deliver.

Beside oil, Gulf countries could also use their standing in global fertilizer markets as an asset in such a situation. The blocked take-over bid of Australian BHP Billiton for Canadian Potash Corp. in 2010 and the hostile Canadian reactions to a potential counter-bid by Chinese state-owned Sinochem have shown that fertilizers can play a role in strategic considerations and stir protectionist sentiments.[33] The three primary macronutrients nitrogen, potassium, and phosphorus can be produced in an inorganic fashion and trade widely internationally.[34] GCC countries are important producers of ammonia

---

[32] For authoritative accounts of the international relations of the Gulf countries in general see Gause 2010; Legrenzi 2011; Ulrichsen 2011.

[33] Massot 2011.

[34] The secondary macronutrients calcium, magnesium, and sulfur are required in roughly similar quantities for plant growth, but their availability is largely managed as part of liming and manuring practices. Thus, their supply is generated locally and not so much by industrial production and international trade. Beside the six macronutrients plants require micronutrients or trace minerals such as iron, manganese, or zinc in smaller qantities.

and urea, which are needed for production of nitrogen fertilizer. They have expanded their petrochemical industries rapidly and there has been a shift of production capacity from Europe and America to the Gulf, at least until the US shale boom.[35] They do not have production of potassium containing potash. Saudi Arabia has a modest output of phosphate fertilizer, though, the main source of phosphorus in modern agriculture. Production will expand dramatically once the phosphate mining project at Al-Jalamid in the north of the country is completed around 2014. Saudi Arabia currently holds a 10 percent share of globally traded urea and aims at a similar market penetration rate in traded di-ammonium phosphate fertilizer once the Al-Jalamid project is fully operational.[36]

While nitrogen fertilizer is mainly produced from natural gas, phosphate and potash are gained from mining rocks. Supply concerns about natural gas have eased decisively with the advent of new production techniques, which have added large unconventional natural gas resources to global supplies. As nitrogen fertilizer only requires air, water, and large amounts of energy for its production, alternatives to natural gas are conceivable and depend on the respective economics and price developments.

Phosphorus on the other hand is a chemical element and without alternative. Based on older reserve figures of the US Geological Service (USGS), some studies have expressed concerns about supply constraints. They argue that a peak in phosphate production could be expected as early as 2033 with negative consequences for agricultural production.[37] However, a study of the International Fertilizer Development Center (IFDC) dramatically upgraded global reserve figures in 2010.[38] It argued that the price assumptions of the USGS estimate were too low and that higher prices would increase reserves by making production of hitherto uneconomical resources profitable. The discrepancy is huge and mostly attributable to a tenfold upgrade of Moroccan reserve figures. The IFDC report has an estimate of 60 billion metric tons of global phosphate rock reserves as compared to the 2010 USGS estimate of only 16 billion mt.

In response to the IFDC report USGS also upgraded its Moroccan reserve estimate and now gauges global reserves at 65 billion mt.[39] According to the new reserve estimates a peak in phosphate production is not imminent. Remaining reserve life would be 300–400 years and Morocco would command over three-quarters of global reserves. Yet, these figures are regarded as preliminary by the IFDC itself because of a deficient database. The findings are

[35] Luciani 2012c; Fattouh and Mabro 2006.
[36] <http://www.maaden.com.sa/en/news_details/32> (accessed 22 April 2012).
[37] Cordell, Drangert, and White 2009.
[38] van Kauwenbergh 2010: 33.
[39] U.S. Geological Survey (USGS) 2011: 119.

based on older secondary literature and assume flattening demand trends without detailed analysis. A more sustainable management of the phosphorus cycle is warranted in any case, not only for environmental reasons: A peak in production will occur long before the remaining reserve life and phosphorus will be indispensable for future generations and their food production.[40] Phosphate fertilizers will likely become increasingly valuable.

The GCC offered Morocco and Jordan membership in 2011. The motivation for this offer was to strengthen Arab monarchies in the wake of the Arab Spring. It had nothing to do with fertilizers and GCC integration of the two countries is not very likely. Yet, it is conceivable that Gulf countries, Morocco, and Jordan could try to leverage their fertilizer resources, particularly phosphate fertilizers in a situation of strained food supplies. Philippine officials have already mentioned fertilizer deliveries from the Gulf countries when discussing the potential for agricultural cooperation. Saudi agro-businessmen have also pondered the possibility of using subsidized diesel and fertilizer deliveries as a tool in foreign agro-investments, similar to the practice of subsidized agriculture at home.[41]

One reason for the GCC countries' preferences for developing countries as investment destinations are the gains in productivity that can be expected in underdeveloped markets.[42] Investments in developing countries with sufficient renewable blue and green water resources can be an important ingredient in the overall GCC strategy of food security, but it should not be the only one. They would need to look at developed agro-markets as well. The bulk of their food imports comes from there. There has indeed been an increasing orientation towards countries like Australia, Brazil, or Ukraine for reasons of practicability. Cooperation in these markets will take different forms and will include joint ventures beside outright land acquisitions.

As GCC countries seek agricultural cooperation in the developing world, they will need to take greater account of the interests of local stakeholders and their food security concerns. Increased communication of investment goals and close cooperation with local governments and communities will be of the essence for any successful implementation of agricultural projects. A necessary precondition for such cooperation would be greater transparency in order to allow local communities to make decisions of free, prior, and informed consent (FPIC). Gulf countries mostly aspire to a plantation model with full control and long-term rights to the land, but there are more promising cooperation models.[43] Contract farming might integrate local farmers better

---

[40] Cordell and White 2011; Global Phosphorus Research Initiative 2010.

[41] *Emirates 24/7*, 5 March 2011; interview, Saudi agro-businessman, Princeton, 27 September 2011.

[42] Interview with executive of Al-Qudra Agriculture, Abu Dhabi, 20 April 2009.

[43] For examples of such schemes in Africa see Cotula et al. 2009: 84–7.

and could take advantage of local production know-how. Outgrower schemes, joint equity with local communities, and local content requirements can not only increase acceptance of foreign agro-investments, they also have the potential to contribute to efficiency gains.

Overall, a picture emerges where trade issues and the integration of legitimate food security concerns of Middle Eastern countries in a more equitable global food system will be of greater importance than the widely publicized international land acquisitions by Gulf countries and their unsustainable domestic agricultural sector. Oil-for-food policies will be an important factor in strategic calculations and international politics for decades to come.

References

Primary Sources

Archives

Burdett, Anita L. P. (ed.). 1997. *Records of Saudi Arabia, 1961–1965.* 6 vols. Slough, UK: Archive Editions.

——1998. *Water Resources in the Arabian Peninsula, 1921–1960.* 2 vols. Slough, UK: Archive Editions.

——2002. *Records of the Emirates, 1966–1971.* 6 vols. Slough, UK: Archive Editions.

——2004. *Records of Saudi Arabia, 1966–1971.* 6 vols. Slough, UK: Archive Editions.

Carter Library, Atlanta, Ga.

Ford Foundation Archive, New York.

Ford Library, Ann Arbor, Mich.

National Archives of Australia (cited as NAA).

National Archive and Record Administration, College Park, Maryland, Series RG 59 and RG 166 (cited as NARA).

Nixon Library, Yorba Linda, Calif.

Preston, Paul, Michael Partridge, and Malcolm Yapp (eds.). 1997. *British Documents on Foreign Affairs—Reports and Papers from the Foreign Office Confidential Print.* Part III, From 1940 through 1945. Series B, Near and Middle East. Bethesda, Md: University Publications of America.

Public Record Office, London:

Foreign Office Record, Series FO 371 (cited as FO).

Records of the Agriculture, Fisheries and Food Departments, and of related bodies, Series MAF 83 (cited as MAF).

Reagan Library, Simi Valley, Calif.

Tuson, Penelope (ed.). 1990. *Records of the Emirates: Primary Documents, 1820–1958.* 12 vols. Farnham Common, Slough, UK: Archive Editions.

——1991. *Records of Qatar: Primary Documents, 1820–1960.* 8 vols. Farnham Common, Slough, UK: Archive Editions.

Tuson, Penelope, and Anita Burdett (eds.). 1992. *Records of Saudi Arabia. Primary Documents, 1902–1960.* 9 vols. Slough, UK: Archive Editions.

US Department of State. Foreign Relations of the United States, Washington, DC, 1861– (cited as FRUS):

FRUS, *The British Commonwealth, the Near East and Africa (1941)*, Vol. III, Washington 1959.

FRUS, *The Near East and Africa (1942)*, Vol. IV, Washington 1963.

FRUS, *The Near East and Africa (1943)*, Vol. IV, Washington 1964.

FRUS, *The Near East, South Asia, and Africa, the Far East (1944)*, Vol. V, Washington 1965.

FRUS, *The Near East and Africa (1947)*, Vol. V, Washington 1971.

FRUS, *Near East Region, Iraq, Iran, Arabian Peninsula (1958–1960)*, Vol. XII, Washington 1993.

FRUS, *Near East Region, Arabian Peninsula, 1964–68*, Vol. XXI, Washington 2000.
US Records on Saudi Affairs, 1945–1959, 6 vols. (Slough, UK: Archive Editions, 1997) (cited as USRSA).

Paper Collections, Oral Histories, and Other Sources

William Alfred Eddy Papers, Seeley G. Mudd Manuscript Library, Princeton University (cited as Eddy Papers).
The Foreign Affairs Oral History Collection of the Association for Diplomatic Studies and Training at the Library of Congress, <http://memory.loc.gov/ammem/collections/diplomacy/index.html>
George Stanley McGovern Papers, Seeley G. Mudd Manuscript Library, Princeton University (cited as McGovern Papers).
William E. Mulligan Papers, Lauinger Library, Special Collections, Georgetown University, Washington, DC (cited as Mulligan Papers).
Karl S. Twitchell Papers, Seeley G. Mudd Manuscript Library, Princeton University (cited as Twitchell Papers).
WikiLeaks US embassy cables.
Personal interviews and newspaper sources are quoted in the respective footnotes.

Government Documents

Agriculture and Agro-Food Canada. 2001. *Saudi Arabia. Bi-Weekly Bulletin* 14(11). 29 June 2001. Market Analysis Division. Ottawa.
——2005. *Saudi Arabia. Bi-Weekly Bulletin* 18(5). 4 March 2005. Market Analysis Division. Ottawa.
British Information Services. 1951. *Britain and Middle East Development*. New York: British Information Services.
Catterson, Thomas, Mersie Ejigu, Malik Doka, Jaden Tongun Emilio, and Luke Ipoto Ojok. 2003. *USAID Integrated Strategic Plan in the Sudan, 2003–2005. Environmental Threats and Opportunities Assessment*. Washington, DC: USAID.
Federal Government of Ethiopia. 2009. Land Rent Contractual Agreement between Ministry of Agriculture and Saudi Star Agricultural Development Plc, Addis Ababa, 29 September 2009. Ministry of Agriculture and Rural Development. Addis Ababa.
Government of Abu Dhabi. 2009. *Abu Dhabi Water Resources Master Plan*. Abu Dhabi.
Government of Sudan. 1977. *The Six Year Plan of Economic and Social Development, 1977/78–1982/83*. Ministry of Culture and Information. Khartoum.
——2008. *The Executive Programme for the Agricultural Revival*. Supreme Council for Agricultural Revival. Secretariat General. Khartoum.
——2010. *Agriculture. Sudan's Indisputable Wealth. A Guide to Investment in Agriculture*. Ministry of Investment (in coordination with Ministry of Agriculture and Forests). Khartoum.
Intelligence Community Assessment. 2012. *Global Water Security: The Intelligence Community Assessment*. Washington, DC.
Kingdom of Saudi Arabia. 1970. *The First Development Plan (1970–1975)*. Central Planning Organization. Riyadh.

——1975. *The Second Development Plan (1975–1980)*. Ministry of Planning. Riyadh.

——1980. *The Third Development Plan (1980–1985)*. Ministry of Planning. Riyadh.

——1985. *The Fourth Development Plan (1985–1990)*. Ministry of Planning. Riyadh.

——1990. *The Fifth Development Plan (1990–1995)*. Ministry of Planning. Riyadh.

——1995. *The Sixth Development Plan (1995–2000)*. Ministry of Planning. Riyadh.

——2000. *The Seventh Development Plan (2000–2004)*. Ministry of Planning. Riyadh.

——2005. *The Eighth Development Plan (2005–2009)*. Ministry of Economy and Planning. Riyadh.

——2009a. "Custodian of the Two Holy Mosques Receives Minister of Commerce and Industry." Ministry of Foreign Affairs, 27 January 2009. Available at: <http://mofa.gov.sa/sites/mofaen/ServicesAndInformation/news/statements/Pages/NewsArticleID88796.aspx> (accessed 10 March 2012).

——2009b. "King Abdulla's Initiative for Agricultural Investment Abroad." Presentation by Taha A. Alshareef at IPC Conference on Food and Environmental Security. The Role of Food and Agricultural Trade Policy, Salzburg/Austria, 10–11 May. Ministry of Commerce and Industry. Riyadh.

——2009c. "Wheat Production in Saudi Arabia (a Three Decade Story)." Presentation by Deputy Minister for Agricultural Research and Development Affairs, Abdullah A. Al-Obaid, Conference on Food and Environmental Security. The Role of Food and Agricultural Trade Policy, Salzburg/Austria, 10–11 May. Ministry of Agriculture. Riyadh.

——2010a. "King Abdullah's Initiative for Saudi Agricultural Investment Abroad: A Way of Enhancing Saudi Food Security." Presentation by Abdullah A. Al-Obaid, Deputy Minister for Agricultural Research and Development Affairs, at the Expert Group Meeting on Achieving Food Security in Member Countries in Post-Crisis World, Islamic Development Bank, Jeddah, 2–3 May. Ministry of Agriculture. Riyadh.

——2010b. *The Ninth Development Plan (2010–2014)*. Ministry of Economy and Planning. Riyadh.

Mousa, Hussein. 2008a. *Saudi Arabia Retail Food Sector. Annual Update 2008.* GAIN Report, USDA Foreign Agricultural Service. Washington, DC: US Department of Agriculture (USDA).

——2008b. *Saudi Arabia to Import Wheat in 2009.* USDA Foreign Agricultural Service. Washington, DC: US Department of Agriculture (USDA).

——2009. *Saudi Arabia Grain and Feed: Saudi Arabia Reduces Import Subsidies on Animal Feed.* GAIN Report, USDA Foreign Agricultural Service. Washington, DC: US Department of Agriculture (USDA).

——2010. *Grain and Feed Annual.* USDA Foreign Agricultural Service. Washington, DC: US Department of Agriculture (USDA).

——2012. *Saudi Arabia: Grain and Feed Annual.* USDA Foreign Agricultural Service. Washington, DC: US Department of Agriculture (USDA).

U.S. Congress. 1973. House. Committee on Foreign Affairs Report of a Study Mission to the Middle East from October 22 to November 3, December 20, 1973, pursuant to H. Res. 267. *The United States Oil Shortage and the Arab-Israeli Conflict.* 93rd Congress, 1st session. Washington, DC: U.S. Government Printing Office.

——1977. House. Congresssional Research Report prepared for House Committee on International Relations. *Uses of US Food for Diplomatic Purposes: An Examination of the Issues*, January 1977. 94th Congress, 2nd session. Washington, DC: U.S. Government Printing Office.

——1979a. Senate. Hearing before the Subcommittee on Foreign Agricultural Policy of the Committee on Agriculture, Nutrition, and Forestry, 14 June 1979. *International Grain Agreements Oversight*. 96th Congress, 1st session. Washington, DC: U.S. Government Printing Office.

——1979b. House. Hearings before the Subcommittees on Department Investigations, Oversight, and Research, and Livestock and Grains on H.R. 4273. Committee on Agriculture, House of Representatives, 5–6 June. *National Grain Board*. 96th Congress, 1st session. Washington, DC: U.S. Government Printing Office.

——1981. Senate. Hearings before the Committee on Energy and Natural Resources, 28 and 30 July. *Government Responses to Oil Supply Disruptions*. Report Number 97-29. 97th Congress, 1st session. Washington, DC: U.S. Government Printing Office.

——1983. Senate. Hearings before the Committee on Agriculture, Nutrition, and Forestry, 17 and 25 February. *Agricultural Export Trade*. HRG-1983-ANF-0002. 98th Congress, 1st session. Washington, DC: U.S. Government Printing Office.

——2004. House. Hearing before the Committee on Agriculture, 16 June. *Review Iraqi Agriculture: From Oil for Food to the Future of Iraqi Production, Agriculture and Trade*. 108th Congress, 2nd session. Washington, DC: U.S. Government Printing Office.

United States Department of Agriculture (USDA). 2008. "Iran: 2008/09 Wheat Production Declines Due to Drought," 9 May. Available at: <http://www.pecad.fas.usda.gov/highlights/2008/05/Iran_may2008.htm> (accessed 11 April 2012).

——2009. "Grain: World Markets and Trade Circular, Series FG-04–09," April. Available at: <http://www.fas.usda.gov/grain/circular/2009/04–09/grainfull04–09.pdf> (accessed 11 April 2012).

——2012a. *Agricultural Projections to 2021*. Washington, DC.

——2012b. Foreign Agricultural Service Database. Production, Supply and Distribution (PSD). Available at: <http://www.fas.usda.gov/psdonline/psdQuery.aspx> (accessed 10 March 2012).

U.S. Census Bureau. 2011. U.S. International Trade in Goods and Services (Ft900) Dataset. Available at: <http://www.census.gov/foreign-trade/Press-Release/current_press_release/index.html> (accessed 14 April 2011).

U.S. Geological Survey (USGS). 2011. *Mineral Commodity Summaries 2011*. Reston, Va.

Vassilieva, Yelena, and Mary Ellen Smith. 2009. *Russian Federation Grain and Feed. Russia's Federal United Grain Company Created 2009*. GAIN Report, USDA Foreign Agricultural Service. Washington, DC: US Department of Agriculture (USDA).

International and Regional Organizations

Arab Authority for Agriculture Investment and Development (AAAID). 2002. *Strategy for the Years 2002–2012*. Khartoum.

Arab Fund for Economic and Social Development (AFESD). 1976. *Basic Programme for Agricultural Development in the Democratic Republic of the Sudan, 1976–1985. Summary and Conclusions*. Kuwait.

Arab Organization for Agricultural Development (AOAD). 2009. *Arab Agricultural Statistics Yearbook*. Khartoum.

Bank for International Settlement (BIS). 2008. *International Banking and Financial Market Developments*. Quarterly Review, June. Basle.

Bruinsma, Jelle, and FAO. 2003. *World Agriculture: Towards 2015/2030: An FAO Perspective*. London: Earthscan Publications.

Cotula, Lorenzo, Sonja Vermeulen, Rebeca Leonard, and James Keeley. 2009. *Land Grab or Development Opportunity? Agricultural Investments and International Land Deals in Africa*. Report. Rome: FAO, IFAD, IEED.

Deininger, K. 2003. *Land Policies for Growth and Poverty Reduction*. Washington, DC: World Bank.

Deininger, Klaus, Derek Byerlee, Jonathan Lindsay, Andrew Norton, Harris Selod, and Mercedes Stickler. 2011. *Rising Global Interest in Farmland Can It Yield Sustainable and Equitable Benefits?* Agriculture and Rural Development. Washington, DC: World Bank.

Economic and Social Commission for Western Asia (ESCWA), and IFPRI. Mimeo 2012. *Food Security Strategies in the Arab Gulf Region*. Beirut and Washington, DC.

Food and Agriculture Organization of the United Nations (FAO). 1949. *Food Balance Sheets*. Washington, DC.

——1951. "Report of the Second Near East Meeting on Food and Agricultural Programs and Outlook," 28 August–6 September, at Bloudane, Syria.

——2005. *Country Profile Sudan*. Aquastat, Version 2005. Rome.

——2008a. *Country Profile Bahrain*. Aquastat, Version 2008. Rome.

——2008b. *Country Profile Kuwait*. Aquastat, Version 2008. Rome.

——2008c. *Country Profile Oman*. Aquastat Version 2008. Rome.

——2008d. *Country Profile Qatar*. Aquastat, Version 2008. Rome.

——2008e. *Country Profile Saudi Arabia*. Aquastat, Version 2008. Rome.

——2008f. *Country Profile UAE*. Aquastat, Version 2008. Rome.

——2010a. *Country Profile Pakistan*. Aquastat, Version 2010. Rome.

——2010b. *The State of Food Insecurity in the World 2010*. Rome.

——2011a. AQUASTAT Database. Available at: <http://www.fao.org/nr/water/aquastat/data/query/index.html> (accessed 12 January 2011).

——2011b. Consultation for the Private Sector on Responsible Agricultural Investment, 2 March 2011. Rome.

——2011c. FAOSTAT Database. Available at: <http://faostat.fao.org/site/291/default.aspx> (accessed 19 August 2011).

——2011d. Fishery and Aquaculture, FIGIS Database. Available at: <http://www.fao.org/fishery/statistics/en> (accessed 11 October 2011).

Food and Agriculture Organization of the United Nations (FAO). 2012a. Role of Imports and Net-Trade (Exports-Imports) in Total Food Consumption, 2006–2008. Available at: <http://www.fao.org/fileadmin/templates/ess/documents/food_security_statistics/Net_Trade_Calories_en.xls> (accessed 15 June 2012).

——2012b. Voluntary Guidelines on the Responsible Governance of Tenure of Land, Fisheries and Forests in the Context of National Food Security, 11 May 2012. Rome.

Habluetzel, H. 1963. *Final Report to the Government of Saudi Arabia on Farm Mechanization and Problems and Services.* Report 1611. Rome: FAO.

HLPE. 2011. *Land Tenure and International Investments in Agriculture.* HLPE 2. Report by the High Level Panel of Experts on Food Security and Nutrition. Rome: FAO.

International Fund for Agricultural Development (IFAD). 2002. *Republic of the Sudan. Country Strategic Opportunities Paper (COSOP).* Executive Board, Seventy-Sixth Session. Rome.

International Labour Organization (ILO), and United Nations Development Programme (UNDP). 1976. *Growth, Employment, and Equity: A Comprehensive Strategy for the Sudan. Employment Mission 1975.* Geneva: International Labour Office.

International Monetary Fund (IMF). 2007. "IMF Backs UAE Statistics Overhaul," 26 November. Available at: <http://www.imf.org/external/pubs/ft/survey/so/2007/num1126a.htm> (accessed 5 April 2012).

——2010. *Sudan: 2010 Article IV Consultation—Staff Report.* Washington, DC.

——2011a. "IMF Executive Board Concludes 2010 Article IV Consultation with Oman." Public Information Notice (PIN) No. 11/44, 1 April. Washington, DC.

——2011b. *Qatar: 2010 Article IV Consultation—Staff Report.* Washington, DC.

——2011c. *Kuwait: 2011 Article IV Consultation—Staff Report.* Washington, DC.

——2011d. *Saudi Arabia: 2011 Article IV Consultation—Staff Report.* Washington, DC.

——2011e. *United Arab Emirates: 2011 Article IV Consultation—Staff Report.* Washington, DC.

——2011f. *Gulf Cooperation Council Countries (GCC). Enhancing Economic Outcomes in an Uncertain Global Economy.* Washington, DC.

——2011g. World Economic Outlook dataset, September 2011.

——2012. "IMF Executive Board Concludes 2012 Article IV Consultation with Bahrain." Public Information Notice (PIN) No. 12/39, 24 April. Washington, DC.

International Trade Center. 2012. Trade Map Statistics. Available at: <www.trademap.org> (accessed 29 June 2012).

Intergovernmental Panel on Climate Change (IPCC). 2007. *Climate Change 2007: Impacts, Adaptation and Vulnerability.* IPCC Fourth Assessment Report (AR4), Contribution of Working Group II. Geneva.

Islamic Development Bank (IsDB). 2011. *Islamic Development Bank Group in Brief.* Jeddah.

Middle East Supply Center (MESC). 1944. *Proceedings of the Conference on Middle East Agricultural Development, Cairo, February 7th–10th, 1944.* Agricultural Report. Cairo.

Müller, C., A. Bondeau, A. Popp, K. Waha, and M. Fader. 2009. *Climate Change Impacts on Agricultural Yields.* Washington, DC: World Bank.

Organisation for Economic Co-operation and Development–Food and Agriculture Organization (OECD–FAO). 2009. *Agricultural Outlook 2009–2018.* Paris.

——2010. *Agricultural Outlook 2010–2019.* Paris.

United Nations Conference on Trade and Development (UNCTAD). 2009. *World Investment Report 2009: Transnational Corporations, Agricultural Production and Development.* New York and Geneva.

United Nations Development Programme (UNDP). 2011. *Human Development Report 2011: Sustainability and Equity: A Better Future for All.* New York.

United Nations. 2010. World Population Prospects: The 2010 Revision. Available at: <http://esa.un.org/wpp/unpp/panel_population.htm> (accessed 22 April 2012).

United Nations. 2011. World Urbanization Prospects: The 2011 Revision. Available at: <http://esa.un.org/unpd/wup/CD-ROM/Urban-Rural-Population.htm> (accessed 29 January 2013).

UN Human Rights Council. 2010. *Promotion and Protection of All Human Rights, Civil, Political, Economic, Social and Cultural Rights, Including the Right to Development.* Report submitted by the Special Rapporteur on the right to food, Olivier De Schutter. Geneva.

Westlake, Michael. 2000. "The Economics of Strategic Crops." In *Syrian Agriculture at the Crossroads,* ed. Ciro Fiorillo and Jacques Vercueil, 137–62. Rome: FAO.

World Food Program (WFP). 2011. *2010 Food Aid Flows.* International Food Aid Information System. Rome.

World Bank. 2007. *World Development Report 2008: Agriculture for Development.* Washington, DC and London: World Bank.

——2008. *Biofuels: The Promise and the Risks.* Washington, DC.

——2010a. *Arab Development Assistance: Four Decades of Cooperation.* Washington, DC.

——2010b. *World Development Report 2010: Development and Climate Change.* Washington, DC.

World Bank, and FAO. 2012. *The Grain Chain: Food Security and Managing Wheat Imports in Arab Countries.* Washington, DC.

World Bank, FAO, and IFAD. 2009. *Improving Food Security in Arab Countries.* Washington, DC.

World Bank, and International Finance Corporation (IFC). 2012. *Doing Buisness 2011: Doing Business in a More Transparent World.* Washington, DC.

Secondary Sources

Note: For Burdett 1997, 1998, 2002, 2004, Preston et al. 1997, Tuson 1990, 1991, and Tuson and Burdett 1992 see Archives. For Catterson et al. 2003, Moussa 2008a, 2008b, 2009, 2010, 2012 and Vassilieva and Smith 2009 see Government Documents. For Bruinsma and FAO 2003, Cotula et al. 2009, Deininger 2003, Deininger et al. 2011, Habluetzel 1963, Müller et al. 2009, and Westlake 2000 see International and Regional Organizations.

Abdullah, Muhammad Morsy. 1978. *The United Arab Emirates: A Modern History.* London: Croom Helm; New York: Barnes & Noble.

Adam, Farah Hassan, El Tayeb Amin Mohamed, and Kamil Ibrahim Hassan. 1983. "Mechanized Agriculture in the Central Rainlands of the Sudan." In—*The Development Perspectives of the Democratic Republic of Sudan: The Limits of the Bread Basket Strategy*, ed. Peter Oesterdiekhoff and Karl Wohlmuth, 54–80. Munich, Cologne, and London: Weltforum.

Adams Jr., Richard H. 2003. "The Political Economy and Distributional Impact of the Egyptian Food Subsidy System." In *Food, Agriculture, and Economic Policy in the Middle East and North Africa*, ed. Hans Lofgren, 105–32. Amsterdam and New York: JAI.

Adelman, M. A. 2004. "The Real Oil Problem." *Regulation* 27(1) (Spring): 16–21.

Ahmad, Mahmood. 2002. "Agricultural Policy Issues and Challenges in Iraq: Short- and Medium-Term Options." In *Iraq's Economic Predicament*, ed. Kamil A. Mahdi, 169–99. Reading: Ithaca Press.

Al-Ahrar. 2010. "Tahaluf ghair Mubashir baina Duwal al-Khalij wa Isra'il wa Amrika fi Manabi' al-Nil didda Masalih Misr." [Indirect Alliance between Gulf Countries, Israel, and America against the Interest of Egypt with regard to the Nile Sources]. *Al-Ahrar*, 29 December.

Aissaoui, Ali. 2010. *MENA Natural Gas: A Paradox of Scarcity Amidst Plenty*. Economic Commentary. Dammam: APICORP.

Al-Alami, Fawaz. 2009. "Hal Yanjah al-Istithmar al-Zira'i al-Khariji?" [Is the Foreign Agro-Investment Successful?]. *Al-Watan*, 29 December.

Al Ameeri, Saeed Mohammad. 2003. "The Baloch in the Arabian Gulf States." In *The Baloch and Their Neighbours: Ethnic and Linguistic Contact in Balochistan in Historical and Modern Times*, ed. Carina Jahani and Agnes Korn, 237–43. Wiesbaden: Reichert.

Alamdari, Kazem. 2005. *Why the Middle East Lagged Behind: The Case of Iran*. Lanham, Md.: University Press of America.

Ali, Mohamed Ahmed. 1998. "Sudan: The Hidden Signs of a Food Crisis." *Sudan Dispatch: Journal of Sudanese Development* 3: 4–5.

Alikhani, Hossein. 2000. *Sanctioning Iran: Anatomy of a Failed Policy*. London and New York: I. B. Tauris.

Allan, Tony. 2001. *The Middle East Water Question: Hydropolitics and the Global Economy*. London and New York: I. B. Tauris.

——2011. *Virtual Water: Tackling the Threat to Our Planet's Most Precious Resource*. London: I. B. Tauris.

Allen, H. B. 1946. *Rural Education and Welfare in the Middle East*. Middle East Supply Centre. Report to the Director General. London: HMSO.

Alpen Capital. 2011. *GCC Food Industry*. Dubai.

Alterman, Jon B., and Michael Dziuban. 2010. *Clear Gold: Water as a Strategic Resource in the Middle East*. Washington, DC: Center for Strategic and International Studies (CSIS).

Amid, Javad. 2007. "The Dilemma of Cheap Food and Self-Sufficiency: The Case of Wheat in Iran." *Food Policy* 32(4): 537–52.

Andræ, Gunilla, and Björn Beckman. 1985. *The Wheat Trap: Bread and Underdevelopment in Nigeria*. Third World Books. London and Totowa, NJ: Zed Books in association with Scandinavian Institute of African Studies.

Anscombe, Frederick Fallowfield. 1997. *The Ottoman Gulf: The Creation of Kuwait, Saudi Arabia, and Qatar, 1870–1914*. New York: Columbia University Press.

Anseeuw, W., M. Boche, T. Breu, M. Giger, J. Lay, P. Messerli, and K. Nolte. 2012. *Transnational Land Deals for Agriculture in the Global South.* Analytical Report based on the Land Matrix Database. Bern, Montpellier, and Hamburg: CDE, CIRAD, GIGA, GIZ, ILC.

Anseeuw, Ward, Liz Alden Wily, Lorenzo Cotula, and Michael Taylor. 2012. *Land Rights and the Rush for Land. Findings of the Global Commercial Pressures on Land Research Project.* Rome: International Land Coalition (ILC).

Arndt, H. W. 1987. *Economic Development: The History of an Idea.* Chicago: University of Chicago Press.

Arnove, Anthony. 2003. *Iraq under Siege: The Deadly Impact of Sanctions and War.* Updated edn. London: Pluto.

Ash, R. 2010. "The Chinese Economy after 30 Years of Reform: Perspectives from the Agricultural Sector." *The Copenhagen Journal of Asian Studies* 28(1): 36–62.

Ashraf, Ahmad. 1991. "State and Agrarian Relations before and after the Iranian Revolution, 1960–1990." In *Peasants and Politics in the Modern Middle East,* ed. John Waterbury Farhad Kazemi, 277–311. Miami: University Press of Florida.

Awad, Mohammed Hashim. 1971. "The Evolution of Landownership in the Sudan." *Middle East Journal* 25(2): 212–28.

Ayoub, A. T. 1999. "Land Degradation, Rainfall Variability and Food Production in the Sahelian Zone of the Sudan." *Land Degradation & Development* 10(5): 489–500.

Bahanshal, Osama M. 1990. "Grain Cartel, How Realistic a Threat?" *Journal King Saud University* 2 (Admin. Sci. 2): 83–105.

Balba, ʿAbd al-Munʿim. 1975. *Adwaʾ ʿala al-Ziraʿa al-ʿArabiyya.* [Spotlights on the Arab Agriculture]. Alexandria: Dar al-Matbuʿat al-Jadida.

Barnett, Tony. 1977. *The Gezira Scheme: An Illusion of Development.* London: F. Cass.

Barnett, Tony, and Abbas Abdelkarim. 1991. *Sudan: The Gezira Scheme and Agricultural Transition.* London and Portland, Or.: F. Cass.

Barrios, Salvador, Bazoumana Ouattara, and Eric Strobl. 2008. "The Impact of Climatic Change on Agricultural Production: Is It Different for Africa?" *Food Policy* 33(4): 287–98.

Bartos, Stephen, Australian Wheat Board, and United Nations Oil-for-Food Program. 2006. *Against the Grain: The AWB Scandal and Why It Happened.* Briefings. Sydney: UNSW Press.

Baxter, Joan, and Frédéric Mousseau. 2011. *Rapport: Mali.* Comprendre les investissements fonciers en Afrique. Oakland: Oakland Institute.

Baxter, Joan, Frédéric Mousseau, Anuradha Mittal, and Shepard Daniel. 2011. *Country Report: Sierra Leone.* Understanding Land Investment Deals in Africa. Oakland: Oakland Institute.

Bayt.Com, and YouGov Siraj. 2007. *Research Results, Rents, Transports and Costs, October 2007.* Available at: <http://img.b8cdn.com/images/uploads/article_docs/rents_bayt_en.pdf_20090609081905.pdf> (accessed 30 January 2012).

Bechtold, Peter K. 1973. "New Attempts at Arab Cooperation: The Federation of Arab Republics, 1971–?" *Middle East Journal* 27(2): 152–72.

Becker, Jasper. 1996. *Hungry Ghosts: China's Secret Famine.* London: J. Murray.

Bertelsmann Transformation Index. 2010. *United Arab Emirates Country Report 2010.* Berlin: Bertelsmann Foundation.

Beutel, Joerg. 2012. "Conceptual Problems of Measuring Economic Diversification, as Applied to the GCC Economies." In *Resources Blessed. Diversification and the Gulf Development Model*, ed. Giacomo Luciani, 29–70. Berlin and London: Gerlach.

Borras, Saturnino M., C. Kay, and E. Lahiff. 2007. *Market-Led Agrarian Reform*. London: Routledge.

Bowen-Jones, H. 1980. "Agriculture in Bahrain, Kuwait, Qatar and UAE." In *Issues in Development: The Arab Gulf States*, ed. May Ziwar-Daftari, 46–64. London: MD Research and Services.

Bowen-Jones, Howard, and Roderick Dutton. 1983. *Agriculture in the Arabian Peninsula*. Special Report. London: Economist Intelligence Unit.

Brabeck-Letmathe, Peter. 2009. "The Next Big Thing: H_2O. Water Is the New Gold, and a Few Savvy Countries and Companies Are Already Banking on It." *Foreign Policy*, 15 April.

Braudel, Fernand. 2000. *The Mediterranean and the Mediterranean World in the Age of Philip II*. Translation of the second revised edition, 1966 edn. 3 vols. London: The Folio Society.

von Braun Joachim, and Ruth Meinzen-Dick. 2009. *"Land Grabbing" by Foreign Investors in Developing Countries: Risks and Opportunities*. IFPRI Policy Brief. Washington, DC: International Food Policy Research Institute (IFPRI).

von Braun, Joachim, and Maximo Torero. 2009. *Implementing Physical and Virtual Food Reserves to Protect the Poor and Prevent Market Failure*. IFPRI Policy Brief. Washington, DC: IFPRI.

von Braun, Joachim, Justin Lin, and Maximo Torero. 2009. *Eliminating Drastic Food Price Spikes: A Three Pronged Approach for Reserves*. Washington, DC: IFPRI.

Brautigam, Deborah. 2009. *The Dragon's Gift: The Real Story of China in Africa*. Oxford and New York: Oxford University Press.

——2012a. "Chinese Engagement in African Agriculture." In *Handbook of Land and Water Grabs in Africa: Foreign Direct Investments and Food and Water Security*, ed. Tony Allan, Jeroen Warner, Suvi Sojamo and Martin Keulertz, 89–101. London and New York: Routledge.

——2012b. "'Zombie' Chinese Land Grabs in Africa Rise Again in New Database!" 30 April. Available at: <http://www.chinaafricarealstory.com/2012/04/zombie-chinese-land-grabs-in-africa.html> (accessed 30 April 2012).

Bray, Francesca. 1994. *The Rice Economies: Technology and Development in Asian Societies*. Berkeley: University of California Press.

Breisinger, Clemens, Olivier Ecker, and Perrihan Al-Riffai. 2011. *Economics of the Arab Awakening: From Revolution to Transformation and Food Security*. IFPRI Policy Brief. Washington, DC: International Food Policy Research Institute (IFPRI).

Breisinger, Clemens, Olivier Ecker, Perrihan Al-Riffai, and Bingxin Yu. 2012. *Beyond the Arab Awakening: Policies and Investments for Poverty Reduction and Food Security*. Food Policy Report. Washington, DC: International Food Policy Research Institute (IFPRI).

Breisinger, Clemens, Teunis van Rheenen, Claudia Ringler, Alejandro Nin Pratt, Nicolas Minot, Catherine Aragon, Bingxin Yu, Olivier Ecker, and Tingju Zhu. 2010. *Food Security and Economic Development in the Middle East and North Africa*.

Current State and Future Perspectives. IFPRI Discussion Paper. Wahington, DC: International Food Policy Research Institute (IFPRI).

Brenner, Robert. 2006. *The Economics of Global Turbulence: The Advanced Capitalist Economies from Long Boom to Long Downturn, 1945–2005.* London and New York: Verso.

Briggs, John A. 1978. "Farmers' Responses to Planned Agricultural Development in the Sudan." *Transactions of the Institute of British Geographers* 3(4): 464–75.

Brinkman, Henk-Jan, and Cullen S. Hendrix. 2010. "Food Insecurity and Conflict: Applying the WDR Framework." World Development Report Background Paper. Washington, DC: World Bank.

Bronson, Rachel. 2006. *Thicker Than Oil: America's Uneasy Partnership with Saudi Arabia.* Oxford and New York: Oxford University Press.

Brown, Lester Russell. 2009. *Plan B 4.0: Mobilizing to Save Civilization.* New York: W. W. Norton, Earth Policy Institute.

——2011. "When the Nile Runs Dry." *New York Times*, 1 June.

Brugmann, Jeb. 2009. *Welcome to the Urban Revolution: How Cities Are Changing the World.* New York: Bloomsbury Press.

Burns, William J. 1985. *Economic Aid and American Policy toward Egypt, 1955–1981.* Albany: State University of New York Press.

Bush, Ray. 1999. *Economic Crisis and the Politics of Reform in Egypt.* Boulder, Colo.: Westview Press.

——2002. "Land Reform and Counter-Revolution." In *Counter-Revolution in Egypt's Countryside: Land and Farmers in the Era of Economic Reform*, ed. Ray Bush, 3–31. London, New York: Zed Books.

——2012. "Food Security in Egypt." Working Paper, Center for International and Regional Studies (CIRS) workshop about Food Security and Food Sovereignty in the Middle East, 22–23 April 2012. Doha: Georgetown University Qatar.

Castelli, Massimiliano, and Fabio Scacciavillani. 2012. *The New Economics of Sovereign Wealth Funds.* Hoboken, NJ: Wiley.

Chaudhry, Kiren Aziz. 1997. *The Price of Wealth: Economies and Institutions in the Middle East.* Cornell Studies in Political Economy. Ithaca: Cornell University Press.

Chulov, Martin. 2009. "Iraq: Water, Water Nowhere." *World Policy Journal* 26 (Winter 2009/2010): 33–40.

Churchill, Winston. 1950. *The Second World War.* 6 vols. Vol. 3. *The Grand Alliance.* Cambridge, Mass.: Houghton Mifflin Co.

Cline, William R. 2007. *Global Warming and Agriculture: Impact Estimates by Country.* Washington, DC: Center for Global Development/Peterson Institute for International Economics.

Clinton, Bill. 2011. *Back to Work: Why We Need Smart Government for a Strong Economy.* New York: Alfred A. Knopf.

Coalition for International Justice (CIJ). 2006. *Soil and Oil: Dirty Business in Sudan.* Washington, DC.

Cobham, Alex. 2005. "Causes of Conflict in Sudan: Testing the Black Book." QEH Working Paper Series. Oxford: Queen Elizabeth House, Oxford University.

Cochrane, Willard Wesley. 1958. *Farm Prices, Myth and Reality.* Minneapolis: University of Minnesota Press.

Cohen, Michael A. 2012. "Reinventing the Future: Designing Urban 3.0." *Harvard International Review* 34(1) (Summer): 52–7.

Collier, Paul. 2008. "The Politics of Hunger: How Illusion and Greed Fan the Food Crisis." *Foreign Affairs* 87(6): 67–79.

Collier, Paul, Gordon Conway, and Tony Venables. 2008. "Climate Change and Africa." *Oxford Review of Economic Policy* 24(2): 337–53.

Collier, Paul, and Stefan Dercon. 2009. "African Agriculture in 50 Years: Smallholders in a Rapidly Changing World?" Paper presented at FAO Expert Meeting on How to Feed the World in 2050.

Collingham, E. M. 2011. *The Taste of War: World War Two and the Battle for Food.* London and New York: Allen Lane.

Collins, Robert O. 2008. *A History of Modern Sudan.* Cambridge and New York: Cambridge University Press.

The Committee of Anti-Dal Kajbar Dams, Nubia-Sudan. 2011. "Protest Letter to Sinohydro and the Chinese Government, 12 January 2011." Available at: <http://www.sudan-forall.org/Anti-Dal-Kajbar-Dams_Executive-Summary.pdf> (accessed 3 July 2012).

Conway, Gordon. 1998. *The Doubly Green Revolution: Food for All in the Twenty-First Century.* Ithaca, NY: Comstock.

Conway, Gordon, and Edward Barbier. 2009. *After the Green Revolution: Sustainable Agriculture for Development.* International Institute for Environment and Development. Sterling, Va.: Earthscan.

Conway, Gordon, and Jules N. Pretty. 2009. *Unwelcome Harvest: Agriculture and Pollution.* International Institute for Environment and Development. Sterling, Va.: Earthscan.

Cook, Michael. 1986. "Early Islamic Dietary Law." *Jerusalem Studies in Arabic and Islam* 7: 217–77.

Cordell, Dana, Jan-Olof Drangert, and Stuart White. 2009. "The Story of Phosphorus: Global Food Security and Food for Thought." *Global Environmental Change* 19: 292–305.

Cordell, Dana, and Stuart White. 2011. "Peak Phosphorus: Clarifying the Key Issues of a Vigorous Debate About Long-Term Phosphorus Security." *Sustainability* 3(10): 2027–49.

Cotula, Lorenzo. 2010. *Getting a Better Deal: How to Make Contracts for Fairer and More Sustainable Natural Resource Investments.* London: International Institute for Environment and Development (IIED).

——2011. *Land Deals in Africa: What is in the Contracts?* London: International Institute for Environment and Development (IIED).

——2012. "The International Political Economy of the Global Land Rush: A Critical Appraisal of Trends, Scale, Geography and Drivers." *Journal of Peasant Studies* 39: 1–32.

Cotula, Lorenzo, and Rebeca Leonard. 2010. *Alternatives to Land Acquisitions: Agricultural Investment and Collaborative Business Models.* Highlights from an International Lesson-Sharing Workshop (Maputo, 17–18 March 2010). London, Bern, Rome, and Maputo: IIED, SDC, IFAD, and CTV.

Crary, Douglas D. 1951. "Recent Agricultural Developments in Saudi Arabia." *Geographical Review* 41(3): 366–83.

Crystal, Jill. 1990. *Oil and Politics in the Gulf: Rulers and Merchants in Kuwait and Qatar.* Cambridge Middle East Library. Cambridge and New York: Cambridge University Press.

Daniel, Shepard, and Anuradha Mittal. 2010. *(Mis) Investment in Agriculture. The Role of the International Finance Corporation in Global Land Grabs.* Oakland: Oakland Institute.

Daoudy, Marwa. 2005. *Le partage des eaux entre la Syrie, l'Irak et la Turquie: Négociation, sécurité et asymétrie des pouvoirs.* Moyen-Orient. Paris: CNRS.

Davidson, Christopher M. 2005. *The United Arab Emirates: A Study in Survival.* The Middle East in the International System. Boulder, Colo.: Lynne Rienner Publishers.

——2008. *Dubai: The Vulnerability of Success.* London: Hurst.

——2009. *Abu Dhabi: Oil and Beyond.* London: Hurst.

Davies, H. R. J. 1991a. "Development Programmes in Non-Irrigated Rainland Areas." In *The Agriculture of the Sudan*, ed. G. M. Craig, 308–38. Oxford and New York: Oxford University Press.

——1991b. "Irrigation Development Programmes." In *The Agriculture of the Sudan*, ed. G. M. Craig, 339–64. Oxford and New York: Oxford University Press.

Davis, Eric. 1983. *Challenging Colonialism: Bank Miṣr and Egyptian Industrialization, 1920–1941.* Princeton Studies on the Near East. Princeton, NJ: Princeton University Press.

Davis, Mike. 2001. *Late Victorian Holocausts: El Niño Famines and the Making of the Third World.* London and New York: Verso.

——2006. *Planet of Slums.* London and New York: Verso.

Dawoud, Mohamed A. 2007. *Water Scarcity in the GCC Countries: Challenges and Opportunities.* Research Papers. Dubai: Gulf Research Center.

De Mestral, Armand L. C., and T. Gruchalla-Wesierski. 1990. *Extraterritorial Application of Export Control Legislation: Canada and the U.S.A.* Research Study/Canadian Council on International Law. Dordrecht and Boston: M. Nijhoff.

De Waal, Alexander. 2005. *Famine That Kills: Darfur, Sudan.* Rev. edn. Oxford Studies in African Affairs. Oxford and New York: Oxford University Press.

DeMars, William E. 2005. *NGOs and Transnational Networks: Wild Cards in World Politics.* London and Ann Arbor, Mich.: Pluto.

Deng, David K. 2011. *The New Frontier: A Baseline Survey of Large-Scale Land-Based Investment in Southern Sudan.* Norwegian People's Aid, Generation Agency for Development and Transfromation-Pentagon (GADET Pentagon). South Sudan Law Society (SSLS).

Deng, David K., and Anuradha Mittal. 2011. *Country Report: South Sudan.* Understanding Land Investment Deals in Africa. Oakland: Oakland Institute.

Devlin, Julia. 2003. "From Citrus to Cellphones? Agriculture as a Source of New Comparative Advantage in the Middle East and North Africa." In *Food, Agriculture, and Economic Policy in the Middle East and North Africa*, ed. Hans Lofgren, 33–52. Amsterdam and New York: JAI.

Dikötter, Frank. 2010. *Mao's Great Famine: The History of China's Most Devastating Catastrophe, 1958–1962.* New York: Walker & Co.

Doran, Anthony. 1980. "Agricultural Extension and Development: The Sudanese Experience." *Bulletin of the British Society for Middle Eastern Studies* 7(1): 39–48.

Dutton, Roderick W. 1980. "The Agricultural Potential of Oman." In *Issues in Development: The Arab Gulf States*, ed. May Ziwar-Daftari, 170–84. London: MD Research and Services.

Ehteshami, Anoushiravan, and Steven M. Wright. 2008. *Reform in the Middle East Oil Monarchies*. Reading, UK: Ithaca Press.

El-Tom, Abdullahi. 2003. "The Black Book of Sudan: Imbalance of Power and Wealth in Sudan." *Journal of African National Affairs* 1(2): 25–35.

El Mallakh, Ragaei. 1982. *Saudi Arabia, Rush to Development: Profile of an Energy Economy and Investment*. Baltimore: Johns Hopkins University Press.

Elhadj, Elie. 2006. "Experiments in Achieving Water and Food Self-Sufficiency in the Middle East: The Consequences of Contrasting Endowments, Ideologies, and Investment Policies in Saudi Arabia and Syria." Ph.D. thesis, History Department, SOAS, London.

——2008. "Saudi Arabia's Agricultural Projects: From Dust to Dust." *MERIA* 12(2). Available at: <http://www.gloria-center.org/2008/06/elhadj-2008-06-03/> (accessed 13 October 2012).

Ellings, Richard. 1985. *Embargoes and World Power: Lessons from American Foreign Policy*. Westview Special Studies in International Relations. Boulder, Colo: Westview Press.

Elnagheeb, Abdelmoneim Hashim, and Daniel W. Bromley. 1992. "Rainfed Mechanized Farming and Deforestation in Central Sudan." *Environmental and Resource Economics* 2(4): 359–71.

Elnur, Ibrahim. 2009. *Contested Sudan: The Political Economy of War and Reconstruction*. Durham Modern Middle East and Islamic World Series. London and New York: Routledge.

Erb, Guy F. 1974. "Controlling Export Controls." *Foreign Policy* 17: 79–84.

Erdkamp, Paul. 2005. *The Grain Market in the Roman Empire: A Social, Political and Economic Study*. Cambridge: Cambridge University Press.

Fabietti, Ugo. 1982. "Sedentarisation as a Means of Detribalisation: Some Policies of the Saudi Arabian Government Towards the Nomads." In *State, Society and Economy in Saudi Arabia*, ed. Tim Niblock, 186–97. London: Croom Helm/Center for Arab Gulf Studies, Exeter.

Fakry, Ahmed Omar, and Karl Saben Twitchell. 1943. *Report of the United States Agricultural Mission to Saudi Arabia*. Cairo.

Al-Fahim, Mohammed. 1998. *From Rags to Riches: A Story of Abu Dhabi*. London: I. B. Tauris.

Al-Faisal, Prince Turki. 2009. "Don't Be Crude: Why Barack Obama's Energy-Dependence Talk Is Just Demagoguery." *Foreign Policy* (September/October).

Fattouh, Bassam, and Robert Mabro. 2006. "The Investment Challenge." In *Oil in the 21st Century: Issues, Challenges and Opportunities*, ed. Robert Mabro, 101–27. New York and Oxford: Oxford University Press for the Organization of the Petroleum Exporting Countries.

FIAN International Secretariat. 2010. *Landgrabbing in Kenya and Mozambique: A Report on Two Research Missions—and a Human Rights Analysis of Land*. Heidelberg.

Field, Michael. 1985. *The Merchants: The Big Business Families of Saudi Arabia and the Gulf States*. Woodstock, NY: Overlook Press.

Fischer, Günther, Eva Hizsnyik, Sylvia Prieler, Mahendra Shah, and Harrij van Velthuizen. 2009. *Biofuels and Food Security*. Vienna: International Institute for Appplied Systems Analysis (IIASA), commissioned by OPEC Fund for International Development (OFID).

Fischer, Günther, Mahendra Shah, Francesco N. Tubiello, and Harrij van Velhuizen. 2005. "Socio-Economic and Climate Change Impacts on Agriculture: An Integrated Assessment, 1990-2080." *Philosophical Transactions of the Royal Society B: Biological Sciences* 360 (1463): 2067–83.

Fitch Ratings. 2008. *External Debts of the Emirates*. International Special Report. Dubai.

Flint, Julie, and Alexander De Waal. 2005. *Darfur: A Short History of a Long War*. London and New York: Zed Books.

Foreign Policy Magazine, and The Fund for Peace. 2012. The Failed States Index 2012. Available at: <http://www.foreignpolicy.com/failed_states_index_2012_interactive> (accessed 18 June 2012).

Franssen, Herman, and Elaine Morton. 2002. "A Review of US Unilateral Sanctions against Iran." *MEES* 45(34): D1–D5.

Friedmann, Harriet, and Philip McMichael. 1989. "Agriculture and the State System: The Rise and Decline of National Agricultures, 1870 to the Present." *Sociologia Ruralis* 29(2): 93–117.

Funk, McKenzie. 2010. "Will Global Warming, Overpopulation, Floods, Droughts and Food Riots Make This Man Rich? Meet the New Capitalists of Chaos." *Rolling Stone Magazine*, 27 May.

Gause, F. Gregory. 2010. *The International Relations of the Persian Gulf*. Cambridge and New York: Cambridge University Press.

Gazdar, Haris, and Athar Hussain. 2002. "Crisis and Response: A Study of the Impact of Economic Sanctions in Iraq." In *Iraq's Economic Predicament*, ed. Kamil A. Mahdi, 31–84. Exeter Islamic Studies Series. Reading, UK: Ithaca Press.

Gelb, Leslie H., and Anthony Lake. 1974. "Washington Dateline: Less Food, More Politics." *Foreign Policy* 17: 176–89.

Ghattas, Hala. 2012. "Food Security, Nutrition and Health in the Arab World: The Case of Marginalized Populations in Lebanon." Paper presented at Food Secure Arab World Conference, ESCWA–UN–IFPRI, Beirut, 6–7 February 2012.

GIZ, Deutsche Gesellschaft für Internationale Zusammenarbeit. 2012. "Artificial Recharge and Utilization of the Ground Water Resource in the Liwa Area, 2008-2013." Available at: <http://www.giz.de/themen/en/13573.htm> (accessed 28 April 2012).

Glaeser, Edward L. 2011. *Triumph of the City: How Our Greatest Invention Makes Us Richer, Smarter, Greener, Healthier, and Happier*. New York: Penguin Press.

Gleckler, James, and Luther Tweeten. 1994. "The Economics of Grain Producer Cartels." International Agricultural Trade Research Consortium.

Gleick, Peter H., and Meena Palaniappan. 2010. "Peak Water Limits to Freshwater Withdrawal and Use." *Proceedings of the National Academy of Sciences* 107(25): 11155–62.

Global Phosphorus Research Initiative. 2010. "GPRI Statement on Global Phosphorus Scarcity." Available at: <http://phosphorusfutures.net/files/GPRI_Statement_responseIFDC_final.pdf> (accessed 15 July 2012).

Glover, Dominic. 2010. "The Corporate Shaping of GM Crops as a Technology for the Poor." *Journal of Peasant Studies* 37(1): 67–90.

Gordon, Joy. 2010. *Invisible War: The United States and the Iraq Sanctions.* Cambridge, Mass.: Harvard University Press.

Görgen, Matthias, Bettina Rudloff, Johannes Simons, Alfons Üllenberg, Sudanne Väth, and Lena Wimmer. 2009. *Foreign Direct Investment (FDI) in Land in Developing Countries.* Division 45. Agriculture, Fisheries and Food. Eschborn, Germany: GTZ.

Gornall, Jemma, Richard Betts, Eleanor Burke, Robin Clark, Joanne Camp, Kate Willett, and Andrew Wiltshire. 2010. "Implications of Climate Change for Agricultural Productivity in the Early Twenty-First Century." *Philosophical Transactions of the Royal Society B: Biological Sciences* 365(1554): 2973–89.

GRAIN. 2008. *Seized! The 2008 Land Grab for Food and Financial Security.* GRAIN Briefing. Barcelona: Grain.

——2009. *The New Farm Owners: Corporate Investors Lead the Rush for Control over Overseas Farmland.* GRAIN Briefing. Barcelona: GRAIN.

——2010a. *Saudi Investors Poised to Take Control of Rice Production in Senegal and Mali?* Against the Grain. Barcelona: GRAIN.

——2010b. *World Bank Report on Land Grabbing: Beyond the Smoke and Mirrors.* Against the Grain. Barcelona: GRAIN.

——2012. Food Crisis and the Global Land Grab. [Collection of Global Media Reports]. Available at: <www.farmlandgrab.org> (accessed 12 Februrary 2012).

Granit, Jakob, Ana Cascao, Inga Jacobs, Christina Leb, Andreas Lindström, and Mara Tignino. 2010. *The Nile Basin and the Southern Sudan Referendum.* Regional Water Intelligence Report. Stockholm: UNDP, SIWI.

Gulf Research Center (GRC). 2009. *Economic Growth in the Makkah Province: The Governorates of Rabigh, Al Leith and Al Qunfudha.* GRC Study for Jeddah Chamber of Commerce and Industry (JCCI) and Governorate of the Makkah Region. Dubai.

Gurdon, C. G. 1991. "Agriculture in the National Economy." In *The Agriculture of the Sudan,* ed. G. M. Craig, 148–61. Oxford and New York: Oxford University Press.

Habib, John S. 1978. *Ibn Sa'ud's Warriors of Islam: The Ikhwan of Najd and Their Role in the Creation of the Sa'udi Kingdom, 1910–1930.* Social, Economic and Political Studies of the Middle East Vol. 27. Leiden: Brill.

Hafiz, Ziyad. 1976. *Azmat al-Ghidha' fi al-Watan al-ʿArabi.* [The Food Crisis in the Arab Homeland]. Dirasat al-Iqtisadiyya al-Istratijiyya. Beirut: Maʿhad al-Inma' al-ʿArabi.

Haggard, Stephan, and Marcus Noland. 2007. *Famine in North Korea: Markets, Aid, and Reform.* New York: Columbia University Press.

Haghayeghi, Mehrdad. 1990. "Agricultural Development Planning under the Islamic Republic of Iran." *Iranian Studies* 23(1/4): 5–29.

Hamdi, Abdelrahim. 2005. "Future of Foreign Investment in Sudan: A Working Paper Delivered by Abdel Rahim Hamdi, a Member of the National Congress Party (NCP) and an Ex-Minister for Economy and Finance, Khartoum, 11–12 September 2005.

Unauthorized Translation by Abdullahi El-Tom. Office of Strategic Planning and Training, Jem Abuja, 10/10/2005." *Sudan Studies Association Newsletter* 24(1).

Hanafi, Muhammad Sayyid Ahmad. 1986. *Mustaqbal al-Tanmiyya al-Zira'iyya fi al-Watan al-'Arabi hatta 'Am 2000.* [The Future of Agricultural Development in the Arab Homeland until 2000]. Beirut: Dar al-Jil.

Hanjra, Munir A., and M. Ejaz Qureshi. 2010. "Global Water Crisis and Future Food Security in an Era of Climate Change." *Food Policy* 35(5): 365–77.

Hansohm, D. 1991. "Agricultural Credit." In *The Agriculture of the Sudan*, ed. G. M. Craig, 117–23. Oxford and New York: Oxford University Press.

Harvey, David. 2003. *The New Imperialism.* Oxford and New York: Oxford University Press.

Hassan, Rashid M., Hamid Faki, and D. Byerlee. 2000. "The Trade-Off between Economic Efficiency and Food Self-Sufficiency in Using Sudan's Irrigated Land Resources." *Food Policy* 25(1): 35–54.

Heard-Bey, Frauke. 1982. *From Trucial States to United Arab Emirates: A Society in Transition.* London and New York: Longman.

Hebebrand, Charlotte. 2011. *Leveraging Private Sector Investment in Developing Country Agrifood Systems.* Policy Paper Series, study commissioned by the Global Agricultural Development Initiative. Chicago: Chicago Council on Foreign Affairs.

Heckscher, Eli F. 1964. *The Continental System: An Economic Interpretation.* Publications of the Carnegie Endowment for International Peace, Division of Economics and History. Gloucester, Mass.: P. Smith.

Henry, Clement M., and Robert Springborg. 2010. *Globalization and the Politics of Development in the Middle East.* 2nd edn. The Contemporary Middle East. Cambridge and New York: Cambridge University Press.

Herb, Michael. 1999. *All in the Family: Absolutism, Revolution, and Democracy in the Middle Eastern Monarchies.* Suny Series in Middle Eastern Studies. Albany: State University of New York Press.

——2009. "Kuwait: The Obstacles of Parliamentary Politics." In *Political Liberalization in the Persian Gulf*, ed. Joshua Teitelbaum, 133–56. New York: Columbia University Press.

Hernandez, Manuel, and Maximo Torero. 2010. *Examining the Dynamic Relationship between Spot and Future Prices of Agricultural Commodities.* IFPRI Discussion Paper. Washington, DC: International Food Policy Research Institute (IFPRI).

Hertog, Steffen. 2010. *Princes, Brokers, and Bureaucrats: Oil and the State in Saudi Arabia.* Ithaca and London: Cornell University Press.

——2011. "The Evolution of Rent Recycling During Two Booms in the Arab Gulf States: Business Dynamism and Societal Stagnation." In *Shifting Geo-Economic Power of the Gulf: Oil, Finance and Institutions*, ed. Matteo Legrenzi and Bessma Momani, 55–74. Farnham, UK and Burlington, Vt.: Ashgate.

Hertog, Steffen, and Giacomo Luciani. 2009. "Energy and Sustainability Policies in the GCC." Kuwait Programme in Development, Governance and Globalisation in the Gulf States. London: London School of Economics.

Heydemann, Steven, and Robert Vitalis. 2000. "War, Keynesianism and Colonialism: Explaining State-Market Relations in the Postwar Middle East." In *War, Institutions and Social Change in the Middle East*, ed. Steven Heydemann, 100–45. Berkeley and London: University of California Press.

Al-Hindi, Adil Ibrahim. 1981. *Al-Maʿalim al-Raʾisiyya li Istratijiyyat al-Tanmiyya al-Ziraʿiyya bi Aqtar al-Watan al-ʿArabi.* [The Main Signposts for a Strategy of Agricultural Development in the Regions of the Arab Homeland]. Alexandria: Munshaʾat al-Maʿarif.

Hinnebusch, Raymond A. (ed.). 2011. *Agriculture and Reform in Syria.* Fife, Scotland, Boulder, CO: University of St Andrews Centre for Syrian Studies and Lynne Rienner Publishers.

Hoagland, Jim. 1975a. "The Arab Money Men: I—Adnan Khashoggi and His Empire." *Washington Post,* 14 September.

——1975b. "The Arab Money Men: V—Private/Public Line Blurs." *Washington Post,* 18 September.

Hoekstra, A. Y., and A. K. Chapagain. 2007. "Water Footprints of Nations: Water Use by People as a Function of Their Consumption Pattern." *Water Resource Management* 21: 35–48.

Hoekstra, Arjen Y., and Mesfin M. Mekonnen. 2012. "The Water Footprint of Humanity." *Proceedings of the National Academy of Sciences* 109(9): 3232–7.

Hoffmann, Clemens. 2012. "The Contradictions of Development: Primitive Accumulation and Geopolitics in the Two Sudans." In *Handbook of Land and Water Grabs in Africa: Foreign Direct Investments and Food and Water Security,* ed. Tony Allan, Jeroen Warner, Suvi Sojamo and Martin Keulertz, 55–68. London and New York: Routledge.

Holden, Stacy E. 2009. *The Politics of Food in Modern Morocco.* Gainesville: University Press of Florida.

Hooglund, Eric J. 1982. *Land and Revolution in Iran, 1960–1980.* Modern Middle East Series. Austin: University of Texas Press.

Hooper, Emma. 2010. "Pakistan's Food Crisis. Water, Energy, Agriculture & Power: The Conflict Ahead." Notes Internacionals. No. 23 Barcelona: Barcelona Centre for International Affairs (CIDOB).

Horne, Felix, Frédéric Mousseau, Obang Metho, Anuradha Mittal, and Shepard Daniel. 2011. *Country Report: Ethiopia.* Understanding Land Investment Deals in Africa. Oakland: Oakland Institute.

Howell, P. P., Michael Lock, and Stephen Cobb. 1988. *The Jonglei Canal: Impact and Opportunity.* Cambridge Studies in Applied Ecology and Resource Management. Cambridge and New York: Cambridge University Press.

Huang, J., and S. Rozelle. 1996. "Technological Change: Rediscovery of the Engine of Productivity Growth in China's Rural Economy." *Journal of Development Economics* 49(2): 337–69.

Hubbard, James P. 2011. *The United States and the End of British Colonial Rule in Africa, 1941–1968.* Jefferson, NC: McFarland & Company.

Hufbauer, Gary Clyde, Kimberley Ann Elliot, and Barbara Oegg. 2008. *Economic Sanctions Reconsidered.* 3rd edn. Washington, DC: Peterson Institute for International Economics.

Hunter, Guy. 1953. "Economic Problems: The Middle East Supply Center." In *The Middle East in the War,* ed. George E. Kirk, 169–93. London, New York, and Toronto: Oxford University Press.

Hussain, ʿAdil. 1982. *Al-Iqtisad al-Misri Min al-Istiqlal ila al-Tabaʿiyya, 1974–1979.* [The Egyptian Economy from Independence to Dependence, 1974–1979]. 2nd edn. 2 vols. Cairo: Dar al-Mustaqbal al-ʿArabi.

Ianchovichina, E., J. Loening, and C. Wood. 2012. "How Vulnerable Are Arab Countries to Global Food Price Shocks?" Washington, DC: World Bank.

Immerzeel, Walter W., Ludovicus P. H. van Beek, and Marc F. P. Bierkens. 2010. "Climate Change Will Affect the Asian Water Towers." *Science* 328(5984): 1382–5.

International Assessment of Agricultural Knowledge, Science and Technology for Development (IAASTD). 2009. *Agriculture at a Crossroads. Global Report.* Washington, DC.

International Food Policy Research Institute (IFPRI). 2006. "Biotech and Biosafety Policy. Note from the Director General." Available at: <http://www.ifpri.org/ourwork/about/biotech-biosafety> (accessed 7 March 2012).

International Food Policy Research Institute (IFPRI), Concern Worldwide, and Welthungerhilfe. 2011. *Global Hunger Index. The Challenge of Hunger: Taming Price Spikes and Excessive Food Price Volatility.* Bonn, Washington, DC, and Dublin.

International Institute for Applied Systems Analysis (IIASA). 2011. *Land Use Change and Agriculture—Agro-Ecological Zoning*, 24 February. Available at: <http://www.iiasa.ac.at/Research/LUC/Research-AEZ/index.html?sb=8> (accessed 15 June 2012).

International Institute for Population Sciences. 2006. *Third National Family Health Survey (NFHS-3) 2005–06.* Mumbai.

Institute of International Finance (IIF). 2008. *Regional Report. Gulf Cooperation Council Countries.* Washington, DC.

International Rice Research Institute (IRRI). 2009. "A Summary of the Meetings Held During the Visit of Dr. Robert Zeigler, Mr. Syeduzzaman, and Abdel Ismail to Saudi Arabia, March 7–8, 2009." Los Baños, Laguna.

Issawi, Charles Philip. 1982. *An Economic History of the Middle East and North Africa.* The Columbia Economic History of the Modern World. New York: Columbia University Press.

——1995. *The Middle East Economy: Decline and Recovery: Selected Essays.* Princeton Series on the Middle East. Princeton, NJ: Markus Wiener Publishers.

Jackson, Ashley. 2006. *The British Empire and the Second World War.* London and New York: Hambledon Continuum.

James, Lawrence. 1997. *Raj: The Making and Unmaking of British India.* London: Little, Brown.

Janardhan, N. 2011. *Boom Amid Gloom: The Spirit of Possibility in the 21st Century Gulf.* Reading, UK: Ithaca Press.

Jansen, Heinz-Gerhard, and Werner Koch. 1982. "The Rahad Scheme—the Agricultural System and Its Problems." In *Problems of Agricultural Development in the Sudan*, ed. Günther Heinritz, 23–36. Göttingen: Edition Herodot.

Johnson, D. Gale. 1999. "North America and the World Grain Market." In *The Economics of World Wheat Markets*, ed. John M. Antle and V. H. Smith, 21–38. New York and Wallingford: CABI Publishing.

Johnson, Douglas H. 2003. *The Root Causes of Sudan's Civil Wars.* African Issues Series. Oxford, Bloomington, and Kampala: Indiana University Press.

Jones, Toby Craig. 2006. "Rebellion on the Saudi Periphery: Mondernity, Marginalization, and the Shia Uprising of 1979." *International Journal of Middle East Studies* 38(2): 213–33.

Jones, Toby Craig. 2010. *Desert Kingdom: How Oil and Water Forged Modern Saudi Arabia*. Cambridge, Mass.: Harvard University Press.

Justice and Equality Movement (JEM). May 2000 and August 2002. *The Black Book: Imbalance of Power and Wealth in Sudan*. 2 vols. Khartoum.

Kaikati, Jack G. 1980. "The Economy of Sudan: A Potential Breadbasket of the Arab World?" *International Journal of Middle Eastern Studies* 11(1): 99–123.

Kameir, El Wathig, and Ibrahim Kursany. 1985. *Corruption as a "Fifth" Factor of Production in the Sudan*. Vol. 72. Research Report. Uppsala: Scandinavian Institute of African Studies.

Kapiszewski, Andrzej. 2006. "Arab Versus Asian Migrant Workers in the GCC Countries." Paper presented at United Nations Expert Group Meeting on International Migration and Development in the Arab Region, Beirut, 15–17 May 2006. Population Division, Department of Economic and Social Affairs, United Nations Secretariat. UN/POP/EGM/2006/02.

Katakura, Motoko. 1977. *Bedouin Village: A Study of a Saudi Arabian People in Transition*. The Modern Middle East Series. Tokyo: University of Tokyo Press.

Kaufmann, Christine, and Simone Heri. 2007. "Liberalizing Trade in Agriculture and Food Security—Mission Impossible?" *Vanderbilt Journal of Transnational Law* 40(4): 1039–70.

van Kauwenbergh, Steven J. 2010. *World Phosphate Rock Reserves and Resources*. Muscle Shoals, Al: International Fertilizer Development Center (IFDC).

Keen, Bernard Augustus. 1946. *The Agricultural Development of the Middle East*. Middle East Supply Centre. Report to the Director General. London: HMSO.

Keen, David. 1994. *The Benefits of Famine: A Political Economy of Famine and Relief in Southwestern Sudan, 1983–1989*. Princeton, NJ: Princeton University Press.

Keen, David, and Vivian Lee. 2007. "Conflict, Trade and the Medium-Term Future of Food Security in Sudan." *Disasters* 31: S9–S24.

Kepel, Gilles. 2002. *Jihad: The Trail of Political Islam*. Cambridge, Mass.: Belknap Press of Harvard University Press.

Khalaf, Abd al-Hadi, and Giacomo Luciani. 2006. *Constitutional Reform and Political Participation in the Gulf*. Dubai: Gulf Research Center.

Khan, Mahmood Hasan. 1981. *Underdevelopment and Agrarian Structure in Pakistan*. A Westview Replica Edition. Boulder, Colo.: Westview Press.

Kherallah, Mylène, Nicolas Minot, and Peter Gruhn. 2003. "Adjustment of Wheat Production to Market Reform in Egypt." In *Food, Agriculture, and Economic Policy in the Middle East and North Africa*, ed. Hans Lofgren, 133–59. Amsterdam and New York: JAI.

Kirk, George E. 1953. *The Middle East in the War*. Survey of International Affairs. London, New York, and Toronto: Oxford University Press/Royal Institute of International Affairs.

Kiss, Judit. 1977. *Will Sudan Be an Agricultural Power?* Studies on Developing Countries. Budapest: Institute for World Economics of the Hungarian Academy of Sciences; New York: distributed in the USA by Stechert-Hafner.

Kissinger, Henry. 1982. *Years of Upheaval*. Boston: Little, Brown.

——1999. *Years of Renewal*. New York: Simon & Schuster.

Kliot, Nurit. 1994. *Water Resources and Conflict in the Middle East.* London and New York: Routledge.

Knox, J. W., T. M. Hess, A. Daccache, and M. Perez Ortola. 2011. *What Are the Projected Impacts of Climate Change on Food Crop Productivity in Africa and S Asia?* DFID Systematic Review Final Report. Cranfield University.

Kombargi, Raed, Otto Waterlander, George Sarraf, and Asheesh Sastry. 2010. "Gas Shortage in the GCC: How to Bridge the Gap." Perspective Booz & Company.

Kontos, Stephen. 1990. "Farmers and the Failure of Agribusiness in Sudan." *Middle East Journal* 44(4): 649–67.

Koopman, Jeanne E. 2004. "Dams, Irrigation, and Neo- Liberalism: The Dismantling of Inter-African Development Dreams in the Senegal River Valley." Paper presented at the Institute for African Development of Cornell University, 23 September. Cornell University.

——2009. "Globalization, Gender, and Poverty in the Senegal River Valley." *Feminist Economics* 15(3): 253–85.

Kostiner, Joseph. 1993. *The Making of Saudi Arabia, 1916–1936: From Chieftancy to Monarchical State.* Studies in Middle Eastern History. New York: Oxford University Press.

Kurz, Robert. 1999. *Schwarzbuch Kapitalismus: Ein Abgesang auf die Marktwirtschaft.* Frankfurt: Eichborn.

Kurzum, Jurj. 1997. *Al-Tanmiyya bi-l-Iʿtimad ʿala al-Dhat.* [Development with Self-Sufficiency]. Silsilat al-Dirasat al-Tanmawiyya. Ramallah: Markaz al-ʿAmal al-Tanmawi, Maʿan.

Lacey, Robert. 1981. *The Kingdom.* New York: Harcourt Brace Jovanovich.

——2009. *Inside the Kingdom: Kings, Clerics, Modernists, Terrorists, and the Struggle for Saudi Arabia.* New York: Viking.

Lackner, Helen. 1978. *A House Built on Sand: A Political Economy of Saudi Arabia.* London: Ithaca Press.

Lahn, Glada, and Paul Stevens. 2011. *Burning Oil to Keep Cool. The Hidden Energy Crisis in Saudi Arabia.* London: Chatham House.

Land Matrix. 2012. Available at: <www.landportal.info/landmatrix> (accessed 4 May 2012).

Landis, J. M. 1945. "Anglo-American Co-Operation in the Middle East." *Annals of the American Academy of Political and Social Science* 240: 64–72.

Legrenzi, Matteo. 2011. *The GCC and the International Relations of the Gulf: Diplomacy, Security and Economic Coordination in a Changing Middle East.* London and New York: I. B. Tauris.

Lesch, Ann M. 2002. "Osama Bin Laden's 'Business' in Sudan." *Current History* 101 (655): 203.

Lippman, Thomas W. 1983. "U.S. Gives Saudis No-Embargo Pledge." *Washington Post*, 10 May.

——2004. *Inside the Mirage: America's Fragile Partnership with Saudi Arabia.* Boulder, Colo.: Westview Press.

——2010. "Saudi Arabia's Quest for 'Food Security'." *Middle East Policy* 17(1): 90–8.

Lipsky, George A. 1959. *Saudi Arabia: Its People, Its Society, Its Culture.* Survey of World Cultures 4. New Haven: HRAF Press.

Little, Ian Malcolm David. 1982. *Economic Development: Theory, Policy, and International Relations*. New York: Basic Books.

Lloyd, E. M. H. 1956. *Food and Inflation in the Middle East, 1940–45*. Studies on Food, Agriculture, and World War II. Stanford, Calif.: Stanford University Press.

Lobell, David B., Wolfram Schlenker, and Justin Costa-Roberts. 2011. "Climate Trends and Global Crop Production since 1980." *Science* 333(6042): 616–20.

Locke, Christopher G., and Fredoun Z. Ahmadi-Esfahani. 1993. "Famine Analysis: A Study of Entitlements in Sudan, 1984–1985." *Economic Development and Cultural Change* 41(2): 363–76.

Luciani, Giacomo. 1987. "Allocation Vs. Production States: A Theoretical Framework." In *The Rentier State: Nation, State, and Integration in the Arab World*, ed. Hazem Beblawi and Giacomo Luciani, 63–82. London and New York: Croom Helm.

——2005. "Private Sector to National Bourgeoisie: Saudi Arabian Business." In *Saudi Arabia in the Balance: Political Economy, Society, Foreign Affairs*, ed. Paul Aarts and Gerd Nonneman, 144–81. New York: New York University Press.

——2010. "From Price Taker to Price Maker? Saudi Arabia and the World Oil Market." Occasional Paper 3. Paper presented at the Rahmaniah Annual Seminar January 2010 in Al-Ghat. Al-Rahmaniah Cultural Center. Abdulrahman al-Sudairy Foundation.

——2012a. "Domestic Pricing of Energy and Industrial Competitiveness." In *Resources Blessed: Diversification and the Gulf Development Model*, ed. Giacomo Luciani, 95–114. Berlin and London: Gerlach.

——2012b. "Introduction." In *Resources Blessed: Diversification and the Gulf Development Model*, ed. Giacomo Luciani, 1–28. Berlin and London: Gerlach.

——2012c. "GCC Refining and Petrochemical Sectors in Global Perspective." In *Resources Blessed: Diversification and the Gulf Development Model*, ed. Giacomo Luciani, 183–212. Berlin and London: Gerlach.

Luttrell, Clifton B. 1981. "A Bushel of Wheat for a Barrel of Oil: Can We Offset Opec's Gains with a Grain Cartel?" St. Louis: Federal Reserve Bank of St. Louis.

Lynch, Marc. 2006. *Voices of the New Arab Public: Iraq, Al-Jazeera, and Middle East Politics Today*. New York: Columbia University Press.

Mabro, Robert. 2006. "Introduction." In *Oil in the 21st Century: Issues, Challenges and Opportunities*, ed. Robert Mabro, 1–18. Oxford and New York: Oxford University Press for the Organization of the Petroleum Exporting Countries.

McLachlan, K. S. 1986. "Food Supply and Agricultural Self-Sufficiency in Contemporary Iran." *Bulletin of the School of Oriental and African Studies, University of London* 49(1): 148–62.

McMichael, Philip. 2009a. "A Food Regime Analysis of the 'World Food Crisis'." *Agriculture and Human Values* 26(4): 281–95.

——2009b. "A Food Regime Genealogy." *Journal of Peasant Studies* 36(1): 139–69.

Magnan, Nicholas, Travis Lybbert, Alex McCalla, and Julian Lampietti. 2011. "Modeling the Limitations and Implicit Costs of Cereal Self-Sufficiency: The Case of Morocco." *Food Security* 3(1): 49–60.

Malaeb, Makram. 2006. *Diversification of the GCC Economies. Analysis of the Preceding Decade (1993-2003)*. Gulf Papers. Dubai: Gulf Research Center.

Martin, Nicolas. 2009. "The Political Economy of Bonded Labour in the Pakistani Punjab." *Contributions to Indian Sociology* 43(1): 35–59.

Massot, Pascale. 2011. "Chinese State Investments in Canada: Lessons from the Potash Saga." *Canada-Asia Agenda* 16, Asia Pacific Foundation of Canada.

Maugeri, Leonardo. 2006. *The Age of Oil: The Mythology, History, and Future of the World's Most Controversial Resource*. Westport, Conn.: Praeger Publishers.

Mazaheri, Nimah. 2010. "Iraq and the Domestic Political Effects of Economic Sanctions." *Middle East Journal* 64(2): 254–68.

Meadows, Donella H., and Club of Rome. 1972. *The Limits to Growth: A Report for the Club of Rome's Project on the Predicament of Mankind*. New York: Universe Books.

Meadows, Donella H., Jørgen Randers, and Dennis L. Meadows. 2004. *The Limits to Growth: The 30-Year Update*. White River Junction, Vt.: Chelsea Green Publishing Company.

Mejcher, Helmut. 1989. "Saudi Arabien's Beziehungen zu Deutschland in der Regierungszeit von König ʿAbd al-ʿAziz Ibn Saʿūd." In *Der Nahe Osten in der Zwischenkriegszeit, 1919–1939. Die Interdependenz von Politik, Wirtschaft und Ideologie*, ed. Linda Schatkowski Schilcher and Claus Scharf, 109–27. Stuttgart: Franz Steiner.

Mekonnen, Dereje Zeleke. 2010. "The Nile Basin Cooperative Framework Agreement Negotiations and the Adoption of a 'Water Security' Paradigm: Flight into Obscurity or a Logical Cul-De-Sac?" *European Journal of International Law* 21(2): 421–40.

Mekonnen, M. M., and A. Y. Hoekstra. 2011. "National Water Footprint Accounts: The Green, Blue and Grey Water Footprint of Production and Consumption." Value of Water Research Report Series. Delft, the Netherlands: UNESCO-IHE.

Meulen, D. van der. 1957. *The Wells of Ibn Sa'ud*. New York: Praeger.

Meyer, Jeffrey A., and Mark G. Califano. 2006. *Good Intentions Corrupted: The Oil-for-Food Program and the Threat to the U.N.* Public Affairs Reports. New York: Public Affairs.

Miller, Aaron David. 1980. *Search for Security: Saudi Arabian Oil and American Foreign Policy, 1939–1949*. Chapel Hill: University of North Carolina Press.

Mishra, Pankaj. 2007. "Exit Wounds: The Legacy of Indian Partition." *The New Yorker*, 13 August.

Mitchell, Richard P. 1993. *The Society of the Muslim Brothers*. New York: Oxford University Press.

Mitchell, Timothy. 2002. *Rule of Experts: Egypt, Techno-Politics, Modernity*. Berkeley: University of California Press.

Molden, David (ed.). 2007. *Water for Food, Water for Life: A Comprehensive Assessment of the Water Managment in Agriculture. Summary*. London: International Water Management Institute, Earthscan.

Moody's. 2008. *Demystifying Dubai Inc.: A Guide to Dubai's Corporatist Model and Moody's Assessment of Its Rising Leverage*. Special Comment. Dubai.

Morgan, Dan. 1975. "Butz Loses Power to Set Food Policy." *Washington Post*, 16 October.

——1979. *Merchants of Grain*. New York: Viking Press.

Mousseau, Frédéric, Anuradha Mittal, and Grace Phillips. 2011. *Country Report: Tanzania*. Understanding Land Investemnt Deals in Africa. Oakland: Oakland Institute.

Müller, Christoph, Wolfgang Cramer, William L. Hare, and Hermann Lotze-Campen. 2011. "Climate Change Risks for African Agriculture." *Proceedings of the National Academy of Sciences* 108(11): 4313–5.

Nanda, Ved P. 2006. "The 'Good Governance' Concept Revisited." *The Annals of the American Academy of Political and Social Science* 603(1): 269–83.

Al-Naqeeb, Khaldun Hasan. 1990. *Society and State in the Gulf and Arab Peninsula: A Different Perspective*. London and New York: Routledge.

Narlikar, Amrita. 2003. *International Trade and Developing Countries: Bargaining Coalitions in the Gatt and WTO*. RIPE Series in Global Political Economy. London and New York: Routledge.

National Alfalfa & Forage Alliance (NAFA). 2008. *Coexistence for Alfalfa Hay Export Markets*. St. Paul.

Naylor, R. T. 2008. *Patriots and Profiteers: Economic Warfare, Embargo Busting, and State-Sponsored Crime*. 2nd edn. Montreal and Ithaca: McGill-Queen's University Press.

NCB Capital. 2010. *GCC Agriculture: Bridging the Food Gap*. Economic Research. Jeddah.

Nelson, Gerald C., Mark W. Rosegrant, Jawoo Koo, Richard Robertson, Timothy Sulser, Tingju Zhu, Claudia Ringler, Siwa Msangi, Amanda Palazzo, Miroslav Batka, Marilia Magalhaes, Rowena Valmonte-Santos, Mandy Ewing, and David Lee. 2009. *Climate Change: Impact on Agriculture and Costs of Adaptation*. Food Policy Report. Washington, DC: International Food Policy Research Institute (IFPRI).

Nelson, Joan M. 1968. *Aid, Influence, and Foreign Policy*. Government in the Modern World Series. New York: Macmillan.

Niblock, Tim. 1987. *Class and Power in Sudan: The Dynamics of Sudanese Politics, 1898–1985*. London: Macmillan.

——2001. *"Pariah States" & Sanctions in the Middle East: Iraq, Libya, Sudan*. The Middle East in the International System. Boulder, Colo. and London: Lynne Rienner Publishers.

Niblock, Tim, with Monica Malik. 2007. *The Political Economy of Saudi Arabia*. London and New York: Routledge.

Nicolini, Beatrice, and Penelope-Jane Watson. 2004. *Makran, Oman, and Zanzibar: Three Terminal Cultural Corridor in the Western Indian Ocean, 1799–1856*. Islam in Africa Series. Boston: Brill.

Al-Nimri, Khalaf ibn Sulaiman ibn Salih ibn Khidr. 1995. *Al-Tanmiyya al-Ziraʿiyya fi Dawʾ al-Shariʿa al-Islamiyya: Maʿa Dirasa Tatbiqiyya ʿala al-Mamlaka al-ʿArabiyya al-Saʿudiyya wa-l-Mamlaka al-Urduniyya al-Hashimiyya*. [Agricultural Development in Light of the Shariʿa. With an Applied Study of Saudi Arabia and Jordan]. 2 vols. Vol. 2. Silsilat Buhuth al-Dirasat al-Islamiyya. Mecca: Ministry of Higher Education, Jamiʿat Umm al-Qura, Maʿhad al-Buhuth al-ʿIlmiyya wa-Ihyaʾ al-Turath al-Islami, Markaz Buhuth al-Dirasat al-Islamiyya.

Al-Nimri, Khalaf ibn Sulaiman ibn Salih ibn Sulaiman. 2002. *Al-Tanmiyya al-Ziraʿiyya fi ʿAhd Khadim al-Haramain al-Sharifain al-Malik Fahd ibn ʿAbd al-ʿAziz al-Saʿud*. [Agricultural Development During the Reign of King Fahd]. Mecca: Ministry of Higher Education, Jamiʿat Umm al-Qura.

Noland, Marcus, and Howard Pack. 2007. *The Arab Economies in a Changing World.* Washington, DC: Peterson Institute for International Economics.

Nowshirvani, Vahid. 1987. "The Yellow Brick Road: Self-Sufficiency or Self-Enrichment in Saudi Agriculture?" *MERIP Middle East Report* 145 (March–April): 7–13.

Nugent, Jeffrey B. 2003. "Yemeni Agriculture: Historical Overview, Policy Lessons and Prospects." In *Food, Agriculture, and Economic Policy in the Middle East and North Africa*, ed. Hans Lofgren, 257–88. Amsterdam and New York: JAI.

O'Brien, Jay. 1981. "Sudan: An Arab Breadbasket?" *MERIP Reports* 99: 20–6.

——1983a. "The Formation of the Agricultural Labour Force in Sudan." *Review of African Political Economy* 10(26): 15–34.

——1983b. "The Political Economy of Capitalist Agriculture in the Central Rainlands of Sudan." *Labour, Capital and Society* 16(1): 8–32.

——1985. "Sowing the Seeds of Famine: The Political Economy of Food Deficits in Sudan." *Review of African Political Economy* 12(33): 23–32.

O'Brien, Jay, and Ellen Gruenbaum. 1991. "A Social History of Food, Famine, and Gender in Twentieth Century Sudan." In *The Political Economy of African Famine*, ed. R. E. Downs, Donna O. Kerner, and Stephen P. Reyna, 177–204. Amsterdam: Gordon Breach.

Oakland Institute. 2009. *Voices from Africa: African Farmers & Environmentalists Speak out against a New Green Revolution in Africa.* Oakland: Oakland Inistitute.

Ochsenwald, William. 1980. "Muslim–European Conflict in the Hijaz: The Slave Trade Controversy, 1840–1895." *Middle Eastern Studies* 13: 115–26.

——1982. "The Commercial History of the Hijaz Vilayet, 1840–1908." *Arabian Studies* 6: 57–76.

Oesterdiekhoff, Peter. 1982. "Problems with Large-Scale Agro-Industrial Projects in the Sudan: The Example of the Kenana Sugar Corporation." In *Problems of Agricultural Development in the Sudan*, ed. Günther Heinritz, 51–68. Göttingen: Edition Herodot.

Oesterdiekhoff, Peter, and Karl Wohlmuth. 1983a. "The 'Breadbasket' Is Empty: The Options of Sudanese Development Policy." *Canadian Journal of African Studies/Revue Canadienne des Études Africaines* 17(1): 35–67.

——1983b. *The Development Perspectives of the Democratic Republic of Sudan: The Limits of the Breadbasket Strategy.* Afrika-Studien. München: Weltforum.

Oi, Jean Chun. 1989. *State and Peasant in Contemporary China: The Political Economy of Village Government.* Berkeley: University of California Press.

Okruhlik, Mary Gwenn. 1992. "Debating Profits and Political Power: Private Business and Government in Saudi Arabia." Ph.D. thesis, Graduate School, University of Texas, Austin.

Onley, James. 2007. *The Arabian Frontier of the British Raj: Merchants, Rulers, and the British in the Nineteenth-Century Gulf.* Oxford and New York: Oxford University Press.

Oreskes, Naomi, and Erik M. Conway. 2010. *Merchants of Doubt: How a Handful of Scientists Obscured the Truth on Issues from Tobacco Smoke to Global Warming.* New York: Bloomsbury Press.

Ottaway, Marina. 1987. "Post-Numeiri Sudan: One Year On." *Third World Quarterly* 9(3): 891–905.

Overington, Caroline. 2007. *Kickback: Inside the Australian Wheat Board Scandal.* Crows Nest, NSW: Allen & Unwin.

Owen, Roger. 1993. *The Middle East in the World Economy, 1800–1914.* London and New York: I. B. Tauris.

——1999. "Inter-Arab Economic Relations During the Twentieth Century: World Market vs. Regional Market?" In *Middle East Dilemma: The Politics and Economics of Arab Integration*, ed. Michael C. Hudson, 215–32. New York: Columbia University Press.

Paarlberg, Robert L. 1980. "Lessons of the Grain Embargo." *Foreign Affairs* 59(1): 144–62.

——2008. *Starved for Science: How Biotechnology Is Being Kept out of Africa.* Cambridge, Mass.: Harvard University Press.

——2010. *Food Politics: What Everyone Needs to Know.* New York: Oxford University Press.

Pampanini, Andrea H. 2010. *Desalinated Water in the Kingdom of Saudi Arabia: The History of the Saline Water Conversion Corporation (SWCC).* New York: Turnaround Associates Inc.

Pearce, Fred. 2012. *The Land Grabbers: The New Fight over Who Owns the Earth.* Boston: Beacon Press.

Peterson, John. 1978. *Oman in the Twentieth Century: Political Foundations of an Emerging State.* London and New York: Croom Helm.

Philby, H. St. J. B. 1928. *Arabia of the Wahhabis.* London: Constable.

——1959. "Riyadh: Ancient and Modern." *Middle East Journal* 13(2): 129–41.

Philipp, Hans-Jürgen. 1984. *Die landwirtschaftliche Modernisierung Saudi-Arabiens im 20. Jahrhundert.* Mitteilungen des Deutschen Orient-Instituts No. 25. Hamburg: Deutsches Orient-Institut, im Verbund der Stiftung Deutsches Übersee-Institut.

Piesse, Jenifer, and Colin Thirtle. 2009. "Three Bubbles and a Panic: An Explanatory Review of Recent Food Commodity Price Events." *Food Policy* 34(2): 119–29.

Pimentel, David, and Marcia Pimentel. 2003. "Sustainability of Meat-Based and Plant-Based Diets and the Environment." *American Journal of Clinical Nutrition* 78(3): 660–3.

Prunier, Gérard. 2007. *Darfur: The Ambiguous Genocide.* Rev. and updated edn. Crises in World Politics. Ithaca, NY: Cornell University Press.

Al-Qahtani, Safar bin Husain. 2009. *Al-Istithmar al-Zira'i al-Khariji.* [The Foreign Agricultural Investment]. Vol. 17. Occasional Papers Series. Riyadh: King Saud University, Department of Agrciulture.

Raboy, David G., Syed Abul Basher, Ishrat Hossain, and Simeon Kaitibie. 2011. "Public–Private Partnerships in Emerging Arab Agriculture Sectors: A Conceptual Market Risk Mitigation System." Working Paper.

Radetzki, Marian. 2010. "Peak Oil and Other Threatening Peaks: Chimeras without Substance." *Energy Policy* 38(11): 6566–9.

Al-Rasheed, Madawi. 2010. *A History of Saudi Arabia.* 2nd edn. New York: Cambridge University Press.

Al-Rasheed, Turki Faisal. 2008. "Al-Takamul: ʿIlaj Fajwat al-ʾAmn al-Ghidhaʾi al-ʿArabi." [Integration: The Treatment of the Arab Food Security Gap]. *Al-Eqtisadiah*, 29 June.

——2010. *Al-Tabaʿa Al-Ula*. [The First Edition]. Riyadh.

——2011. "Al-Istithmar al-Ziraʿi al-Khariji Darura . . . wa lakin!" [Foreign Agricultural Investment Is a Necessity . . . But!], 30 April. Available at: <http://www.tfrasheed.org/ara/?p=1501> (accessed 3 October 2011).

——2012. *Agricultural Development Strategies: The Saudi Experience—The Role of Agriculture to Enhance Food Security, Alleviate Poverty and Promote Economic Growth*. Saarbrücken, Germany: Lambert Academic Publishing (LAP).

Ravallion, M. 2009. "Are There Lessons for Africa from China's Success against Poverty?" *World Development* 37(2): 303–13.

Reisner, Marc. 1993. *Cadillac Desert: The American West and Its Disappearing Water*. Rev. and updated edn. Vancouver: Douglas & McIntyre.

Rende, Mithat. 2007. "Water Transfer from Turkey to Water-Stressed Countries in the Middle East." In *Water Resources in the Middle East: The Israeli-Palestinian Water Issues—From Conflict to Cooperation*, ed. Hillel I. Shuval and Hassan Dwiek, 165–74. Berlin, Heidelberg, and New York: Springer.

Rice, Andrew. 2009. "Is There Such a Thing as Agro-Imperialism?" *New York Times*, 16 November.

Richards, Alan. 1991. "Syrian Food Security in the 1970s and 1980s." *Food Policy* 16(6): 487–92.

Richards, Alan, and John Waterbury. 2008. *A Political Economy of the Middle East*. 3rd edn. Boulder, Colo.: Westview Press.

Richards, Paul, Matteo Rizzo, Meredith L. Weiss, Claudia Steiner, and Sarah England. 2010. "Do Peasants Need GM Crops?" *Journal of Peasant Studies* 37(3): 559–74.

Riedel, Bruce. 2011. "The New Bahrain–Pakistan Alliance." *National Interest*, 2 August.

Rifkin, Jeremy. 1992. *Beyond Beef: The Rise and Fall of the Cattle Culture*. New York: Dutton.

Riyadh Chamber of Commerce and Industry. 2009. "Saudi Importers May File Suit against Indian Rice Exporters," 16 May. Available at: <http://www.riyadhchamber.com/newsdisplay.php?id=631> (accessed 7 March 2011).

——2010. "Muqtarahat li Muʿalajat ʾAthar Waqf Ziraʿa al-Qamh." [Proposals for the Treatment of the Termination of Wheat Farming], 24 December. Available at: <http://www.riyadhchamber.com/newsdisplay.php?id=1028> (accessed 24 March 2011).

Robbins, John. 2001. *The Food Revolution: How Your Diet Can Help Save Your Life and Our World*. Berkeley, Calif.: Conari Press.

Rodman, Peter W. 2009. *Presidential Command: Power, Leadership, and the Making of Foreign Policy from Richard Nixon to George W. Bush*. New York: Alfred A. Knopf.

Rothschild, Emma. 1976. "Food Politics." *Foreign Affairs* 54(2): 285–307.

Rozanov, Andrew. 2005. "Who Holds the Wealth of Nations?" *Central Banking Journal* 15(4): 52–7.

——2008. "A Liability-Based Approach to Sovereign Wealth." *Central Banking Journal* 18(3): 37–41.

Ruel, Marie. 2012. "Opportunities and Challenges for Achieving Nutrition Security in Low and Middle Income Countries." Paper presented at Food Secure Arab World Conference, ESCWA-UN-IFPRI, Beirut, 6–7 February.

Runge, Carlisle Ford, and Carlisle Piehl Runge. 2010. "Against the Grain: Why Failing to Complete the Green Revolution Could Bring the Next Famine." *Foreign Affairs* 89(1): 8.

Rural Modernity. 2012a. "ILC Response to Critique," 5 May. Available at: <http://ruralmodernity.wordpress.com/2012/05/05/88/> (accessed 3 June 2012).

——2012b. "Karuturi: Why the Hype?," 7 April. Available at: <http://ruralmodernity.wordpress.com/2012/04/07/karuturi-why-the-hype/> (accessed 23 June 2012).

——2012c. "Land Matrix: Ethiopia Data Update," 5 May. Available at: <http://ruralmodernity.wordpress.com/2012/05/05/land-matrix-ethiopia-data-update/> (accessed 3 June 2012).

——2012d. "The Land Matrix: Much Ado About Nothing," 27 April. Available at: <http://ruralmodernity.wordpress.com/2012/04/27/the-land-matrix-much-ado-about-nothing/> (accessed 27 April 2012).

Ruttan, Vernon W. 1996. *United States Development Assistance Policy: The Domestic Politics of Foreign Economic Aid*. The Johns Hopkins Studies in Development. Baltimore: Johns Hopkins University Press.

Safran, Nadav. 1985. *Saudi Arabia: The Ceaseless Quest for Security*. Cambridge, Mass.: Belknap Press of Harvard University Press.

Salerno, Tania. 2010. "Land Deals, Joint Investments and Peasants in Mindanao, Philippines." MA Thesis, Graduate School of Development Studies, Institute of Social Studies, The Hague.

Salman, Salman M. A. 2011. "The New State of South Sudan and the Hydro-Politics of the Nile Basin." *Water International* 36(2): 154–66.

Sanger, Richard H. 1947. "Ibn Saud's Program for Arabia." *Middle East Journal* 1(2): 180–90.

——1954. *The Arabian Peninsula*. Ithaca: Cornell University Press.

Sauer, S., and S. P. Leite. 2011. "Agrarian Structure, Foreign Land Ownership, and Land Value in Brazil." Paper presented at the International Conference on Global Land Grabbing, University of Sussex, UK, 6–8 April.

Saunders, Doug. 2010. *Arrival City: The Final Migration and Our Next World*. Toronto: Knopf Canada.

Al-Sayyid, ʿAbd Allah Muhammad Qasam. 1994. *Al-Tanmiyya fi al-Watan al-ʿArabi: Al-Nazariyya wa-l-Tatbiq: Al-Tajriba al-Sudaniyya*. [Development in the Arab Homeland: Theory and Practice, the Sudanese Experience]. Cairo: Dar al-Kitab al-Hadith.

Schatkowski-Schilcher, Linda. 1989. "Die Weizenwirtschaft des Nahen Ostens in der Zwischenkriegszeit: Der Einfluß der Ökonomie auf die Politik am Beispiel Syriens." In *Der Nahe Osten in der Zwischenkriegszeit, 1919–1939. Die Interdependenz von Politik, Wirtschaft und Ideologie*, ed. Linda Schatkowski-Schilcher and Claus Scharf, 241–59. Stuttgart: Franz Steiner.

——1992. "The Famine of 1915–1918 in Greater Syria." In *Problems of the Modern Middle East in Historical Perspective: Essays in Honor of Albert*

Hourani, ed. John Spagnolo, 229–58. Reading, UK: Ithaca Press (for Garnet Publishing Ltd.).

Schmitz, Andrew, Alex F. McCalla, Donald O. Mitchell, and Colin Carter. 1981. *Grain Export Cartels*. Cambridge, Mass.: Ballinger.

Schnepf, Randy. 2003. *Iraq Agriculture and Food Supply: Background and Issues*. Congressional Research Service Report. Washington, DC.

Schutter, Olivier de. 2010a. *Food Commodities Speculation and Food Price Crises: Regulation to Reduce the Risks of Price Volatility*. Briefing Note. Geneva: United Nations Special Rapporteur on the Right to Food.

——2010b. "Responsibly Destroying the World's Peasantry." *Project Syndicate*, 4 June.

Sen, Amartya. 1981. *Poverty and Famines: An Essay on Entitlement and Deprivation*. Oxford and New York: Oxford University Press.

Serels, Steven. 2012. "Famines of War: The Red Sea Grain Market and Famine in Eastern Sudan, 1889–1891." *Northeast African Studies* 12(1): 73–94.

Setser, Brad, and Rachel Ziemba. 2009. "GCC Sovereign Funds: Reversal of Fortune." Working Paper. New York: Council on Foreign Relations.

Sfakianakis, John. 2008. *Eating into the Economy: Food Price Inflation in the Kingdom*. Research Report. Riyadh: Saudi British Bank.

——2009. *Prudent Overspending: Saudi State Spending and Signs of Recovery*. Research Note. Riyadh: Banque Saudi Fransi.

Shah, Mahendra. 2010. "Gulf Cooperation Council Food Security: Balancing the Equation." Nature.com, 25 April. Available at: <http://www.nature.com/nmiddle-east/2010/100425/full/nmiddleeast.2010.141.html> (accessed 22 April 2012).

Shakoori, Ali. 2001. *The State and Rural Development in Post-Revolutionary Iran*. Basingstoke and New York: Palgrave Macmillan.

Shaw, D. John. 2007. *World Food Security: A History since 1945*. New York: Palgrave Macmillan.

——2009. *Global Food and Agricultural Institutions*. Routledge Global Institutions. London and New York: Routledge.

Sheehan, John, Terri Dunahay, John Benneman, and Paul Roessler. 1998. *A Look Back at the US Department of Energy's Aquatic Species Program: Biodiesel from Algae*. Report of the National Renewable Energy Laboratory. Washington, DC: US Department of Energy.

Shepherd, Andrew. 1988. "Case Studies of Famine: Sudan." In *Preventing Famine: Policies and Prospects for Africa*, ed. Donald Curtis, Michael Hubbard, and Andrew Shepherd, 28–72. London and New York: Routledge.

Shepherd, Benjamin. 2010. "Above Carrying Capacity: Saudi Arabia's External Policies for Securing Food Supplies." Paper presented at World Congress of Middle Eastern Studies in Barcelona, July.

——2012. "Thinking Critically About Food Security." *Security Dialogue* 43(3): 195–212.

Simpson, I. G., and M. C. Simpson. 1991. "Systems of Agricultural Production in Central Sudan and Khartoum Province." In *The Agriculture of the Sudan*, ed. G. M. Craig, 252–79. Oxford and New York: Oxford University Press.

Smil, Vaclav. 2001. *Enriching the Earth: Fritz Haber, Carl Bosch, and the Transformation of World Food Production.* Cambridge, Mass.: MIT Press.

——2006. "Peak Oil: A Catastrophist Cult and Complex Realities." *World Watch* (Jan./Feb): 22–4.

Sojamo, Suvi, Martin Keulertz, Jeroen Warner, and John Anthony Allan. 2012. "Virtual Water Hegemony: The Role of Agribusiness in Global Water Governance." *Water International* 37(2): 169–82.

Solidarity Movement for a New Ethiopia (SMNE). 2012. "Pakistani and Ethiopians Killed in Gambella," 30 April. Available at: <http://www.solidaritymovement.org/downloads/120430-Pakistani-and-Ethiopians-Killed-in-Gambella.pdf> (accessed 4 June 2012).

Solomon, Jay. 2002. "In This Philippine Town, Muslim, Jews, Rebels Set Aside Their Differences for Bananas." *Wall Street Journal*, 21 March.

Spiro, David. 1989. "Policy Coordination in the International Political Economy: The Politics of Petrodollar Recycling." Ph.D. thesis, Department of Politics, Princeton University, Princeton.

——1999. *The Hidden Hand of American Hegemony: Petrodollar Recycling and International Markets.* Cornell Studies in Political Economy. Ithaca, NY: Cornell University Press.

Springborg, Robert. 1986. "Impediments to the Transfer of Australian Dry Land Agricultural Technology to the Middle East." *Agriculture, Ecosystems & Environment* 17(3–4): 229–51.

——2012. "Governance in Egypt." In *Governance in the Middle East and North Africa: A Handbook*, ed. Abbas Kadhim. London and New York: Routledge.

Steinberg, Guido. 2004. "Ecology, Knowledge and Trade in Central Arabia (Najd) During the Nineteenth and Early Twentieth Centuries." In *Counter Narratives: History, Contemporary Society, and Politics in Saudi Arabia and Yemen*, ed. Madawi Al-Rasheed and Robert Vitalis, 77–102. New York and Basingstoke: Palgrave Macmillan.

——2005. "The Wahhabi Ulama and the Saudi State: 1745 to the Present." In *Saudi Arabia in the Balance: Political Economy, Society, Foreign Affairs*, ed. Paul Aarts and Gerd Nonneman, 11–34. New York: New York University Press.

Steinberg, Guido Walter. 2002. *Religion und Staat in Saudi-Arabien: Die Wahhabitischen Gelehrten 1902–1953.* Mitteilungen zur Sozial- und Kulturgeschichte der Islamischen Welt. Würzburg: Ergon.

Strobl, Staci. 2011. "From Colonial Policing to Community Policing in Bahrain: The Historical Persistence of Sectarianism." *International Journal of Comparative and Applied Criminal Justice* 35(1): 19–37.

Al-Sultan, Abdul Rahman. 2010. "Al-Istithmar al-Zira'i al-Khariji la Yad'am al-'Amn al-Ghidha'i al-Khaliji" [Foreign Agro-Investment Does Not Support Gulf Food Security]. *Al-Ru'ya al-Iqtisadiyya*, 20 January.

Supersberger, Nikolaus, Dennis Taenzler, Kerstin Fritzsche, Dietmar Schuewer, and Daniel Valentin. 2009. *Energy Systems in OPEC Countries of the Middle East and North Africa: System Analytic Comparison of Nuclear Power, Renewable Energies and Energy Efficiency.* Wuppertal, Berlin: Wuppertal Institute for Climate, Environment, Energy, in cooperation with Adelphi Consult.

Taryam, Abdullah Omran. 1987. *The Establishment of the United Arab Emirates, 1950–85.* London and New York: Croom Helm.

Tauger, Mark B. 2003. "Entitlement, Shortage and the 1943 Bengal Famine: Another Look." *Journal of Peasant Studies* 31(1): 45–72.

Taylor, Jerry, and Peter van Doren. 2006. *Economic Amnesia: The Case Agaist Oil Price Controls and Windfall Profit Taxes.* Policy Analysis. Washington, DC: Cato Institute.

Teitelbaum, Joshua. 2001. *The Rise and Fall of the Hashimite Kingdom of Arabia.* London: Hurst and New York: New York University Press.

——(ed.). 2009. *Political Liberalization in the Persian Gulf.* New York: Columbia University Press.

Tell, Tariq. 2000. "Guns, Gold, and Grain: War and Food Supply in the Making of Transjordan." In *War, Institutions and Social Change in the Middle East,* ed. Steven Heydeman, 33–58. Berkeley and London: University of California Press.

Tétreault, Mary Ann. 2009. "Kuwait: Slouching Towards Democracy?" In *Political Liberalization in the Persian Gulf,* ed. Joshua Teitelbaum, 107–32. New York: Columbia University Press.

Thesiger, Wilfred. 1959. *Arabian Sands.* New York: Dutton.

Thurow, Roger. 2010. "The Fertile Continent: Africa, Agriculture's Final Frontier." *Foreign Affairs* 89(6): 102–11.

Tignor, Robert L. 1987. "The Sudanese Private Sector: An Historical Overview." *Journal of Modern African Studies* 25(2): 179–212.

Tooze, J. Adam. 2007. *The Wages of Destruction: The Making and Breaking of the Nazi Economy.* New York: Viking.

Transparency International. 2011. *Corruption Perception Index (CPI) 2011.* Berlin.

Truman, Edwin M. 2010. *Sovereign Wealth Funds: Threat or Salvation?* Washington, DC: Peterson Institute for International Economics.

Twitchell, K. S. 1944. "Water Resources of Saudi Arabia." *Geographical Review* 34(3): 365–86.

——1958. *Saudi Arabia, with an Account of the Development of Its Natural Resources.* 3rd edn. Princeton, NJ: Princeton University Press.

Ulrichsen, Kristian. 2011. *Insecure Gulf: The End of Certainty and the Transition to the Post-Oil Era.* London: Hurst.

University of London. Centre of Islamic and Middle Eastern Law. 1995. *Yearbook of Islamic and Middle Eastern Law.* London and Boston: Kluwer Law International.

U.S.-Saudi Arabian Business Council. 2008. *The Agriculture Sector in the Kingdom of Saudi Arabia.*

Valeri, Marc. 2009. *Oman: Politics and Society in the Qaboos State.* The CERI/Science Po Series in Comparative Politics and International Studies. New York and Paris: Columbia University Press.

Van Rooy, Alison. 2004. *The Global Legitimacy Game: Civil Society, Globalization, and Protest.* Palgrave Texts in International Political Economy. Basingstoke and New York: Palgrave Macmillan.

Verhoeven, Harry. 2011a. *Black Gold for Blue Gold? Sudan's Oil, Ethiopia's Water and Regional Integration.* Briefing Paper. London: Chatham House.

Verhoeven, Harry. 2011b. "Climate Change, Conflict and Development in Sudan: Global Neo-Malthusian Narratives and Local Power Struggles." *Development and Change* 42(3): 679–707.

———2012a. "Sudan and Its Agricultural Revival: A Regional Breadbasket at Last or Another Mirage in the Desert?" In *Handbook of African Land- and Watergrabs*, ed. Tony Allan, Jeroen Warner, Suvi Sojamo, and Martin Keulertz, 41–54. London and New York: Routledge.

———2012b. "Water, Civilisation and Power: Sudan's Hydropolitical Economy and the Al-Injaz Revolution." Ph.D., Department of Politics and International Relations, St. Cross College, Oxford University, Oxford.

Vermeulen, Sonja, and Lorenzo Cotula. 2010. "Making the Most of Agricultural Investment: A Survey of Business Models That Provide Opportunities for Small-holders." Report. London and Rome: IIED, FAO.

Via Campesina, GRAIN, et al. 2011. *It's Time to Outlaw Land Grabbing, Not to Make It 'Responsible'!* Report.

Vick, Margaret J. 2006. "The Senegal River Basin: A Retrospective and Prospective Look at the Legal Regime." *Natural Resources Journal* 46 (Winter): 211–43.

Vicker, Ray. 1975. "Tycoon Khalil Osman Builds a Conglomerate with Oil-Money Help." *Wall Street Journal*, 5 August.

Vidal, F. S. 1954. "Date Culture in the Oasis of Al-Hasa." *Middle East Journal* 8(4): 417–28.

Vitalis, Robert. 1999. "Review of Kiren Aziz Chaudhry, *The Price of Wealth: Economies and Institutions in the Middle East*." *International Journal of Middle East Studies* 31(4): 659–61.

———2007. *America's Kingdom: Mythmaking on the Saudi Oil Frontier*. Stanford Studies in Middle Eastern and Islamic Societies and Cultures. Palo Alto, Calif: Stanford University Press.

Voll, John Obert, and Sarah Potts Voll. 1985. *The Sudan: Unity and Diversity in a Multicultural State*. Profiles: Nations of the Contemporary Middle East Series. Boulder, Colo.: Westview Press.

Wallach, Bret. 1988. "Irrigation in Sudan since Independence." *Geographical Review* 78(4): 417–34.

Wallensteen, Peter. 1976. "Scarce Goods as Political Weapons: The Case of Food." *Journal of Peace Research* 13(4): 277–98.

Wallerstein, Mitchel B. 1980a. *Food for War–Food for Peace: United States Food Aid in a Global Context*. Cambridge, Mass.: MIT Press.

———1980b. "Foreign–Domestic Intersections in US Food Policy." *Food Policy* 5(2): 83–96.

Walsh, R. P. D., M. Hulme, and M. D. Campbell. 1988. "Recent Rainfall Changes and Their Impact on Hydrology and Water Supply in the Semi-Arid Zone of the Sudan." *Geographical Journal* 154(2): 181–97.

Waterbury, John. 1976a. "The Sudan in Quest for a Surplus. Part I: Dreams and Realities." *North East Africa Series, American Universities Field Staff Reports* 8: 1–33.

Waterbury, John. 1976b. "The Sudan in Quest for a Surplus. Part III: Capital Packages and Regional Prospects." *North East Africa Series, American Universities Field Staff Reports* 21(10): 1–27.

Waterbury, John. 1979. *Hydropolitics of the Nile Valley.* Contemporary Issues in the Middle East. Syracuse, NY: Syracuse University Press.

——1983. *The Egypt of Nasser and Sadat: The Political Economy of Two Regimes.* Princeton Studies on the Near East. Princeton, NJ: Princeton University Press.

——2002. *The Nile Basin: National Determinants of Collective Action.* New Haven: Yale University Press.

Weis, Anthony. 2007. *The Global Food Economy: The Battle for the Future of Farming.* London and New York: Zed Books.

Wheatcroft, Andrew. 2005. *With United Strength: H. H. Shaikh Zayid Bin Sultan Al Nahyan, the Leader and the Nation.* Abu Dhabi: Emirates Center for Strategic Studies and Research (ECSSR).

Whelan, John (ed.). 1981. *Saudi Arabia.* MEED Special Report. London: Middle East Economic Digest (MEED).

Wiggins, Steve, Johann Kirsten, and Luis Llambí. 2010. "The Future of Small Farms." *World Development* 38(10): 1341–8.

Wilmington, Martin W. 1952. "The Middle East Supply Center: A Reappraisal." *Middle East Journal* 6(2): 144–66.

——1971. *The Middle East Supply Centre.* Albany: State University of New York Press.

Wilson, Peter W., and Douglas Graham. 1994. *Saudi Arabia: The Coming Storm.* Armonk; NY: M. E. Sharpe.

Winders, Bill. 2011. "The Food Crisis and the Deregulation of Agriculture." *The Brown Journal of World Affairs* 18(1): 83–95.

Woertz, Eckart. 2006. "The Mineral and Mining Industry of the GCC." *GRC Economic Research Bulletin* no. 2.

——2007. *GCC Stock Markets: Managing the Crisis.* Gulf Papers. Dubai: Gulf Research Center.

——2010. "The Gulf Food Import Dependence and Trade Restrictions of Agro Exporters in 2008." In *Will Stabilisation Limit Protectionism?*, ed. Simon J. Evenett, 43–56. London: Center for Economic Policy Research.

——2012a. "Gulf Sovereign Wealth Funds in International Comparison." In *GCC Financial Markets: The World's New Money Centers*, ed. Eckart Woertz, 229–54. Berlin and London: Gerlach.

——2012b. "Oil, the Dollar and the Stability of the International Financial System." In *Handbook of Oil Politics*, ed. Robert Looney, 375–400. London and New York: Routledge.

——2012c. "Repercussions of Dubai's Debt Crisis." In *GCC Financial Markets: The World's New Money Centers*, ed. Eckart Woertz, 137–64. Berlin and London: Gerlach.

Woertz, Eckart, Samir Pradhan, Nermina Biberovic, and Chan Jinzhong. 2008. *The Potential for GCC Agro Investments in Africa and Central Asia.* GRC Report. Dubai: Gulf Research Center.

Wohlmuth, K. 1991. "National Policies for Agriculture." In *The Agriculture of the Sudan*, ed. G. M. Craig, 436–54. Oxford and New York: Oxford University Press.

Wolfe, Robert. 1998. *Farm Wars: The Political Economy of Agriculture and the International Trade Regime.* International Political Economy Series. Basingstoke and New York: St. Martin's Press.

World Economic Forum. 2011. *The Global Competitiveness Report 2011–2012.* Geneva.

Worthington, E. Barton. 1946. *Middle East Science: A Survey of Subjects Other Than Agriculture.* Middle East Supply Center. Report to the Director General. London: HMSO.

Yamauchi, Akira 2002. "Toward Sustainable Agricultural Production System: Major Issues and Needs in Research." Paper presented at Proceedings of the Forum on Sustainable Agricultural System in Asia.

Yergin, Daniel. 1991. *The Prize: The Epic Quest for Oil, Money, and Power.* New York: Simon & Schuster.

Yizraeli, Sarah. 1997. *The Remaking of Saudi Arabia: The Struggle between King Sa'ud and Crown Prince Faysal, 1953–1962.* Dayan Center Papers. Tel Aviv, Israel: Moshe Dayan Center for Middle Eastern and African Studies, Tel Aviv University.

——2012. *Politics and Society in Saudi Arabia: The Crucial Years of Development, 1960–1982.* London: Hurst and New York: Columbia University Press.

Al-Zaydi, Mshari. 2005. "History of the Jordanian Muslim Brotherhood. Part One." *Al-Sharq al-Awsat*, 27 December.

Zeitoun, Mark, and Jeroen Warner. 2006. "Hydro-Hegemony: A Framework for Analysis of Trans-Boundary Water Conflicts." *Water Policy* 8: 435–60.

Zoomers, Annelies. 2010. "Globalisation and the Foreignisation of Space: Seven Processes Driving the Current Global Land Grab." *Journal of Peasant Studies* 37(2): 429–47.

Zurayk, Rami. 2011. *Food, Farming and Freedom. Sowing the Arab Spring.* Charlottesville, Va: Just World Books.

Zurayk, Rami, Jad Chaaban, and Alia Sabra. 2011. "Ensuring that Potential Gulf Farmland Investments in Developing Countries are Pro-Poor and Sustainable." *Food Security* 3 (Supplement 1): 129–37.

Index

Note: Page numbers in italics indicate figure, *t* indicates a table and an *n* a footnote.

Al-Abdali 91
Abdul Majid bin Abdulaziz 82
Abdulaziz, King of Saudi Arabia. *See* Ibn Saud
Abdullah Abbar & Ahmed Zainy Co. (NEH) 203
Abdullah al-Faisal 82
Abdullah bin Abdulaziz 13–14
Abdullah, Ahmed Abdullah 161
Abidin, Abdul Hakim 72–3
Abraaj Capital 225
absentee landlords 36, 67, 81
Abu Dhabi Fund for Development
 (ADFD) 199, 213, 216, 218, *220-2*, 228
Abu Dhabi Group 225
Abu Dhabi Investment House (ADIH) 245
Abu Hamad 200, 228
accumulation by dispossesion. *See* original
 accumulation
Afghanistan 114, 133, 200
 food basket proposal for Gulf countries 194
Agadi scheme 183, 229
Agricultural Market Information System
 (AMIS) 260
agricultural production growth 20–2
Agricultural Revival Programme (ARP),
 Sudan 191–3, 200
agricultural treadmill 21–4, 26, 154
Agrinuture Industries 203
Al-Ahmad, Nasser Sabah 176
Ahmadinejad administration 101
Al-Ain 38, 93, 96
Al-Ain National Wildlife 199
Al-Alami, Fawaz 185, 259, 262
Al-Anhar Group 229
Aleppo 56, 263
Alexander Gibb & Partners 91
Alfa Laval 82
alfalfa 32, 80, 84, 87, 96, 200, 207, 225, 228
 as substitute for wheat phase-out 88
 East Africa as potential source of 83
 Gulf imports of 29–30, 206
Algeria 11, 12*t*, 18*t*, 112, *197*, 222, 225
Alireza, Abdullah 117
Alireza, Abdullah A. Zainal 201
Alireza, Muhammad 69, 70*n*42
Alliance for a Green Revolution in Africa
 (AGRA) 198
Almarai 82, 87, 202, 207, 224
Altima 151
American Agriculture Movement (AAM) 127

Americana Group 205, 224
Amery, Leo 52
Al-Amoudi, Mohammed Hussein 202, 230
Amstutz, Daniel 137
Amtar 200
Anglo-Egyptian Condominium over Sudan
 (1899–1955) 173
Angola 147
Aquaculture 25, 86
Arab Authority for Agricultural Investment
 and Development (AAAID) 174, 176,
 179, 183, 193, 199, 263
 $2bn fund of (2009) 249
 Agadi scheme and 183, 229
 as shareholder of Kenana SC 176
 Camp David funding freeze and 178
 Dubai office and commercial control
 of 180*n*86
 establishment of 171
 project implementation since 1980s 180
 strategic outlook and assessment of
 (2002) 180
Arab Bank for Economic Development in
 Africa (BADEA) 199, 216, *220-1*
Arab Fund for Economic and Social
 Development (AFESD) 174, 176, 179,
 183, 193, 195, *220*
 AAAID proposal of 171
 as host of CSANRDI 221
 Basic Programme for Agricultural
 Development (1976-85) of 171
 Sudan bread-basket plan of 171–3
 Sudan dam program 2000s and 190
Arab Gulf Programme for United Nations
 Development Organizations
 (AGFUND) 221
Arab Investment Corporation (AIC) 176
Arab League 18*t*, 161, 171, 199
Arab Liberation Front 111
Arab Monetary Fund (AMF) 216
Arab oil embargo 81, 108, 114–18, 125, 139,
 180, 265
Arab Organization for Agricultural Development
 (AOAD) 26, 28*t*, 161, 199, 263
Arabian American Oil Company
 (ARAMCO) 61, 68, 70, 73, 110
 Al-Kharj farm and 64–6
 establishment of 42–3
 oil pricing of 215–16

Arabian American Oil (*cont.*)
  water drilling and 78, 84
Arab-Israeli conflict 111–12, 118, 124, 259
Aral Sea 240
Archer Daniels Midland (ADM) 153, 238, 261
Argentina 32, 129, 153, 195, 198n5, 225
  as possible member of grain cartel 127
  Cairns group and 149
  changes in tax code of 217
  export restrictions of 139, 195, 225
  feedstock supplies to Almarai and 224
  food exports to the Gulf and 29
  Gulf agro-investments and 197, 204–5
  land reserves of 147–8
  US grain embargo against USSR and 114
Ashraf, Ahmad 100
Asir 36, 60, 80, 88
  terraced fields of 38–40
Atatürk Dam 252
Atbara River 190
Australia 129, 132, 139, 143, 147, 151, 195,
    215, 223, 225, 234, 241
  as possible member of a grain cartel 127
  barley export ban of (2004) 259
  Cairns group and 149
  dryland farming projects Middle East and 263
  food exports to the Gulf by 30–2, 39n14,
    46, 54, 261
  Foreign Investment Review
      Framework 244
  governance indicators and 235t, 237
  grain exports to UK 19th century 35
  Gulf agro-investments and 32, 197–8, 204–5,
    207–8, 243, 267
  MESC and 46, 54
  proposed Saudi oil for food deal and
    117–18, 265
  US grain embargo against USSR and 114
  US pressures for food embargo against Iran
    and 118–20
  virtual water exports of 238
  water situation of 24, 147, 238, 239t, 240
Australian Wheat Board 132, 137, 261

Badr bin Sultan 199
Baghdad Pact 111
Bahr al-Ghazal province 169
Bahrain 10t, 15t–19, 28t, 38, 47, 56, 89t, 93,
    95, 208, 221, 245, 263–4
  agricultural development of 92
  peak oil in (1977) 10, 214
  reform of sponsorship system in 247
  special interest in Philippines of 203,
    214, 246
Bahrain Petroleum Company 47
Balghunaim, Fahd 84, 87, 199, 212

Baluchistan 200, 214, 246
barley 52, 63, 79, 80, 103, 206, 241
  as livestock fodder in Saudi Arabia 29, 84, 87
  Australian export ban (2004) 259
  imports of Iran 28
  imports of Saudi Arabia 19, 28, 30, 31–2, 77
  Iraqi exports prior to WWII 46
  price controls Saudi Arabia 14
  regional trade WWII 39, 46, 54, 56
  subsidy regime in Saudi Arabia 74, 77–8, 83
barter trade 102, 120, 126, 174, 215–16, 265
Al-Bashir, Omar 161, 169, 187, 191
  power struggle with Al-Turabi 169, 189
Basra 39, 56
Al-Bateel 85
Bayt, recruitment firm 15
Baz, Abdulaziz ibn 65
Beja 188
Bellmon, Henry 127
Bengal famine (1943) 51–2, 186
BHP Billiton 265
Bhutto, Benazir 200
Bilateral Investment Treaties (BIT) 212,
    214, 230
Bin Laden, Muhammad 82
Bin Laden, Osama 170, 188
biofuels 143, 150, 153, 160
  abstention of Gulf countries 206
  impact on food prices 20, 25, 31–2, 146
Black Book pamphlet
    (*al-kitab al-aswad*) 169, 171
Block, John 131–3
Blue Nile province 164, 168–9, 183, 188, 191–2,
    248, 250
Bowen-Jones, Howard 95
Brabeck-Letmathe, Peter 147
Brazil 23n49, 25, 113n28, 131, 152–3, 161,
    229, 241, 243, 253
  Cairns group and 149
  cerrado and land reserve 147–8
  governance indicators of 235t, 237
  Gulf agro-investments and 32, 197–8, 204–5,
    225, 234, 267
  ineqality of land ownership in 154, 157, 246
  restrictions on foreign land ownership
    in 231, 244
  soybean investments by Japan (1970s) 114
  sugar and poultry exports to the Gulf 30–1
  superfarms 155
  water situation of 238–40
Bretton Woods system 110, 121
British Government of India 89
Brown & Root Company 252
Bunge 153, 238, 261
Burdana 190
Burma 51–2

Bush, George W. 133
Bush, Ray 99
Butler, Bobby "So Fine" 126
Butz, Earl 110, 123-4

Cairns group 149
California Arabian Standard Oil Company (CASOC) 42, 47, 49, 61
Caliph, title and alleged pan-Islamic influence 43n43
Cambodia 111n18, 113n29, 143, 148
    Gulf agro-investments and 195, 197-8n5, 202, 216
Canada 109, 129, 198n5, 206
    as a possible member of a grain cartel 127
    Cairns group and 149
    food exports to the Gulf of 30-2, 261
    grain trade WWII and 46, 54
    limits on foreign ownership in 244
Canadian Potash Corp. 265
Canadian Wheat Board 127, 132, 261
Cape of Good Hope 43
Carbon Capture and Storage (CCS) 259
carbon fertilization effect 24, 242-3
Cargill 24, 127, 137-8, 153, 203, 228, 238, 261
Carter administration 115n36, 118-19, 128, 147
Carter Library 177t
Central Banking Journal 218
Central Intelligence Agency (CIA) 121
cereal programs
    Egypt 98-100, 251
    Iran 100-02
    Saudi Arabia 75-83
    Sudan 103-04, 187-8, 192
    Syria 102-03
Ceyhan River 252
Ceylon 51, 54, 113n28
Chamber of Commerce and Industry
    Islamic 205
    Jeddah 70n42, 212
    Riyadh 200, 211
Chaudhry, Kiren Aziz 59
Chicago Council on Global Affairs 158
Chile 44, 113n28
China 11, 17, 20, 22, 31, 85n119, 133, 135, 147-9, 156, 164, 195, 216, 219, 259, 264
    agricultural demonstration centers in Africa 152
    diets in 26t
    land investment policies of 145, 151-3, 246, 251
    soybean imports from Brazil of 152
China Investment Corporation 218
Churchill, Winston 52
Clean Development Mechanism (CDM) 262
climate change 189

attitudes of Gulf countries towards 239, 259, 262
    Copenhagen and Cancun summits 262
    impact on agriculture 20, 24-5, 32, 146
    impact on target countries 169, 233, 237, 240-3, 253
Clinton administration 133
Clinton, Bill 133
Club of Rome 19
Cochrane, Willard Wesley 21, 154
Collier, Paul 23, 155-6
Colorado River 70
Common Agricultural Policy (CAP) 20
Conference on Middle East Agricultural Development, Cairo (1944) 57
Congo 112, 144, 147, 157, 198n5, 228, 237
Consultative Group on International Agricultural Research (CGIAR) 203, 263
Consumer Price Index (CPI), share of food in Gulf countries 14
Continental System 107
Coordination Secretariat of Arab National and Regional Development Institutions 221
Corn Laws, UK (1846) 35
Corruption Perception Index (CPI) 235t, 237
cotton agreement (1933) 129
Council of Economic Advisers (CEA) 123
Crane, Charles A. 63
Cuba 113n28, 134, 176
customary land rights 3, 146, 155, 158, 160, 193, 245, 248, 253, 265
    conflicts in Sudan 161, 167-70, 194n147, 229
    land titling and 158
    primitive accumulation and 155

Daewoo 144, 153, 246
Al-Dahra 204, 207, 213, 225
Dal Dam 328
DAL group 145, 250
Dalla Albarakah Group 205
Damazin 174-5, 188
Daoud, Osama, 331
Darfur 162, 168n35, 169-70, 172, 191, 199
Davao 203
Davis, Mike 156
Al-Dawasir 85
DeGolyer, Everette Lee 51
deregulation of agriculture in US and EU 20-1
desalination 19, 69, 76, 79, 97, 252
    dependence of Gulf countries on 19, 257
    energy mix and 209, 257
    first plant in UAE 96
    MoWE Saudi Arabia and 79
    Qatar self-sufficiency plans and 93, 97, 208-9
    water storage and 257
Deutsche Bank 150

dhows 49, 56
diabetes 3, 16–17*n*24, 258
dietary change 46
    environmental impact of 24
    from dates to rice 39–40
    to meat, dairy, sugar, and packaged
        food 16, 20, 152
    from sorghum to wheat and rice 167, 205.
        See also wheatification
diets
    Gulf countries, China, India, USA, Sudan
        (2005–07) 26*t*
    Middle East WW II 46*t*
Diouf, Jacques 155
diversification. *See* economic diversification
Doha round 149
Dole 150
Dongola 191
drainage. *See* soils
Dreyfus 153, 238, 261
drip irrigation 27, 84, 105, 136, 257
drought resistant crops 23, 25, 102, 242, 257
dryland farming 102, 147, 229, 243, 261.
        See also rain-fed agriculture
    Australian methods of 263
Dubai Aluminum (DUBAL) 207
Dubai Holding 207
Dubai World 222, 232
Dubai World Trading Company 202, 206
dust bowl farm crisis 109, 167
Dutch disease 102, 189
dynastic monarchy 71

Ease of Doing Business Index (EDBI) 235*t*–7
East African Community (EAC) 250
economic diversification 10*t*–11, 97, 99, 103,
        121, 209, 214, 219, 255–7, 259, 265
Economic Salvation Programme (ESP) 187–8
Eddy, William Alfred 57
Egypt 9, 11–12*t*, 14, 17, 18*t*, 30–2, 35*n*1–37,
        39–41, 49, 50–58, 64, 72, 73*n*56, 103, 105,
        132, 138, 148, 164, 229–32, 259
    absentee landlords 36–7
    cereal crisis in (1942) 45
    cereal program of 98–100
    governance indicators and 235*t*–7
    Gulf agro-investments and 197–8, 204,
        217, 222, 225, 245, 247, 263
    impact of climate change on 243
    opposition to dam funding by 190, 251
    Sudan policies of 162, 170, 172–4, 176, 178,
        180, 188–90, 248
    US food aid as a foreign policy tool
        towards 107–24
    water situation of 238–41, 249–51, 253
Egyptian Council for Foreign Affairs 251

Egypto-Sudanese Company for Agricultural
        Integration 174
Egypto-Sudanese Company for Irrigation and
        Construction 174
Eilts, Hermann Frederick 112–13
Eisenhower administration 111
Elfora Agro-Industries 202
Elhadj, Elie 81
Emami Biotech 153
Emirates Center for Strategic Studies and
        Research (ECSSR) 95
Emirates Investment Group 225
Enders, Thomas 134
Entente 41, 43*n*43, 108
entitlements and food accessibility 16, 24, 52,
        151, 186. *See also* food security
Eritrea 16, 24, 52, 151, 186
ethanol 25, 31, 192, 206
Ethiopia 16, 32, 45, 55, 56, 73*n*57, 148, 166
    agriculture led industrialization and 248
    conflict with Sudan 170, 177, 188
    contract documentation in 143
    food exports to Gulf WWII 53–4
    governance indicators of 235*t*–7
    Gulf agro-investments and 197–9, 201–203,
        206–8, 216, 225, 228, 230, 244, 253
    Indian agro-investments and 153
    job creation of projects in 157
    opposition to Nile Waters Agreement 190,
        243, 249–51
    Red Sea economic union plan and 173
    villagization programs 247
    water situation of 239–41
Euphrates 138, 240, 252, 265
European Community/ European Union 114,
        120, 131–2
expatriates. *See* migrant workers
Export Enhancement Program (EEP) 132
Exxon Mobil 151

Fahd bin Abdulaziz 72, 117
Failed States Index (FSI) 235*t*–7
Faisal bin Abdulaziz 49, 66, 71, 73, 82, 111,
        113, 117
Faisal Islamic Bank (FIB) 186–7
Faisal scheme 183
Al-Faisal, Muhammad 186
falaj (pl. *aflaj*), canals 40, 93
Far East Agricultural Investment Corporation
        (FEAICO) 203, 228
Faruk, King of Egypt 57
Al-Fayed, Mohammed 176
Federal Reserve Bank 131
Federation of Arab Republics (FAR) 174
fertilizer 3, 20, 21–2, 24, 39,
        136, 150, 205

application in Saudi Arabia 63–5, 70,
74*t*–6, 82, 216
application in Sudan 165, 179*n*85, 187, 189
disruptions of nitrate imports from Chile
WWII 44
impact on agricultural productivity 25–6,
109, 128
phosphates and role of Morocco 265–7
production of Gulf countries 75, 209, 265–6
Flint, Julie 170
FMC 82
Food and Agriculture Organization of the
United Nations (FAO) 26, 26*t*, 46*t*, 58,
79, 89*t*, 155, 161, 239*t*
Committee on World Food Security 158
consultancy to Gulf countries 70, 92, 95
definition of food security of 2
delegation to Sudan (1973) 171
estimate of Saudi rural population
(1953) 60–1
food price projections of 19
foundation of 57
international food reserve proposal of 124
national inventories in target countries
(with IFAD and IIED) 144, 146
office in Abu Dhabi of 223
statistics about land use in Gulf
countries 95
Voluntary Guidelines for Governance of
Land Tenure and RAI 158, 160, 261
food balance sheets 25
Food City 209
Food for Peace Program 107, 109, 122–4,
130, 132
and Egypt 110–14
food prices 9, 32, 110, 114, 121, 124–5, 150,
195, 231, 255, 261
in the Gulf countries 12–16
Middle East WW II 49, 52, 54–6
OECD and FAO projections 19
paradigm shift globally 18–25, 146–7, 160
food regime theory and post war food
regime 58, 109–10
food riots 12–13, 45
food security
equation with self-sufficiency 19, 32, 36,
63, 73, 76, 81, 86, 88, 95–108, 117, 132–3,
149, 151–3, 172–3, 179, 187, 192, 204,
208–9, 251
export restrictions and 9, 29, 31, 36, 88,
107, 114, 120, 122–3, 131–9, 179, 195,
204, 208–9, 213, 217, 225, 230, 259–61
food accessibility and 12, 16, 52*n*93, 54, 56,
108, 136, 151, 186–7, 189, 210.
See also entitlements
lack of transportation and 36, 56–7, 199

land grabs and 68, 146, 154–5, 158–60, 168,
182, 198, 205–6, 212, 248*t*
levels in the Middle East 18*t*
stunting and lack of micronutrients and 17
trade-based approach to 73, 104, 105, 108,
132–3, 238
urbanization and 9, 36n4, 40, 61, 72–3,
80–1, 92, 100, 102, 104, 136, 149, 152,
155–8, 205, 258
water security and 9, 79, 238–41, 257–8
food subsidies 11, 20, 73, 246
Egypt 98
Gulf countries 9, 13–14, 16, 73–6, 83–4
Iran 101–2
USA 12, 131
food trade
during WWI 41–2
liberalization since 1970s 24, 153
of Gulf countries 28–32
of target countries 239*t*–41
politicization of since WWII 107–39
Sudan famine and 186–7
under the MESC 45–7, 53–57
Foras International Investment
Company 205
Ford Foundation 74–6
Ford, Gerald 114, 125–6
foreign direct investment (FDI) 235–6
Foreign Economic Administration (FEA) 64, 66
Foreign Policy Magazine 235*t*–6
France 30, 39*n*14, 50*n*84, 116, 135, 261
Free Prior Informed Consent (FPIC) 159, 267
Freedom and Justice Party 247
Funj Kingdom 162

G20 260–2
Gaddafi, Muammar 83, 84*n*108, 177
Gambela 202, 248
Gassim Agricultural Co. (GACO) 82
Gates Foundation, Bill and Melinda 198
Gazprom 130
Geithner, Timothy 257
General Agreement on Tariffs and Trade
(GATT) 20, 261
Genetically Modified Organisms (GMO) 23–4
geopolitics. *See* international relations
Germany 30–1, 45, 50, 69, 90, 144, 164, 244
Hungerplan 107
Ibn Saud and 49
U-boat campaign of 43
Gezira scheme 36*n*3, 56, 104, 164–7*n*26, 184,
187, 200, 250
Ghana 197–8*n*5
Ghawar oil field 68
Gini-coefficient 16*n*23
GIZ, German consultancy 144

Glencore 153, 261
Global Competitiveness Report (GCR) 235t–7
Global Dry Land Alliance (GDLA) 209
Global Hunger Index (GHI) 17
Google Earth 229
Al-Gosaibi group 232
governance indicators, ranking of target
    countries 233–7
GRAIN (NGO) 144, 197, 215, 245
grain cartel 107–8, 120
    plans for and problems of
        implementation 126–30
grain embargo
    against Arab countries (planned) 114–17,139
    against Iran (planned) 118–20
    against the USSR (1980) 102, 114, 118, 120,
        131, 133
grain export moratorium to the USSR and
    Poland (1975) 126
Grain Silos and Flour Mills Organization
    (GSFMO) 76–8, 83, 215
Great Depression 40–2, 131
Green Revolution 20, 22–3, 29, 100, 151, 198
Guillame, François 130
Gulf agro-investments
    by target country 197–9
    in Sudan 174–8, 189–93
    lack of implementation of 227–31
    preference for developed markets 185,
        204–5, 267
    resistance by NGOs 245–9
Gulf countries
    belief in international standards 209, 233–4
    domestic energy consumption of 209, 256
    political liberalization and backlash 263–4
Gulf Finance House (GFH) 245
Gulf Fisheries 176
Gulf International (GI) 175

Haber-Bosch process 25
Haggard, Stephen 133
Hail Agricultural Development Corp.
    (HADCO) 82, 200, 224
Hajar Mountains 88
hajj, pilgrimage 31, 41, 56–7, 59, 61, 84
Al-Hamad, Abdellatif Youssef 190
Hamdi, Abdelrahim 187, 190–1
Hanbali School 85
Haradh Agricultural and Animal Production
    Corp. 82
Al-Hasa 38–40, 42, 53, 59, 60, 67, 70, 75, 77, 80, 83
Hashemite monarchy 111
Hassad Food 200, 208–9, 211, 217, 220,
    222–3, 228, 249
Heath, Edward 176
Heffernan, Bill 244
Heilberg, Phil 143

Hejaz 38, 41–2, 57, 59–60, 67, 70, 80, 173
Herb, Michael 71
Hertog, Steffen 72
Heydemann, Steven 44, 58
High Dam at Aswan 112, 190
Higher Petroleum Committee, Saudi Arabia 117
hijra (pl. hijar), Bedouin settlement 60, 66
Al-Hofuf Agricultural Research Company 87
horse and camel trade 41
Human Development Index (HDI) 235t–7
Human Rights Watch 246, 263
Hussain, the Sharif of Mecca 41–2
Hussein, Saddam 134, 136–7, 91n154
hydrocarbon revenues
    Saudi Arabia post WWII 71
    share of GDP, budget and exports 10t–11
    Sudan (after 1999) 168n34, 170
hydropolitics 231, 240, 243, 249–53, 265
hydroponics 19, 91, 105, 208
Hyundai 153

Ibn Saud 41–2, 50, 59, 65, 68, 70, 73,
    90, 108, 113
    Al-Kharj farm and 72
    British stipends to, 47, 54, 57, 73, 76
    CASOC royalty payments to 43, 47–9, 56, 61
    centralization of land control by 60–1
    food and legitimacy of his rule 43, 47–9,
        56, 61
    Kuwaiti exile of 60
    Lend-Lease refusal and 48
    on food inflation 56
    on transportation crisis 57
    patrimonial rule and nascent institution
        building of 71–2
    reaction to British food quotas by 49–50
    sedentarization policies of 60, 66
    shopping for alliances by 49
    view of agriculture of 61
Ickes, Harold 51
Idriss, King of Libya 71
IFFCO 202
Ikhwan 60, 66
Imperial Valley 69
import-substituting industrialization (ISI) 55,
    57–8, 98, 162, 165, 178, 259
India 16–17, 22, 24, 27t, 35, 38, 40–1, 47, 89,
    102, 109, 133, 149, 152, 175, 195, 197–8,
    200–1, 207, 223n126, 225, 264
    Bengal famine (1943) 51–3, 56, 186
    investments in Ethiopia of 153, 248
    land investment policies of 145, 151, 153
    migrant workers in the Gulf from 15n19
    rice exports to Gulf of 29–31, 39, 49–51, 54,
        73n57, 113n28
    water situation of 147, 240, 251–2
Indonesia 111n18, 113n28, 157, 235t, 239–41

food export restrictions of (1997) 259
Gulf agro-investments and 197, 204,
 216, 232
housemaid plight and 201, 246-7, 263
palm oil exports and production 30-1, 147
rice imports of 28, 31, 204
settlement policies on Irian Jaya 246, 265
Indus River 240, 265
Indus Water Treaty (1960) 240, 251
inequality of land ownership. See also original
 accumulation
Brazil 112
Iran 101, 102
Latin America vs. Asia 22
Pakistan 201, 245
Philippines 246
Saudi Arabia 81
Institute of International Finance
 (IIF) 231n21, 232
Intergovernmental Panel on Climate Change
 (IPCC) 262
International Assessment of Agricultural
 Knowledge, Science and Technology for
 Development (IAASTD) 22
International Center for Agricultural Research
 in the Dry Areas (ICARDA) 224, 263
International Center for Biosaline
 Agriculture 95
International Energy Agency (IEA) 260
International Finance Corporation
 (IFC) 145, 235
International Food Policy Research Institute
 (IFPRI) 17, 23
 on climate change adpatation 242
 on population policies 258
 on strategic storage 260
international food reserve 124, 260. See also
 strategic storage
International Fund for Agricultural
 Development (IFAD) 125, 144, 146, 158,
 160, 189, 222, 240, 251
International Institute for Applied Systems
 Analysis (IIASA) 146, 149
International Institute for Environment and
 Development (IIED) 144, 146
International Labour Organization (ILO) 171
International Land Coalition (ILC) 144
International Monetary Fund (IMF) 10t, 15,
 18t, 57, 121, 259
 and Sudan 165, 177t-80, 182, 186-8,
 194, 233
international relations 246, 249, 255, 265
 climate change negotiations and 262
 counter threats to Arab oil embargo 114-20
 establishment of international postwar
 system 57-8
 establishment of MESC and 43-5

food aid as foreign policy tool 109-14
global imbalances and petrodollar
 recycling 120-2
guidelines for agro-investments 158-9, 261
hydropolitics and 249-53
international food politics 1970s 120-6
Iranian hostage crisis and food trade 118-20
Iraqi oil for food program 134-8
NGOs as factor of 263-4, 245-6
of Gulf countries and food security
 policies 255-68
politics of Islamic development and 111,
 186, 188-9, 191, 200, 247
regional dynamics in Cold War years 110-11
Saudi post-war situation and 70
US food export promotion 1980s 130-3
US grain cartel plans 126-8
WTO issues and 83, 87, 130, 149, 259-60
International Rice Research Institute
 (IRRI) 203, 205, 223, 263
International Wheat Agreement
 (1949-65) 129
Interstate Commission for Water
 Coordination of Central Asia
 (ICWC) 240
Iran 14, 18t, 30-1, 36n3, 43, 45, 50n84,
 53-4, 71, 78n77, 92, 102, 105, 138, 189,
 252n107, 259
 cereal imports of 9, 11, 28, 112, 204
 cereal program of 100-2
 population policies 11-12t, 258
 sanctions against 118-20, 133
Iraq 9, 12t, 18t, 43, 50n84, 58, 100, 103, 107,
 132, 139, 173, 263
 absentee landlords 36-7, 164
 Arab opposition to UN embargo 137
 barley exports to UK pre WWII 46
 cereal imports of 11, 28, 204
 food exports to Gulf and Middle East
 39-40, 46, 52, 54, 56
 funding share AAAID 180
 hydropolitics along the Euphrates and
 Tigris 240, 252
 imports of camels and horses from Gulf 41
 Oil-for-Food Program 11, 134-8
 safety of Saudi frontier with 57, 60
 scientific mission to Saudi Arabia
 (1939) 63-4
 and Sudan issues 170, 176n72, 177, 188-9
 US assistance grain export marketing
 (1958) 135
 water exports to Kuwait and planned water
 pipeline (1925-1950s) 90-1
 withdrawal Baghdad pact 111
Iraq Petroleum Company 42
Iraq Sanction Committee of the UN 135
Irrigation and Drainage Project (IDP) 75

Islamic Development Bank (IsDB) 85, 111,
    199, 205, *220*-1, 247
Islamic law. *See* Sharia law
Israel 16, 108, 111, 113, 115, 117–18, 124, 176,
    178, 203, 240, 251, 252*n*109, 257, 259
  share of P.L. 480 (1960–73) 112
Italy 41, 43, 46*t*, 50
Ithmaar Bank 245
Itochu 153

Al-Jaber, Sabah al-Ahmad 175
Jackson, Robert 44
Al-Jahra 91
Al-Jalamid phosphate mining project 266
Japan 85, 116, 131, 148, 206
  friendship treaty with Ibn Saud 49
  invention of artifical pearls 41
  land investment policies of 151, 153–4
  occupation of Burma by 51–2
  soybean investments in
      Brazil 1970s 114, 153
  US naval blockade against 107
Jawf 85
Jazan 72, 85
Jazan Company for Agricultural Development
    (JAZADCO) 82
Al Jazeera 137, 210
Jebel Aulia Dam 190
Jeddah 37–9, 42, 49, 50–1, 53–4, 56–7, 63, 65,
    69–70, 73, 86, 118, 205, 212, 215, 221
Al-Jenat 202
Jerusalem 45
jihad 43*n*43, 100, 169
job creation 13, 80, 156, 188, 232, 256
  of land investments 157, 159, 216, 248
John Deere 82
Jones, Jesse 48
Jones, Toby 59
Jonglei Canal 172, 174, 191, 250
Jordan 18*t*, 39*n*14, 58, 148
  Abdul Hakim Abidin and 73*n*56
  as wheat producer prior WWII 40
  food weapon WWI and 42
  offered GCC membership (2011) 267
  proposed integration with Saudi Arabia 173
  safety of Saudi frontier with 57, 60
  smuggling to Iraq 135
  subsidized wheat production in 98
  US food aid promises and peace
      negotiations 124
  water situation of 240, 252*n*109
Al-Jouf Agricultural Development Co.
    (JADCO) 82, 202

Kahn, R. F. 55
Kajbar Dam 190, 248

Kamel, Saleh 205, 234
Karuturi 153, 248
Kassala 56
Kazakhstan 32, 130, 139, *197*–8*n*5, 204, 207,
    235*t*, 237–41
Kenana Sugar Company 184, 187, 193, 199
  criticism of 181*n*86, 185
  ethanol production of 192, 206
  foundation of 175–6
  role in ARP of 192–3
  shareholder structure of 176
  Sudan's "sugar system" and 185
Kennedy, John F. 109, 111–12
Kenya 188, *197*–8, 208, 237
  corn exports WWII 53
  Tana River project by Qatar 216, 228, 246
Keynes, John Maynard 44, 55, 58
Khafs Daghra 65
Khaibar 38
Khaled bin Abdullah 82
Khalil, Abdullah Bey 173
Khamenei, Sayyed Ali Hosseini 101
Kharafi, Nasser 205
Al-Kharj Agricultural Project 79
Al-Kharj farm 58–9, 61, 80, 104
  Aramco role in 64–6
  food supplies to palace by 59, 61, 66
  imitation of farming in S-W USA by 69–70
  social conflict and 67–8
  US agricultural mission and beginnings
      of 63–4
  visit of Emir of Kuwait to 90
Khashm al-Girba Dam 190
Khashoggi, Adnan 175, 179*n*82, 183
Khomeini, Sayyed Ruhollah Musavi 100
Al-Khorayef brothers 82
King Abdullah Initiative for Saudi
    Agricultural Investment Abroad
    (KAISAIA) 175, 179*n*82, 183, 202, 208,
    210–3, 241
  interagency coordination and 211–12
  private sector and 224, 230
King Saud University 202
Kingdom Holding 99, 100, 193, 204, 207, 245,
    261. *See also* Al-Waleed, bin Talal
Kissinger, Henry 115–17, 122–6
knowledge economy 256
Kontos, Stephen 183
Kordofan 168, 191, 223, 248
Korean War 109, 166
Kosti 176
Kuwait 10*t*, 14, 15*t*, 17*n*24, 18*t*–19, 27*t*, 28*t*,
    38, 42, 53, 56, 60, 89*t*, 95*n*174, 103, 118,
    134–5, 137, 170–1, 208, 221, 224, 231,
    233–4, 247, 263–4
  agricultural development of 90–2

investments in Sudan 174–7*t*, 180, 185,
   188, 190, 222, 248
   agro-investments elsewhere 203, 205,
      213–16
Kuwait Department of Agriculture 91
Kuwait Development Board 91
Kuwait Foreign Trading Contracting and
   Investment Co. (KFTCIC) 175
Kuwait Investment Authority (KIA) 176,
   213–14, 218–*20*, 222
Kyoto Protocol 262
Kyrgyzstan 237, 240

La Via Campesina 245
labor rights 247, 263
Lackner, Helen 65
Lake Nasser 99, 204
Lancashire 164
land grabs 104. *See also* customary land rights
   and colonialism 155
   and food insecurity 155, 159, 198
   and mechanized agriculture in Sudan 182–3
   and water grabs 147
   foreignisation of space and 145
   global phenomenon of 143–4
   implementation gaps and media
      misrepresentation 227–31
Land Matrix 144
land reform debates 67, 81, 101, 157, 246, 265
land tenure and titling
   in Africa 158
   in Saudi Arabia 60, 74, 77, 81
   in Sudan 167–9
Landis, J. M. 43
Al-Leith 85
Lend-Lease 48, 50–1, 55, 57, 61, 69
Liberation and Justice Movement 199
Libya 2–3, 18*t*, 56, 71, 119*n*54
   Arab oil embargo and 115
   conflict and reconciliation with
      Sudan 177, 188
   OAU summit 2009 in 161
   project implementation gap 145
   subsidized wheat production in 98, 172
Lloyd, E. M. H. 45
Lonhro 151, 176

Madagascar 50n84, 144, 198n5, 237, 246
Mahd al-Dhahab 63
Mahdi rule (1885–1898) 164
Majlis al-Shura 13, 87
Malawi 148
Malaysia *197*, 204, 113*n*28, 148
   food export restrictions of (1997) 259
   palm oil exports and production of *30*–1, 147
Mali *197*–8*n*5, 205, 246
Malthusian fears 20, 22–3, 170

Managil scheme 165
Mao, Tse-tung 151
Marubeni 153
Marx, Karl 155
Matip, Paulino 143
Mauritania 1718*t*, 85, *197*–8
Mawashi 223–4
Maxwell-Stamp 261
McGovern, George Stanley 109, 127
McGuckian, Alastair and Paddy 82
Merowe Dam 190, 214, 222, 248
Meulen, D. van der 39, 65–8
Mexipak 75–6
micronutrients
   as fertilizer 265*n*34
   dietary lack of 16
Middle East Supply Center (MESC) 43, 62,
   98, 135
   anti-locust campaign of 38
   countries of remit of 45–7
   dissolution of 58
   establishment of 43–4
   gold sales of 55
   Keynesian influences and 44, 58
   managment of interregional food trade 45,
      52–7
   strategic storage and 44–5, 260
   supplies to the Gulf by 47
Middle East, naissance of the term 45
migrant workers 96, 156, 169–70, 184, 200, 264
   in Saudi agriculture 81
   plight of 201, 227, 246–7, 263
   share in Gulf population 15*n*19, 15
   vulnerability to food price shocks 15*t*
Millenium Dam 250
millet 23, 27*t*, 39–40, 53, *79*, 172,
   181, 205, 243
Mindanao 203, 217, 247
Ministers of Finance of the Arab League
   Summit in Rabat (1976) 171
Ministry of Agriculture (MoA, Saudi
   Arabia) 74*t*, 80*n*92
   agro-lobby and 79, 87, 211–12, 259
   creation of (1953) 72
   effective demotion of 79
   name change to MoAW (1965) 72
Ministry of Agriculture (Sudan) 171, 179*n*85
Ministry of Agriculture (UAE) 94, 96
Ministry of Agriculture and Water (MoAW,
   Saudi Arabia) 72, 76
   name change to MoA (2001) 79
Ministry of Commerce and Industry (MoCI,
   Saudi Arabia) 76
   leadership role in KAISAIA 211–12
   name change (2003) 259*n*11
   WTO process and 259
Ministry of Economy (UAE) 215

Ministry of Education (Saudi Arabia) 72
Ministry of Electricity and Water (Sudan) 191
Ministry of Finance (Saudi Arabia) 71, 76
    foreign aid and 221
    role in KAISAIA 211
Ministry of Foreign Affairs (Saudi
        Arabia) 211, 221
Ministry of Interior (Saudi Arabia) 76
    creation of (1951) 71
    foreign aid and 221
    wheat phase out and 87
Ministry of Investment (Sudan) 228
Ministry of Irrigation and Water Resources
        (MoIWR, Sudan) 179n82
    effective demotion of 191–2
Ministry of Labor and Social Affairs (Saudi
        Arabia) 76
Ministry of Municipal and Rural Affairs
        (Saudi Arabia) 79
Ministry of Planning (Saudi Arabia) 76–7
Ministry of War Transport (UK) 44
Ministry of Water (MoW, Saudi Arabia),
        creation of (2001) 79
Ministry of Water and Electricity (MoWE,
        Saudi Arabia) 241
    creation of (2004) 79
Mitsubishi 153
Mitsui 153
Moffet, James A. 47–8
Monsanto 24
monsoon 38, 40
Moose, James S. Jr. 63
Morgan, Dan 109
Morgan Stanley 150
Morocco 11, 18t, 36n4, 112, 173
    Gulf agro-investments and 197, 200–1,
        206, 225, 263
    offered GCC membership (2011) 267
    phosphate rock reserves 266–7
    subsidized wheat production 98
Mosul 56
motor pumps 38, 62, 68, 74t, 75, 89, 92, 104
    decline of *aflaj* and terraced fields and 40, 93
Mottl, Ron 127
Moynihan, Daniel 127
Mozambique 147, 198n5, 237
Mubarak, Hosni 99, 170, 251
Muqrin bin Abdulaziz 82
Al-Murraba 84
Muscat 94
Muslim Brotherhood 72–3n56, 247
Mussolini, Benito 49

Nader & Ebrahim S/O Hassan 203
Najd 39, 41, 60–1, 80–1
    definition of 39n19
Najran 38, 85

nakba (1948) 251
Nasir al-Said 110
Nasser, Gamal Abdel 110–13, 174
Al-Nasser, Nassir Abdulaziz 261
National Agricultural Development Corp.
        (NADEC) 82
National Association of Wheat Growers 127
National Barrel for a Bushel Committee 127
National Broadcasting Associated Press 126
National Congress Party (NCP) 191, 251
National Farmers Union (NFU) 127
National Grain Board proposal 127
National Islamic Front (NIF) 169–70,
        187–9, 191
National Prawn Company (NPC) 85
National Security Study Memoranda
        (NSSM) 123–4
National Water Company (NWC), Saudi
        Arabia 257
naval blockade
    Entente WWI 41–2, 107–8
    German U-boat campaign 43
    of Red Sea by Italy WWII 50
    US against Japan 107
Nayef bin Abdulaziz 87
Nazer, Hisham 173
Nestlé 24, 147
Net Food Importing Developing Countries
        (NFIDC) 261
New Halfa scheme 165
New York Times 263
New Zealand 30, 238
NGOs 136, 143–5, 156, 197, 215, 253
    resistance to Gulf agro-investments 245–6,
        263–4
    Government Organized NGOs
        (GONGOs) 264
Nigeria 197, 204, 222, 237
Nile basin 100, 204
    water rights after separation of South
        Sudan 250–1
Nile Basin Initiative 9, 190, 240
Nile Valley Authority for River
        Navigation, 228
Nile Waters Agreement (1959) 190, 243,
        249–51
Al-Nimeiri, Gaafar Muhammad 165, 180,
        182, 186–9
    Adnan Khashoggi and 175, 179
    as strategic parter of US 176–8
    downfall of regime (1985) 187
    political instrumentalization of mechanized
        rain-fed farming by 168–70
    Sudanese civil war and 174
Noland, Marcus 133
nomadism 36, 41, 88, 162, 168, 172, 181
    failed nomads 170

sedentarization and 59–61, 65, 68, 83, 93
North Korea and US food aid 113n28, 133
Nuba Mountains 169, 191
Nubia 164n8, 192, 248
nuclear politics 102, 133, 259
nuclear power 209, 256

O'Brien, Jay 168n35, 181–3
Al-Obaid, Abdullah 87, 213
obesity 16, 17n24, 24, 32, 151, 258
Oesterdiekhoff, Peter 182, 187
Office of Management and Budget (OMB) 123
Ogalalla aquifer 70
oil pricing 215–16
oil revenues. *See* hydrocarbon revenues
Oil-for-Food Program 134–8
    Syrian perception of 137
Olayan, Sulaiman 82
Oman 10t–12t, 15t, 17, 18t, 19, 28t, 30, 38–9,
    41, 86, 208, 221, 231n21, 264
    agricultural development of 36, 88–9t, 92–4
    close relationship with Baluchistan and
        Zanzibar 200, 214
    peak oil in (2001) 10, 214
    strategic storage in 214–15
OPEC Fund for International Development
    (OFID) 220–1
Organization of African Unity (OAU) 83,
    161, 176
Organization of the Islamic Conference
    (OIC) 111, 205
Organization of the Petroleum Exporting
    Countries (OPEC) 123n73, 139, 255
    IFAD foundation OPEC share 125, 222
    loss of market share in 1980s 115, 129
    power shift in oil markets 1970s 117, 120–1
    US bushel for barrel proposal to USSR
        and 126–7
    US grain cartel proposals and 127–8, 130
    World Food Conference 1974 and 124–5
original accumulation 155
orphan crops 23
Oryx gazelle 39
Osman, Khalil 174–6
Ostriches 39
Ottoman government 38, 40–3n43, 67
outgrower schemes 157, 267
Ozal, Turgut 252

P.L 480. *See* Food for Peace Program
Paarlberg, Robert 23
Pakistan 16n19, 29, 92, 102, 111n18, 113n28,
    147, 202–3, 207–8, 241, 264
    governance indicators of 201, 235t, 237
    Gulf agro-investments in *197*–201, 207–8,
        217, 223, 225, 228, 230, 246
    rice exports to Gulf of 29–*30*, 32

water situation and impact of climate
    change 238–41, 242–3, 251–3
zamindar system in 201, 245
Palestine 45–6, 54n113
Palestinian occupied territories 11–12, 108
palm oil 147, 150, 152, 241
    imports of Gulf countries 30–1
Palmer, Martin 127
Paraguay *30*, 32
Patolichev, Nikolai 126
Paulson, Henry 257
Peace Pipeline 252
peak oil debate 10, 22, 51, 129, 214
peak phosphorus debate 266–7
peak water debate 238
pearl fishing 39–41, 52
petrodollar recycling 121
Pharaon, Rashad 113
Philippines 28, *30*–1, 148, 246, 253
    BITs with Saudi Arabia and
        Bahrain 212, 214
    export restrictions of (1997) 259
    fruit exports to the Gulf 31–2, 203
    governance indicators of 235t, 237
    Gulf agro-investments 195, *197*–8, 203–4,
        215, 225, 228, 230
    housemaid plight 201, 246–7, 263
    land reform in 157, 265
pilgrimage. *See* hajj
Poland 111n18, 114, 126, 131n110, 198n5
political legitimacy and food provision 12–13,
    35–6, 43, 61, 72, 94, 97, 126, 136, 178,
    191, 232
population growth 20, 29, 32, 124, 146,
    148, 152
    in target countries 151, 172–3, 225, 238–9t,
        241, 253
    in the Middle East 11–12, 19, 96, 100, 102,
        135, 138
    population policies 258
    pre WWII 38
Port Said 112
Port Sudan 170, 172, 188, 199
ports
    Asmara 73n57
    Bahrain 56
    Bandar Abbas 100
    Bandar Khomeini 100
    Dammam 215
    Djibouti 199, 50n84
    Gwadar 199, 225
    Jeddah 56, 215
    Jubail 215
    Khorramshahr 100
    Lamu 216
    Massawa 50
    Mombasa 216

ports (*cont.*)
  Ras Tanura 56
  Salalah 214
  Sohar 214
  Yanbu 215
poultry 25, 27*t*, 28*t*, 29, *30*–1, 66, 76, 82, 92, 206, 208
precious metals as currency 55–6, 110, 121
price controls 9, 14, 54, 115*n*36, 246
primitive accumulation. *See* original accumulation
private sector 101, 124, 130, 145, 153, 166
  role in agro-investments 210–12, 223–6
  role in Gulf economies 12–13, 81*n*96, 85, 154, 207–8, 214–15, 217, 230, 232–3
Public Investment Fund (PIF) 211, 220
Punjab 29, 240, 251

Qassim 85
Qassim, Abdul Karim 91*n*154, 111
Qatar 10*t*, 14–15*t*, 16, 18*t*–19, 28*t*, 38, 89*t*, 118, 153, 205, 208, 214, 221, 223, 231, 244, 247, 255
  agricultural development of 19, 89*t*, 92–3, 95*n*174, 97, 255, 257
  agro-investments of 216, 228, 246, 248
  food security situation in WWII 52–3
  foreign policy of 199, 210, 261, 264,
  National Water Resources Management and Development Strategy 89*n*141, 93
Qatar Investment Authority (QIA) 219–20, 222. *See also* Hassad Food
Qatar National Food Security Programme (QNFSP) 205, 208–10, 213, 224, 241
Qatar Steel Company (QASCO) 207
Al-Qatif 38–40, 42, 59, 67, 70, 77
Al-Qudra Agriculture 199, 206, 213, 225
Al-Qunaybit, Mohammad 13

Rahad scheme 165, 193
railways 35, 56, 165, 172, 199
rain-fed agriculture 146–8
  in Sudan 161, 165–72, 179, 181–3, 186–9, 193, 229, 243
  in target countries 239*t*–41, 249
  on the Arabian Peninsula 36, 88
Al-Rajhi, Abdulaziz 82
Al-Rajhi family 82, 85, 203, 228, 230
Al-Rajhi International 193, 200, 228
Al-Rajhi, Sulaiman Abdulaziz 82
Rajputana Desert, India 38
Al-Rasheed, Turki Faisal 87, 108, 132, 197, 230, 234
Rashidis 60
rawdat (sing. *rawda*) 92
Reagan doctrine of agricultural trade 130–3

Reagan, Ronald 132
Red Sea 36*n*3, 38–40, 42, 49–50*n*84, 53, 56, 85, 208
Red Sea economic union plan 173
renewable energy 10, 209, 257, 262*n*24
rentier state 196
  and transparency of companies 196
  early beginnings pre WW II 59–60
  in Kuwait 214
  in Sudan 170
  segmented clientelism and 71–2, 76
  ruling bargain of 12, 43, 207
Responsible Agricultural Investments (RAI) 158, 261
Rhodes, Cecil 155
Rhodes grass 96
rice 13, 15, 98, 101–2, 112, 119, 148, 152–3, 172, 198, 202, 204–7, 212, 214, 216, 227*n*1, 229–30, 232, 241–4, 246
  as C3 crop 243
  dietary change from dates 39
  futures and global market 29, 31
  Gulf preference for basmati rice 29, 201, 203, 217, 232
  imports of Gulf countries 29–*30*, 32, 74*t*–6
  trade during WWII 39, 49, 51–2, 54, 56
Richards, Alan 257
Riyadh 39*n*19, 38*n*8, 58, 60, 66*n*17, 68, 112–13, 176, 201, 221, 246, 257
Robinson, Charles 126
Rockefeller Foundation 198
Rommel, Erwin 45
Roosevelt, Franklin D. 47–8, 50, 57, 61
Roosevelt Dam 70
Roseires Dam 174, 188, 190, 248
Rowland, R. W. "Tiny" 175–6
Rozanov, Andrew 218
Rumela 190
Rusk, Dean 113
Russia *30*–1, 35, 50, 107*n*1, 109, 126, 131, 133, 135, 139, 195, 225, 242. *See also* Soviet Union
  arms for sesame deal with Sudan 188
  grain cartel proposal of 130, 139
  land and water reserves of 147, 240
Al-Ru⊠ya al-Iqtisadiyya 210
Rwanda 148, 250

Sahara Agricultural Venture (SAV) 183
Sahelian drought (1968–73) 181
sanctions 9. *See also* Soviet Union
  Egypt 113
  historic overview 107–8
  Iran 102, 118–20, 133
  Iraq 11, 103, 134–38

Sudan 188
Syria 102–3, 137*n*141
Sanger, Richard H. 64
Sanitation Authority at Al-Ahsaa 79
Saqqaf, Omar 116–17
Saud bin Abdulaziz 66, 69, 72–3, 173
Al-Saud, Mohammed 79
Saudi Agricultural Development Corp. 82
Saudi Arabia 9–10, 12*t*–19, 27*t*–8*t*, *30*–1,
  36, 38–9, 41, 43, 47–51, 53, 55–6,
  58–65, 68–*79*, 81*t*-9, 92, 94, 96–8,
  101, 104–5, 127, 153–4, 170, 175–7*t*,
  178, 180, 183, 185–6, 192–4, 200–6,
  208, 210, 212–19, 221–6, 230–3, 238,
  240, 249, 255–9, 261–6
 Accelerated Wheat Production Program 75
 agricultural census (1960–64) 72
 Agricultural Development Fund 84
 Agricultural Units 72, 74*t*
 agro-lobby 81–2, 86–8, 211
 Council of Ministers Resolution No. 33583
 Directorate of Agriculture 71
 EDBI and 236
 Eighth Development Plan
  (2005–2009) 79, 85
 Fifth Development Plan (1990–95) 78
 fisheries of 85–6
 housemaid plight in 246–7
 Kilo Ten Government Farm 70
 Land Registration Law (1952) 60
 Ninth Development Plan (2010–14) 83–4
 oil embargo and counter threats 115–18
 oil for food program stance of 137–8
 Public Lands Distribution Ordinance
  (1968) 74, 77, 81
 Red Sea economic unon proposals and 173
 rivalry with Nasser 110–14
 Royal Court of 221
 Second Development Plan (1975–1980) 76
 Third Development Plan (1980–85) 76, 78,
  86, 215
 urbanization rate of 81*t*
 visit of John Block to 132–3
 Water Desalination Organization 76, 79
 wheat program 75–83
 wheat program phase-out 74*t*, 83–4
Saudi Arabian Agricultural and Dairy
  Corp. 82
Saudi Arabian Agricultural Bank (SAAB) 74,
  76–7, 84
Saudi Arabian Fertilizer Company
  (SAFCO) 75
Saudi Arabian Government Investment
  Authority (SAGIA) 236
Saudi Arabian Mining Syndicate 63, 70

Saudi Arabian Monetary Authority
  (SAMA) 175, 219–21, 231
Saudi Basic Industries Corporation
  (SABIC) 75, 219–21
Saudi Binladin Group 205, 232
Saudi Company for Agricultural Investment
  and Animal Production (SCAIAP) 211,
  212, 224
Saudi East African Forum in Addis Ababa
  (2009) 202
Saudi Industrial Development Fund
  (SIDF) 220, 224
Saudi Star 202, 207, 216, 244*n*71, 248
Saunders, Doug 156
Savola 224
de Schutter, Olivier 159
self-sufficiency ratios
 China 152
 Egypt 99
 Gulf countries 27–8*t*, 78, 81, 87*n*133, 94,
  96, 208
 Middle East WW I and II 40, 42, 46, 53
 Sudan 28*t*, 103, 187–8, 192
Sen, Amartya 16, 51
Senegal *197*–8*n*5, 205–6, 227*n*1
Senegal River Development Organization
  (SRDO) 205
Sennar 162, 191, 248
Sennar Dam 190
Setait River 190
Seyhan River 252
Shah, Mahendra 149, 205
Sharaf, Issam 251
Sharia law 60, 101, 164, 186, 201
 rulings on aquatic animals as food 85*n*121
Sharif, Nawaz 200
Al-Sharqiyah Development Co.
  (SHADCO) 82
Shatt El Arab 90, 100
Sheikh Mohammed 231
Sheikh Zayed 19, 89, 93–5, 105, 201
Al-Sheikh, Mohammed Ibrahim 117
Sheikha Fatima 201
Shultz, George 121–2, 123*n*73
Sime Darby 150
Sirhan 38
slave trade 41, 162, 164, 200*n*17
slums 80, 156
Small and Medium-sized Enterprises
  (SMEs) 236
small-scale farming 23, 26, 149, 159, 245
 agricultural modernization and 21, 61,
  67–8, 76, 166, 168*n*35, 181
 productivity vs. large-scale farming 155–8
Smil, Vaclav 25

soils 24–5, 39, 58, 90–2, 100, 146–7, 167–8, 172, 183, 192, 229. *See also* fertilizer
    moisture and climate change 181, 243
    sabkha salt marshes 86
    salinity problem of 88, 93, 95, 136, 138, 182, 204
    soil water 238. *See also* water
Sojitz 85
Somalia 11, 18*t*, 45, 198, 216, 223, 237
sorghum 23, 27t, 39, 52, 79–80, 103–4, 205
    as C4 crop 243
    production in Sudan 103–4, 166–7, 170, 172, 181, 184, 186–7, 189, 190, 229
de Soto, Hernan 156
South Africa *30*–1, 149, 198–9
South Korea 111*n*18, 144, 148, 151, 206
    land investment policies of 153, 246
sovereign wealth funds (SWFs) 207–8.
    See also petrodollar recycling
    asset allocation and global financial crisis 231–2, 257
    liability based analysis of 218–19
    typology of Gulf SWFs 220–1
Soviet Union 49–50, 102, 111–14, 119–20, 133–4, 135, 148, 152, 167, 200. *See also* Russia
    as US food export market 131
    cooperation with Egypt 112–13
    US bushels for barrels proposal and 126
    US grain embargo against (1980) 114, 118, 120, 133–4
    US grain export moratorium against (1975) 114, 126
Spain *30*, 32
sponsorship system 19, 77, 207, 244, 247
Springborg, Robert 236
Standard & Poor's 232
Standard Oil of California (SOCAL) 42, 47, 63
State Trading Company (STD, India) 153
statistics in the Gulf, lack of reliability of 15, 96, 196
steamships 35, 40
strategic storage 9, 253
    Arab perceptions of 108, 234, 260
    Ford Foundation proposal of 74
    IFPRI proposal of international food reserve and 342
    in Gulf countries 9, 73, 195, 213–15
    MESC and 45, 52, 56, 260
    oil for food proposal to Australia and 117
    Sudan famine 1984–85 and 186
stunting as indicator for food insecurity 17–18*t*
subsidies
    for food in Gulf countries 16–17
    for wheat production in Saudi Arabia and their reduction 97–8

subsistence farming 21, 103–4, 159, 172, 181
Al-Sudairi family 85
Sudan 8, 11, 12*t*, 17–18*t*, 20, 27*t*, *30*, 32, 36*n*3, 39*n*14, 45, 53–4, 56, 58, 81, 108, 117, 124, 138–9, 143–8, 155*n*58, 160–94, 195, *197*–200, 202–3, 207–8, 213–17, 221–5, 228–30, 233–5*t*, 243, 245, 248–51, 253, 263, 265. *See also* Agricultural Revival Programme (ARP)
    Ansar and Khatmiyya 164, 169
    balance of payments crisis of 177
    Camp David and foreign aid to 178–9
    cereal program of 103–5, 187–8
    Civil Transactions Act (1990) 169
    civil war of 166, 168*n*34, 169, 172, 174, 248
    Comprehensive Peace Agreement (CPA) 190
    counterinsurgency on the cheap 170
    Dam Implementation Unit (DIU) 191
    Development Act (1972) 165
    Encouragement of Development Act (1974) 165
    expansion of irrigated agriculture after independence 165–6
    expansion of rain-fed agriculture under Nimeiri 167–70
    famine in (1984–85) 186–7
    food exports to Gulf in WWII 49–50
    Food Investment Strategy (FIS) 171
    governance indicators of 235*t*–7
    IMF structural adjustment program (1978) 178–80, 182, 186–7
    Nile water rights after separation 250–1
    Northern Axis within 191
    rain-fed agriculture and environmental degradation 167–8
    rentier state structures and 170
    Six Year Plan (1977/78–1982/83) (SYP) 171, 180
    Strategy for Development of Rain-fed Agriculture (1986) 179
    sudd swamps 172
    Three Year Plan (1978–1981) 180
    Unregistered Land Act (1970) 166, 169
    water situation of 240–1
    withholding of oil deliveries by Iraq and Kuwait 177–8
Sudan bread-basket plan 20, 81, 108, 117, 139, 160, 162, 167, 171, 173–4, 176, 179–81, 183–4, 186–8, 196, 198–9, 221, 233–4, 265
Sudan Defence Force 56
Suez Canal 11, 35, 43, 50
sugar 24, 27*t*-9, 44, 46*t*, 52, 54, 102, 117, 135, 150, 153, 157, 161, 172–3, 175–6, 184, 192, 199, 206, 214, 229, 246, 258. *See also* Kenana Sugar Company
    as C4 crop 243

Brazil's role in Gulf and world markets 25, 31
dietary change and 17, 29, 39, 46, 100, 258
government regulations Egypt 98
imports of Gulf countries 30–1
political power in Sudan and 165, 185
Suki scheme 193
Sulaibiyya 90
Al-Sulaiman, Abdullah 58, 63, 67, 69–70
Sultan bin Abdulaziz 72
Sultanate of Darfur 162
Sumitomo 153
Syr Darya 240
Syria 9, 18t, 30–1, 41–2, 50, 54, 56, 98, 105,
    122, 138, 164, 174, 223, 229, 259, 261, 263
cereal program of 102–3
Greater Syria famine (1915–18) 42, 55
net oil trade of 11
oil embargo and 115–16
perception of Oil-for-Food Program 137
Special Agricultural Investment Agreement
    with Sudan (2002) 208
US food aid promises and peace
    negotiations 124
US plan for food cooperation with Arabian
    Peninsula 58
water situation of 240, 252

Tabuk Agricultural Development Corp.
    (TADCO) 82, 202
Tajikistan 237, 240
Talal bin Abdulaziz 111
Tana River 216, 228, 246
Tanzania 83, 148, 153, 197–8n5, 204,
    244n71, 250
Tapline 68
Al-Tariki, Abdullah 71n48, 73, 110
Tenneco Inc. 175, 183
Texas A&M University 224
Texas Department of Agriculture 121
Thailand 29, 30, 31, 73n57, 85n119,
    197–8n5, 203–4, 231
Cairns group and 149
Restrictions on foreign
    ownerhsip 230–1, 244
rice production by smallholders 147–8
Al-Thani, Hamad bin Khalifa 210
Al-Thani, Tamim bin Hamad 208
The Fund for Peace 235t–4
Tigris 69, 138, 240, 265
Toshka Valley 99–100, 204, 245
Transnational Corporations (TNCs) 24,
    150–1, 158, 160
Transparency International 235t, 237
treasuries, US 121, 232
Trucial states 39–40, 56, 89–90, 93
Tunisia 11, 18t, 112

Al-Turabi, Hassan 169, 186–7, 189
Turkey 11–12t, 18t, 36n3, 40, 111n18
Governance indicators 235t, 237
Gulf agro-investments and 197–8, 204,
    207, 245
hydropolitics and 69, 138, 240, 252
MESC and 45
smuggling to Iraq 135
Southeastern Anatolia Project
    (GAP) 240, 252
water situation of 239t–41
Turkiyya (1821–85) 162, 164, 173
Turkmenistan 240
Tuwaiq Mountains 58
Twitchell, Karl S. 41, 61, 63, 65, 67, 69

U.S.-Saudi Arabian Business Council 84
Uganda 153, 250
Ukraine 130, 139, 148
food exports to the Gulf 30, 32
Gulf agro-investments and 195, 197–8n5,
    204–5, 235t, 237, 239t–41, 267
UN embargo against Iraq 134–8
UN General Assembly 125, 135, 261
UN Security Council 119, 134–5
UN Special Rapporteur on the right to
    food 159
Unilever 150
United Arab Emirates (UAE) 10t, 12t, 14–19,
    27t–8t, 30, 36, 38–9, 41, 86, 105, 153, 219,
    222, 264
agricultural development of 88–9t, 92–7
agro-investments and 199–201, 206, 208,
    213–15, 217, 225, 229, 231–2, 244–7
alfalfa and Rhodes grass demand 96, 206
Office for the Coordination of Foreign
    Aid 221
re-exports via Dubai 10, 31, 256
Sudan and 176, 185, 229–30
Supreme Petroleum Council 213
United Grain Company (UGC) 130
United Kingdom (UK) 35, 46, 48–51, 55, 58,
    62, 70, 89, 109, 145, 168n34
United Kingdom Commercial Corporation
    (UKCC) 44
United Nations Children's Fund (UNICEF)
    (formerly International Children's
    Emergency Fund) 151
United Nations Conference on Food and
    Agriculture in Hot Springs, Virginia
    (1943) 58
United Nations Conference on Trade and
    Development (UNCTAD) 158, 160
United States 12, 27t, 30, 38, 46t, 70, 102,
    198n5, 251, 264
Agricultural and Food Act (1981) 131

United States (*cont.*)
  Agriculture and Consumer Protection Act
    (1973) 122
  Food for Peace Act (1966) 132
  Food Security Act (1985) 132
  soybean embargo of (1973) 114, 122.
    See also Soviet Union
United States Agency for International
  Development (USAID) 111, 122
United States Congress 112, 116, 124, 127
United States Department of Agriculture
  (USDA) 28, 122–4, 132, 204
United States Geological Survey
  (USGS) 266
United States Information Service 112
United States National Foreign Assessment
  Center 119–20
United States Senate Committee on Foreign
  Relations 127
United States Technical Cooperation
  Administration 70
United States Treasury Department 110, 121,
  123, 256–7
Unity of the Nile Valley 173–4
Upper Nile province 169
urbanization 72, 80, 81t, 104, 136, 149,
  155–8, 258
Uruguay 148, 195
Uruguay round 20, 261
US agricultural mission to Saudi Arabia
  (1942) 38, 41, 48, 61, 63–5, 67, 69
US-UK rivalry 48, 51, 62, 70
Uzbekistan 237, 240

Verhoeven, Harry 228
Vietnam 31, 85n119, 110, 111n18,
  133, 139, 196
  food for war program and 113n29, 124
  Gulf agro-investments and 29, *197*–8n5,
    203–4, 208, 216, 225
  land reform and smallholder rice
    production in 147–8, 157
virtual water 108, 238–9, 252, 255, 261.
  See also water
  exports by North and South America,
    Australia and New Zealand 238
Vision 3245
Vitalis, Robert 58–9, 64

Waal, Alex de 168n35, 170
Wad Rawah 229
Wadi Fatima 38, 68n30, 70
Al-Waleed, bin Talal 99, 193, 261
Wali, Yousef 99
Al-Wataniyya Poultry 82
water. *See also* desalination, motor pumps

impact of early Gulf agriculture on 40, 62,
  67–9, 89, 92–3, 104
impact of Saudi wheat program on 83–4,
  87–8
leakage loss in pipeline system 257
physical and economic shortage of 29, 198,
  240–1
situation in target countries 238–41, 243
typology of, blue, green, grey, renewable
  and virtual 238
water footprint 96, 238n46
Waterbury, John 161, 257
Wathen, Albert L. 69
Wavell, Archibald Percival, Viceroy of
  India 52
Weaver, Jim 127–8
Weis, Tony 149
wheat. 9, 19, 27t, 28t, 74t, 79t. *See also* cereal
  programs, grain cartel, grain embargo,
  Saudi Arabia
  globalization of market 35, 238, 261
  imports Middle East 9, 29–31, 76, 99, 102,
    112, 132, 137, 152, 188, 204
  production in Sudan 170, 172, 178, 182,
    186–90, 192–3, 200
  regional trade and production Middle East
    WWII and before 36, 39, 40, 45–6, 52–4
  subsidized production in Libya, Morocco,
    Jordan 98
  trade during Roman Empire 35n1
  wheatification of diets in LDCs 40, 100,
    112, 167
  yields 22, 24n58, 36n3, 44, 63–4, 75,
    99–100, 102–4, 136, 146, 242–3
wheat agreement (1933) 129
White Nile Sugar Company 192
WikiLeaks 185, 201, 202, 216, 233
Wohlmuth, Karl 187
Wolde-Giorgis, Girma 201
World Bank 23, 57, 70, 157–8, 160, 220t, 223,
  245, 259
  good governance concept and 235–6
  hydropolitics and 251
  on job creation of land
    investments 157, 216
  report about land investments of 144–5,
    147–9, 159, 228
  Sudan and 182, 188, 241
World Economic Forum (WEF) 235
World Food Conference (1974) 19, 123–4,
  128, 198, 222
World Food Programme (WFP) 11, 159, 198,
  243, 261
World Investment Report (2009) 158
World Trade Organization (WTO) 83, 87,
  130, 149, 185, 259, 262

Yamani, Hashim 13
Yamani,
   Zaki 115–16
Yemen 11, 12*t*, 14, 17–18*t*, 36, 38, 40–1, 53,
   55, 63, 77, 88, 110–13
yield gaps typology 148
YouGov, polling
   company 15

Zad Holding Company 220, 223–4
Al-Zafra company 229
Zambia 148, *197–8n5*, 237
Zanzibar 83, 214
Zayed al-Khair project 229
Zeigler, Robert 263
Zenawi, Meles 202
ZTE 144

Printed and bound by CPI Group (UK) Ltd, Croydon, CR0 4YY